NIETZSCHE
—— AND THE ——
QUESTION OF INTERPRETATION

NIETZSCHE
—— AND THE ——
QUESTION OF INTERPRETATION

Between

Hermeneutics

and

Deconstruction

ALAN D. SCHRIFT

Routledge

New York • London

Published in 1990 by

Routledge
An imprint of Routledge, Chapman and Hall, Inc.
29 West 35 Street
New York, NY 10001

Published in Great Britain by

Routledge
11 New Fetter Lane
London EC4P 4EE

Copyright © 1990 by Routledge, Chapman and Hall, Inc.

Printed in the United States of America

Library of Congress Cataloging in Publication Data

Schrift, Alan D., 1955–
    Nietzsche and the question of interpretation : between
hermeneutics and deconstruction / Alan D. Schrift.
        p.   cm.
    Includes bibliographical references.
    ISBN 0-415-90311-4. — ISBN 0-415-90312-2 (pbk.)
        1. Nietzsche, Friedrich Wilhelm, 1844–1900—Contributions in
hermeneutics. 2. Nietzsche, Friedrich Wilhelm, 1844–1900–
–Influence. 3. Hermeneutics—History—19th century.
4. Heidegger, Martin,
1889–1976—Contributions in hermeneutics. 5. Derrida, Jacques–
–Contributions in hermeneutics. 6. Deconstruction. I. Title.
B3318.H44S37   1990
193—dc20   90-33979

British Library Cataloguing in Publication Data
Schrift, Alan D.
    Nietzsche and the question of interpretation : between
hermeneutics and deconstruction.
    1. German philosophy. Nietzsche, Friedrich, 1844–1900
I. Title
193

ISBN 0-415-90311-4
ISBN 0-415-90312-2 pbk

iv

To Joan, Leonard and Mitchell Schrift,
and again, to Jill

Table of Contents

List of Abbreviations

All references to Nietzsche's writings have been included in the body of the text, denoted by the following abbreviations. Unless otherwise specified, Roman numerals denote the volume number of a set of collected works or a standard subdivision within a single work in which the sections are not numbered consecutively, and Arabic numerals denote the section number rather than the page number. While the available English translations of Nietzsche's texts, especially those of W. Kaufmann and R. J. Hollingdale (see Bibliography), have been consulted, these translations frequently have been altered to reflect more accurately the emphasis and style of the original German texts, and the ultimate responsibility for the translations which appear in the following pages must be mine. In a number of instances, I have found it helpful to include parts of the original German text in addition to the translation. In these cases, the original is placed within brackets immediately following its English translation. Also, in order to differentiate Nietzsche's use of ellipsis points from my editorial omissions of certain words or passages within a citation, I have marked all editorial omissions with ellipsis points between brackets as follows: [. . .].

Collected editions of Nietzsche's work.

GOA = *Nietzsches Werke (Grossoktavausgabe).*

MA = *Nietzsches Gesammelte Werke (Musarionausgabe).*

KGW = *Nietzsche Werke, Kritische Gesamtausgabe.* Edited by Giorgio Colli and Mazzino Montinari. I have used the accepted convention in citing references from this edition: Roman numeral (designating volume number), followed by Arabic numeral (designating band number), followed by the fragment number. For example, the abbreviation "*KGW,* VI, 2: 4[78]" refers to Abteilung VI, Band 2, fragment 4[78].

WDB = *Werke in drei Bänden.* Edited by Karl Schlechta.

Writings not published by Nietzsche.

HCP = "Homer and Classical Philology" (*Homer und die klassische Philologie*), 1869.

P = "The Last Philosopher. The Philosopher. Reflections on the Struggle between Art and Knowledge" (*Der letzte Philosoph. Der Philosoph. Betrachtungen über den Kampf von Kunst und Erkenntniss*), 1872.

PT = "On the Pathos of Truth" (*Ueber das Pathos der Wahrheit*), 1872.

FEI = "On the Future of our Educational Institutions" (*Ueber die Zukunft unserer Bildungsanstalten*), 1872.

HC = "Homer's Contest" (*Homer's Wettkampf*), 1872.

Rh = "Introduction to Rhetoric" (*Rhetorik*), 1872/74.

PCP = "The Philosopher as Cultural Physician" (*Der Philosoph als Arzt der Cultur*), 1873.

OTL = "On Truth and Lies in an Extramoral Sense" (*Ueber Wahrheit und Lüge im aussermoralischen Sinne*), 1873.

PHT = "Thoughts on the Meditation: Philosophy in Hard Times" (*Gedanken zu der Betrachtung: Die Philosophie in Bedrängniss*), 1873.

PTAG = "Philosophy in the Tragic Age of the Greeks" (*Die Philosophie im tragischen Zeitalter der Griechen*), 1873.

WPh = "We Philologists" (*Wir Philologen*), 1874/75.

SSW = "The Struggle between Science and Wisdom" (*Wissenschaft und Weisheit im Kampfe*), 1875.

WP = *The Will to Power* (*Der Wille zur Macht*), a selection of excerpts from Nietzsche's notebooks of the 1880s.

Works published or prepared for publication by Nietzsche.

BT = *The Birth of Tragedy* (*Die Geburt der Tragödie*), 1872.

DS = *David Strauss, the Writer and the Confessor* (*David Strauss, der Bekenner und der Schriftsteller*), 1873.

H = *On the Use and Disadvantage of History for Life* (*Vom Nutzen und Nachtheil der Historie für das Leben*), 1874.

SE = *Schopenhauer as Educator* (*Schopenhauer als Erzieher*), 1874.

WB = *Richard Wagner in Bayreuth* (*Richard Wagner in Bayreuth*), 1876.

HAH = *Human, All-too-Human* (*Menschliches, Allzumenschliches*), 1878.

AOM = *Assorted Opinions and Maxims* (*Vermischte Meinungen und Sprüche*), 1879.

WS = *The Wanderer and his Shadow* (*Der Wanderer und sein Schatten*), 1880.

D = *Daybreak* (*Morgenröte*), 1881.

GS = *The Gay Science (Die fröhliche Wissenschaft),* 1882.

Z = *Thus Spoke Zarathustra (Also sprach Zarathustra),* 1883/84/85.

BGE = *Beyond Good and Evil (Jenseits von Gut und Böse),* 1886.

GM = *On the Genealogy of Morals (Zur Genealogie der Moral),* 1887.

CW = *The Case of Wagner (Der Fall Wagner),* 1888.

TI = *Twilight of the Idols (Götzen-Dämmerung),* 1888.

NCW = *Nietzsche contra Wagner (Nietzsche contra Wagner),* 1888.

A = *The Antichrist (Der Antichrist),* 1888.

EH = *Ecce Homo (Ecce Homo),* 1888.

Preface

This text arose out of a desire to work on a project that merged my two primary philosophical interests: Nietzsche's philosophy and hermeneutic theory. I saw in Nietzsche's various comments on interpretation an untapped resource for furthering our understanding of what happens when we interpret texts. In addition, the multiplicity of diverse interpretations of Nietzsche's thought made his works a promising prospect for exploring a pluralistic approach to interpretation. As I read the interpretations of Kaufmann, Danto, Heidegger, Jaspers, Deleuze, Derrida, Magnus, Nehamas, Kofman, Granier, and others, one thing became increasingly clear to me: as much can be learned about what goes on in Nietzsche's texts from interpretations that one believes to be largely, if not entirely, a misreading of those texts as can be learned from interpretations with which one is in complete sympathy. Moreover, it struck me that this was itself a very Nietzschean phenomenon.

What interested me in particular about hermeneutic theory was the problem of avoiding interpretive dogmatism without relinquishing all hope for judging between interpretations. The tension between the dogmatic assertion of one correct interpretation and the relativistic acceptance of any interpretation seemed to me to be not only the central issue in hermeneutics. It was also the point of conflict between two of the most powerful styles of interpreting Nietzsche: those of Heidegger and various French post-structuralists. Moreover, this tension appeared to me to be at the heart of Nietzsche's own philosophizing, and the fact that he had been and could be read as a relativist or as a dogmatist did not seem to be insignificant.

To bring both of these issues to the fore, I tried to construct a text that would enact a pluralistic interpretive approach. This meant refraining from refuting all of the other Nietzsche interpretations currently in circulation, while arguing that my interpretation of Nietzsche was the correct one. For the reader who is looking for definitive refutations of the Heideggerian or French interpretations of Nietzsche, what follows will be disappointing, for that is not what I sought to do. Instead, I wanted to display Heidegger's, Derrida's and several other post-structuralist interpretations at their best, articulating both what they offer the reader and what I find they miss. To do this meant, especially in the cases of Heidegger and Derrida, lengthy and detailed exegeses which would introduce their interpretations to those who, by training or disposition, were unable or unwilling to read their interpretations. I try to provide clear restatements that follow the text's own developments while holding my critical comments to a few selective intrusions during the exposition and several discussions in the notes. I believe that my success in clarifying these interpretations is a function of not interrupting their explication with frequent objections and digressions. While these exegetical summaries might not be necessary for the Nietzsche specialist, who in addition to Part Three, may be more interested in the opening and concluding remarks to each of the first two parts and the critical comments and intertextual connections drawn in the notes, my hope is to make Heidegger's and Derrida's readings accessible to anyone who might pick up my work with the intention of reading about Nietzsche's own perspectives on interpretation.

The real novelty of my discussion, I believe, is to be found in the third part, where I work out a Nietzschean approach to interpretation. Although there have been many books written on Nietzsche in the last two decades, and many more books will no doubt be written in the next few years, there has not been a discussion in English that focuses on Nietzsche's interpretive practices. This is not to say that Nietzsche's impact on current interpretation theory has gone unrecognized. In fact, precisely the opposite is the case, as most philosophical interpretations of Nietzsche at the very least mention Nietzsche's influence, and it is almost *de rigueur* for literary theorists to invoke Nietzsche when discussions of interpretive practices arise. But what is missing in all these invocations is a sustained analysis of the various things Nietzsche says about and does with interpretation. I hope that this work will at least begin to fill this gap in the literature on Nietzsche's impact on current interpretive practices.

This study has evolved over many years, and has undergone both major and minor changes in response to the thoughtful comments of several people. In particular, I would like to single out four individuals whose conversations helped me to understand, and whose friendship and encouragement gave me the confidence to continue working on this project and seek its publication: Bernd Magnus, Gayle L. Ormiston, Richard E. Palmer, and Calvin O. Schrag. I am certain they will each continue to question certain of my formulations, but I hope they also see and take some pleasure in those places where my own understanding of the texts I discuss has been informed by our conversations together. Many others have had an impact on the construction of this text, both directly and indirectly, and I would like to acknowledge and thank David B. Allison, David C. Hoy, Djelal Kadir, David F. Krell, Virgil Lokke, William L. McBride, Richard Schacht, Richard Schmitt, Charlene and Hans Siegfried, two anonymous reviewers at Routledge, the Program Committees and members of the Nietzsche Society and the North American Nietzsche Society who heard parts of this work presented in several forums, and my colleagues at Grinnell College, Purdue University, and Clarkson University.

I am also grateful to my editor, Maureen MacGrogan, for her support of this project, and I would like to acknowledge the staff at Routledge, especially Max

Zutty, Michael Esposito, and Karen Sullivan, and my assistants at Grinnell: Peter Simon, David McCammond-Watts, and Carl Thelin.

The research for and writing of this work was supported by the financial assistance provided by several institutions and I would like here to formally acknowledge the support of the Trustees of Grinnell College, the Grinnell College Grant Board, the American Council of Learned Societies Fellowships for Studies in Modern Society and Values, the National Endowment for the Humanities Summer Seminars for College Teachers, and the David Ross Research Foundation of Purdue University.

Finally, I would like once again to acknowledge the encouragement and love of my parents Joan and Leonard, my brother Mitchell, and my wife Jill. Without your support, this book would not have been possible and to all of you it is dedicated.

Parts of this work have been published previously: several paragraphs from the Introduction appear in a slightly different form in the "Editors' Introduction" to *The Hermeneutic Tradition: From Ast to Ricoeur,* edited by Gayle L. Ormiston and Alan D. Schrift, 1990 by The State University of New York Press; an earlier version of part of Chapter One appears in "Violence or Violation? Heidegger's Thinking 'about' Nietzsche," *Tulane Studies in Philosophy,* Vol. XXXII (Fall 1984); an earlier version of Chapter Two appears in *The Journal of the British Society for Phenomenology,* Vol. 14, No. 3 (1983); parts of Chapter Three appear in "Foucault and Derrida on Nietzsche and the 'end(s)' of 'man,' " in *Exceedingly Nietzsche: Aspects of Contemporary Nietzsche-Interpretation,* edited by David Farrell Krell and David Wood, 1988 by Routledge and Kegan Paul, Ltd.; an earlier version of Chapter Four appears in *Research in Phenomenology,* Vol. 14 (1984), by Humanities Press International, Inc.; an earlier version of Chapter Five appears in *Journal of the History of Philosophy,* Vol. 23, No. 3 (July 1985); parts of Chapters Six and Seven appear in "Between Perspectivism and Philology: Genealogy as Hermeneutic," *Nietzsche-Studien,* Band 16, 1987 by Walter de Gruyter, and "Genealogy and the Transvaluation of Philology," *International Studies in Philosophy,* Vol. XX, No. 2 (1988); several paragraphs from Chapter Seven appear in different form in "Reading, Writing, Text: Nietzsche's Deconstruction of Author-ity," *International Studies in Philosophy,* Vol. XVIII, No. 2 (1985). I thank the editors and publishers for their kind permission to republish these sections.

An aphorism, properly stamped and molded, has not been "deciphered" when it has simply been read; rather one has then to begin its interpretation, *for which is required an art of interpretation.*

—Nietzsche, *On the Genealogy of Morals*

Because I still like him, I can foresee the impatience of the bad *reader: this is the way I name or accuse the fearful reader, the reader in a hurry to be determined, decided upon deciding (in order to annul, in other words to bring back to oneself, one has to wish to know in advance what to expect, one wishes to expect what has happened, one wishes to expect (oneself)). Now, it is bad, and I know no other definition of the bad, it is bad to predestine one's reading, it is always bad to foretell. It is bad, reader, no longer to like retracing one's steps.*

—Derrida, *The Post Card*

Introduction

Nietzsche, in whose light and shadow all of us today, with our "for him" or "against him," are thinking and writing [. . . .]
                                        —Martin Heidegger, *Zur Seinsfrage*

[O]ne is much more of an artist than one knows.
                                        —*Beyond Good and Evil,* 192

In the past half-century, philosophers on the European continent have, with increasing frequency, come to characterize their investigations as "hermeneutical" or "interpretive." This hermeneutical turn indicates a rejection of the traditional concept of philosophy as the pursuit of metaphysical or epistemological foundations upon which to erect a philosophical system. Such metaphysical and epistemological foundationalism appears incapable of satisfactorily solving many of the problems with which it confronts itself, and the reason for this incapacity has come to be viewed not as a function of the particular systems which have been propounded, but rather as a function of the project of seeking metaphysical and epistemological foundations itself. We thus find many proponents of the hermeneutical turn describing their various projects in such terms as a *rethinking* of metaphysics[1] or a moving *beyond* epistemology.[2] However, by emphasizing the interpretive nature of all understanding instead of the traditional pursuit of firm foundations, the proponents of this view are themselves faced with the problem of devising some standard or standards by which to adjudicate competing interpretations. This is to say, if there are no foundations of knowledge or, to put this another way, if there is no single "correct" interpretation, does it make any sense to speak of "incorrect" interpretations? This problem in effect confronts any approach to interpretation with the following basic dilemma: if we are to avoid positing one interpretation as correct (which would ultimately entail a return to some sort of foundationalism), then how can we avoid lapsing into an unmitigated relativism in which all interpretations are regarded as equally legitimate? Any successful approach to interpretation must confront this basic hermeneutical dilemma, and in Parts One and Two of this study, I examine two leading interpretive approaches (those of Heidegger and deconstruction) in an effort to discern whether or not they succeed in resolving this dilemma. In Part Three, I show that Nietzsche's text provides some important insights for a successful resolution, and I develop these insights into an approach which, while

1

drawing on the resources of deconstruction, nevertheless provides an alternative to the Heideggerian and deconstructive approaches examined in Parts One and Two. Before moving to these analyses, it will be helpful first to contextualize this problem by briefly surveying the recent history of hermeneutic theory[3] with an eye toward disclosing the pervasiveness of this hermeneutical dilemma.

Although the term "hermeneutics" as an approach to textual interpretation has a history which dates back to Aristotle (who found the topic of sufficient importance that he devoted to it an entire treatise: *Peri Hermēneias* [*On Interpretation*]), the modern use of the term can be traced more directly to the work of two nineteenth-century thinkers: Friedrich Schleiermacher and Wilhelm Dilthey. Schleiermacher is credited with taking the first steps toward developing a *general* hermeneutic methodology, in contrast to a variety of *regional* hermeneutic approaches.[4] Prior to Schleiermacher, the task of textual interpretation was thought to require different interpretive methods depending on the type of text to be interpreted. Thus, legal texts gave rise to a juridical hermeneutic, sacred scripture to a biblical hermeneutic, literary texts to a philological hermeneutic, etc. Schleiermacher's project of a "general hermeneutics" sought to uncover the interpretive techniques which operate *universally* within understanding. For our present purposes, the techniques uncovered by Schleiermacher are not as significant as the end toward which they were directed. In Schleiermacher's view, the task of hermeneutics is essentially psychological: the goal of hermeneutics is to understand the "original" meaning of the text, which is to say, "to understand the text at first as well as and then even better than its author."[5] To attain this goal, one must psychologically reconstruct the author; the interpreter must project her- or himself "inside" the author and reconstruct the author's original imposition of a univocal sense.[6] This conception of hermeneutics reveals a basic limitation on the activity of interpretation: interpretation is always guided by the author's intended meaning and all interpretive activity aims to approximate as closely as possible this "original" authorial intent.

Dilthey, for his part, follows Schleiermacher in calling for a general hermeneutics, but in so doing, he broadens the scope of hermeneutical application. Like Schleiermacher, Dilthey sees hermeneutics as the "methodology of the understanding of recorded expressions,"[7] but he criticizes Schleiermacher for limiting hermeneutics to the analysis of "understanding which is a reshaping or reconstruction on the basis of its relationship to the process of literary creation."[8] Dilthey regards hermeneutics as having a wider epistemological application than that acknowledged by Schleiermacher, and he broadened the scope of the methodology of understanding to facilitate the acquisition of knowledge of *all* aspects of mental (*geistige*) life. Dilthey thus writes that, in addition to Schleiermacher's "philological procedures," hermeneutics has

> a second task which is indeed its main one: it is to counteract the constant irruption of romantic whim and skeptical subjectivity into the realm of history by laying the

historical foundations of valid interpretation on which all certainty in history rests. Absorbed into the context of epistemology, logic and methodology of the human studies the theory of interpretation becomes a vital link between philosophy and the historical disciplines, an essential part of the foundations of the human sciences.[9]

In this remark, we see Dilthey's central task: in an effort to respond to the anti-Hegelian positivism of his day, Dilthey's hermeneutic method will put the human sciences (*Geisteswissenschaften*) on as secure a foundation as the scientific method had provided for the natural sciences (*Naturwissenschaften*). It will do so by providing a definitive answer to the question "How is historical knowledge possible?" For Dilthey, the question of the possibility of historical knowledge raises the question of how a knowing subject comes to know *objectively* that which has been subjectively created. Dilthey answers that we will attain such objective knowledge "if the individual processes which combine in the creation of this system can be sorted out and it can be shown what part each of them plays, both in the construction of the historical course of events in the mind-constructed world and in the discovery of its systematic nature."[10] Unfortunately, the way Dilthey explicates this answer reiterates, at the level of historical understanding, the psychologistic mistake of which he had accused Schleiermacher at the level of literary understanding:

> Understanding is a rediscovery of the I in the Thou: the mind rediscovers itself at ever higher levels of complex involvement: this identity of the mind in the I and the Thou, in every subject of a community, in every system of a culture and finally, in the totality of mind and universal history, makes successful cooperation between different processes in the human sciences possible.[11]

Dilthey avoids the problems of psychologism associated with Schleiermacher's hermeneutics by directing understanding toward the reconstruction of the historical product, whether it is an event or an object, rather than toward the reproduction of the psychic state of the author. Nevertheless, he continues to locate the meaning of historical events in the mental processes of the historical agents involved, in their productions, and in our objective psychological reconstruction of them.

In the move from Dilthey to Martin Heidegger, a fundamental shift in the approach to hermeneutics takes place. Whereas Dilthey and Schleiermacher had conceived hermeneutics to be at bottom an epistemological endeavor, Heidegger situates hermeneutics in the realm of ontology. This is to say, for Heidegger hermeneutics is no longer directed toward discovering the epistemological foundations of the human sciences or the methodological principles which can lead to objective knowledge in the human sciences. Rather, it seeks to uncover the ontological conditions which underlie such claims to knowledge. As a methodology of understanding, Heidegger views the hermeneutic projects of Dilthey and Schleiermacher as having evolved from hermeneutics in its primordial signification, "through which the authentic meaning of Being, and also those basic structures of Being which Dasein itself possesses, are *made known* to Dasein's understanding of Being."[12] The hermeneutic of Dasein, "as an analytic of *existence*," is thus, for Heidegger, the point of departure for philosophy conceived as "universal phenomenological ontology."[13] This is to say, the first step on the way to fundamental ontology, as the uncovering of the meaning of Being, will be a hermeneutic inquiry into the structures of Being implicated in the activities of understanding and interpretation.

Although Heidegger stopped speaking of his own project as "hermeneutical" shortly after the publication of *Being and Time,* the importance and influence of his situating hermeneutics within ontology rather than epistemology should not be underestimated, and it would not be incorrect to view much of subsequent hermeneutical reflection as, in part, entangled within the controversy over whether hermeneutics belongs in one or the other of these realms. A number of different camps within the hermeneutic tradition have developed since Heidegger's move beyond the conception of hermeneutics as a methodology of understanding, and between these camps a number of critical dialogues have emerged.[14] Hans-Georg Gadamer most clearly follows the Heideggerian program of phenomenological hermeneutics in his elaboration of the later Heideggerian insight into the "linguisticality" (*Sprachlichkeit*) of understanding and ontology. For Gadamer, "language is the universal medium in which understanding itself is realized [and] the mode or realization of language is interpretation."[15] Like Heidegger, Gadamer rejects limiting the scope of hermeneutical inquiry, conceived as the study of "the phenomenon of understanding and of the correct interpretation of what has been understood," to problems "proper to the methodology of the human sciences."[16] Rather, insofar as all understanding is mediated through language, the task of hermeneutics is conceived as a descriptive ontological analysis of the linguistically-mediated dialogue between the tradition and the reflective appropriation of it.[17] Gadamer thus concludes that "language constitutes the hermeneutical event proper not as language, whether as grammar or as lexicon, but in the coming into language of that which has been said in the tradition: an event that is at once assimilation and interpretation."[18] Insofar as language is a central point where "I" and world "manifest their original unity," Gadamer locates within language a "universal ontological structure." Language is "Being that can be understood,"[19] and the ontological significance of linguisticality for Gadamerian hermeneutical reflection cannot be overestimated.

In the debates and dialogues which have surrounded Gadamerian hermeneutics, we can see the focus on issues of interpretive dogmatism and relativism. On the one hand, Gadamer has been accused by the objectivist camp of being relativistic in his approach to interpretation. Both Emilio Betti and E. D. Hirsch, Jr., two major spokespersons for "objective hermeneutics," have objected to Gadamer's rejection of method on the grounds that such a lack of methodology threatens the objective status of interpretation. Both Betti and Hirsch argue for the essential autonomy of the object to be interpreted and they criticize Gadamer's dialogical approach for inserting the subject into the hermeneutic circle. This insertion, in their views, inevitably leads to both subjectivism and relativism, with the consequence that hermeneutics is unable to distinguish correct from incorrect interpretations. For Betti, Gadamer's subjectivist position

> tends toward the confounding of interpretation and meaning-inference [*Sinngebung*] and the removing of the canon of the autonomy of the object, with the consequence of putting into doubt the objectivity of the results of interpretive procedures in all the human sciences. It is my opinion that it is our duty as guardians and practitioners of the study of history to protect this kind of objectivity and to provide evidence of the epistemological condition of its possibility. [. . .] The obvious difficulty with the hermeneutical method proposed by Gadamer seems to lie, for me, in that it enables a substantive agreement between text and reader—i.e., between the apparently easily accessible meaning of a text and the subjective conception of the reader—to be formed without, however, guaranteeing the correctness of understanding; for that it would be necessary that the understanding arrived at corresponded fully to the meaning underlying the text as an objectivation of mind. Only then would the objectivity of the result be guaranteed on the basis of a reliable process of interpretation.[20]

Betti concludes that whereas Gadamer concerns himself with a *quaestio facti,* that of "ascertaining what actually happens in the activity of thought apparent in interpretation," the proper task of hermeneutics is to provide a solution to the *quaestio juris,* "i.e., what one should aim for in the task of interpretation, what methods to use and what guidelines to follow in the correct execution of this task."[21]

Hirsch follows Betti in this critique of Gadamer's subjectivism and relativism, as we can see in the following explication of the goal of interpretation:

> The interpreter's primary task is to reproduce in himself the author's "logic," his attitudes, his cultural givens, in short, his world. Even though the process of verification is highly complex and difficult, the ultimate verificative principle is very simple— the imaginative reconstruction of the speaking subject.[22]

As the title of Hirsch's major work makes clear, the task of hermeneutics is to achieve *validity* in interpretation: "The activity of interpretation can lay claim to intellectual respectability only if its results can lay claim to validity."[23] To be valid, an interpretation must reproduce the "determinate meaning" of the object being interpreted and, in Hirsch's view, the only meaning which will satisfy this condition of determinacy is the author's intended meaning: "On purely practical grounds, therefore, it is preferable to agree that the meaning of a text is the author's meaning."[24] For Betti, the appeal to authorial intent is justified on more than "practical" grounds. In fact, it follows directly from the "canon of the hermeneutical autonomy of the object." To be regarded as autonomous means, for Betti, that the object

> should be judged in relation to the standards immanent in the original intention: the intention, that is, which the created forms should correspond to from the point of view of the author and his formative impulse in the course of the creative process; [. . .][25]

In determining the validity of interpretation according to the degree of correspondence to the author's original intention, the dogmatic character of "objective hermeneutics" is clearly revealed: the text has a single, determinate meaning and any interpretation that does not reproduce this meaning is judged, on this ground alone, to be incorrect.

In addition to this objectivistic critique of Gadamer's alleged relativism, we also find a critique of Gadamerian dogmatism. This criticism comes from the perspective of "critical hermeneutics" and has been most forcefully propounded by Jürgen Habermas in his debate with Gadamer. Habermas objects to what he sees as Gadamer's uncritical acceptance of the tradition. For Habermas, the tradition is always appropriated as an authority, and all authority is by its nature authoritarian. Within tradition, certain forces of repression and domination are always operating and in our appropriation of the tradition, we are in danger of appropriating the ideological interests which the tradition has sanctioned. This is not to say, however, that we should simply discard the tradition. Rather, Habermas argues for our appropriating the tradition *critically:* in our discourse with the tradition, we must critically attend to the ideological forces of repression and domination that are always at work *within* the tradition. In refraining from a critique of what the tradition hands down, Habermas sees Gadamer unavoidably accepting the interests which traditional authority has surreptitiously incorporated into language itself. That is, in uncritically apprehending the language of the tradition, he cannot avoid appropriating the authoritarian values that have infiltrated the language of the tradition itself. Whether Habermas is right in regarding the tradition as necessarily a medium of domination, and whether or not Gadamer has successfully replied to Habermas's criticism of his uncritical acceptance of the ideological domination transmitted through the medium of the linguistic tradition, is not as significant for the present study as is the fact that this debate again focuses our attention on the question of dogmatism and relativism in interpretation.[26] Thus, while on the one hand, Gadamer finds himself responding to Betti and Hirsch's charges of relativism and subjectivism, on the other hand, he is forced to respond in his dialogue with Habermas to the charge of dogmatism.[27]

This debate concerning dogmatism and relativism has recently resurfaced with the appearance of a new interpretive approach, one that consciously seeks to distance itself from the hermeneutic tradition precisely in regard to the question of dogmatism. This "deconstructive" approach draws on the insights of both phenomenological hermeneutics and structuralist linguistics in an effort to move beyond the hermeneutic circle to a view of interpretation as infinite play. Jacques Derrida has emerged as the leading spokesperson for this deconstructive approach and, unlike Betti and Hirsch, he does not shy away from but, rather, embellishes the relativistic tendency within phenomenological hermeneutics. For Derrida, reading as a "transformational" activity[28] develops a multiplicity of interpretations from the fundamental polysemy inherent in both linguistic and non-linguistic signs. The deconstructionists thus broaden the scope of interpretive activity to the limit, as the world itself is now viewed as a text to be read and reading becomes a model for all perceptual acts. Regarding the Heideggerian hermeneutic, deconstructionists criticize what they view as a nostalgic longing for the presence of an authentic meaning that serves to guide the hermeneutic procedures of textual deciphering. In criticizing this dogmatic Heideggerian tendency on the grounds that it will put an end to the proliferative play of creative, transformational interpretation, Derrida and other deconstructive interpreters have been frequently criticized for advocating an unmitigated relativism that results in the acceptance of all interpretations as equally legitimate.

The debate between Heideggerian hermeneutics and Derridean deconstruction, which once again manifests the difficulty of avoiding both dogmatism and relativism in interpretation, is at present a central issue in hermeneutic theory that, in addition, raises important questions concerning how we should interpret the history of philosophy. The following study attempts to show that Nietzsche's text can help us to avoid the noxious consequences of this interpretive dilemma in two distinct yet interconnected ways. First, Nietzsche's text will be considered as an object of interpretation. In Parts One and Two, we will examine closely the interpretations of Nietzsche that have been generated from Heidegger's hermeneutic method, as well as a number of post-structural and deconstructive interpretations. Our task, in the first two parts, will not be to confront these interpretive approaches directly. Rather, we will operate on the assumption that a careful examination of what these interpreters actually *do* in their readings, the interpretive moves that they make, may be more significant for evaluating the respective approaches they propose than a critical examination of the methodological procedures which they explicitly claim to be following. Thus, while Heidegger no longer explicitly claims to be engaged in "hermeneutic" analysis when he interprets Nietzsche's thinking, the way his interpretation proceeds reveals a number of implicit methodological assumptions at work within his reading of Nietzsche. The same is true of the deconstructive readings: although they refrain from enumerating the acceptable "protocols of reading," their interpretations implicitly sanction certain protocols and foreclose others. Therefore, in what follows we will examine the *ways* Heidegger and several post-structuralists interpret the Nietzschean text, and through a careful examination and exposition of their interpretive practices, the dogmatic tendency of Heidegger and the relativistic tendency of deconstruction will be displayed.

The second contribution which Nietzsche's text makes toward circumventing this dilemma of dogmatism and relativism in interpretation will be explored in Part Three. While there are frequent references to Nietzsche as a forerunner of contemporary hermeneutics, little attention has been paid to the specific contributions to interpretation theory which can be found in the Nietzschean text. The present study is, in large part, an attempt to rectify this situation. The phenomenon of interpretation is a recurrent theme throughout Nietzsche's writings, and within Nietzsche's remarks on interpretation a tension is present which anticipates the current dilemma of dogmatism and relativism. In examining Nietzsche's exposition of this tension, I will propose a pluralistic approach to interpretation and I will argue that this interpretive pluralism circumvents the current hermeneutic dilemma by refusing to be situated within the traditional hermeneutic alternatives of fidelity and violation.

Insofar as pluralism shares with relativism a basic assumption as to the multiplicity of possible interpretations, it should come as no surprise that the approach developed in Part Three will occasionally resemble deconstruction. This resemblance is not unintended, and there will be several points in the discussion where my own reconstruction of a Nietzschean interpretive approach will approximate the approach of Derrida and other deconstructive interpreters. At times, Nietzsche claimed himself to be a relativist or pluralist, and he was consistent in his renunciation of interpretive dogmatism. As a result, the interpretive approach I develop will have much more in common with Derrida's approach than with Heidegger's. This is not to say that Derrida's interpretive practices are without problems, or that pluralism and relativism are the same. Rather, it is to acknowledge that while affinities exist between my Nietzschean approach and Derrida's, there are also several differences that will emerge as we compare these respective interpretive practices.

Before concluding this introduction, one final disclosure of strategy is in order, and it concerns Nietzsche's remark cited as one of the epigraphs to this introduction regarding one's being more of an artist than one knows. In the interpretation of Nietzsche's text provided in Part Three, I have attempted to exercise a method of interpretive pluralism and, in so doing, this study attempts to dismantle the traditional border which has separated the activity of interpretation from that of original creation. That is to say, the interpretation which I provide is both a "mere" commentary *and* an "original" creation, but, in being *both at once,* this interpretation seeks to show that no commentary is ever a *mere* reproduction nor is any act of creation ever wholly original. By affirming an active, transformational approach, the pluralistic account of interpretive construction advocated here seeks to situate itself outside the traditional hermeneutic disjunctions of fidelity/violation, true/false, accurate/inaccurate. Sartre writes, in *What is Literature?* that "for the reader, all is to do and all is already done."[29] I take this, as well as Nietzsche's remark, quite seriously. The interpretation here provided is thus, on the one hand, an exegetical commentary on a number of

Nietzsche's remarks on language, metaphor, and rhetoric, perspectivism and philology, and genealogy and interpretation. But, on the other hand, by organizing these various remarks in the ways I do, I produce not a repetition of the Nietzschean text but a new construction of that text which, I believe, *is* original to the extent that it brings to the fore aspects of this text heretofore unrecognized by many of Nietzsche's English-speaking readers. In so doing, my interpretation seeks to situate itself alongside the Heideggerian and Derridean interpretations in accordance with the following strategy. Both Heidegger and Derrida view the Nietzschean text as an occasion for something other than mere exegesis. That is, in addition to their viewing Nietzsche's text as an object of interpretation, for Heidegger this text also provides a space in which he seeks to pursue his own task of the overcoming of metaphysics and the oblivion of Being while, for Derrida, the Nietzschean text opens a space in which he can critically confront Heidegger's hermeneutic method. In a similar fashion, the interpretation of Nietzsche which follows should be read both as an interpretation *of* Nietzsche's text and as the space in which I seek to confront both the Heideggerian and the deconstructive methods of interpretation, in an effort to contribute to a resolution of the seemingly intractable hermeneutic dilemma of avoiding both dogmatism and unmitigated relativism in interpretation. Whether or not this new construction fits the Nietzschean text, and whether or not it contributes to resolving this hermeneutic dilemma, are questions left to the readers' interpretive play to decide.

Part 1
Heidegger's Nietzsche

Chapter 1

Heidegger Reading Nietzsche

In the usual present-day view what has been said here is a mere product of the farfetched and one-sided Heideggerian method of exegesis, which has already become proverbial. But here we may, indeed, we must ask: Which interpretation is the true one, the one which simply takes over a perspective into which it has fallen, because this perspective, this line of sight, presents itself as familiar and self-evident; or the interpretation which questions the customary perspective from top to bottom, because conceivably—and indeed actually—this line of sight does not lead to what is in need of being seen.
—Martin Heidegger, *An Introduction to Metaphysics*

Rather than protect Nietzsche from the Heideggerian reading, we should perhaps offer him up to it completely, underwriting that interpretation without reserve.
—Jacques Derrida, *Of Grammatology*

To appropriate one of Nietzsche's more famous chapter headings, Heidegger's entire philosophical project can be viewed as an examination of "The History of an Error." This error is metaphysics, whose history Heidegger recounts as the story of the forgetfulness of Being. In this history, Nietzsche occupies a place of singular importance, evidenced by the fact that Heidegger published a greater volume of material on Nietzsche (over 1,200 pages devoted specifically to interpretations of Nietzsche) than any other figure in this history. Nietzsche's paramount importance for Heidegger emerges in his viewing Nietzsche's work as the "completion of metaphysics"; Heidegger finds in Nietzsche the most complete expression of the forgetfulness of Being. If Being is to be recovered from this oblivion, philosophy must "overcome metaphysics" and the first step on this path must be a confrontation (*Aus-einander-setzung*) with the thought of Nietzsche, seen as the greatest expression of the oblivion of Being.

In what follows, we will examine Heidegger's confrontation with Nietzsche as it is presented in three of Heidegger's discussions: his discussion of Nietzsche's proclamation of the death of God; his answer to the question "Who is Zarathustra?"; and his interpretation of Nietzsche's discussion of art as exhibiting most explicitly Nietzsche's bringing metaphysics to completion through the overturning of Platonism. This examination will be prefaced by a discussion of several basic methodological choices that guide Heidegger's reading, and it will be followed in Chapter Two by a critical response to Heidegger that returns to these methodological choices and appraises the overall success of Heidegger's method in his interpretation of Nietzsche, while offering several alternative interpretations. The examination itself, which comprises the majority of this first chapter, is largely exegetical and a word of explanation as to the function it serves in my argument is called for. In this chapter, I want to *demonstrate* through a careful exegesis of Heidegger's works on Nietzsche what many readers either *assume* or take on the word of other commentators or critics of Heidegger. As a scholarly work, I think it is important to actually look at what Heidegger says and point out the places where he makes the dogmatic interpretive moves that I, and many others, find problematic. This explication is, therefore, a necessary step in confronting the Heideggerian interpretation: it both exemplifies the methodological choices discussed in the first section of this chapter and supports my critical comments in the following chapter.

Before beginning this examination, another word regarding my approach to the reading of Heidegger is in order. At the simplest level, there would seem to be two distinct yet interconnected ways to approach a reading of Heidegger's works on Nietzsche. One can view these works from the perspective of Heidegger's philosophical project of overcoming metaphysics and retrieving Being from its oblivion, in which case these works speak primarily about Heidegger, and any insights into Nietzsche's philosophy are incidental and derivative. Or one can view these works as an exegesis of Nietzsche's philosophical corpus, in which case they speak to us primarily about Nietzsche, and only incidentally about Heidegger. While it will often be impossible to keep separate these two strategies of reading, I will emphasize the latter, viewing Heidegger's works on Nietzsche to be works about Nietzsche and *not* about Heidegger. Therefore, these works will be read critically only in terms of their being interpretations of Nietzsche's philosophy and, as such, as examples of Heidegger's method of interpretation; any critical remarks regarding Heidegger's reading of the history of philosophy and his task of overcoming metaphysics will, for the most part, be deferred. William J. Richardson, one of Heidegger's most sympathetic commentators, told the following story when he delivered the 1965 "Suarez Lecture" at Fordham University: "When confronted with the history of criticisms of his interpretation of Kant, Heidegger simply said: 'it may not be good Kant, but it's excellent Heidegger.' "[1] The following examination will not concern itself *per se* with what is "excellent Heidegger," but will continually raise the question of whether or not Heidegger's interpretation is "good Nietzsche." The question of Heidegger's philosophy proper will be raised only in those sections where we will locate the methodological principles which ground Heidegger's hermeneutic.

Heidegger's Methodological Choices

Broadly viewed, Heidegger's reading of Nietzsche unfolds out of three methodological choices drawn from his meditations on thinking. The first of these choices grounds Heidegger's decision to locate what he calls "Nietzsche's philosophy proper" in his unpublished *Nachlass*, part of which appeared under the title *The Will to Power*. Heidegger writes that "The 'doctrine' of a thinker is that which is left unsaid in what he says."[2] There is a significant ambiguity in the Heideggerian conception of the "unsaid" as it unfolds in his reading of Nietzsche. The "unsaid" alludes to what, as a simple matter of fact, did not come to be expressed by Nietzsche in the works which he saw published. At the same time, it also makes reference to that which *cannot* be said in any form from within the Western metaphysical tradition of which Nietzsche is seen to be a part. Heidegger's application of each of these two senses is revealed in his discussion of the Nietzschean "unsaid." First, the primacy of the unsaid justifies his focusing on Nietzsche's *Nachlass*. If the texts which Nietzsche himself had published are what he said, then to his literary remains, the *Nachlass*, falls the characterization of being unsaid. Heidegger resorts to the idea of the primacy of what remains unsaid in a thinker when he asserts that *The Will to Power*—by which he refers to the "text" that Nietzsche intended to publish with that title, and not merely that book titled *The Will to Power* which was constructed from his notebooks by his literary executors—is Nietzsche's philosophical "main structure," his *Hauptwerk*, to which all his published texts stand as an entrance way (*Vorhalle*).

> Nietzsche's philosophy proper, the fundamental position on the basis of which he speaks [. . .] in all the writings he himself published, did not assume a final form and was not itself published in any book, neither in the decade between 1879 and 1889 nor during the years preceding. What Nietzsche himself published during his creative years was always foreground. [. . .] His philosophy proper was left behind as posthumous, unpublished work.[3]

The second use Heidegger makes of the essentiality of what remains unsaid in what a thinker says can be understood in terms of his related notion of the unthought. After *Thus Spoke Zarathustra*, Heidegger tells us, "Nietzsche never did publish what he really thought."[4] Rather, all his published writings after *Zarathustra* are polemical responses to the event of European nihilism. What Nietzsche really thought is to be found in his *Nachlass*, and even there we find what Nietzsche thought only in the form of what is unthought. "What is unthought in a thinker's thought is not a lack inherent in his thought. What is *un*-thought is there in each case only as the un-*thought*. The more original the thinking, the richer will be what is unthought in it" (*WCT*, p. 76). As we will see, what remains unthought in Nietzsche's thinking is the same as what remains unthought in the thinking of Western history as the history of metaphysics: the Truth of Being. Heidegger's principal aim in his exposition of Nietzsche will be to think the thought of the Truth of Being which remains unthought in Nietzsche as the culmination of Western thinking as metaphysics.

Before moving to Heidegger's second methodological choice, a few critical remarks on Heidegger's emphasis upon the *Nachlass* and the unthought in Nietzsche are called for. Although there is no clear consensus among Nietzsche's commentators as to where to locate Nietzsche's "philosophy proper," Heidegger's emphasis on the *Nachlass* is both extreme and idiosyncratic. Karl Schlechta, for instance, writes in the postscript to his edition of Nietzsche's works: "I omit the already published *Nachlass,* because to my knowledge no *new* central thought is to be found there" (*WDB, III,* p. 1433). Schlechta finds in the *Nachlass* only new variations and different expressions of the basic themes which Nietzsche put forth in his published works. Karl Jaspers, on the other hand, does not assent to the primacy of either the published or posthumous works. In his work on Nietzsche, Jaspers writes that "it must be realized that none of Nietzsche's forms of communication has a privileged character. [. . .] Nowhere is Nietzsche's work truly centralized: there is no *magnum opus.*"[5] This debate concerning which texts of Nietzsche, if any, are to be given primacy raises some important questions regarding Nietzsche interpretation, as well as some interesting philosophical questions on the nature of textuality. On this question, Bernd Magnus has suggested a helpful distinction.[6] He divides Nietzsche's principal commentators into two camps: "lumpers" (including Heidegger, Jaspers, Danto, Schacht, Deleuze, Müller-Lauter), for whom the status of the *Nachlass* is unproblematic, and who treat it on at least a par with Nietzsche's published writings; and "splitters" (including Alderman, Hollingdale, Strong, Montinari and himself), who "distinguish sharply between published and unpublished writings." According to this scheme, I might suggest that rather than being a "lumper," Heidegger is an "inverse splitter": he, too, separates sharply between published and unpublished writings, but he gives priority to the *unpublished* writings. It will suffice to say at this point that Heidegger's almost exclusive focus on the unpublished notes should be regarded with suspicion. The extreme care that Nietzsche took in the publishing of those works that appeared during his lifetime must be taken into account when considering what *Nietzsche* thought. And the status of the unpublished notes vis-à-vis his published works must be questioned. Why did some notes remain unpublished? Nietzsche's notes often take the form of "experiments in thought." He follows the progress, on paper, of some of his ideas and, if this progress results in failure, the notes are set aside, sometimes returned to and sometimes not. One must, in reading the unpublished notes, attend to the question of why the notes remained unpublished. The answer may be that he never got around to finalizing them, or that he found himself in disagreement with the results of his "thought-experiment."[7] To value these notes *en masse* as the site of Nietzsche's philosophy proper, as Heidegger does, does not do justice to the stylistic care which Nietzsche devoted to bringing his works to publication.

A few remarks are also called for regarding Heidegger's thinking of what remains unthought in the history of Western philosophy, and this brings us back to the issue raised earlier as to whether Heidegger's exposition of Nietzsche is "good Heidegger" or "good Nietzsche." Richardson characterizes Heidegger's reading of the history of Western thinking as the endeavor "to comprehend and express not what another thinker thought/said, but what he did not think/say, could not think/say, and why he could not think/say it."[8] With this idea in mind, we can grasp Heidegger's strategy in his exposition of Nietzsche. What Nietzsche did not and could not think/say is the question of the Truth of Being, and the reason why Nietzsche did not/could not think/say the question of the Truth of Being is that he remained within the metaphysical tradition. Heidegger writes that it is only by conceiving Nietzsche as the culmination of this metaphysical tradition, and then proceeding to the question of the Truth of Being, that we can succeed in arriving at Nietzsche's philosophy proper, a philosophy that, while leaving unthought the question of the Truth of Being, nevertheless opens up the path by which subsequent thinking will be able to think this hitherto unthought thought (see *N* I, p. 10). While we shall defer a discussion of this conception of Nietzsche's place in the history of Western thinking until we have examined more carefully Heidegger's situating Nietzsche as the culmination of metaphysics, nevertheless we must here point out the danger that such a strategy poses for the hermeneutic enterprise. Heidegger declares that our thinking on the tradition requires that we recognize and acknowledge that tradition. "Respecting and acknowledging [*Anerkennen*, recognizing, admitting] is not yet agreement; but it is the necessary precondition for any confrontation" (*WCT*, p. 81. Translation altered.). Yet it is not at all clear that Heidegger's thinking adheres to this requirement. What we come to find in Heidegger's reading of Nietzsche is the uniform character of the tradition of Western thinking as the forgetfulness of Being and the identity of what is unthought in all thinkers within this tradition, viz., what is unthought is in each case the question of the Truth of Being. Whereas this provides an interesting vantage-point from which to view the unfolding of the tradition of Western metaphysics, the appropriateness of such a vantage-point to each figure within that tradition is a dubious claim. Heidegger argues that what is unthought in Plato and Aristotle is the *same* as what is unthought in such figures as Descartes, Leibniz, Hegel and Nietzsche. The danger that such a strategy poses for hermeneutics is that of dogmatism: the willful reading of a text in accordance with a pre-existing schema of interpretation that is superimposed on the text and with which the text is made to cohere. In our evaluation of Heidegger's reading of Nietzsche, we must be attentive to this willful appropriation of Nietzsche by Heidegger, and we must be aware of a possible tendency in Heidegger's reading of *ap*propriation's becoming *ex*propriation.[9] We will be guided in this task by a remark of Nietzsche's regarding the theologian's *"incapacity for philology."*

> Philology is to be understood here in a very wide sense as the art of reading well— of being able to read off a fact *without* falsifying it by interpretation, *without* losing caution, patience, subtlety in the desire for understanding. Philology as *ephexis* [undecisiveness] in interpretation. (*A*, 52)[10]

That is to say, we must inquire whether or not Heidegger's confrontation with Nietzsche's thought suffers from this "incapacity for philology";[11] whether in his desire to understand Nietzsche as the completion of the metaphysical tradition, Heidegger falsifies Nietzsche's thinking by viewing it under the interpretation of the history of metaphysics as the oblivion of Being.

The second methodological principle that guides Heidegger's reading of Nietzsche is that "every thinker thinks only one single thought"[12] (*WCT*, p. 50). Nietzsche, Heidegger tells us, "belongs to the essential thinkers." Heidegger echoes his conclusion from the meditation on thinking when he writes:

> With the name "thinker" we name those individuals chosen among men who are destined to think a single thought—this thought always "about" *beings as a whole*. Every thinker thinks only a *single* thought.[13]

Using this principle as a point of departure, Heidegger seeks to systematize the admittedly unsystematic expressions that Nietzsche has given us. Nietzsche thinks his one and only thought, Heidegger tells us, as the thought of the eternal recurrence of the same (*WCT*, p. 50). The eternal recurrence "is seen to coincide with the very center of Nietzsche's metaphysical thinking" (*N* I, p. 23). Around this center revolve all of Nietzsche's other major themes: will to power, *Übermensch*, transvaluation of values, and nihilism. Heidegger's systemization of Nietzsche does not stop here, however. Rather, following from the principle that Nietzsche's *one* and *only* thought is the eternal recurrence, Heidegger goes on to assert the *unity* of Nietzsche's five major themes: they are the *same*.

> The so-called five major themes—"nihilism," "transvaluation of all values," "will to power," "eternal recurrence of the same," "*Übermensch*"—each portrays Nietzsche's metaphysics in *one* respect, but at any given time, each also shows a determinate view of the whole. Thus Nietzsche's metaphysics is grasped only when what are named in these five themes are thought—that is, essentially experienced—in their primordial and heretofore merely intimated unity [*Zusammengehörigkeit*].[14]

As we will see, the unity of these themes comes to light when Nietzsche's thought of the eternal recurrence is examined in terms of the unthought question that it raises: the question of Being and Time (cf. *N* I, p. 20). Here Nietzsche rejoins Plato and Aristotle, who also thought Being as Time in terms of their thinking Being as *ousia* (presence), and he brings to completion the tradition which they began. Nietzsche is seen as joining Plato and Aristotle rather than going beyond them in that "Nietzsche thinks that thought [i.e., Being as Time] but does not think it as the *question* of Being and Time" (*N* I, p. 20). It is the *question* of Being and Time, which is to say, the question of the Truth of Being, that remains unthought in Nietzsche as in Plato and Aristotle, and it is only through the thinking of this question *as* a question that metaphysics will be overcome.

We shall return to this question of Being and Time which remains unthought at the center of the unity of all Nietzsche's major themes when we examine

Heidegger's discussion of this unthought unity. At this point, we must restrict ourselves to two preliminary remarks. First, Heidegger's attempt to unify Nietzsche's fragmented thoughts is a monumental effort, and he achieves no small success in his conceptual organization of Nietzsche's philosophy. But second, we must ask what in Nietzsche's thinking is lost in this attempt at systemization. The unity of Nietzsche's five themes, focused as they are around his thought of the eternal recurrence as the thought of Being and Time, is achieved at the cost of the complete "metaphysicalization" of Nietzsche. Heidegger's systematic unity works only so long as Nietzsche's themes are conceived metaphysically, that is, viewed in terms of the question of the Truth of Being. While Nietzsche's philosophy may be subject to a metaphysical interpretation, and Heidegger's reading would seem to be *prima facie* evidence that it is, it seems to be a mistake to assert, as Heidegger does throughout his interpretation, that Nietzsche is *only* a metaphysical thinker. If Nietzsche's five themes (will to power, *Übermensch,* transvaluation, eternal recurrence and nihilism) can be interpreted in a non-metaphysical manner, and if Heidegger's desire to systematize or totalize Nietzsche in terms of his "one and only thought" leads to the exclusion of all interpretations other than the metaphysical one, this will reveal something of great significance in appraising Heidegger's hermeneutic attempt at systemization. Nietzsche himself expressed a mistrust of all systematizers, and we shall follow him in this mistrust. If a hermeneutic method places unjustifiable constraints upon the play of interpretation, this will be grounds for the rejection of that method. Following the examination of Heidegger's interpretation, we shall return to this question of the effects of Heidegger's attempt at totalization and see what constraints it imposes on the interpretation of Nietzsche's philosophy.

This brings us to the third methodological choice guiding Heidegger's reading of Nietzsche, the choice to view *all* serious philosophical thinking as metaphysics. In the preceding pages, we saw Heidegger's metaphysicalization of Nietzsche as the consequence of his desire to focus Nietzsche's philosophy around his "one and only thought" of the eternal recurrence. Here we see Heidegger's metaphysicalization as the consequence of his desire "to take Nietzsche seriously as a thinker."[15] Heidegger wants to rescue Nietzsche from the common, yet erroneous, judgment that he is a "poet-philosopher" or a "philosopher of life" (see *N* I, p. 5). Rather, for Heidegger, Nietzsche is a thinker and *eo ipso* his thinking is determined by what is to be thought: Being. Nietzsche is not, however, able to think Being *as Being*. According to Heidegger, he can only think Being "metaphysically," that is, "as the truth of beings as such" (*NW,* p. 54). The answer Nietzsche provides to the question "What beings are?" is "will to power": will to power *is* what is, beings, *das Seiende*. Heidegger writes that "to think means this for Nietzsche: to represent what is as what is [*das Seiende als das Seiende vorstellen*]. Any metaphysical thinking is onto-logy or it is nothing at all" (*NW,* p. 55). If we are to take Nietzsche seriously as a thinker, we must view his thinking as the *logos* of *ontos,* as "that kind of thinking which everywhere provides and accounts for the ground of beings as such within the whole in terms of Being as the ground (*logos*)."[16] Only by viewing Nietzsche's thought in this way can we succeed in rescuing it from its mistaken interpretation as "poet-philosophy" or a "philosophy of life." Nietzsche's thought will then take its rightful place in the history of Western thinking as the last and greatest expression of that thinking, a thinking which in every true expression thinks, although only in the form of what remains "unthought" in its thinking, the same: the Being of beings.

The hermeneutic consequences of Heidegger's metaphysicalization of Nietzsche *qua* serious thinker are enormous. All of Nietzsche's psychological, anthropological, and axiological (aesthetic, ethical) insights are subsumed under the rubric of metaphysics. While these consequences have led many of Nietzsche's interpreters to reject, or at the very least, to modify Heidegger's methodological procedures in approaching Nietzsche's texts, Heidegger makes no attempt to mitigate this subsumption of Nietzsche's psychology, anthropology, and axiology to his metaphysics; on the contrary, he affirms these reductionist consequences of his methodological procedure:

> Judged by their wording, and even by their headings, Nietzsche's discussions do indeed move in the traditional conceptual framework of ethics and psychology. But in substance, Nietzsche thinks everything that falls under the headings of "ethics" and "psychology" in terms of metaphysics, that is, with a view to the question how the Being of beings as a whole is determined, and how it concerns man. "Ethics" and "psychology" are grounded in metaphysics. (*WCT,* p. 89)

In the examination of Heidegger's interpretation that follows, we will see how he unfolds Nietzsche's thinking as always and in each case grounded in metaphysics. However, in this examination, it will become apparent that Nietzsche's conception of metaphysics is seriously at odds with that of Heidegger. For Nietzsche, metaphysics borders on the nonsensical, and he expresses his opposition to all philosophies guided by the question of Being. We must therefore see how and if Heidegger's Nietzsche, who thinks everything with a view to the question of Being and the Being of beings, can be made to fit with the Nietzsche who sees in Being Platonic-Christian otherworldliness and who affirms the "radical repudiation of the very concept 'Being' " (*EH,* BT3). The answer to this question, as well as the other questions raised in these introductory remarks, can be resolved only through a careful examination of Heidegger's confrontation with the thought of Nietzsche, and to this task we must now turn.

"Nietzsche's Word: 'God is Dead' "

Heidegger's first published work devoted specifically to an interpretation of Nietzsche appeared in 1950 in *Holzwege,* with the title "Nietzsche's Word: 'God is Dead.'" In this essay, the major portions of which were frequently delivered to small groups in 1943, Heidegger summarized the bulk of his lectures on Nietzsche delivered at the University of Freiburg between 1936 and 1940 (which were themselves to be later reworked and published in 1961 as the two-volume *Nietzsche*). Although Heidegger's aim in this essay, as in virtually all his published work on Nietzsche, is not merely to provide an interpretation of Nietzsche's thought, he does restrict the discussion and focuses primarily on Nietzsche. In so doing, he avoids the frequent digressions into the metaphysical tradition that usually characterize his lectures. At the same time, this essay does take into account all those themes in Nietzsche's philosophy that Heidegger felt to be central, and thus provides us with more than the limited vantage-point on Nietzsche's thought which characterizes, for example, Heidegger's essay on Zarathustra.[17] Because of its concentration on and comprehensive view of Nietzsche's philosophy, and because it clearly displays how Heidegger brings to his reading of the history of philosophy his own agenda for exposing and overcoming the forgetting of Being, "Nietzsche's Word: 'God is Dead'" will serve as the site for our first examination of the results of Heidegger's confrontation with Nietzsche.

Heidegger opens his essay on Nietzsche's word of the death of God with a declaration of intent: "The following exposition attempts to point the way toward the point from which it may be possible someday to ask the question concerning the essence of nihilism" (*NW*, p. 53).[18] The meditation on Nietzsche's thought is the first step toward that point from which the question of the essence of nihilism may be asked, because Nietzsche recognized that reflection on the essence of nihilism is necessarily historical reflection. "Nietzsche himself interprets the course of Western history metaphysically, and indeed as the rise and development of nihilism" (*NW*, p. 54). Metaphysics is here thought not as the doctrine of any particular thinker, but rather "as the truth of what is as such and in its entirety [*die Wahrheit des Seienden als solchen im Ganzen*]" (*NW*, p. 54). Heidegger proceeds to elaborate the aim and scope of the reflection on Nietzsche as confining itself "to the sphere of one experience from out of which [the book] *Being and Time* is thought": the experience of the forgetting of Being.

> In the history of Western thinking, indeed continually from the beginning, what is [*das Seiende*] is thought in reference to Being; yet the truth of Being remains unthought, and not only is that truth denied to thinking as a possible experience, but Western thinking itself, and indeed in the form of metaphysics, expressly, but nevertheless unknowingly, veils the happening of that denial. (*NW*, p. 56)

Nietzsche, as well, veils the happening of this denial and therefore his thought, *qua* metaphysical, is a part of the history of Western thinking, i.e., is a part of the historical movement of the forgetting of Being which is named by "nihilism." But Nietzsche occupies a unique place within this history for two reasons. First, because "Nietzsche's thinking sees itself as belonging under the heading 'nihilism' " (*NW*, p. 57). And, second, because Nietzsche recognizes nihilism as a historical movement which has dominated and determined the history of the West. Nietzsche's interpretation of this historical movement whereby nihilism has achieved dominion is, for Heidegger, summed up in the brief statement "God is dead" (see *NW*, p. 57).

Heidegger's explication of the meaning of this brief statement takes us along a path traversing the entirety of Nietzsche's thinking. The first moment of this journey explores the interrelatedness in Nietzsche's philosophical thinking of nihilism, transvaluation, value, life, becoming, and will to power. Nietzsche's pronouncement of the death of God is not *merely* a personal expression of his atheistic attitude, and it should not therefore be understood as a mere formula for unbelief. "God" names not only the Christian God, but designates in addition the supersensory world in general, the world of Ideas and ideals which, since Plato, has been taken to be the true and genuinely real world. "God" designates the *meta*-physical world in the Kantian sense, that is, the world which is *beyond* the physical, sensory world. In this sense, Nietzsche's pronouncement "God is dead" means: the metaphysical, supersensory world has lost its effective power, and "God" as the name for this supersensory world of ideals no longer functions as the effective authority that determines the sensory, physical world from above and from without. Elucidating Nietzsche's pronouncement in this way shows how Nietzsche's "God is dead" functions as an interpretation for the historical movement of nihilism. Heidegger quotes Nietzsche: "What does nihilism mean? *That the highest values devaluate themselves*" (*WP*, 2). In this quote, Heidegger sees Nietzsche's understanding of nihilism as an ongoing historical event, under which is subsumed the entire history of Western thinking. What are these highest values which are now seen to be devaluating themselves? Metaphysics has given them many names: "the supersensory world, the Ideas, God, the moral law, the authority of reason, progress, the happiness of the greatest number, culture, civilization" (*NW*, p. 65). And what metaphysics understands by these names are "the true, the good, and the beautiful: the true, i.e., that which really is; the good, i.e., that upon which everything depends; the beautiful, i.e., the order and unity of that which is in its entirety" (*NW*, p. 66). By nihilism Nietzsche thus names the ongoing history of these highest values, the history of the becoming-ineffective of the true, the good, and the beautiful. But by nihilism, says Heidegger, Nietzsche does not mean merely the decay and ruin of these highest values. Rather, Nietzsche takes the first step in thinking nihilism essentially; that is, as the "intrinsic law" and the "inner logic" of Western history as the becoming-valueless of these highest values (see *NW*, p. 67). As such, Nietzsche recognizes the essential ambiguity that lies at the heart of the ongoing historical event of nihilism.

For Heidegger, Nietzsche's recognition of the ambiguity of nihilism is found in his distinction between "completed" and "incomplete" nihilism, and the consequent identification of nihilism with the transvaluation of all values. Incomplete nihilism says no to those values that have hitherto been regarded as most valuable, and thus founders in its desperate recognition of the devaluation of all values. Incomplete nihilism leads to the establishment of the dictatorship of Nothing, and recognizes in the devaluation of all values that Nothing remains. But for Nietzsche incomplete nihilism becomes subsumed under completed nihilism. "The no to the values hitherto comes out of a yes to the positing of new values" (*NW*, p. 67). In completed nihilism Heidegger sees the unity of nihilism and transvaluation in that Nietzsche recognizes that the *de*-valuation of all previous values requires the counter-movement of a *re*-valuation of new values. But the difference between incomplete and completed nihilism is not just the difference between *de*-valuation and *re*-valuation. In incomplete nihilism the old values are replaced by new ones, but these old values remain as the standard by which the new values are judged; that is, the supersensory world remains as the unattainable *telos* toward which the new values are directed. Completed nihilism brings not only the positing of new values but, in addition, there is posited a new principle of valuation, one grounded upon "the ideal of superabundant life" (*WP*, 14). In other words, not only does completed nihilism provide us with a new set of values, it provides us with a set of values no longer to be appraised in terms of a supersensory world. Rather, these new values will be judged according to the determining essence of everything living, that is, in accordance with the standard of life. To understand what Nietzsche means by completed nihilism, we must first understand what he means by "value" and "life."

Understanding what Nietzsche means by "value," Heidegger tells us, is the key to understanding his metaphysics because his metaphysics is "the metaphysics of value" (*NW*, p. 71). Heidegger quotes the following to exemplify Nietzsche's understanding of value: "The point-of-view of 'value' is the point-of-view constituting the *preservation-enhancement* conditions with respect to complex forms of relative duration of life within becoming" (*WP*, 715). The essence of value, Heidegger concludes, lies in its being a point-of-view (*Gesichtspunkt*) and, as such, there is a fundamental ambiguity which resides at the essence of value: "as a point-of-view, value is posited at any given time by a seeing and for a seeing" (*NW*, p. 71). In other words, to be a "point-of-view" can mean two things: to be a point from which a view is to be had, in the sense of a vantage-point, standing-point, or subjective opinion; or to be a point which is *in view*, the focal point of an act of seeing. And, in Nietzsche's characterization of the transvaluation of values in completed nihilism, we see clearly that "value" is used in its full ambiguity. In completed nihilism, the new values as points-of-view in the sense of focal-points are posited upon the grounds of a new point-of-view in the sense of a new vantage-point. Life, whose fundamental tendencies are preservation and enhancement, is both the new focal-point and the new vantage-point; in other words, life, for Nietzsche, as the aim and ground of values, *is* value.

Heidegger concludes the first moment of his exposition by linking the above discussion of life and value with becoming and will to power. The concept of seeing has undergone the "change of *idea* from *eidos* to *perceptio*. Seeing is that representing which since Leibniz has been grasped more explicitly in terms of its fundamental characteristic of striving (*appetitus*)" (*NW*, p. 72). By concluding his characterization of the essence of value with the word "becoming," Heidegger sees Nietzsche providing a clue as to the fundamental realm within which values belong. "Becoming," in Nietzsche's language, is not just the flowing together of things in the endless flux of change. Rather, "becoming means the passing over from something to something" which results from the strivings of will to power. "Becoming" *is* "will to power" and "will to power" *is* the fundamental characteristic of "life." "'Will to power,' 'becoming,' 'life' and 'Being' in the broadest sense—these mean, in Nietzsche's language, the Same" (*NW*, p. 74).

Having shown the essential connection of nihilism, transvaluation and will to power in Nietzsche, Heidegger begins the second moment of his exposition with a discussion of will to power. He begins with a hermeneutic of the combination of words "will to power." His intent is to show how the common "psychological" elucidation of this expression misses in every respect both what Nietzsche thinks with this expression and the manner in which he thinks it. Everyone knows, says Heidegger, that to will is to strive after something which is lacking, and that power means the exercise of rule and authority. Accordingly, "will to power" is taken to mean the striving which originates out of a feeling of lack for the exercising of authority which is not yet a possession. This understanding misses the essential metaphysical significance of Nietzsche's philosophy, which can be called the metaphysics of the will to power (see *NW*, p. 76). To understand the will to power as Nietzsche thinks it, that is, metaphysically, Heidegger looks first at the two terms individually. Willing is thought essentially not as desiring or striving, but rather as commanding. "To will is to will-to-be-master" (*NW*, p. 77). Willing as commanding is to be distinguished from the mere ordering about of others, for what willing essentially commands is itself as the gathering together of itself for a given task. The will's task is self-conquest, and willing thus has its origin not in a lack but in a plenitude. What the will wills it already has, for the will wills itself as the will to be more. Willing is fundamentally a willing beyond itself, a willing to be stronger. "Stronger" means here "more power." As the will essentially wills itself, "to the essence of power belongs the overpowering of itself" (*NW*, p. 78). Power, like will, does not originate from a lack. Rather, it is directed by the goal of self-enhancement: power overpowers itself toward the goal of attaining more power. What Heidegger thus finds at the essence of "will to power" is the identity of will and power. He concludes:

> In the name "will to power" the word "power" connotes nothing less than the essence of the way in which the will wills itself inasmuch as it is a commanding. [. . .] will and power are, in the will to power, not merely linked together; but rather the will, as the will to will, is itself the will to power in the sense of the empowering to power. But power has its essence in the fact that it stands to the will as the will standing within that will. The will to power is the essence of power. It manifests the unconditional essence of the will, which as pure will wills itself. (*NW*, pp. 78–79)

Having exposed the essential understanding of will to power, Heidegger links this understanding with his previous discussion of values as the positing of preservation-enhancement conditions for life. Life, we are told, is the will to will (*Wille zum Willen*). What life wills are the conditions for its own preservation and enhancement, that is, the making secure of the particular level of power already attained and the positing of conditions that will facilitate the heightening of that level of power. These preservation-enhancement conditions are what Nietzsche names "values." Heidegger thus concludes that life, as will to power, is in its essence the value-positing will. And the value-positing will, as the essence of the will to power, is the fundamental trait of everything real.

This discussion once again demonstrates, according to Heidegger, Nietzsche's entanglement within the tradition of metaphysics insofar as Nietzsche thinks "everything real" as the essence of Being, understood as the Being of what is—beings. Heidegger summarizes what has been shown above in terms of the metaphysical distinction between *essentia* and *existentia* and in so doing relates will to power to the eternal recurrence.

> The way in which that which is, in its entirety—whose *essentia* is the will to power—exists, i.e., its *existentia*, is "the eternal returning of the same." The two fundamental terms of Nietzsche's metaphysics, "will to power" and "eternal returning of the same," define whatever is, in its Being—*ens qua ens* in the sense of *essentia* and *existentia*—in accordance with the views that have continually guided metaphysics from ancient times. (*NW*, pp. 81–82)

In other words, the relation Heidegger sees in Nietzsche's thinking between will to power and eternal recurrence is the traditional metaphysical relation between essence and existence: the will to power, as the essence of all Being, exists in the form of the eternal recurrence. Although Heidegger does not elaborate upon the traditional *essentia-existentia* distinction in this essay, one problem needs to be raised at this point. In *Being and Time,* he brings up this distinction once, in the context of distinguishing the existence (*Existenz*) of Dasein from the traditional concept of *existentia*. The latter is "ontologically [. . .] tantamount to *Being-present-at-hand* [*Vorhandensein*], a kind of Being which is essentially inappropriate to entities of Dasein's character."[19] Heidegger's extension of this distinction needs to be questioned, however, in terms of his characterizing the eternal recurrence as *existentia*. For Nietzsche, *everything* recurs and if Heidegger is correct when he claims that Nietzsche conceives the eternal recurrence as the *existentia* of what is (i.e., will to power), it would seem that Nietzsche must conceive the *Übermensch,* and everything else, for that matter, as Being-present-at-hand. The problem then is this: whatever else Nietzsche might mean by "*Übermensch,*" it seems clear that he does not understand by "*Übermensch*" something present-at-hand. Yet Heidegger's interpretation would appear to commit him to this problematic conclusion.

Rather than explore the metaphysical link between will to power and eternal recurrence, Heidegger instead develops the anthropomorphism inherent in Nietzsche's discussion of the will to power as the essence of what is. He views this anthropomorphism as the culmination of a tendency within Western thinking that is made most explicit in Descartes' search for certain truth and the consequent development of philosophical anthropology. For Heidegger, modern metaphysics begins with and has its essence in the Cartesian search for certainty. This search desires to find something unconditionally indubitable, something firmly fixed and enduring. As such, this search continues the metaphysical tradition, which sees the essence of what is "as the constantly presencing [*Wesen des Seienden als des beständig Anwesenden*], which everywhere already lies before (*hypokeimenon, subiectum*)" (*NW*, p. 83). Descartes seeks this *subiectum* (*Subjektität, subjectness*) and he locates it in the *ego cogito* as that which "presences as fixed and constant." In so doing, "the *ego sum* is transformed into the *subiectum*, i.e., the subject becomes self-consciousness," subjectness becomes subjectivity and philosophical anthropology is born (*NW*, p. 83).[20]

According to Heidegger, Nietzsche's transformation of Being and truth into value attests to his remaining entangled within the metaphysical tradition he inherited. Nietzsche, says Heidegger, thinks certainty (*Gewissheit*) as security (*Sicherheit*). Heidegger thus unpacks Nietzsche's remark that "the question of value is more fundamental than the question of certainty" (*WP*, 588) in the following way. The will to power posits the conditions for its own preservation. To preserve is to make secure, i.e., the preservation of the will to power secures the constancy and stability of this will to power. This securing of constancy is what the tradition has named by "certainty." And what is secured as constant is designated by the metaphysical tradition as Being (*ousia*, enduring presence). Heidegger concludes:

> Despite all his overturnings and revaluings of metaphysics, Nietzsche remains in the unbroken line of the metaphysical tradition when he calls that which is established and made fast in the will to power purely and simply Being, or what is in being, or truth [*das Sein oder das Seiende oder die Wahrheit*]. Accordingly, truth is a condition posited in the essence of the will to power, namely, the condition of the preservation of power. (*NW*, p. 84).

As we have already seen, in Heidegger's Nietzsche the conditions for the preservation of power are named "values" and, thus, he concludes that truth and Being are transformed by Nietzsche into values.

The consequences for Nietzsche's thought of the becoming-value of truth and Being are what occupy Heidegger in the remainder of this essay. The first consequence discussed is what Heidegger calls the grounding value-principle of the metaphysics of the will to power. Heidegger cites two forms in which Nietzsche articulates this value-principle: "Art is *worth more* than truth" (*WP*,

853) and "We possess *art* lest we *perish of the truth*" (*WP*, 822). What this value-principle asserts is that while both art and truth are values, the value of art is greater than the value of truth. Heidegger understands this hierarchy of values in terms of the preservation-enhancement conditions of will to power. As we have seen, the value of truth resides in truth's being a condition for the preservation of will to power. The essence of art, on the other hand, lies in its providing conditions for the enhancement of will to power. Art, says Nietzsche, is "the great stimulant to life" (*WP*, 851). Art stimulates life, conceived as will to power, both to itself and beyond itself. The enhancement of will to power, the willing and empowering beyond itself of will to power is of greater value than the preservation and making secure of the level of power already established, and this is what Nietzsche means when he asserts that "art is *worth more* than truth."[21]

The second consequence of the becoming-value of truth and Being follows from the first. In Nietzsche's formulating the grounding value-principle of the metaphysics of the will to power in terms of art's being worth more than truth, "art and truth are thought as the primary forms of the holding-sway [*die ersten Herrschaftsgebilde*] of the will to power in relation to man" (*NW*, p. 93). Heidegger cautions us not to think the relation between will to power and man from out of the tradition of philosophical anthropology, for in so doing, we will miss what is essential in Nietzsche's thinking. Nietzsche never philosophizes existentially, Heidegger tells us, but he does think metaphysically (see *NW*, p. 94). By thinking will to power and man metaphysically, we will understand what Nietzsche thinks by the "*Übermensch*" and will be able to relate the *Übermensch* to Nietzsche's thought as Heidegger has hitherto presented it. By "*Übermensch*," Nietzsche does not name any particular man, nor does he name the form of man that will result from the practical application of Nietzsche's philosophy to life. "The name '*Übermensch*' designates the essence of humanity" which wills itself as its self-preservation and self-enhancement, that is, which wills itself *as* will to power. While man is essentially determined "by the will to power as the fundamental characteristic of all that is, he has still not experienced and accepted the will to power as that principal characteristic" (*NW*, p. 98). In Nietzsche, Heidegger finds the distinction between man and *Übermensch* to be a question of cognition. The *Übermensch* recognizes and experiences itself as will to power, whereas this ontological fact has gone unrecognized in man as he has hitherto existed.

The reason for Heidegger's viewing the distinction between man and *Übermensch* in this way becomes clear in the concluding pages of the essay, when Heidegger returns to the question of the essence of nihilism and its relation to Nietzsche's proclamation "God is dead." In this discussion, the third and most important consequence of the becoming-value of truth and Being comes into view; viz., in his viewing truth and Being as values, Nietzsche shows himself to be the supreme nihilist and, insofar as nihilism is the essence of metaphysics, Nietzsche's philosophy thus situates itself as the completion and culmination of the history of Western thinking as metaphysics. By viewing the distinction between man and *Übermensch* as one of cognition, Heidegger sees Nietzsche's metaphysics of the will to power as a metaphysics of subjectivity. For Heidegger, the metaphysics of subjectivity views the essence of consciousness as self-consciousness, and all that is not self-consciousness (subject) is viewed as object. The bifurcation of subject and object appears in Nietzsche's philosophy as well when this philosophy is thought metaphysically. The *Übermensch* is distinguished from man in terms of self-consciousness, that is, the *Übermensch* is conscious of itself as will to power. With this consciousness of self, all that is not self becomes an object over which dominion is to be exercised. This, says Heidegger, is the essential meaning of the *Übermensch's* struggle for dominion over the earth.

When Nietzsche proclaims that God has been killed so that the *Übermensch* can live, it is a mistake, says Heidegger, to understand by this that the *Übermensch* will now occupy the place formerly occupied by God. Nietzsche's thinking, Heidegger claims, is more radical. God's place in the supersensory world beyond this one, from which God formerly exercised dominion over the earth, is to remain empty. This is the *metaphysical* meaning of Nietzsche's proclamation of the death of God, and the *Übermensch's* appropriation of God's dominion must therefore be understood in terms of Nietzsche's metaphysics of subjectivity. In this metaphysics "all that is, is now either what is real [*das Wirkliche*] as the object or what works the real [*das Wirkende*], as the objectifying within which the objectivity of the object takes shape" (*NW*, p. 100). The *Übermensch*, conscious of itself as will to power, proves to be the *subiectum* and exercises dominion over the earth in that the earth is transformed into an object for its objectifying. This is to say, the *Übermensch's* dominion over the earth manifests itself in the *Übermensch's* positing the value (truth and Being) of the earth as an object for its subjectness (*Subjektität*) as self-consciousness of self as will to power.

Whereas Nietzsche sees the retrieval of the earth's dominion from the supersensory world as the overcoming of nihilism, for Heidegger it is the culmination of nihilism. It is significant, says Heidegger, that Nietzsche's word does not merely say that there is no God, but rather that we have *killed* God. By transforming God from a superior Being to a superior value, we have brought this Being closer to its end. Viewed in this light, Nietzsche's transvaluation is, in reality, the transformation of Being into a value. Whereas Nietzsche felt this transformation to be an exaltation of Being, in fact, it is the obliteration of Being, and so completes the history of metaphysics as the history of the oblivion of Being:

> [T]his supposed overcoming is above all the consummation of nihilism. For now metaphysics not only does not think Being itself, but this not-thinking of Being clothes itself in the illusion that it does think Being in the most exalted manner, in that it esteems Being as a value. (*NW*, p. 104)

By viewing Nietzsche's philosophy in this way, i.e., by thinking it essentially, we see, according to Heidegger, that Nietzsche's transvaluation and proclamation of the death of God announces not the *Übermensch* but the essence of nihilism. God's death, in other words, completes the history of the transformation from "God as highest being" to "God as highest value" to the devaluation of that highest value, i.e., to nihilism. With God's death, now "Nothing is befalling Being" (*NW*, pp. 104, 110: "*Mit dem Sein ist es nichts.*"). Nietzsche's philosophy, in announcing the completion of the forgetting of Being, thus poses a challenge to the future of thinking, one to which thinking must respond if it is to proceed along its way. In this challenge we can see the tremendous importance of Nietzsche for Heidegger's later philosophy. If philosophy is to be able to proceed beyond the epoch of metaphysics, whose essence is nihilism, it must first confront what is essential in Nietzsche's thought and retrieve Being from the culmination of its oblivion in that thought. Heidegger concludes his essay with this exhortation to future thinking to confront what is essential in Nietzsche's thinking. What remains undeveloped in this essay, however, is the elucidation of the eternal recurrence as Nietzsche's "one and only thought," and before we can begin our appraisal of Heidegger's interpretation, we must first examine how he understands the eternal recurrence. The beginnings of the answer to this question are found in Heidegger's essay on Zarathustra.

"Who is Nietzsche's Zarathustra?"

In his essay "Who is Nietzsche's Zarathustra?" Heidegger addresses the two main themes in Nietzsche's philosophy not discussed at length in "Nietzsche's Word: 'God is Dead'": the *Übermensch* and the eternal recurrence of the same. In this brief essay, Heidegger's reading unfolds out of the same methodological framework utilized in the longer essay examined above. Specifically, this essay makes explicit the metaphysical reductionism that guides Heidegger's reading of the tradition of Western thinking in general and his reading of Nietzsche in particular, a reductionism that dogmatically overdetermines Heidegger's interpretation of the history of philosophy by seeing in all previous philosophical thinking a reflection upon the Being of beings.

Heidegger's meditation on the persona of Zarathustra opens with a reflection upon Zarathustra as a spokesman. The title *Thus Spoke Zarathustra* is significant: Zarathustra is a speaker, and a speaker of a special sort: Zarathustra is an "advocate," a *Fürsprecher*. Heidegger distinguishes three senses of being an advocate. An advocate speaks *for* something; he is a spokesman who advocates. An advocate also speaks "for the benefit of, or in behalf of," that is, an advocate is the spokesman for what cannot speak in its own behalf. Finally, an advocate speaks "in justification of." Zarathustra is an advocate in this threefold sense as "the man who interprets and explains that of and for which he speaks" (*NZ*, p. 64). But what does Zarathustra advocate? Heidegger quotes Nietzsche: "I, Zarathustra, the advocate of life, the advocate of suffering, the advocate of the circle" (*Z*, "The Convalescent," 1). Heidegger initially unpacks this citation in the following terse remark: "Zarathustra presents himself as the advocate of the fact that all being is will to power, which suffers as creative, colliding will and thus wills itself in the eternal recurrence of the same" (NZ, p. 65). This is to say, "life" for Nietzsche means the will to power as the essence ("whatness," *quidditas*) of all beings; "suffering" means that life as will to power is essentially conflict; and "circle," the sign of the ring which turns back upon itself, means that the way to overcome the essential suffering of life is achieved through willing the recurrence of the same. Having thus explained what Zarathustra thinks by "life," "suffering," and "circle," Heidegger proceeds to ask how it is that Zarathustra advocates these three things. Zarathustra advocates them through his teachings. And what does Zarathustra essentially teach? He is the teacher of the *Übermensch* (Z, "Prologue," 3) and the teacher of the eternal recurrence (Z, "The Convalescent," 2). Through an understanding of *what* Zarathustra teaches and *how* he teaches these two thoughts which are, when correctly understood, the same, we will find the answer to the question "Who is Nietzsche's Zarathustra?" Heidegger finds this answer, and locates what is essential in Zarathustra's teaching of the *Übermensch* and the eternal recurrence, in Zarathustra's remarks on revenge (*Rache*).

Heidegger's interpretation of revenge centers on Zarathustra's metaphor of the bridge in his proclaiming that man is a bridge between beast and *Übermensch* (Z, "Prologue," 4). To understand this metaphor, we must attend to three things: that from which the bridge departs, the passage of the bridge itself, and the destination to which the bridge leads. The key to deciphering this metaphor is revenge: what the bridge leads from is the last man, characterized as he is by the spirit of revenge; to pass over the last man requires deliverance from the spirit of revenge, and this deliverance is the bridge itself; what one passes over to is the *Übermensch*, who delivers itself from the spirit of revenge through affirming the eternal recurrence of the same. It is in this sense that the *Übermensch* is Zarathustra's greatest hope and the object of his great longing, for it is the *Übermensch* who, through being delivered from revenge, surpasses man as he has hitherto existed. This discussion is still metaphorical, cautions Heidegger, and to get at what is essential in Nietzsche's thought, we must think revenge as Nietzsche thinks it, that is, we must think revenge *metaphysically* "as the spirit that attunes and determines man's relation to beings" (NZ, pp. 70–71). By thinking revenge metaphysically, Heidegger will be able to discover the answer to the question which guides his meditation: Who is Nietzsche's Zarathustra? And in so doing, we will see that Heidegger's answer to this question is two-fold: within Nietzsche's philosophy proper, Zarathustra is the teacher of the belonging-together of the eternal recurrence of the same and the *Übermensch;* at the same time, within the history of Western thinking as metaphysics, Zarathustra, by virtue of this teaching, is the "being who appears within metaphysics at its stage of completion" (NZ, p. 77).

Heidegger's first claim, that Zarathustra is the teacher of the belonging-together of the eternal recurrence and the *Übermensch,* is relatively straightforward and non-controversial. It follows from two passages in *Thus Spoke Zarathustra*. The first, discussed above, claims that deliverance from revenge is the bridge that must be crossed if man is to surpass himself and become *Übermensch* (Z, "The Tarantulas"). In the second passage, Zarathustra tells us what he means by revenge: "This, yet this alone, is *revenge* itself: the will's aversion to time and its 'It was' " (Z, "On Redemption"). Heidegger reads this "and" in "time and its 'It was' " not as singling out the passage of time as one feature of time, i.e., the Past, and distinguishing it from the Present and the Future. On the contrary, this "and" asserts the foundational identity of time and its passage (see *NZ*, p. 73). Nietzsche, like all metaphysical thinkers since Aristotle, conceives time as an endless succession of "nows" in which the future (the not-yet-now) passes through the present (the now of the moment [*Augenblick*][22]) and immediately becomes past (the no-longer-now which is called "It was"). Thus, transience (*Vergehen*), the ceasing to be of the now—the becoming "It was" of the "Moment"—designates the essence of time; and revenge is conceived by Nietzsche as the will's aversion to transience and the passage of time. Understood in this way, deliverance from revenge is deliverance from the will's aversion to the passage of time, and the *Übermensch*, as the one delivered from revenge, is the one who liberates the vengeful "No" said to time's passage unto an affirmation of that passage. The doctrine affirming time's passage is, of course, the eternal recurrence of the same, and Heidegger can conclude that Zarathustra teaches the belonging-together of eternal recurrence and *Übermensch* in his teaching that the *Übermensch*, as the being delivered from revenge, is delivered through the affirmation of the eternal recurrence of the same.

Heidegger's second claim, that Zarathustra is the "being who appears within metaphysics at its stage of completion," is more problematic. He begins by relating Zarathustra's claim that revenge is the will's aversion to transience to Nietzsche's view of the metaphysical tradition, and he quotes the following: "*The spirit of revenge, my friends, has so far been the subject of man's best reflection, and wherever there was suffering, there punishment was also wanted*" (Z, "On Redemption"). Heidegger interprets this remark to mean that, for Nietzsche, all previous reflection, insofar as it has been reflection upon what *is*, i.e., *metaphysical* reflection, has been grounded on the spirit of revenge and the will's aversion to the passage of time. The result of this vengeful metaphysical reflection always takes the same form: the positing as true Being of some eternal, absolute, immutable ideal that is not subject to time's passage, along with the consequent denigration of all that is subject to temporal alteration as non-Being. Characterizing metaphysical reflection this way, it is clear that Nietzsche's metaphysical adversary here (as everywhere, according to Heidegger's reading) is Platonism, and the deliverance from revenge is also a deliverance from the Platonic world of *Ideas* and its ensuing degradation of the world of Becoming.

To view Nietzsche's philosophy in this way, however, as the successful overcoming of the spirit of revenge that has hitherto guided metaphysical reflection would be, claims Heidegger, a mistake. We can recognize this mistake if we notice that Zarathustra characterizes revenge as the *will's* aversion to transience. By characterizing the will to power as the Being of beings, Nietzsche thereby situates himself within the tradition of modern metaphysical thinking, a thinking which expresses the essential character of the Being of beings generally as will. Heidegger finds the classic expression of modern metaphysics in a few sentences of Schelling's *Philosophical Investigation Concerning the Nature of Human Freedom and Its Object:*

> In the final and highest instance there is no being other than willing. Willing is primal being and to it [willing] alone belong all [primal being's] predicates: being unconditioned, eternity, independence of time, self-affirmation. All philosophy strives only to find this highest expression. (Quoted in *NZ*, p. 71)

In these sentences, Schelling attributes to willing all the essential predicates that metaphysics has traditionally attributed to Being: being unconditioned, eternal, independent of time and self-affirming. What Schelling here expresses is, for Heidegger, what Leibniz thought when he defined the Being of beings as the unity of *perceptio* (representation) and *appetitus* (striving); what Kant and Fichte expressed as rational will; what Hegel called absolute spirit; what Schopenhauer had in mind "when he titles his major work *The World* (not man) *as Will and Representation,* [and] Nietzsche thinks the same thing when he recognizes the primal Being of beings as the will to power" (*NZ*, p. 72).

By viewing Nietzsche as belonging both to the modern metaphysical legion, in which the Being of beings appears as will, and to the ancient metaphysical tradition, which views time as an endless succession of "nows," Heidegger concludes that Nietzsche's apparent deliverance from revenge through affirming the eternal recurrence repeats what Nietzsche himself had rejected in Plato: the positing of eternal ideals. More specifically, Heidegger asks, is this not precisely what Nietzsche does when he conceives the *eternal* recurrence as the permanent within Becoming? Heidegger quotes Section 617 of *The Will to Power* here, to substantiate his claim that Nietzsche himself recognized this focal point of his thinking: "To *impress* the character of Being upon Becoming—that is *the highest will to power.*" This note, which Heidegger calls one of Nietzsche's "most decisive,"[23] and which is made to do a great deal of work in Heidegger's reading of Nietzsche as the culminating figure in the history of metaphysics, is interpreted here to mean that "the highest will to power—that is, the life force in all life— is to represent transience as a fixed Becoming within the eternal recurrence of the same, and so to render it secure and stable" (*NZ*, p. 75). And it is the *Übermensch* who wills this highest will to power. The *Übermensch* is delivered from the spirit of revenge by itself willing what has hitherto been beyond its will: the past. The *Übermensch* does this by willing the eternal recurrence and affirming time's passage itself as an eternal and immutable ideal. This deliverance thereby reveals itself to be the most "supremely spiritualized spirit of revenge" (*NZ*, p. 76), in that the past can only be willed in terms of its being no-longer-merely-past. Thus, the past must be made eternal, transience must be made permanent. This is the riddle and the vision Zarathustra teaches in his teaching the belonging-together of the eternal recurrence of the same and the *Übermensch*. And by teaching the belonging-together in this way, *as* a vision and a riddle, Zarathustra completes metaphysics insofar as he raises a question which has guided all previous metaphysical thinking, but which has itself remained unthought in that thinking. This question is not asked explicitly by Nietzsche but it nevertheless hovers around all his thinking. It is the question of the belonging-together of Being and human being. This, says Heidegger, is what Zarathustra unknowingly asks when he teaches the belonging-together of the eternal recurrence of the same and the *Übermensch,* inasmuch as the eternal recurrence, as the highest will to power, is thus the "name of the Being of beings [and] '*Übermensch*' is the name of the human being who corresponds to this Being" (*NZ*, p. 77).

Nietzsche could not answer this question because he was still too much a part of the metaphysical tradition whose destiny it was to forget such a question. But his recognizing that the belonging-together of Being and human being was worthy of questioning places him in a position of singular importance within that tradition, as this recognition brings the metaphysical tradition to completion and points the way toward the path of thinking beyond metaphysics. It was this path that Heidegger spent his philosophical life pursuing and, to those who were to follow him, he offered the advice of beginning their journey with a lengthy confrontation with the thought of Nietzsche. This confrontation, if it is to be successful, must not proceed haphazardly through Nietzsche's writings. Rather, a careful meditation on what is *essential* in Nietzsche's thinking is required if the way out of metaphysics is to be opened. Heidegger provided with his lecture courses examples of how such a careful meditation upon Nietzsche's thinking was to proceed and we shall conclude the examination of his Nietzsche interpretation with an exploration of the first of these lectures.

"The Will to Power as Art"

Heidegger delivered his first lecture course on Nietzsche at the University of Freiburg in the winter semester of 1936–37. Entitled "The Will to Power as Art," these lecture notes were later reworked and published as the first chapter of his two-volume *Nietzsche.*[24] In these notes, Heidegger focuses on the significance of art in Nietzsche's thinking as the context in which to set Nietzsche's thinking over against Plato's. In so doing, he attempts to demonstrate that Nietzsche's self-proclaimed overturning of Plato (*KGW,* III, 3: 7[156]: "*Meine Philosophie umgedrehter Platonismus*[. . . .]") in fact brings to completion the tradition which Plato began. Insofar as many of Heidegger's remarks repeat points noted earlier in my discussion, I will begin by briefly summarizing the general structure of this lecture, and will focus my examination on a few key passages in Heidegger's text.

Heidegger's published text is composed of twenty-five unnumbered sections, organized around three themes. In the first ten sections, Heidegger introduces the theme of Nietzsche as metaphysician, and he explores Nietzsche's conceptions of will, power, and will to power. In the twelfth through eighteenth sections, Heidegger examines Nietzsche's conception of art, and the metaphysical significance of art in Nietzsche's thought as exhibited in his "*magnum opus*" *The Will to Power* (Sections 794–853). In the last six sections, he compares Nietzsche's and Plato's conceptions of art, and from this comparison concludes that Nietzsche's thought is both the reversal and completion of Platonist metaphysics. These three themes are linked by two crucial sections: the eleventh, entitled "The Grounding Question and the Guiding Question of Philosophy"; and the nineteenth, entitled "The Raging Discordance between Truth and Art." These two sections are the hermeneutical "hinges"[25] on which Heidegger's interpretation turns. In them, he provides what might be called his *meta*-interpretive insights, in that they go *beyond* the texts of Nietzsche and Plato, and provide the groundwork for the movement of Heidegger's interpretation as a whole.

Heidegger opens his lecture with a number of assertions regarding how one should confront the thought of Nietzsche. Because Nietzsche is not a philosopher-poet or philosopher of life but a metaphysical thinker, he asks the same question that has guided all metaphysical thinking since antiquity: What is a being? Nietzsche's answer is will to power, by which he names "what constitutes the basic character of all beings" (*N* I, p. 3). Heidegger summarizes Nietzsche's metaphysical thinking of will to power in the following abrupt manner:

> The question as to what being is [*was das Seiende sei*] seeks the Being of beings. All Being is for Nietzsche a Becoming. Such Becoming, however, has the character of action and the activity of willing. But in its essence will is will to power. (*N* I, p. 7)

Following some remarks on the structure and significance of Nietzsche's book (or more accurately, his non-book) *The Will to Power,* Heidegger proceeds to assert the unity of will to power, eternal recurrence, and transvaluation. When Nietzsche thinks the eternal recurrence, his "most difficult thought," he goes beyond the guiding question of philosophy (What is a being?) and approaches the "decisive question [. . .] of 'the meaning of Being' " (*N* I, p. 18). For Heidegger, when Nietzsche thinks "his "most difficult thought," he is meditating on "Being, that is, on will to power as eternal recurrence" (*N* I, p. 20). What he names the "transvaluation" is just this "intrinsic coherence" of the two doctrines, that is, the thinking of Being as Time. In conceiving the unity of will to power, eternal recurrence, and transvaluation, however, Nietzsche does not ask but only *approaches* the decisive question. Like Plato and Aristotle, who also thought

Being as Time (Being = *ousia* [presence]), Nietzsche fails to think the decisive question of the "meaning of Being" as "the *question* of Being and Time" (*N* I, p. 20). Thus, at this preliminary stage, we begin to see how Heidegger views Nietzsche as completing and not overcoming the metaphysical tradition which originates in Plato: to overcome this tradition, Nietzsche would have to have asked the decisive question of philosophy *as* a question and, Heidegger will argue, this question cannot be asked from within that tradition in which Nietzsche remained entangled.

Heidegger concludes these early sections with a meditation on "will" as the name modern metaphysics has given to the Being of beings, and on Nietzsche's conceptions of will and power. For Nietzsche, all willing is self-willing. What the activity of willing wills is self-mastery, that is, power over itself. Power is therefore the essence of will. According to Heidegger, when Nietzsche speaks of "will to power," he does not add something—power—to the will. Rather, he elucidates the essence of will as that which reaches out beyond itself: all willing is willing-to-be-more. When Nietzsche speaks of "power," says Heidegger, what he means is the self-enhancement of the will, for power has as its essence the enhancement and heightening of power: "power itself only *is* inasmuch as, and so long as, it remains a willing to be more power" (*N* I, p. 60). For Heidegger, when Nietzsche names the will to power, he is in fact being redundant, for will is power and power is will (cf. *N* I, p. 41). Yet by naming the basic character of beings "will to power," Nietzsche makes explicit the impulse to self-overcoming and self-mastery that animates all beings: what will to power wills in each case is its own enhancement. The importance of this conclusion will become apparent in Heidegger's explication of the significance of art in Nietzsche's thinking, in which he will attempt to demonstrate that art, as "the greatest *stimulans* of life" (*WP*, 808), is esteemed by Nietzsche to the extent that it facilitates the enhancement of the will to power.

Heidegger makes the transition from the meditation upon Nietzsche's conception of will to power to the reflection upon his conception of art in the first of the two hermeneutical "hinges" mentioned above, the eleventh section, entitled "The Grounding Question and the Guiding Question of Philosophy." In this section, he sharpens the "basic philosophical intention" of his interpretation while at the same time making clear why an interpretation of the essence of the will to power must begin with art. Western philosophy has been guided from its beginnings by the question "What is the being?" ("*Was ist das Seiende?*"). This, however, is only the penultimate (*vorletzte*) question. "The *ultimate,* i.e., *first* question is: What is Being itself?" (*N* I, p. 67: "*Die* letzte *und d. h.* erste *lautet: Was ist das Sein selbst?*"). It is this latter question which Heidegger's lecture seeks to unfold. He calls this the "grounding question of philosophy because in it philosophy first inquires into the ground of beings [*Seienden*] as *ground*." This is to say, in the grounding question, philosophy first inquires into the meaning of beings *and*

Being. And it will be Heidegger's intention as well to show that the grounding question remains as foreign to Nietzsche's thinking as it does to his predecessors in the history of Western philosophy.

Heidegger concludes this section by making explicit just what the guiding and grounding questions ask: "What beings and Being in truth are?" The guiding question (What is the being?) and the grounding question (What is Being?) both ask: What is . . . ? The "is" brings beings as a whole and Being itself into the open. Beings are brought into the openness of Being, and Being is brought "into the open region of its essence. The openness of beings we call unconcealment [*Unverborgenheit*]: *alētheia, truth*" (*N* I, p. 68). Thus, what the guiding question essentially asks is the question "What is true?" And the grounding question? It asks the question of the essence of truth, which, at the same time, is the question of the truth of essence. Although this language of Being and essence may seem foreign to Nietzsche's thinking, and its connection to art may appear strained, Heidegger assures us that they are not. The essential link between Being and essence, although unsaid, is nevertheless present in Nietzsche's thinking in that he thinks beings as will to power. "If will to power determines beings as such, which is to say, in their truth, then the question concerning truth, i.e., the question of the essence of truth, must always be inserted into the interpretation of beings as will to power" (*N* I, p. 68). What is significant in Nietzsche, however, and what, according to Heidegger, distinguishes him from the metaphysical tradition to which he nonetheless belongs, is that the convergence in Nietzsche's philosophy of will to power (beings) and truth takes place not in knowledge but in art. If art is the highest expression of will to power, then precisely here we must endeavor to discern the decisive role which the question of truth *must* play.

Heidegger's inquiry into the relationship between truth and art begins by exhibiting a sequence of five statements in which Nietzsche discloses his conception of the essence of art:

1. Art is the most perspicuous and familiar configuration of will to power;

2. Art must be grasped in terms of the artist;

3. According to the expanded concept of artist, art is the basic occurrence of all beings; to the extent that they are, beings are self-creating, created;

4. Art is the distinctive countermovement to nihilism;

5. Art is worth more than "the truth." (see *N* I, p. 75)

The first three statements are interconnected and unfold out of a single passage from *The Will to Power* (797): "The phenomenon 'artist' is still the most *perspicuous* [*durchsichtig*]:—from that position to scan the *basic instincts of power,* of nature, etc.! Also of religion and morals!" This passage, Heidegger tells us, should open the section of *The Will to Power* entitled "The Will to Power as Art," for it shows us the decisive importance of art as the ground for a new principle of valuation. The phenomenon "artist" is "the most perspicuous." But what is this phenomenon "artist"? "To be an artist is to be able to bring something forth, [that is,] to establish in Being something that does not yet exist" (*N* I, p. 69). What the artist brings forth and establishes in Being is, of course, art. Art, however, is not here conceived merely as "fine art." Rather, following Nietzsche's conception of Being as will to power, the artist brings forth art as a configuration of will to power, indeed its most perspicuous and familiar configuration. We should note, Heidegger tells us, that in opposition to traditional aesthetic thinking, Nietzsche locates the essence of art not in the work or in its reception but in the artist as the one who brings forth the work. The essence of art resides in the artist's creation of new configurations of will to power, and any creation is art to the extent that it is brought forth into Being as a configuration of will to power. In this conception of the essence of art we begin to see how, for Nietzsche, "art is the basic occurrence of all beings," and we here get a preliminary glance at the importance of the artist in Nietzsche's thinking. The phenomenon "artist," as "most perspicuous," gives us an important insight into how we should observe other configurations of will to power—e.g., nature, religion, morals. These configurations correspond in a certain way to the being of art and to being created, and they will become transparent to thinking only if viewed as having been brought forth into Being in a way analogous to artistic creation.

The final two statements, that art is the distinctive countermovement to nihilism and, as such, is worth more than "the truth," also belong together. These thoughts animate most of the remarks on art found in *The Will to Power,* and Heidegger cites a number of sections where Nietzsche expresses them outright (e.g., *WP,* 794, 795, 822, 853). Although Nietzsche's statements may strike the reader as "perverse," Heidegger asserts that they will lose their foreignness when read in the right way, as Nietzsche's attempt to reverse the supremacy of Platonic-Christian metaphysics and morality. The first principle of these "decadence-forms of humanity" is that there must be a "better" world beyond this one. This "supersensuous" world beyond judges that this world, the world of the senses, is merely a world of appearance whose value is nil. As we have already seen, Nietzsche characterizes nihilism, that uncanniest of guests now standing at the door of the modern epoch, as the consequence of this judgment. Art stands as the distinctive countermovement to nihilism in that it affirms precisely what the judgment of the supersensuous world negates: the value of the senses and of appearance. Because "art is the will to semblance as the sensuous" (*N* I, p. 74), when Nietzsche claims that "art is *worth more* than the truth," he means that "the sensuous stands in a higher place and *is* more genuinely than the supersensuous" (*N* I, p. 74).[26]

Heidegger completes the preliminary discussion of Nietzsche's five statements on art by linking them to "Nietzsche's *major statement on art*" (*N* I, p. 76): art as "the greatest *stimulans* of life" (*WP,* 808). A "stimulant" lifts a thing beyond itself, it enhances. Art, as the basic configuration of will to power, is the "greatest *stimulans* of life" in that it reveals to life its Being as will to power and opens the way for the enhancement of that power. To understand *how* art stimulates life, we must examine what Nietzsche understands to be the basic artistic phenomenon: *der Rausch,* rapture.[27]

Before introducing what Nietzsche means by rapture, Heidegger first situates Nietzsche within the history of aesthetic thinking. In its originary significance, aesthetics designated *aisthētikē epistēmē,* knowledge of *aisthēsis,* of one's state of feeling in its relation to the beautiful and the way this relation to the beautiful determines one's behavior. Within the tradition of "aesthetics," however, aesthetic thinking has lost its originary nature as a type of knowledge of human behavior, insofar as the artwork has come to be represented as an "object" for a "subject." With this view of aesthetic thinking as determined by the subject's feelings in response to an art-object, Heidegger proceeds to sketch out the five basic developments in the history of aesthetics that precede Nietzsche: the great art of pre-Platonic Greece, art understood as a kind of *technē,* the aesthetics of taste, Hegel's announcement of the end of great art, and Wagner's "collective artwork," whose function was to arouse the experiences of its audience to the level of redemptive frenzy. Wagner thus completes an aesthetic development that began with the aesthetics of taste: the criterion by which art is to be judged is now the effects which it has on the *psyche* of its audience, and aesthetic states come to be seen as a type of psychological state.

Heidegger develops the theme of Wagnerian aesthetics as a "psychology of art" to make clear the context out of which the sixth aesthetic development, that found in Nietzsche's thinking, unfolds. Nietzsche expresses his aesthetic theory in two ways, thereby making explicit his reversal of *both* nineteenth-century aesthetic developments. For Hegel, art fell victim to nihilism and became a thing of the past. For Nietzsche, art, in opposition to Hegel, is pursued as the distinctive countermovement to nihilism. At the same time, and in opposition to Wagner's psychologistic aesthetics, Nietzsche's aesthetic meditation is conceived as a "physiology of art." But here a problem arises. Physiology, conceived as the realm of natural processes, would seem to admit of no hierarchy of standards. In the area of physiology, the question of value does not seem to arise. Things are the way they are; nervous stimuli and responses may be essential or non-essential, but the question of decisions regarding their value would seem to be superfluous. As such, making art the object of physiology, i.e., reducing art to the level of brain states, would seem to be the apotheosis of nihilism rather than its countermovement. If we are to understand Nietzsche's aesthetics and his conception of art as a configuration of will to power, we must, says Heidegger, try to grasp *by way of* physiology how art, as the distinctive countermovement to nihilism, is to provide the principle for the establishment of new values.

Heidegger finds the key to unifying these two thoughts on art (art as countermovement to nihilism and art as object for physiology) in Nietzsche's remarks on rapture as the basic aesthetic state. Nietzsche writes that "What is essential in rapture is the feeling of enhancement of force and plenitude" (*TI*, "Skirmishes of an Untimely Man," 8). When Nietzsche proclaims that rapture, as the basic aesthetic feeling, is to be an object for physiology, he reveals his having overcome the fatal metaphysical distinction between mind and body. By "feeling" (*Gefühl*), Nietzsche understands what Heidegger, in *Being and Time,* understood by "mood" (*Stimmung*). Feelings and moods are not something we have, but a way in which we are bodily. When Nietzsche, therefore, speaks of rapture as a feeling, he does not understand by this a characterization of the goings on of our "inner lives"; instead he describes "a mode of the embodying, attuned stance towards beings as a whole" (*N* I, p. 105). For Heidegger, this understanding of rapture as "embodying attunement" underlies Nietzsche's basic aesthetic opposition between the Apollonian and the Dionysian.

Heidegger recalls that Nietzsche's thinking on the opposition between Apollonian and Dionysian undergoes an important transformation. In *The Birth of Tragedy,* Nietzsche designates by the Apollonian and Dionysian the two basic aesthetic states. The Apollonian is exemplified in the image world of dreams, whose fundamental force is that of illusion and deception. The Apollonian strives for the creation of the eternally beautiful. The Dionysian is juxtaposed to the Apollonian as its necessary counterpart, characterized by the creative-destructive world of rapture. The fundamental forces of the Dionysian are those of sensuality, frenzy, and superabundant animality. It strives not for the eternally beautiful but rather for continual creativity as the ever-ongoing process of world-construction and world-destruction.

When Nietzsche returns to the Apollonian-Dionysian opposition in *Twilight of the Idols,* a fundamental change has taken place. Rapture is now *the* basic aesthetic state, grasped in a unified way. With the Dionysian and Apollonian, Nietzsche no longer designates the bifurcation of aesthetic states that grounded the aesthetics of *The Birth of Tragedy.* On the contrary, the Dionysian and Apollonian now designate two kinds of rapture: the rapture of enchantment and the rapture of dream. For Heidegger, the transformed Apollonian-Dionysian opposition now names two ways rapture is embodied. The opposition designates a difference, within the basic aesthetic state of rapture, of *tempo:* Apollonian rapture is calm, calculating; Dionysian rapture is explosive and overflowing. Yet what is essential in both the Dionysian and Apollonian remains what is essential in rapture itself: the feeling of enhancement of force and the feeling of plenitude.

These feelings, moreover, are ultimately reflected in what we regard as "beautiful." For Nietzsche, the "beautiful" reflects what the ascent beyond ourselves holds in store, an ascent which occurs in the state of rapture and is accompanied by feelings of enhancement of force and of plenitude. The "beautiful" is what is disclosed in rapture and what transports us into this feeling. Nietzsche has in mind this understanding of the relation between beauty and rapture, according to Heidegger, when he says "It is a question of *strength* [*Kraft,* force] (of an individual or a nation), *whether* and *where* the judgment 'beautiful' is made" (*WP*, 852). By this, he means that strength, the level to which one's force has ascended, is the decisive factor in decisions regarding what is to be esteemed "beautiful."

With this insight into Nietzsche's conception of the "beautiful," we arrive at the vantage-point necessary for understanding how art is conceived to be an object of physiology. Nietzsche provides the final clue in the following passage quoted by Heidegger: "The fundament of all aesthetics [is given in] the general principle that aesthetic values rest on biological values, that aesthetic delights are biological delights" (Quoted in *N* I, p. 114). If we recall that life as will to power means for Nietzsche the process of the will's willing the enhancement of its own power, and if we recall that Nietzsche often uses power (*Macht*) and force (*Kraft*) interchangeably, we can understand how beauty is a "biological value" and aesthetic pleasure a "biological delight." Nietzsche does not understand biology in the way it is understood by the biologist. On the contrary, he understands "biological" in a more originary way, as referring to *bios*, "life." Aesthetic values are values for life and what is esteemed "beautiful" is so esteemed by virtue of its enhancement of will to power as the creative and procreative will to life.

This rapturous creation involves decisions with respect to standards and rankings, decisions grounded on the level of one's feelings of force and plenitude. In creation, one puts one's will to power into things, one decides which features will be emphasized and which overlooked. The conceptual language of the aesthetic tradition, which Nietzsche in this instance speaks as well, refers to these emphasized features as "form." Form is, for Nietzsche, the true content of art (see *WP*, 818). It is form itself which is aesthetic, and not what the form expresses (its "content"). "Form founds the realm in which rapture as such becomes possible [in that] form defines and demarcates for the first time the realm in which the state of waxing force and plenitude in being comes to fulfillment" (*N* I, p. 119). What is essential in Nietzsche's thinking on form, however, is not the particular form brought into Being by the artist. Rather, the essence of art lies in the rapturous comporting itself, in the life-process of the becoming-form of art as a configuration of will to power. This becoming-form is the source of delight in art, for in the artistic comportment to form, human beings experience their most basic pleasure: the pleasure of ordering. By understanding the pleasure in ordering as the ground of aesthetic pleasure, we get our first insight into how Nietzsche understands in a unified way art as an object of physiology and art as the countermovement to nihilism. Nietzsche says of the pleasure of ordering that it is nothing other than

> the pleasurable feelings among all organic creatures in relation to the danger of their situation or to the difficulty of finding nourishment; the familiar does one good, the sight of something that one trusts he can easily *overpower* does one good, etc. (*GOA*, XIV, p. 133; quoted in *N* I, p. 121)

These pleasures are pleasures of life, *bios;* they are the *bio*-logical pleasures of preservation and enhancement which characterize everything that is alive. The pleasure of ordering is valued as well in terms of these standards of preservation and enhancement of "life"; as such, it stands in opposition to nihilism as the negation and decline of life.

Heidegger explicates Nietzsche's unified understanding of art by means of an examination of the highest form of the basic aesthetic state of rapture: creation in the grand style. For Heidegger, the concept of the grand style provides the "unifying center" of Nietzsche's aesthetics in that art in the grand style exhibits the essence of art as a concept of rank. In the grand style, there comes to pass "a triumph over the plenitude of living things; *measure* becomes master, [. . .]" (*WP*, 819). In the grand style is experienced the "supreme feeling of power" in the subjugation and containment of chaos through its being willed into form. Creation in the grand style is not, however, the mere subjugation of chaos into form. It is, rather, that mastery which allows chaos and form (law) to unfold together in their mutual necessity. As such, creation in the grand style reveals the necessity of formal lawfulness (*Formgesetzlichkeit*); it reveals that art is not only subject to laws but is legislation (*Gesetzgebung*) itself. Art in the grand style is thus the *supreme* stimulant of life in that it manifests art's legislative, form-grounding aspect as that which is "properly creative."

Heidegger further explicates the "properly creative" in art by contrasting Nietzsche's remarks on grand style with his comments on classical and romantic style (in *WP*, 843–850). Like the classical and the romantic styles, the grand style is directed toward Being, but in a unique way. Whereas in the romantic style, the reactive longing for Being negates Becoming, and in the classical style, the active longing for Being requires a suppression of Becoming, "the grand style is the active will to Being which takes up [*aufhebt*] Becoming into itself" (*N* I, p. 135). This is to say, the grand style affirms *both* Being and Becoming; Being is willed as the assimilation and not the suppression of Becoming. As such, the antithesis of Being and Becoming does not disappear but, rather, comes to its essential unfolding in the determination of what is "properly creative" as art in the grand style.

Characterizing the grand style in this way brings Heidegger to the peak of Nietzsche's "aesthetics," which, for Heidegger, when *properly* understood, is no longer "aesthetics" at all. Viewing the grand style as the essential unfolding of the original unity of Being and Becoming, we see that Nietzsche's aesthetics mirrors his basic metaphysical position. Art, we recall, is a configuration of will to power, and the grand style, as the highest form of art, is conceived as the supreme configuration of will to power. But will to power *is* as eternal recurrence. "In the latter Nietzsche wants his thinking to fuse Being and Becoming, action and reaction, in an original unity" (*N* I, p. 136). We can thus see why Nietzsche places supreme value upon the grand style, which, as the assimilation of Being and Becoming in the properly creative, unfolds what is thought in the eternal recurrence. This is the "metaphysical horizon upon which we are to think what Nietzsche calls the grand style and art in general," and Heidegger concludes that just as the will to power, the essence (*essentia*) of beings, exists (its *existentia*) as eternal recurrence, so too the essence of art becomes actual in the grand style (see *N* I, pp. 136–137).

Having concluded his metaphysical interpretation of Nietzsche's thinking on art, Heidegger returns to the five basic statements on art with which his inquiry began, in an attempt to ascertain their ground. The first two statements are grounded without difficulty. The first statement, that art is the most familiar and perspicuous configuration of will to power, is grounded in the fact that art, grasped aesthetically as the state of embodied rapture which we ourselves *are,* reveals to human being its innermost nature as will to power creating beyond itself. The first statement is thus linked to the second, that art must be grasped in terms of the artist. The focus upon the artist, as the productive moment in the aesthetic process, effectively guarantees access to creation in general; it thus grounds the inquiry into art in will to power as a constant creating. With the third statement, however, a number of problems arise. The third statement says that art is the basic occurrence within beings as a whole. In order to ground this statement, we must first answer two questions: "First, in what does the beingness of beings [*das Seiendsein am Seienden*] consist? What is the being itself in truth? Second, to what extent can art, among beings, be more in being [*seiender sein*] than others?" (*N* I, p. 140). To answer these questions, thereby grounding the third as well as the fourth (art is the countermovement to nihilism) statements, requires that we first ground the fifth statement, which proclaims that art is worth more than truth. It is upon this grounding, Heidegger claims, that everything hangs, and to ground Nietzsche's fifth statement is to ask the question of the essence of truth. The question of the essence of truth is, for Heidegger, "the preliminary question of philosophy [*die Vorfrage der Philosophie*]," and it is always already included in both philosophy's guiding question (What is the being?) and its grounding question (What is Being?).

The effort to discover the ground for Nietzsche's fifth statement on art brings us to Heidegger's second hermeneutical "hinge," in the nineteenth section, entitled "The Raging Discordance between Art and Truth." This section marks the transition from the meditation on Nietzsche's aesthetics to the meditation on Nietzsche's thinking as the completion of metaphysics. Heidegger's meta-interpretive remarks here draw on, and are analogous to, his remarks in the first hermeneutical hinge. In that earlier section, Heidegger focused upon the guiding and grounding questions of philosophy and attempted to demonstrate that Nietzsche, following the tradition from which he could not extricate himself, asks only the former question (What are beings?), and does not raise the latter question of the essence of Being itself. These two questions, which ask the question of the ontological difference (the difference between beings and Being), give way in this second hinge to what might be called the "veritological difference"—the difference between the true and Truth.

Heidegger attempts to demonstrate that Nietzsche again remains entangled within the tradition, asking only the question "What things are true?" while unable to raise the question of the essence of Truth *as* a question. "Truth" is a basic word (*Grundwort*), and the attempt to clarify what is named by such a basic word must take heed of two things. First, because human Dasein is inextricably caught up in relations with the essences of what are named by such words, these essences will inevitably be concealed. And second, we must attend to the way such basic words vary in meaning. This is to say, basic words are historical, which means both that "they have various meanings for various ages [and that] they ground history now and in times to come in accordance with the interpretation of them that comes to prevail" (*N* I, p. 144). The examination of basic words can thus proceed along two principal routes: "the route of the essence, and that which veers away from the essence and yet is related back to it" (*N* I, p. 146). In the case of the basic word "Truth," we observe the ambiguity that results from these two routes. "Truth" names both the one essence as well as the many which satisfy this essence. That is, "truth" can mean the essence of the true (as "justice" means the essence of the just, "beauty" the essence of the beautiful, etc.), thereby designating something singular and universal. At the same time, "truth" can mean those many particular things which are "true" by virtue of satisfying this one essence.

Returning to Nietzsche, Heidegger asserts that Nietzsche's thinking on truth, like the entire history of Western thinking since Plato, deviates from the "essential route" of inquiring into the essence of truth, and inquires only into the truth as that which is true, that which satisfies the essence of truth. To be sure, the interpretation provided for the concept of "truth" changes as the tradition unfolds. For Descartes, truth is certitude. Kant distinguishes between empirical and transcendental truth. Hegel adds a new distinction, that of concrete and abstract truth. Nietzsche says that truth is an "error." Each insight advances the inquiry of the tradition, but in what is essential, they stand close together in following a particular route of the meaning of truth and, without exception, they leave untouched the question of the essence of truth itself. When viewed from the "correct vantage-point," we discover that, in each case, truth is pursued as proper to the realm of knowledge. "The true is what is truly known, the actual. The true is established as something true in, by, and for knowledge alone" (*N* I, p. 149). Thus, for Heidegger, an "oversight" pervades the entire Western philosophical tradition. By pursuing the question of truth as an epistemological inquiry, the tradition has overlooked the fundamental ontological questions of the essence of truth and the truth of essence, which is to say, the question "What Being in truth is?" Nietzsche, too, fails to ask this question in that he also takes truth to be determined by knowledge. But, for Heidegger, Nietzsche's failure is unlike any other, for if one attends to what remains unthought in Nietzsche's thinking, the first faint glimmering of this question can be found. It appears in the "raging discordance [*der erregende Zwiespalt*]" between art and truth, in the face of which Nietzsche stands in "holy dread." Although Nietzsche continues to think truth as properly belonging to the realm of knowledge, his affirming that art is worth more than truth discloses the implicit recognition that the truth of knowledge must be subordinated to the truth of Being. For when he says that art is worth more than truth, Nietzsche means that art, as the basic occurrence of beings whose Being is will to power, is more valuable than the so-called "truths" of knowledge. This essential Nietzschean insight emerges in his attempted overturning of Platonism.[28]

Defining the essential concept of truth depends on how we conceive the essence of knowing. Heidegger begins to clarify Nietzsche's conception of the essence of knowing by briefly examining the ways Platonism and positivism conceive this essence. In so doing, he attempts to demonstrate that Nietzsche's inversion of Platonism differs from the positivistic inversion. Knowing, in the tradition, is always an approximation to what is to be known and, as such, implies as a consequence a relation to some sort of standard. In Platonism, what is to be known is the being, whose Being is determined on the basis of Ideas and as the *ideai*. The *ideai*, the Platonist standard for knowing, is non-sensuous and, at the same time, stands above the sensuous. Thus, in Platonism, knowledge is defined as the "presentative measurement of self [*vorstellendes Sichanmessen*] upon the supersensuous" (*N* I, pp. 151–152). This pure non-sensuous presentation is called *theoria,* and the Platonist conception of knowledge is theoretical, grounded upon a particular interpretation of Being as *idea*. In positivism, knowing is also a measuring, but based upon a different standard, that of the *positum,* the sensuous, what is given in sensation. Positivism therefore stands in relation to Platonism as its inversion. For positivism, what is true is the sensuous, which acts as the standard against which the supersensuous is measured and judged as not properly belonging to Being, while for Platonism, the supersensuous is what is true and, measured against the standard of the supersensuous, it is the sensuous which may not be addressed as Being.

While Nietzsche's inverted Platonism appears on the surface to repeat the positivistic project, this is not, in fact, the case. Like the positivists and the Platonists, Nietzsche accepts truth as an object of theoretical knowledge. And like the positivists, Nietzsche affirms the sensuous as a standard. But unlike the positivists, who continue to accept the basic hierarchical structure of Platonism, Nietzsche's inversion of the Platonist hierarchy is made on *historical* rather than theoretical grounds. That is to say, Nietzsche's inversion of the Platonist standards is grounded in history and in the fundamental historical event of nihilism, that is, in the event of the highest values devaluing themselves. Nietzsche's overturning of Platonism is thus the *result* of his inquiry into the history of philosophy as the history of the devaluation of the highest values (nihilism). It is a mistake, says Heidegger, to interpret Nietzsche's inversion of Platonism as that which led him to affirm the sensuous over the supersensuous. On the contrary, Nietzsche's inversion of Platonism must be understood in terms of the overcoming of nihilism: the Platonist affirmation of the supersensuous has, as a matter of historical fact, given rise to our present nihilistic situation and, if nihilism is to be overcome, we must, therefore, overcome the affirmation of the supersensuous as the standard of the true. To overcome this standard returns us to the senses as the ground out of which art, as the countermovement to nihilism, creates. To properly understand Nietzsche's overturning of Platonism, therefore, we must return to the relation between art and truth, and discover how and if Nietzsche's conception of this relation differs from the relation in Platonism.

For Nietzsche, the relation between art and truth is one of discordance, in the face of which Nietzsche stands in holy dread. If Nietzsche's philosophy is the inversion of Platonism, we must, says Heidegger, find a similar conflict between art and truth in Plato, but one which reverses the hierarchy asserted by Nietzsche. We appear to find such a reversal in Book X of *The Republic,* where Plato asserts that all art is *mimēsis* (imitation). Although Plato does indeed claim that truth is worth more than art in that it lies closer to Being, what is more significant than this judgment, for Heidegger, is the manner in which it is presented. If Nietzsche's philosophy is, as he himself claimed, an "inverted Platonism," then his discordance must reverse an analogous discordance in Plato. But throughout Plato's discussion in *The Republic,* the metaphor of *distance* is used to describe the relation between art and truth. Distance, however, is not discordance. Discordance is, for Heidegger, ambiguous: it can mean either a severance between two things which essentially belong together as one; or the necessary conflict between things of equal necessity and rank. So long as art is subordinated to truth and is devalued by virtue of its distance from truth, Heidegger asserts that no discordance can exist between art and truth. Such a discordance could arise only if Plato thought truth and art out of a common origin and as beings of equal rank. While this thought is not to be found in *The Republic,* Heidegger locates just such a thought in Plato's *Phaedrus.*

In the *Phaedrus,* Plato reflects upon, among other things, the essence of the beautiful in the context of man's relation to beings as such. Although Plato does not explicitly discuss the relations of beauty to art and truth, Heidegger claims we can reconstruct the movement of the *Phaedrus* in a way that makes clear the originary severance between art and truth that Nietzsche attempts to overturn. In the *Phaedrus,* Plato presupposed the definition of man as the essence that comports itself to beings as such; that is, beings show themselves to man *as* beings. In order to do so, man's "soul" must have already viewed Being, since Being cannot be grasped by the senses. However, the "soul" is exiled in the body, and from this vantage-point Being can never be held in its pure, unclouded radiance. The consequence for man of this concealment of Being is that man is overcome by *lēthē,* "forgetting," which gives rise to the illusion that there is no such thing as Being. The majority of men thus lapse into oblivion of Being, and are no longer able to recognize appearances as appearances. It is the essence of the beautiful to initiate the rectification of the situation of man's fallenness into oblivion of Being. The beautiful, for Plato, is therefore that in the appearances which draws man toward what conceals itself in the appearance: Being. To beauty alone is allotted the role of captivating man's attention in the sensuous, and through this captivation beauty draws man beyond the sensuous toward the supersensuous, toward Being itself. In the radiance of the beautiful in the sensuous realm, man is thus liberated to catch a glimpse of the radiant brilliance of Being itself.

In this characterization of the essence of beauty, Heidegger finds Plato's answer to the question of the relation of beauty and truth.

> The view upon Being opens up what is concealed, making it unconcealed; it is the basic relation to the true. That which truth essentially brings about, the unveiling of Being, that and nothing else is what beauty brings about. (*N* I, p. 198)

Beauty and truth essentially belong together, related as they are to what is decisive: Being itself. Truth is the openedness of Being, and beauty is that which brings about this openedness. But this belonging together of beauty and truth is quickly severed in Plato: truth, the openedness of Being, can only be nonsensuous while the beautiful, as that which opens up Being in truth, is situated in the sensuous realm. Art, therefore, by bringing forth the beautiful in the realm of the sensuous, is far removed from truth. This separation is, for Plato, a discordance, but a discordance which does not arouse dread. On the contrary, the severance is a felicitous one in that "the beautiful elevates us beyond the sensuous and bears us back into the true" (*N* I, p. 198). If, therefore, we are to understand Nietzsche's philosophy, as an "inverted Platonism," we must understand how Nietzsche conceives the discordance between art and truth to be not a felicitous discordance, but one which arouses dread.

Heidegger turns to this task in the penultimate section, "Nietzsche's Overturning of Platonism," which, in many ways, marks the climax of his lecture on the will to power as art. In this section, he returns to the theme with which he opened the third moment of his lecture, namely how Nietzsche's inversion of Platonism differs from the positivist inversion. The answer, we were told earlier, is to be found in the relation between the overturning of Platonism and the overcoming of nihilism. The positivist merely stands the Platonist hierarchy of the supersensuous and the sensuous on its head, thereby affirming the supreme value of the sensuous over the supersensuous. By preserving the formal structure of Platonism, however, and merely inverting the "above and below," the essence of Platonism is preserved. But for Nietzsche, it is the *essence* of Platonism which is nihilism. If, therefore, Nietzsche is to overcome Platonism, and thereby to overcome nihilism, he must invert Platonism in such a way that his philosophical thinking twists free of the essential Platonist structure. This is to say, he must collapse the hierarchization of the sensuous and the supersensuous. According to Heidegger, Nietzsche's philosophical task in his last creative years was directed toward overturning Platonism by twisting free from it, and this task underlies Nietzsche's attempt to collapse the distinction between the "true world" and the "apparent world." Heidegger focuses our attention on a single section of Nietzsche in which he most clearly manifests what is at issue in the overcoming of Platonism. This section, from *Twilight of the Idols,* is entitled "How the 'True World' Finally Became a Fable: The History of an Error." In this section, Nietzsche chronicles the six stages in the history of Platonism, from its inception in Plato to the emergence from Platonism announced by Zarathustra. In Heidegger's lengthy exegesis of this section is located the core[29] of his Nietzsche interpretation, and we must examine this exegesis in some detail.

Heidegger begins by examining each of the six stages in Nietzsche's history of Platonism individually.

> 1. The true world, attainable for the wise, the pious, the virtuous man—he lives it, *he is it.*
> (Oldest form of the idea, relatively sensible, simple, convincing. Circumlocution for the sentence "I, Plato, *am* the truth.")

This first stage recounts the establishment of Plato's doctrine. What is significant is that the true world itself is dealt with only in relation to man and to the extent that it is attainable for man. The true world *is* attainable, here and now, not for all men, but for the virtuous man. Heidegger draws the implication that virtue consists in the repudiation of the sensuous, since the virtuous man *is* the true, i.e., supersensuous world. The parenthetical comment makes clear that Plato's "true world" is not yet Platonist. The supersensuous is the *idea,* not merely an unattainable "ideal," and the *idea,* as the essence of Being, is attainable for the virtuous man who comports himself to its radiant truth.

The second stage marks the transition from Plato to Platonism.

> 2. The true world, unattainable for now, but promised for the wise, the pious, the virtuous man ("for the sinner who repents").
> (Progress of the idea: it becomes more subtle, more insidious, ungraspable—*it becomes woman,* it becomes Christian . . .)

With the origin of Platonism, the harmfulness of the doctrine of the supersensuous as true Being makes its first appearance. The supersensuous is separated from the sensuous; it is no longer attainable, but only promised as the "beyond." As such, true Being is no longer present to human existence, and the realm of sensuous human existence is thereby denigrated. We have, at this stage, two worlds, and to affirm the supersensuous world beyond entails a denial of the sensuous world of human existence. It is this cleavage between the two worlds and the denigration of the sensuous world in favor of the "true world" that Nietzsche finds insidious in the Christianizing progress of Plato's *idea* becoming an "ideal."

> 3. The true world, unattainable, indemonstrable, unpromisable, but even as thought, a consolation, an obligation, an imperative.
>
> (The old sun, basically, but seen through haze and skepticism; the idea rarefied, grown pallid, Nordic, Königsbergian.)

The third stage marks the Kantian contribution to the history of Platonism. With Kant, the supersensuous becomes a postulate of practical reason: while outside the realm of possible experience, its existence is necessary in order to provide adequate grounds for the lawfulness of reason. Kant changes nothing of substance in the Christianized view of the "true world": he gazes upon the same supersensuous realm, but with the eyes of a skeptic. This realm is, by the standards of natural science, unknowable and inaccessible, but its existence is necessary and, therefore, not subject to doubt.

> 4. The true world—unattainable? In any case, unattained. And as unattained also *unknown*. Consequently, also, not consolatory, redemptive, obligating: to what could something unknown obligate us? . . .
>
> (Gray morning. First yawnings of reason. Cockcrow of positivism.)

The fourth stage chronicles the positivist overcoming of Kantian Platonism. The Kantian system is unmasked and exploded with the help of its own chief principle: the theoretical unknowability of the supersensuous. Removing the supersensuous from the realm of cognition reveals the theological presupposition of Kantian philosophy. The "true world" is not an object of knowledge, but one of faith. In the positivist's hands, the unknowable becomes the unknown, the nonsensuous becomes nonsense. For Nietzsche, the positivist announces the coming of a new day; reason is beginning to awake from its Christian slumber and is once again coming to its senses.

> 5. The "true world"—an idea which is of use for nothing, which is no longer even obligating—an idea become useless, superfluous, consequently, a refuted idea: let us abolish it!
>
> (Bright day; breakfast; return of *bon sens* and of cheerfulness; Plato's embarrassed blush; pandemonium of all free spirits.)

The fifth stage marks Nietzsche's first path into philosophy, the path of the free spirit, which occupied his thinking in the series of writings from *Human All-too-Human* (1878) to *The Gay Science* (1882). The "true world" is now set in quotation marks. It is no longer effective as an ideal and should be abolished. Plato has been found out and blushes at the discovery of his indiscretion. The bright dawn of this new day is marked by a return of "good sense" and the free spirit's cheerful affirmation of the sensuous world as the new standard. Nietzsche does not dwell in this new dawn, however, for he quickly realizes that, although the supersensuous world has been removed from its position of supremacy, the vacant site of the "true world" remains as a standard. Therefore, a further step is required if thinking is to free itself of Platonism's dominion.

> 6. The true world we abolished: which world was left? the apparent one perhaps?
> . . . But no! *along with the true world we have also abolished the apparent one!*
> (Midday; moment of the shortest shadow; end of the longest error; highpoint of humanity; INCIPIT ZARATHUSTRA.)

This sixth stage marks the arrival of Nietzsche's philosophy proper, a philosophy which announces the end of the Platonist error. This end becomes visible on the basis of a new beginning, marked by the appearance of Zarathustra, who confronts human beings with a decision regarding their own transformation. This is the meaning of "highpoint of humanity." With the abolition of the "true world," human beings are faced with a momentous decision: will they succumb to nihilism, in the form of the type which Nietzsche designates as the "last man"; or will they overcome nihilism, thereby overcoming themselves as they have hitherto existed, and become *"Übermensch"*? The *Übermensch* does not designate a superman. Rather, by *"Übermensch,"* Nietzsche designates the type of being who has overcome the relation between man and Being hitherto determined by Platonism in one or another of its forms. The overcoming of Platonism marks the beginning of the *Übermensch* as the being who has freed the sensuous from its deprecation when judged according to the unjustifiably elevated standard of the supersensuous. When the "true world" is abolished, the "apparent world" is abolished as well, in that the "apparent world" is apparent only by virtue of comparison with the "true" one. The *Übermensch* avoids the mistake of positivism in that it does not merely invert the hierarchy of the supersensuous and the sensuous, viewing the former as "apparent" and the latter as "true." The *Übermensch's* abolition of the true-apparent distinction requires a new interpretation of the sensuous and the supersensuous, one grounded upon a new ranking of values, freed once and for all from the dominion of the Platonist hierarchy. It is this new interpretation of the sensuous, affirmed on the basis of a new ordering structure, that is unfolded in the dread-inspiring discordance between art and truth.

Nietzsche's new interpretation of the sensuous as the "genuine" reality, Heidegger tells us, directs Nietzsche's project of overturning Platonism and is made manifest in his affirming the value of art over truth. For Nietzsche, the "sensuous" is now demarcated as the perspectival-perceptual. "The *perspectival* [is] the basic condition of all life" (*BGE,* Pr.). Everything alive is perspectival in itself, and asserts itself in its perspective against other beings and other perspectives. By viewing life in this way, as the concatenation of perspectives, Nietzsche brings semblance (*Schein*) itself into the essence of the real. The real, that is to say, the sensuous, is itself composed of semblances insofar as, in the unity of a real being, there is a multiplicity of forces, each possessing its own perspective. The sensuous is deemed "apparent" only when semblance is viewed as mere appearance, that is, "when what becomes manifest in one perspective petrifies and is taken to be the sole, definitive appearance" (*N* I, p. 214). Out of the fixity and constancy of certain appearances emerges the concept of the "object," a concept which creatures need in order to get their bearings and organize their world. But according to the Platonist conception, the entire range of the fixed and constant is the range of "Being," the range of "the true." In Nietzsche's overturning of Platonism, therefore, truth, when viewed perspectivally, is seen as the petrification of a single perspective which has been unduly esteemed. Thus, Nietzsche says *"Truth is the kind of error* without which a certain kind of living being could not live. The value for *life* ultimately decides" (*WP*, 493).

Truth, i.e., the true as the constant, is itself a kind of semblance that is justified as a necessary condition for life. Semblance for Nietzsche is thus not opposed to reality. Rather, "reality, Being, is *Schein* [semblance] in the sense of a perspectival letting-shine [*Scheinenlassen*]" (*N* I, p. 215). Semblance appears only to the extent that something shows itself. What shows itself is reality as perspectival shining. The unity of the belonging-together of art and truth is grounded in this one reality, for "both art and truth are modes of perspectival shining" (*N* I, p. 216). And it is here that we begin to see why, for Nietzsche, art is worth more than truth. Truth, as the fixation of semblance, allows life to preserve itself in resting firmly upon a particular, fixed perspective. Being fixed, truth preserves life at the expense of inhibiting its possible expansion. Art, as the will to semblance, "induces reality [. . .] to shine most profoundly and supremely in scintillating transfiguration" (*N* I, p. 216). Art, as the transfiguration of perspectives, is more enhancing to life than truth, as the fixation of perspective, in that it opens life up for the creation of more life. Thus, Nietzsche claims that art is "the proper task of life, art as its *metaphysical* activity—" (*WP*, 853) and that "we have *art* so that we *do not perish from the truth*" (*WP*, 822). A life guided exclusively by the "will to truth" and its goal of mere preservation would lead to stagnation and decay. Life requires enhancement and expansion, and it is art rather than truth which opens life up for the possibility of such enhancement.

Yet art and truth remain equally necessary for life, in that life is directed toward both its own enhancement *and* preservation. As equally necessary, they nevertheless stand in discordance by virtue of their diverging from one another in their essential belonging-together as two modes of the one reality: perspectival shining. According to Heidegger, this discordance, unlike Plato's felicitous severance, arouses dread "when we consider that creation, i.e., the metaphysical activity of art, receives yet another essential impulse the moment we descry the most tremendous event—the death of the God of morality" (N I, p. 217). With the death of God, an event which accompanies and announces the advent of nihilism, creation takes its place as the only means by which existence can be endured. God and the "true world" had hitherto been the guarantors of Being. With God's death, man experiences dread at being thrown back upon his own resources. Art, as creation, now becomes man's "highest metaphysical activity." Through creation alone is Being now to be guaranteed; it is no longer God but creation that conducts reality "to the power of its rule and of its supreme possibilities." It is in this sense that art is the supreme configuration of will to power, and on this understanding of the metaphysical activity of creation is grounded Nietzsche's proclamation that art is worth more than truth.

Heidegger concludes his lecture with a summary put forth in the context of correcting a prevalent misinterpretation of a key passage in Nietzsche. In the "Attempt at a Self-Criticism," appended as a preface to the new edition of *The Birth of Tragedy*, Nietzsche wrote that his task now (1886) was the same as that undertaken in his first work (1872): "*to see science under the optics of the artist, but art under that of life*" (BT, SC2). The dominant (mis)interpretation of Nietzsche's task, extracted from this passage, has been that scientific inquiry is not to be pursued as the value-free, sterile acquisition of information, but should be "artistically" shaped in such a way as to insure that scientific findings will be readily useful for "life." To correct this misinterpretation, Heidegger focuses on four points in the passage cited. First, by "science," Nietzsche means knowing as such, conceived as the relation to truth. Second, the two-fold reference to the "optics" of the artist and of life refers to the essentially "perspectival character" of Being. Third, the passage equates art with the artist, thereby expressing the fact that Nietzsche conceives art in terms of the artist, creation, and the grand style. And fourth, Nietzsche conceives "life" in terms of a new interpretation of Being, one which undercuts the traditional opposition between Being and Becoming by conceiving of Being *as* Becoming. That is to say, Nietzsche conceives "life" metaphysically, as will to power which "is in itself that Being which wills itself by willing to be Becoming" (N I, p. 218).

With these four points in view, Heidegger provides a "correct reading" of Nietzsche's passage, that is, a reading directed by the grounding question of philosophy: What is Being? Nietzsche's passage suggests "that on the basis of the essence of Being, art must be grasped as the fundamental occurrence of beings, as the properly creative" (N I, p. 219). It is the *Übermensch* who will be able to grasp art in this way, as "essential legislation for the Being of beings." The *Übermensch* will thus view science "under the optics of the artist" and esteem it according to its creative force. The *Übermensch* will view art, creation, "under the optics of life" and evaluate it "according to the originality with which it penetrates to Being" (N I, p. 220). The *Übermensch*, recognizing the truth of Zarathustra's proclamation that "To esteem is to create" (Z, "On the Thousand

and One Goals"), will thus be free for creation of the highest order: creation in the grand style. As the highest creator, the *Übermensch* thus appears as that being who is able to esteem and act in accordance with the standard of Being.

Heidegger ends his lecture on "The Will to Power as Art" on this note, and we will end our close reading of his Nietzsche interpretation on this point as well. We have taken the time to lay out selected sections of Heidegger's reading in such detail for several reasons which warrant summarizing before we proceed to evaluate this reading. First, it is important to read Nietzsche *with* Heidegger to appreciate the strength of the Heideggerian interpretation. Taking random remarks out of the context of his argument, one can easily make of Heidegger's reading a caricature. By examining the details of Heidegger's reading, we can see the strength of this interpretation, but we also see the dogmatic interpretive moves he makes in overdetermining Nietzsche's philosophy as essentially metaphysical. These exegetical "summaries" show how Heidegger's reading follows from the methodological choices discussed earlier in this chapter. They show as well how Heidegger reads into Nietzsche's text his own view of the history of philosophy in order to tell us what Nietzsche *really* meant and what he *really* thought. And in so doing, they will provide the textual "data" to support the critical commentary of Heidegger's hermeneutic method offered in the following chapter.

Chapter 2

Nietzsche's Psycho-Genealogy: A Ludic Alternative to Heidegger's Reading

I mistrust all systematizers and avoid them. The will to a system is a lack of integrity.
—*Twilight of the Idols*, "Maxims and Arrows," 26

[I]n wishing to restore a truth *and an originary or fundamental* ontology *in the thought of Nietzsche, one risks misunderstanding, perhaps at the expense of everything else, the axial intention of his concept of interpretation.*
—Jacques Derrida, *Of Grammatology*

Having followed the path of Heidegger's confrontation with Nietzsche, we are now in a position to appraise critically his interpretation. In this appraisal, I do not intend to provide a systematic refutation of Heidegger's interpretation. There is much that is important and enlightening in Heidegger's interpretation for an understanding of Nietzsche's thought. Making a unified whole of the scattered ideas found in Nietzsche's writings is a difficult task, and Heidegger succeeds in providing a consistent interpretation of Nietzsche's thinking as a whole. While many of the particular assertions about Nietzsche's philosophy in Heidegger's reading are subject to question, the benefits to be gained from offering alternatives to Heidegger's interpretation of particular themes in Nietzsche would be of only limited importance for an investigation of Heidegger's hermeneutic methodology. For the same reason, the following discussion will not attempt to rescue Nietzsche's thinking from Heidegger's charge of being the culmination of the Western metaphysical tradition. Rather, this discussion will show that Heidegger's reading, proceeding as it does from the presuppositions discussed in the previous chapter (i.e., that "every thinker thinks only a *single* thought [. . .] and this [is] always 'about' *beings as a whole*"[1]), dogmatically systematizes Nietzsche in a way that discounts or ignores much of what was central to Nietzsche's philosophical project. In particular, the discussion will focus on three aspects of Heidegger's interpretation: the dogmatic reduction of Nietzsche's anthropological, psychological, and ethical insights to metaphysical claims; the (mis)interpretation of Nietzsche's conception of will; and the (mis)interpretation of his conception of Being as belonging to a metaphysical tradition in which Nietzsche not only does not belong, but against which he was expressly struggling. The discussion will conclude by demonstrating that Heidegger's attempt to *center* Nietzsche's philosophy around his "one and only thought" of the eternal recurrence occurs at the expense of ignoring a fundamental theme in Nietzsche's thinking: the theme of play. In the discussion of Nietzsche's conception of play, it will be suggested that only a decentered reading of Nietzsche's philosophy, one that does not try to totalize or ground it on a single central theme or thesis, can hope to follow the path of his thinking as the Dionysian play of world-construction and world-destruction (cf. *BT*, 24).

We have already seen that, according to Heidegger, the substance of Nietzsche's thinking on "anthropology," "ethics," and "psychology" is grounded in metaphysics and in how "the Being of beings as a whole is determined" (*WCT*, p. 89; see above pp. 19–20). This metaphysical reductionism fits neither with the spirit nor the letter of Nietzsche's philosophical project, as Heidegger's metaphysicalization fails to attend to the *genealogical* character of Nietzsche's remarks. By focusing exclusively on will to power as Nietzsche's "new" interpretation of the Being of beings, Heidegger fails to recognize Nietzsche's project as the attempt to discern the origins of the contemporary anthropological, psychological, and ethical manifestations of will to power. This failure becomes most apparent when we examine Nietzsche's remarks concerning "psychology."

That Nietzsche considered himself a psychologist, in a sense which must be determined, is clear to even the most casual reader. His writings abound in references to his thinking's being "psychological." "Reflection on the human, all-too-human" is Nietzsche's name for what, in a more scholastic context, is called "psychological observation" (*HAH*, 35). *The Antichrist* investigates the "psychology of the redeemer" (28, 29) and the "psychology of 'belief,' or 'believers' " (50). *On the Genealogy of Morals* takes as its point of departure the "bungled moral genealogy" of the "English psychologists" (*GM*, I, 1–2). *Twilight of the Idols* was originally entitled "*Müssiggang eines Psychologen*" ("A Psychologist's Leisure") and, along with *The Birth of Tragedy*, seeks to discover the "psychology of the artist." We find similar passages in virtually all of Nietzsche's writings. Rather than dismiss them, as Heidegger does, as disguised metaphysics, we must endeavor to grasp Nietzsche's conception of his work as "psychology."

Let us take, as our point of departure, the following remark, which appears initially to substantiate Heidegger's reading.

> All psychology so far has got stuck in moral prejudices and fears; it has not dared to descend into the depths. To understand it as morphology and *the doctrine of the development of the will to power,* as I do—nobody has yet come close to doing this even in thought. (*BGE,* 23)

If, following Heidegger, we take "will to power" to name for Nietzsche, always and only, "the Being of beings as a whole," then this remark would, in fact, appear to ground Nietzsche's psychology in metaphysics. However, this is not the only way to understand "will to power," nor is it the only possible way to interpret Nietzsche's understanding of psychology. Nietzsche concludes this passage from *Beyond Good and Evil* with the claim that the psychologist, as he conceives him or her,

> will at least be entitled to demand [. . .] that psychology shall again be recognized as the queen of the sciences, for whose service and preparation the other sciences exist. For psychology is now again the path to the fundamental problems.

The fundamental problems are, contra Heidegger, not metaphysical problems but axiological problems—problems of value. And the solutions to these problems of value are to be discovered along the path of psychology. Psychology as the doctrine of the structure and development of will to power does not seek the Being of beings. It seeks, rather, to discover whether existing manifestations of will to power have arisen from sources which are life-enhancing or life-negating. And psychology seeks these sources not simply to obtain knowledge, but in order to discern the value of the existing manifestations themselves. Psychology, as genealogy, is thus linked, for Nietzsche, to the question of the assignment of value and not, as Heidegger assumed, to questions of ontological status. This is the goal, for example, in his attempted psychology of the artist. Asking whether the artist creates out of superabundance or out of lack reveals that the origin of the artist's creative impulse will ultimately serve as the criterion through which the artist's work is to be valued. And the task of the psychologist is to discover this origin, to decipher in the symptoms of existing manifestations of will to power (art, religion, morality, etc.) their genesis out of impulses which are life-affirming or life-negating.

We see this conception of genealogical psychology in Nietzsche's discussion of nihilism. Nietzsche's use of "nihilism" exhibits an important polysemy: he distinguishes among at least four senses of nihilism as a *psychological* state. These distinctions are made in terms of the sources, the causes of nihilism; that is, the distinctions are drawn from the results of Nietzsche's genealogical inquiry. The first three forms of nihilism, which together Nietzsche labels "incomplete nihilism," are outlined in Section 12 of *The Will to Power*. The first form of "nihilism as a psychological state" is reached "when we have sought a 'meaning' in all events that is not there." The seeker becomes discouraged. Nihilism here is the "recognition of the long *waste* of strength, the agony of the 'in vain.' " This "meaning" could have been any goal, as long as something was "to be achieved through the process—and now one realizes that becoming aims at *nothing* and achieves *nothing*." At this stage, the "disappointment regarding an alleged aim of becoming" is the cause of nihilism. This first form of nihilism is, for Nietzsche, the nihilism of pessimism.

The second form of nihilism is reached when "one has posited a totality, a schematization, indeed any organization in all events" that will serve as a "sort of unity." This faith in some unity gives man the feeling of "being dependent upon some whole that is infinitely superior to him, and he sees himself as a mode of the deity," thereby attributing a value to himself by virtue of this dependence. But there is no such universal, and by losing faith in this unity, man also loses faith in his own value, as "infinitely valuable whole works" can no longer be brought about through him. This loss of unity is what characterizes the second form of nihilism: skeptical nihilism.

There is, however, yet a third psychological form of nihilism. Having seen that becoming has no aim and that beneath all becoming there lies no unity in which the individual can immerse himself, "an escape remains: to pass sentence on this whole world of becoming as a deception and to invent a world beyond it, a *true* world," the world of Being. When man realizes, however, that this world of Being is

> fabricated solely from psychological needs, and that he has absolutely no right to it, the last form of nihilism comes into being; it includes disbelief in any metaphysical world and forbids itself any belief in a *true* world.

We are here at the level of what Nietzsche calls "passive nihilism": "the categories 'aim,' 'unity,' 'Being' which we used to project some value into the world—we *pull out* again; so the world looks *valueless*." Nietzsche concludes that "the *faith in the categories of reason* is the cause of nihilism. We have measured the value of the world according to categories *that refer to a purely fictitious world*."

In opposition to these three forms of "incomplete nihilism" stands what Nietzsche calls "complete" or "active nihilism." The contrast between complete and incomplete nihilism makes clear the necessity of attending to Nietzsche's *genealogical* method if one is to understand his conception of "nihilism as a psychological state." The world exhibits a fundamental ambiguity, which means that "the very same symptoms could point to *decline* and to *strength*" (*WP*, 110). This ambiguity is reflected in the distinction between these two basic types of nihilism.

> Nihilism. It is *ambiguous:*
> A.   Nihilism as a sign of increased power of the spirit: as *active* nihilism.
> B.   Nihilism as decline and recession of the power of the spirit: as *passive* nihilism.
> (*WP*, 22)

In other words, the modern world exhibits the symptoms of nihilism—the highest values have become devalued. But this event, alone, is not sufficient for passing judgment on the modern world. Genealogy is needed to decipher these symptoms, to discover whether this devaluation is an expression of decline or of strength. As symptom of decline, "passive nihilism" is the expression of a weary, exhausted will which has searched in vain to locate the highest values: aim, unity, Being. Having grown dissatisfied with the unsuccessful search for these highest values, passive nihilism devalues not only these values but goes on to devalue the world as well insofar as the world *ought* to have manifested these values.

Active nihilism, as a sign of strength, also devalues the categories of aim, unity, and Being. But in doing so, it shows them to no longer apply to the world, and their absence no longer serves as grounds for the devaluation of the world. Active nihilism has outgrown and overflown these highest values and their devaluation is viewed as a necessary, transitional stage in the creation of new values. Like passive nihilism, active nihilism is destructive. But, unlike passive nihilism, it is not *merely* destructive. Nietzsche notes the "overall insight" that "every major growth is accompanied by a tremendous crumbling and passing away: suffering, the symptoms of decline *belong* in the times of tremendous advances" (*WP*, 112). The destructive moment of active nihilism is essentially linked with the creative moment. Unlike the incomplete forms of nihilism, in which the devaluation of the highest values results in a devaluation of the world as a whole, in active nihilism the destructive moment of devaluation arises out of the overflowing strength of will to power on the way to a revaluation.

This characterization of nihilism displays a movement similar to that which Jacques Derrida finds in the term *pharmakon*.[2] The *pharmakon*, "which acts as both remedy and poison, [. . .] can be—alternatively or simultaneously—beneficent or maleficent."[3] The term *pharmakon* plays between the poles of remedy and poison, and to render *pharmakon* as either "remedy" or "poison" cancels out the resources of signification reserved in that sign. For Derrida, the movement of the *pharmakon* is noteworthy in that it exposes the limits of metaphysical thinking, for this movement cannot be thought in the binary fashion that characterizes the metaphysical tradition. This is to say, metaphysics proceeds by means of an "either . . . or . . . ," organizing its concepts according to one or the other pole of the binary opposition. Terms like *pharmakon,* however, cannot be conceived by means of this binarism, for the movement of the *pharmakon*[4] is not that of a disjunctive "either . . . or . . ." but a conjunctive "both . . . and . . . ": the *pharmakon* is *both* remedy *and* poison, both a remedial poison and a poisonous remedy. Derrida's point is that we should not, in our effort to understand, overdetermine the meaning of *pharmakon* and thereby erase its inherent ambiguity.

This is instructive for our interpretation of nihilism because nihilism, for Nietzsche, is also a *pharmakon*. Nihilism, as Platonism and Christianity ("Platonism for 'the people' " [*BGE*, Pr.]), is a poison. It is the expression of a decadent and decaying will to power which brings with it all of those noxious consequences that Nietzsche catalogues. Nihilism, however, can also be a remedy: "nihilism, as the **denial** of a truthful world, of being, might be *a divine way of thinking*" (*WP*, 15). This complete nihilism recognizes the noxious effects of its own incomplete forms, thereby opening the path for will to power to revalue those values which have come to be devalued. This is why, for Nietzsche, nihilism is a necessary, pathological, *transitional* stage. Nihilism, as poison, becomes its own remedy. Only through suffering the poison is the way cleared for recovery from this pathological condition. Or, to use Nietzsche's language, only through suffering at the hands of Being is the path opened for the affirmation of the Dionysian play of becoming.[5]

Heidegger, it seems, by reading Nietzsche's *pharmakon* (nihilism) only as a poison, the poison of Being, fails to attend to the psycho-genealogical distinction between the forms of nihilism just outlined.[6] This failure is the consequence of his grounding Nietzsche's psychology in metaphysics. This grounding brings us to our second point of criticism: Heidegger's misinterpretation of Nietzsche's conception of will. This (mis)interpretation or overdetermination of will as Nietzsche's answer to the question of the Being of beings leads Heidegger to view Nietzsche as a reductive psychologist rather than a psycho-genealogist. That is to say, Heidegger's reduction of Nietzsche's psychology to metaphysics is derived from the mistaken belief that Nietzsche's psychology is directed toward the goal of reducing everything to will *qua* the Being of beings.

We have already seen that, for Heidegger, post-Cartesian metaphysics is characterized as "voluntaristic" in the sense that the Being of beings is determined as will. Nietzsche, in thinking will to power, the "essential will" (see *N* I, p. 61) as the Being of beings, thus stands in the voluntaristic metaphysical tradition. This tradition stretches from Schopenhauer through Hegel, Schelling, and Kant to its inception in Leibniz, who "defined the essence of Being as the original unity of *perceptio* and *appetitus,* representation and will" (*N* I, p. 35). Heidegger's inclusion of Nietzsche in this tradition, however, is not without problems, for it is not at all clear that Nietzsche's conception of "will" is the same as the conception of will found, for example, in Schelling or Schopenhauer. These problems become acute when one recognizes that, in Nietzsche's writings, one finds an extended critique of the existence of the "will." For Nietzsche, the existence of a simple, unitary entity "will" is a linguistic fiction that arises from our applying to diverse impulses a single name.

> Willing seems to me to be above all something *complicated,* something that is a unit only as word—and it is precisely in this one word that the popular prejudice lurks, which has defeated the always inadequate caution of philosophers. (*BGE,* 19)

The "will," for Nietzsche, is a "misleading metaphor" through which diverging effects are systematically attributed to a single cause.

> The logical-metaphysical postulates, the belief in substance, accident, attribute, etc., derive their convincing force from our habit of regarding all our deeds as consequences of our will—so that ego, as substance, does not vanish in the multiplicity of change.— But there is no such thing as will. (*WP,* 488; see also *WP,* 46, 485)

Heidegger is not unfamiliar with these passages. In fact, he cites them along with others in which Nietzsche asserts that "There is no will" (see *N* I, pp. 38– 39). How, then, can he nevertheless assert that Nietzsche belongs within the tradition of voluntaristic metaphysics? The answer can be found in a Heideggerian reading of passages like the following:

Is "will to power" a *kind* of "will" or identical with the concept "will"? Is it the same thing as desiring? or *commanding?* Is it that "will" of which Schopenhauer said it was the "in-itself of things"?

My proposition is: that the *will* of psychology hitherto is an unjustified generalization, that this will *does not exist at all,* that instead of grasping the idea of the development of *one definite* will into many forms, one has *eliminated* the character of the will by subtracting from it its content, its whither? [*Wohin?*]—this is in the highest degree the case with *Schopenhauer:* what he calls "will" is a mere empty word. (*WP,* 692)

From this passage, the Heideggerian interpretation concludes that Nietzsche's rejection of the *"will* of psychology" is *ipso facto* a rejection of all psychological inquiry into the will. This opens the way for his reduction of Nietzsche's psychology to metaphysics and his consideration of will to power exclusively as a metaphysical concept.

Such conclusions are suspect in light of some of Nietzsche's other remarks regarding the denial of the will. In particular, we can take exception to Heidegger's drawing the conclusion that Nietzsche rejects psychological inquiry in rejecting the *"will* of psychology." To be sure, for Nietzsche, the *"will* of psychology" does not exist. But this only means that the "old psychology" is mistaken in pursuing the will as a faculty of the soul. Nietzsche clearly rejects the static concept of will as an object of "faculty-psychology." In fact, for Nietzsche this "faculty-psychology" is itself submitted to a new type of psychological examination. What is today required, according to Nietzsche, is a meta-psychology, a "psychology of the psychologist" (*WP,* 426); that is, a psycho-genealogical inquiry into the origin of the illusion of the will as simple substance. This psycho-genealogy reveals that the *"will* of psychology" is the product of Christianity's "hangman's metaphysics."

One has deprived becoming of its innocence if being in this or that state is traced back to will, to intentions, to accountable acts: the doctrine of will has been invented essentially for the purpose of punishment, that is, of *finding guilty.* The whole of the old-style psychology, the psychology of will, has as its precondition the desire of its authors, the priests at the head of the ancient communities, to create for themselves a *right* to ordain punishments—or their desire to create for God a right to do so. . . . Men were thought of as "free" so that they could become *guilty:* consequently, every action *had* to be thought of as willed, the origin of every action as lying in the consciousness (—whereby the most *fundamental* falsification *in psychologicis* was made into the very principle of psychology . . .) Today, we have started to move in the *reverse* direction[. . . .] (*TI,* "The Four Great Errors," 7)

This conclusion concerning the tainted origin of the will echoes Nietzsche's genealogical connection between the origin of punishment and the creation of the concepts "soul" and "subject" (see *GM*, I, 13; II, 12–16). On the basis of his judgment as to these perversions of psychological inquiry, the task will fall to the "*new* psychologists" to put an end "to the superstitions which have so far flourished with almost tropical luxuriance around the idea of the soul" and the doctrine of will which accompanies it (*BGE*, 12).

These remarks regarding Nietzsche's genealogical critique of the will raise some serious questions for Heidegger's interpretation. While Heidegger acknowledges many of these remarks, his dogmatic assertion of will to power as Nietzsche's concept of the Being of beings keeps him from recognizing their importance for situating Nietzsche vis-à-vis the voluntaristic metaphysical tradition. Heidegger fails to recognize that Nietzsche criticizes the metaphysical concept of will on *axiological* grounds. Instead, he sees in Nietzsche's thinking the metaphysical concept of will giving way to a new metaphysical concept: will to power. But we must recall that it is not metaphysics but the "new psychology" which is to be understood "as morphology and *the doctrine of the development of the will to power*" (*BGE*, 23). Vis-à-vis the tradition, this indicates that Nietzsche, in thinking will to power, is not providing us with a new interpretation of the determination of the Being of beings as will. Rather, it shows that Nietzsche is fundamentally engaged in a project quite different from that of metaphysics. Nietzsche's thinking is not primarily directed toward metaphysically determining the essence of will to power. In fact, he at times suggests that will to power itself might be only an interpretation (see *BGE*, 22, 36). The essential question, therefore, is not that of the *Being* of will to power. It is, rather, the question of the whither (*Wohin?*) and whence (*Woher?*) of will to power: out of what do these impulses that we call "will to power" arise and toward what ends are these impulses directed? This is to say, Nietzsche's essential thinking is not metaphysical but *axiological* in the originary sense of this term (*axioein* = to hold worthy): it is the question of the *value* of will to power and not the *Being* of will to power that is of primary importance in Nietzsche's thinking, and this primacy of value-inquiry is lost within Heidegger's overdetermined metaphysical reading.

The question of the relationship between axiology and metaphysics in Nietzsche's thinking is also at issue in my third point of criticism: Heidegger's (mis)interpretation of Nietzsche's conception of Being. As we have seen, for Heidegger, Nietzsche's thinking marks the culmination of metaphysics: in his transforming Being into value, Nietzsche sets beings in the complete abandonment of Being, thereby completing metaphysics as the oblivion of Being. This judgment is drawn from Heidegger's thinking will to power as Nietzsche's name for the Being of beings. Heidegger offers this interpretation of will to power as "what is essential in Nietzsche's thinking." Yet this interpretation follows only from Heidegger's fundamental assumption regarding Nietzsche, i.e., that he is essentially a "metaphysical thinker." Such an assumption is, as has been shown, subject to question.

One might say, in this regard, that whereas Heidegger reads the history of philosophy from the point of view of the *Seinsfrage,* the question of Being, Nietzsche confronts that same tradition with the *Wertsfrage,* the question of value. Or to put this another way, although Heidegger recognizes Nietzsche's *Wertsfrage,* he is intent on reducing it to the *Seinsfrage:* "The question about value and its essence is grounded in the question of Being."[7] If we view Nietzsche's thinking as axiological rather than metaphysical, we can make the following response to Heidegger's claim that Nietzsche completes the oblivion of Being: Nietzsche does not *forget* Being, for there is no Being to be forgotten. In his view, "Being" is simply an interpretation whose construction was motivated by the inability or unwillingness to confront becoming, an interpretation, moreover, that has outlived its usefulness and can now be discarded. To say that there is no Being does not mean, however, that there is on the contrary non-Being or nothingness. Rather, it indicates that the question of Being is not germane to Nietzsche's thinking. What is foremost at issue for Nietzsche is the question of value (cf. *KGW,* VII, 3: 40[23]), and finding a solution to the "problem of value" defines "the future task of the philosophers" (*GM,* I, 17 note). Only because Heidegger is himself metaphysical in his reading of the tradition as always asking the *same* question ("What beings and Being in truth are" [*N* I, p. 68: *"was das Seiende und was das Sein in Wahrheit ist."*]) does he see in Nietzsche a reduction of Being to value. But there is no such reduction, at least not in the way that Heidegger suggests. Far from being a metaphysical thinker who has forgotten Being in characterizing will to power as all there is, we can view Nietzsche's thinking as fundamental axiology which, having subjected "Being" to a radical genealogical critique, sets Being aside as an interpretation which is judged to no longer be of value.

This reading is supported by Nietzsche's numerous critical comments regarding Being and the philosophical project of metaphysics. For Nietzsche, the faith of the metaphysicians parallels the faith of religious believers: having judged this world harshly, they assert the primacy of a better world beyond this one. For religion, this world beyond is the world of God; for metaphysics, it is the world of Being. Of German philosophy, Nietzsche writes that it has "always brought forth only 'unconscious' counterfeiters (Fichte, Schelling, Schopenhauer, Hegel and Schleiermacher deserve this epithet as well as Kant and Leibniz: they are all mere veilmakers [*es sind Alles blosse Schleiermacher*])" (*EH,* CW3). The play on words with the name "Schleiermacher" (*Schleier-macher* = veil-maker) makes explicit Nietzsche's judgment that German philosophy has come forth as a disguised theology. Like religion, philosophy suffers from the " 'beyond' corruption: as if outside the actual world, that of becoming, there were another world of Being" (*WP,* 51).

Heidegger correctly points out that Nietzsche sees in Being an answer to the metaphysical need for security, but he is clearly mistaken in asserting that "Nietzsche remains in the unbroken line of the metaphysical tradition when he calls that which is established and made fast in the will to power purely and simply Being [. . .]" (see *NW*, p. 84). For Nietzsche makes no such assertion of the enduring presence (*ousia*) of will to power. Rather, after having pointed out the metaphysical need for security, Nietzsche offers will to power and the world of becoming as an alternative to the world of Being, a challenging alternative that results not in security but risk. Nietzsche writes:

> Metaphysics is still needed by some; but so is that impetuous *demand for certainty* that today discharges itself among large numbers of people in a scientific-positivistic form. The demand that one *wants* by all means that something should be firm [. . .]— this, too, is still a demand for a support, a prop, in short, that *instinct of weakness* which, to be sure, does not create religious, metaphysical systems, and convictions of all kinds but—conserves them. (*GS*, 347)

For Nietzsche, "the doctrine of Being, of thing, of all sorts of fixed unities is a hundred times easier than the doctrine of becoming, of development" (*WP*, 538). Because knowledge requires static, fixed, and unchanging objects, the myth of Being arose to satisfy the knowing man's need for *possessions,* while philosophy and religion are responses to our "longing for *property*" (*KGW*, III, 4: 29[224]; *PHT*, 60).

Because the world of becoming and change is not subject to possession by the man of knowledge, he creates another world, that of Being, in which he puts his faith. The world of Being is, for Nietzsche, "*The fiction of a world* that corresponds to our desires; psychological trick and interpretation with the aim of associating everything we honor and find pleasant with the *true world*" (*WP*, 585A; also *WP*, 579). Nietzsche criticizes the philosophy of Being for its lack of "historical sense," i.e., it refuses to recognize that everything *becomes* (see *HAH*, 2). His conception of becoming stands opposed to the concept of Being: "What is, does not *become;* what becomes, *is* not" (*TI*, " 'Reason' in Philosophy," 1: "*Was ist,* wird *nicht; was wird,* ist *nicht.*"). For Nietzsche, the affirmation of becoming must be accompanied by "a radical repudiation of the very concept 'Being' " (*EH*, BT3), a concept whose origin resides in human beings' inability to feel secure in the ever-changing play of the world.

It should be evident from this brief discussion of "Being" and "will" that Heidegger's interpretation has some serious problems. Heidegger's reading follows from Nietzsche's inclusion in a metaphysical tradition which Nietzsche quite explicitly criticizes. It seems clear that Nietzsche's conception of "will" and "will to power" is quite different from the Schelling-Schopenhauerian conception of "will" that determines, according to Heidegger, "voluntaristic" metaphysics. And it seems equally clear that when Nietzsche says, for example, "*This world is the will to power—and nothing besides*" (*WP*, 1067), he need not be making a metaphysical assertion about the Being of beings. It is easy to see why Heidegger claims that Nietzsche names Being by "will to power." If, as he says in the *Letter on Humanism,* "thinking is the thinking of Being,"[8] then Nietzsche, insofar as he is a thinker, *must* be thinking of Being. And if Nietzsche thinks the will to power, then the will to power must be what Nietzsche thinks *as* Being. But this reasoning, it seems, says more about Heidegger than it does about Nietzsche, and from Nietzsche's perspective, one could argue that it is Heidegger who, in proclaiming the unity of the metaphysical tradition and dogmatically reducing all thinking to thinking of Being, is the consummate metaphysician. At the very least, Nietzsche's genealogical critique of the concept of Being makes dubious Heidegger's claim that what Nietzsche essentially means by "will to power" is the Being of beings.

At this point, we must ask how Heidegger could have so systematically misinterpreted Nietzsche's philosophical project? We glimpse an answer to this question when we recognize that, for all his thoroughness, by dogmatically maintaining that Nietzsche is *always* and *only* thinking metaphysically, Heidegger neglects to attend to a fundamental theme in Nietzsche's philosophy: the theme of play. Play is a Nietzschean theme in a two-fold sense: it operates in his thinking both as a stylistic device and as a philosophical "concept." Had Heidegger better understood Nietzsche's playfulness, his interpretation might very well have turned out significantly different. Eugen Fink, Heidegger's student and colleague at Freiburg, provides such an interpretation. For Fink, "Heraclitus remains the originary root of Nietzsche's philosophy."[9] "In Heraclitus' conception of play, Nietzsche finds his deepest intuition of the reality of the world as grandiose cosmic metaphor."[10] In the final chapter of his work on Nietzsche, "Nietzsche's Relation to Metaphysics as Imprisonment and Liberation," Fink offers a response to Heidegger's Nietzsche interpretation. For Fink, rather than being the culmination of metaphysics, Nietzsche's thinking operates at the boundary of metaphysics, sometimes imprisoned within and sometimes liberated from metaphysics. Insofar as Nietzsche's thinking arises in response to the metaphysical tradition, valuing, as it does, becoming and appearance as alternatives to Being and Truth, Fink sees Nietzsche as remaining imprisoned within metaphysics. But when Nietzsche's thinking arises out of his Heraclitean insight into the cosmic play of the world "beyond all valuation, precisely because all values emerge *within* this play," his thinking liberates itself from the tradition.[11] Fink thus concludes that "where Nietzsche grasps being and becoming as *Spiel,* he no longer stands in the confinement of metaphysics."[12]

But how does Nietzsche "grasp being and becoming as *Spiel*"? We can begin to answer this question by understanding Nietzsche's view of Heraclitus[13] and the contrast he develops between Heraclitus and Socrates. Whereas Nietzsche is ambivalent regarding how we should value Socrates' contribution to philosophy, his positive estimation of Heraclitus persists from his earliest writings to his latest. In Heraclitus, Nietzsche finds a kindred spirit "in whose company [he feels] altogether warmer and better than anywhere else" (*EH,* BT3). Heraclitus exhibits, for Nietzsche, the tragic wisdom that he otherwise finds lacking in the history of philosophy. This tragic wisdom is the decisive move towards a Diony-sian philosophy which affirms "passing-away and annihilating, [. . .] the yea-saying to contrariety and struggle, becoming, with a radical repudiation of the very concept 'Being' " (*EH*, BT3). Even the doctrine of the eternal recurrence "*might* in the end have been taught already by Heraclitus" (*EH*, BT3). For these and other reasons, Nietzsche

with the highest respect [accepts] the name of *Heraclitus*. When the rest of the philosophic folk rejected the testimony of the senses because they showed multiplicity and change, he rejected their testimony because they showed things as if they had permanence and unity. Heraclitus too did the senses an injustice. They lie neither in the way the Eleatics believed, nor as he believed—they do not lie at all. What we *make* of their testimony, that alone introduces lies; for example, the lie of unity, the lie of thinghood, of substance, of permanence. "Reason" is the cause of our falsifica-tion of the testimony of the senses. Insofar as the senses show becoming, passing away, and change, they do not lie. But Heraclitus will remain eternally right with his assertion that being is an empty fiction. The "apparent" world is the only one: the "true" world is merely *added by a lie*. (*TI*, " 'Reason' in Philosophy," 2)

In addition to the denial of Being, Nietzsche admires Heraclitus' "aesthetic fundamental-perception [*aesthetische Grundperception*] as to the play of the world" (*PTAG*, 7). While watching the games of noisy children, Heraclitus "had been pondering something never before pondered by a mortal on such an occasion, viz., the play of the great world-child Zeus, and the eternal game of world destruction and origination" (*KGW*, III, 2: p. 252; *PT*, p. 64). From this ponder-ing, Heraclitus comes to the realization that "everything is illusion and play" (*KGW*, III, 4: 23[8]; *PCP*, 168). This realization and the manner in which it was unfolded leads Nietzsche to proclaim Heraclitus one of the three "purest types" of pre-Platonic philosophy: "Pythagoras, Heraclitus, Socrates—the sage as religious reformer, the sage as proud and lonely truth-finder, the sage as the eternal and extensive seeker" (*MA*, IV, p. 296).

In this description we see the beginnings of the distinction which Nietzsche will draw between Heraclitus and Socrates. The pure Socratic type, eternally searching for the truth, stands opposed to Heraclitus, the proud and solitary philosophical type who recognizes the Dionysian play of the world. Whereas Nietzsche consistently praises Heraclitus throughout the course of his philosophi-cal reflection, a profound ambivalence marks Nietzsche's estimation of Socrates. In his early writings, Nietzsche's opinion of Socrates is, for the most part, quite positive. Socrates is the master of irony and "the first philosopher of *life* [Lebens-*philosoph*]," the first thinker to subordinate thought to life and not life to thought (*MA*, IV, p. 357). Nietzsche's model of the philosopher as "cultural physician" is drawn from the *Apology*, about which he approvingly remarks that "Plato seems to have received the decisive thought as to how a philosopher ought to behave toward men from the apology of Socrates: as their physician, as a gadfly on the neck of man" (*MA*, IV, p. 404). Even in *The Birth of Tragedy*, often cited as evidence of Nietzsche's hostility toward Socrates, he is introduced into the dialectic of the Apollonian and the Dionysian as the *deity* that spoke through the mask of Euripides (see *BT*, 12). The introduction of this new deity marks the beginning of the end of Greek tragedy, as the Dionysian no longer stands opposed to the Apollonian. On the contrary, the Dionysian is now opposed to the Socratic: the logical, the scientific, the serious. The Socratic dictum "Knowledge is virtue" is transformed into the supreme law of "aesthetic Socratism," which reads "To be beautiful, everything must be intelligible" (*BT*, 12). In this regard, Nietzsche writes: "At a moment when truth was *closest*, Socrates *upset everything:* that is especially *ironic*" (*KGW*, IV, 1: 6[7]; *SSW*, 189). What Socrates upsets is the Greeks' instinctive ability "to play around life with lies [*umspielen das Leben mit Lügen*]" (*KGW*, IV, 1: 5[121]; *WPh*, 138). The Heraclitean play of becoming is thus dealt a fatal blow by Socratic seriousness. In his early works, Nietzsche can only respond to this seriousness with puzzlement: "It is strange to take everything so seriously" (*KGW*, IV, 1: 6[7]; *SSW*, 189). One could go so far as to view Nietzsche's early philological period as the attempt to understand the necessity of the fall of Greek culture resulting from its confrontation with Socratic scientism and seriousness. Yet, while Nietzsche clearly recognized the harmfulness of Socratism (his notebooks abound in such references; see *KGW*, III, 4: 19[27, 97, 216], 23[14–16]; IV, 1: 6[13–26]; *PCP*, 175; *P*, 31, 70; *SSW*, 192–196), there nevertheless remained something compelling in the figure of Socrates: "*Socrates* is so close to me that I am almost constantly fighting with him" (*KGW*, IV, 1: 6[3]; *SSW*, p. 127).

In Nietzsche's later writings, however, a different conception of Socrates emerges. While occasional references to Socrates in a positive light remain (see *WS*, 86; *GS*, 340; *GM*, III, 7), they are not nearly as laudatory as those of the earlier period. And these few positive remarks are greatly outnumbered by Nietzsche's critical comments. Socrates comes to be identified as a symptom of decadence (*WP*, 432–435). He is singled out as the origin of the decline of Greek philosophy: "The real philosophers of Greece are those before Socrates (—with Socrates something changes)" (*WP*, 437). What changes is that Socrates initiates the identity of "reason = virtue = happiness," an identity that Nietzsche sees as standing opposed to the instincts and at the origin of moral philosophy (*WP*, 432–433). About *The Birth of Tragedy*, Nietzsche remarks:

> Socrates is recognized for the first time as an instrument of Greek disintegration, as a typical decadent. "Rationality" *against* instinct. "Rationality" at any price as a dangerous force that undermines life. (*EH*, BT1; see also *TI*, "The Problem of Socrates")

In both *Ecce Homo* and *Twilight of the Idols*, the discussion of the anti-instinctual decadence of rationality is followed immediately by praise of Heraclitus' affirmation of the play of becoming and the denial of "Being" (see *EH*, BT3; *TI*, " 'Reason' in Philosophy," 2). This makes clear the opposition of Heraclitean play and Socratic seriousness, an opposition less explicit but analogous to that drawn between Dionysus and the Crucified (see *EH*, IV, 9). In each case, we see Nietzsche affirm becoming and play, over against the moralistic, life-negating tendencies of philosophy and religion. Taking these oppositions as a point of departure, let us see how a reading of Nietzsche can proceed based upon the theme of play.

This theme perhaps more than any other save that of becoming, is one with which Nietzsche concerned himself through the entirety of his philosophical life, and we can locate references to play from his earliest writings through his final notebooks. In his writings on Greek philosophy and tragedy, we find play as a specific topic of Nietzsche's reflections, both in terms of his fascination with the Heraclitean idea of "the play in necessity" (see *PTAG*, 8), and as a fundamental concept in his attempt to construct an "artist's metaphysics." In one essay (*"Die dionysische Weltanschauung," KGW*, III, 2: pp. 45–69) dating from the time of *The Birth of Tragedy*, Nietzsche distinguishes among five senses of play at work in the dialectic of the Apollonian and Dionysian, as he toys with a playful definition of tragedy. First, he discerns two senses of Apollonian play: "While the dream is the play of the individual with the real, the art of the sculptor is, in another sense, *playing with the dream*" (*KGW*, III, 2: p. 46). He then isolates two senses of Dionysian play: "If, now, rapture is the play of nature with man, then the creation of the Dionysian artist is a playing with rapture" (*KGW*, III, 2: p. 47). To these four senses of play, Apollonian artistic activity as playing with dreams, which are themselves a form of playing with the real, and Dionysian artistic activity as playing with rapture, which is itself understood as nature's playing with man, Nietzsche adds a fifth sense: the play of tragedy, understood as the interplay (*Widerspiel*) of the Apollonian and the Dionysian (see *BT*, 21–25).

In Nietzsche's later writings, the theme of play no longer comes to the fore as an explicit subject of discussion, as it did in his early works. Rather, Nietzsche draws the veil of play over us as we attempt to enter into the movement of his discourse. That is, while we no longer find extended discussions of the role of play in his thinking, there are sufficient allusions to indicate the role that play serves in his own understanding of his philosophical project. Nowhere is this role more explicitly indicated than in the following remark: "I know of no other way of associating with great tasks than *play:* as a sign of greatness, this is an essential presupposition" (*EH*, II, 10). While this remark notes the essential function play serves in his thinking, it does not take us very far toward understanding what Nietzsche understands by "play." To this task, we must now turn.

Although he does not provide us, in his later works, with an explicit typology of play like that found in his early writings, there are, in these later works, three distinct yet interrelated conceptions of play. First, there is *Schauspiel*, theatrical play. Human beings are advised to view their condemnation to the world of appearance and illusion as they would an entertaining theatrical performance. We are all actors equipped with an assortment of masks, and laughter and dance are the most joyful, most *fröhlich*, and most highly valued responses to our participation in this *Schauspiel*. "In the end one would live among men and with oneself as in *nature*, without praising, blaming, contending, gazing contentedly, as though at a spectacle (*Schauspiel*), upon many things for which one formerly felt only fear" (*HAH*, 34). In opposition to the "metaphysical comforts" (the beyond) which human beings have sought as compensation for the horrors of existence and becoming, Nietzsche suggests instead that we learn to enjoy our participation in the *Schauspiel:*

> You ought to learn the art of *this-worldly* comfort first: you ought to learn to laugh, my young friends, if you are hell-bent on remaining pessimists. Then perhaps, as laughers, you may some day dispatch all metaphysical comforts to the devil— metaphysics in front. Or, to say it in the language of that Dionysian monster who bears the name of Zarathustra:
>
> "Raise up your hearts, my brothers, high, higher! And don't forget your legs! Raise up your legs, too, good dancers; and still better: stand on your heads!
>
> "This crown of the laugher, the rose-wreath crown: I crown myself with this crown; I myself pronounced holy my laughter. I did not find anyone else today strong enough for that.
>
> "Zarathustra, the soothsayer [*Wahrsager*]; Zarathustra, the sooth-laugher [*Wahrlacher*]; not impatient; not unconditional; one who loves leaps and side-leaps; I crown myself with this crown.
>
> "This crown of the laugher, the rose-wreath crown: to you, my brothers, I throw this crown. Laughter I have pronounced holy: you higher men, *learn*—to laugh!" (*BT*, SC7)

Second, there is the play of the world, *Weltspiel*. The world is a play of forces, a chaotic world in which nothing stands fast (cf. *WP*, 1067). And humans are a part of this play of forces. In fact, a human being is *itself* a play of forces. As such, human beings' task in the world is that of a legislator: they must create rules for this play.

> It is a measure of the degree of strength of will to what extent one can do without meaning in things, to what extent one can endure to live in a meaningless world *because one organizes a small portion of it oneself.* (*WP*, 585A)

Just as persons must organize the play of the world, so too must they organize the forces which make up themselves. Of Goethe, Nietzsche's model of the great individual as self-legislator, he writes:

> What he wanted was *totality;* he fought the mutual extraneousness of reason, senses, feeling and will; [. . .] he disciplined himself to wholeness, he *created* himself. (*TI*, "Skirmishes of an Untimely Man," 49)

Third, there is the play of the child, *Kinderspiel*. This is, for Nietzsche, the most significant sort of play and, in a sense, it animates both *Schauspiel* and *Weltspiel*. *Kinderspiel* is a *serious* play, a play which, while recognizing that human matters are not worthy of seriousness, nevertheless affirms the game and one's part in it, and takes the game seriously (cf. *HAH*, 628). The *Kinderspieler* is, for Nietzsche, the ideal: " 'Play,' the useless—as the ideal of him who is overfull of strength, as 'childlike,' the 'childlikeness' of God, *pais paizon*" (*WP*, 797). Elsewhere, he writes: "A man's maturity—consists in having found again the seriousness one had as a child, at play" (*BGE*, 94). The seriousness of *Kinderspiel* is qualitatively different from the all-too-heavy seriousness of the metaphysical comforters who preach salvation. It is the seriousness of the child building castles in the sand, meticulously creating a world in the full knowledge that the sea may rise up at any moment and wash this world away.

With this three-fold conception of play in view, we can provide an alternative to Heidegger's interpretation of Nietzsche's five main themes. The context of this interpretation will be the first of Zarathustra's speeches: "On the Three Metamorphoses." In this discourse, Zarathustra describes three stages of the development of the spirit: "how the spirit becomes a camel; and the camel, a lion; and the lion, finally, a child." The first stage, that of the camel, is characterized by unconditional obedience to the values and laws of tradition. The guiding word of the camel is "Thou shalt," and following this word, the reverent camel-spirit stands well-loaded with the burdensome weight of the laws of the tradition. The camel has the strength to bear this load, and is rewarded with freedom from responsibility, and with the security of knowing what to do.

In the second stage, that of the lion, the spirit takes hold of its freedom. From the lion issues forth a "sacred No" to the "Thou shalt" which stands in its way as an obstacle to its freedom. For the lion, "I will" is the guiding word. While not yet sufficient for the creation of new values, the lion's power is strong enough to reject the old values. In them, it now finds "illusion and caprice." Yet, the lion must remain in the empty domain of freedom: having overcome the dominion of the old values, something is still lacking for the creation of new values: the lion must become a child.

In the metamorphosis from lion to child, the "sacred No" is transformed into a "sacred Yes." The child, taking off from the freedom secured by the lion, is no longer restricted to the mere negation of the old values. The child now "wills its own will" and takes up the task of the creation of new values. Zarathustra, in this speech, provides the following description of the child:

The child is innocence and forgetting, a new beginning, a game, a self-propelled wheel, a first movement, a sacred Yes. For the play of creation, my brothers, a sacred Yes is needed: the spirit now wills *its own* will, and he who had been lost to the world now conquers *his own* world.

While these two sentences are the only description offered in Zarathustra's first speech, the remainder of *Thus Spoke Zarathustra* unfolds out of this description, filling in the details of the spirit's (and perhaps Zarathustra's own) metamorphosis to the level of the child. And in this description of the child, opposed as it is to that of the lion and the camel, we arrive at a vantage-point from which to see the relation between play and Nietzsche's "five major themes."

Taking nihilism first, we see it as the situation which confronts the child. For what is the outcome of the lion's "sacred No" but the reactively nihilistic devaluation of the hitherto highest values, the values ordained by the camel's "Thou shalt"? While the lion must remain at this reactive level of the highest values having been devalued, the child, through the play of creation (*Spiele des Schaffens*), advances to the level of active nihilism by giving itself the freedom to create new values. This is to say, creative play is here affirmed as the spirit's highest activity and the means by which reactive nihilism will be overcome.

The object of this creative play, as Zarathustra's first speech makes clear, is value; that is to say, what is played *with* are values. The child's creative play makes possible the *transvaluation* of values: while the camel could only accept those values given to it (passive nihilism), and the lion was capable only of devaluing those given values (reactive nihilism), the child is capable of a revaluation (active nihilism). By means of this *revaluation* one creates a world over which one stands as master/legislator. At this point, we must ask: who is this world-creating playful child and what capacity does it have that allows for its playing with values? Nietzsche's answer to the first question is, of course, the *Übermensch*, and the capacity which the *Übermensch* masters is will to power. For Nietzsche, "will to power" is the name given to the world conceived as a non-directed play of forces.

> This world: a monster of energy, without beginning, without end; a firm iron magnitude of force that does not grow bigger or smaller, that does not expend itself but only transforms itself; [. . .] a play of forces and waves of forces, at the same time one and many, increasing here and at the same time decreasing there; a sea of forces flowing and rushing together, eternally changing, eternally flooding back, with tremendous years of recurrence, [. . .] out of the play of contradictions back to the joy of concord, still affirming itself in this uniformity of its courses and its years, blessing itself as that which must return eternally, as a becoming that knows no satiety, no disgust, no weariness; [. . .] (*WP*, 1067)

Human beings, too, are named by this play of forces called "will to power," and with the name "*Übermensch*" Nietzsche designates those who recognize themselves as will to power *qua* play of forces. Zarathustra, as the teacher of the *Übermensch*, thus proclaims himself to be a "prelude to better players" (Z, "On Old and New Tablets," 20: "*Ein Vorspiel bin ich besserer Spieler.*"), and the

Übermenschen, as superior players, will be the ones who can master the play of forces which they themselves are. This interpretation of the *Übermensch* as superior player can be sharpened by returning to Zarathustra's speech and drawing a distinction between player and play-thing.[14] What distinguishes the camel from the lion and child is that while all three are understood as a play of forces, i.e., as will to power, the camel is passively *played by* will to power while the child actively *plays with* will to power. The lion occupies an intermediate level, reactively playing with will to power to the extent that it can negate values, but not having a level of power sufficient to create new values. In other words, while the lion is not a mere play-thing like the camel, it is not as skillful a player as the child. The *Übermensch,* as the superior player, masters the play of forces which is will to power, and is thus free to give meaning to him- or herself and to the earth (cf. *Z,* "Prologue," 3).

Following out this interpretation, the eternal recurrence stands as the ultimate game which the *Übermensch* must play. Nietzsche himself uses the metaphor of play in describing the eternal recurrence. He speaks of the "great dice game of existence [*grossen Würfelspiel ihres Daseins*] [. . . ,] the world as a circular movement that has already repeated itself infinitely often and plays its game *in infinitum* [*sein Spiel in infinitum spielt*]" (*WP,* 1066). The *Übermensch* as a superior player will be willing to play when the stakes of the game are raised to the limit: eternity. He or she will play in the knowledge that the game will be repeated for all eternity. While this interpretation of eternal recurrence begs off the question of the fatality of the *Übermensch's* moves in the play of creation, it is in keeping with the existential challenge[15] of the eternal recurrence as the heaviest of burdens and the weightiest of thoughts. Whereas the eternal recurrence is often discounted as Nietzsche's naive or absurd attempt at cosmology, this view misses the existential significance of this "most terrible thought" which, at the same time, stands as the "highest formula of affirmation that is at all attainable" (*EH,* Z1).

Nietzsche was never satisfied with his attempts at a scientific proof of the validity of this doctrine, and no such cosmological demonstration is to be found outside his unpublished notebooks.[16] Yet the failure of these proofs does not lessen the challenge issued by the *thought* of the eternal recurrence. In fact, it may be precisely the failure of these proofs that rescues Nietzsche's doctrine from the paradoxes and charges of absurdity so often leveled against it. For perhaps what is essentially at issue is not the *fact* of the eternal recurrence, i.e., the cosmological fact that time is an infinitely repeating circle from which there is no escape, but the *thought* of the eternal recurrence, that is, the (possibly counterfactual) thought that one commits oneself to performing eternally the actions that one chooses. It is this thought, as a test of one's will to power, that is at issue in the eternal recurrence viewed as an existential challenge and selective principle (see *WP,* 1058). The "truth" of the promise/threat of an apocalyptic Day of Judgment has not been a necessary condition for its world-historical effectiveness. Similarly, the "truth" of the thought of the eternal recurrence may be no more relevant to the challenge it poses or its potential efficacy. In the *Nachlass,* we find the following remark to support this interpretation.

> Even if the circular repetition is only a probability or possibility, even the *thought of a possibility* can shatter and transform us—not only experiences or definite expectations! How the *possibility* of eternal damnation has worked. (*KGW*, V, 2: 11[203])

And in *Ecce Homo,* Nietzsche writes that the "fundamental conception" of *Thus Spoke Zarathustra* is "the *thought of the eternal recurrence* [*der* Ewige-Wiederkunfts-Gedanke], the highest formula of affirmation that is at all attainable (*EH,* Z1)."

The hypothetical status of this thought comes to the fore in his first published aphorism concerning the eternal recurrence:

> *The greatest weight.*—What if, some day or night a demon were to steal after you into your loneliest loneliness and say to you: "This life as you now live it and have lived it, you will have to live once more and innumerable times more; and there will be nothing new in it, but every pain and every joy and every thought and sight and everything unutterably small or great in your life will have to return to you, all in the same succession and sequence—even this spider and this moonlight between the trees, and even this moment and I myself. The eternal hourglass of existence is turned upside down again and again, and you with it, speck of dust!"
>
> Would you not throw yourself down and gnash your teeth and curse the demon who spoke thus? Or have you once experienced a tremendous moment when you would have answered him: "You are a god and never have I heard anything more divine." If this thought gained possession of you, it would change you as you are and perhaps crush you. The question in each and every thing, "Do you desire this once more and innumerable times more?" would lie upon your actions as the greatest weight. Or how well disposed would you have to become to yourself and to life *to crave nothing more fervently* than this ultimate eternal confirmation and seal? (*GS,* 341)

When understood in this context, the hypothetical status ("What if . . . ") of this aphorism does not lessen the difficulty of the challenge which the doctrine poses. For it is put forth as an alternative to another hypothesis, the hypothesis of the beyond which has come to dominate Platonist metaphysics and Christian morality. The challenge of the eternal recurrence is thus the challenge to renounce our promised rewards in an eternal beyond in favor of our pleasures and pains in an eternal now. The doctrine thus asks: "Are you living your life in such a way that you would will to live everything again the same way for all eternity?" It is in this sense that the eternal recurrence stands as the "highest formula of affirmation" (*EH,* Z1), for to say "Yes" to the eternal recurrence is to say "Yes" to the entirety of one's existence. It is the *Übermensch* who will proclaim such an affirmation of existence and who, as the superior player, will still choose to play when the stakes of the game are raised to the limit, when "*Eternity* is at stake!" (*KGW*, V, 2: 11[163]).[17]

Summarizing, we find that for Nietzsche, play is the highest form of human activity. As such, play is directed toward the overcoming of nihilism in that, through creative play, what is created are new values. The *Übermensch* takes on the significance of the superior player, the player from whom is issued the creative response to the devaluation of values. This is to say, the play of the *Übermensch* is playing with values, is transvaluing values. On this reading, will to power emerges as the creative capacity of humans and world for play, and the highest expression of this creative capacity, i.e., the *Übermensch's* transvaluation of all values, is the creation of a world as the structured interplay of will to power as creative force, that is, the creation of a play-world. The eternal recurrence designates this play-world as the structured interplay of the *Übermensch's* will to power and, as an existential challenge, raises the stakes of the game which the *Übermensch* plays to its highest limit: eternity.

This reading of Nietzsche does not refute but rather supplements the Heideggerian interpretation. As an interpretation of Nietzsche's thought that overflows Heidegger's reading, however, it does raise serious questions regarding Heidegger's attempt to center his reading around Nietzsche's "one and only thought" of the eternal recurrence as the Being of beings as will to power. For when we understand Nietzsche's conception of play, we see that his philosophical style resists Heidegger's attempt at centering. This is to say, Nietzsche offers his philosophy as an example of play. If there is a central flaw in Heidegger's interpretation, it is this: he misunderstands the playfulness of Nietzsche's thinking and overdetermines his thinking as entirely and exclusively metaphysical. As we have seen, for Heidegger, *all* thinking is "thinking of Being." Yet Nietzsche proclaims that he knows of no way of associating with great tasks other than play (*EH*, II, 10). The conclusion we can draw is that, for Nietzsche, thinking is itself a form of play. This conclusion is substantiated by Nietzsche's writings:

> Our *thinking* is really nothing other than a very refined interwoven play of *seeing, hearing, feeling*[. . . .] (*KGW*, V, 1: 6[433])

> The *playful pondering of materials* is our continuous fundamental activity[. . . .] This spontaneous play of phantasizing force is our fundamental intellectual life. (*KGW*, V, 1: 10[D79])

> My style is a dance; it plays with all sorts of symmetries only to leap over and scoff at them. (Letter to E. Rohde, Feb. 22, 1884)

Numerous other passages could be cited. We will cite only one more, for it anticipates, in an interesting way, the Derridean critique of Heidegger's reading to be examined in Chapter Four.

Learning to *think:* our schools no longer have any idea what this means. [. . .] Thinking has to be learned in the way dancing has to be learned, *as* a form of dancing [. . .] for *dancing* in any form cannot be divorced from a *noble education,* being able to dance with the feet, with concepts, with words: do I still have to say that one has to be able to dance with the *pen*—that *writing* has to be learned?—But at this point I should become a complete enigma to German readers . . . (*TI,* "What the Germans Lack," 7)

The metaphor of dance, like that of play, is found throughout Nietzsche's writings, and we must attend to the images of play and dance if we are to understand both the content and style of Nietzsche's thinking. As we will see, these images play a part in his theory of language, his doctrine of perspectivism, and his philological suggestions as to how one should read. It is just these aspects of Nietzsche's philosophy, his "dance with the *pen*," that have been overlooked in Heidegger's interpretation, and these aspects have become a focal point for many of Nietzsche's contemporary French interpreters. It will be the task of the third part of this study to locate, within these three aspects of Nietzsche's thinking, his contribution to the current dialogue concerning interpretation. But first we will examine some of the terrain covered by these contemporary French readings of Nietzsche's text. In distancing themselves from the Heideggerian project of dogmatically overdetermining and deciphering the "essential truth" of Nietzsche's text, these deconstructive readings have opened Nietzsche's text to a proliferation of new fields of interpretive inquiry. In the next two chapters, we will explore some of these fields and ask whether these French readings of Nietzsche are more successful than the Heideggerian reading in circumventing the basic interpretive dilemma of dogmatism and relativism.

Part 2
Nietzsche in France

Chapter 3

The French Scene

[T]he content of the Nietzschean discourse being almost lost for the question of being, its form regains its absolute strangeness, where his text finally invokes a different type of reading, more faithful to his type of writing: Nietzsche has written what he has written. He has written that writing—and first of all his own—is not originally subordinate to the logos and to truth. And that this subordination has come into being during an epoch whose meaning we must deconstruct.

—Jacques Derrida, *Of Grammatology*

Approximately fifteen years after the appearance of Georges Bataille's influential *Sur Nietzsche,*[1] and immediately following the publication of Heidegger's two-volume *Nietzsche* in 1961, French interest in Nietzsche increased dramatically, and the next two decades saw a wide range of new approaches to Nietzsche interpretation. In 1962, Gilles Deleuze's *Nietzsche et la philosophie*[2] appeared. Two years later, an international philosophy colloquium on Nietzsche was held at Royaumont, with such figures as Deleuze, Michel Foucault, Henri Birault, Jean Wahl, Gabriel Marcel, Jean Beaufret and Karl Löwith in attendance. The next ten years saw books dealing exclusively or primarily with Nietzsche by, among others, Jean Granier, Maurice Blanchot, Pierre Klossowski, Jean-Michel Rey, Bernard Pautrat, Pierre Boudot, Sarah Kofman, and Paul Valadier;[3] special issues on Nietzsche by some of France's leading journals;[4] and a second major conference, at Cerisy-la-Salle in 1972, addressing the theme "Nietzsche aujour-d'hui," with many of France's leading philosophers in attendance.[5]

This proliferation of Nietzsche interpretation in the 1960s and 1970s exhibits two basic trends of a new generation of French philosophers. First, these interpretations reflect the passage away from the preceding generation's preoccupation with Hegel, Husserl, and Heidegger. Although the "three H's" continue to exert a great influence on contemporary French philosophy, the problems which engage this new generation are framed by another influential triumvirate: the "masters of suspicion"—Nietzsche, Freud, and Marx. Second, these interpretations reflect a heightened awareness of the *style* of philosophical discourse, bringing questions of literary *form* to bear on the *content* of philosophical issues. To understand the particular, and often peculiar, claims made by Nietzsche's French interpreters, therefore, we must first survey Nietzsche's place in the general intellectual context in which these interpretations appear.

Broadly viewed, these interpretations can be situated around four basic themes: the hermeneutics of suspicion; the reflection upon the nature of language; the end of "man"; and the critical response to Heidegger's early onto-phenomenology. To elaborate on the first three themes, we will briefly examine the situation of Nietzsche in the work of Michel Foucault. Insofar as the response to Heidegger is a central aspect of Derrida's reading of Nietzsche, we will defer our discussion of this fourth theme until we confront the Derridean reading in the next chapter. At this point, let us just acknowledge that whereas Derrida has claimed, regarding his own philosophical project, that "what I have attempted to do would not have been possible without the opening of Heidegger's questions,"[6] so too the entirety of contemporary French Nietzsche interpretation has arisen in response to Heidegger's seminal work on Nietzsche.

At the Seventh International Philosophical Colloquium at Royaumont in 1964, Michel Foucault presented a paper entitled "Nietzsche, Freud, Marx."[7] In these three thinkers, Foucault locates a profound change in the nature of the sign and the way signs in general are interpreted. This change, which Foucault views as breaking the ground for the modern epoch,[8] involves a transformation from an emphasis on the representative function of the sign, toward a view of the sign as already a part of the activity of interpretation. This is to say, signs are no longer viewed as the reservoir of some deep, hidden meaning; rather, they are surface phenomena, linked in an inexhaustible network which condemns interpretation to an infinite task:

> Interpretation can never be brought to an end, simply because there is nothing to interpret. There is nothing absolutely primary to interpret, because at bottom everything is already interpretation. Each sign is in itself not the thing that presents itself to interpretation, but the interpretation of other signs.[9]

In Marx's talk of phenomena as "hieroglyphs," Freud's view of the dream as always already an interpretation, and Nietzsche's theory of masks and the essential incompleteness of the interpretive act, Foucault locates a movement away from the "hegemony of the sign" as a univocal relation between a signifier and a signified, toward the properly hermeneutical view of the sign as always already interpreted and interpreting. It is in this sense that the hermeneut must be suspicious, for the naive view of the sign as a simple relation of signifier and signified obscures relations of domination (Marx), neurotic desire (Freud) and decadence (Nietzsche).

This is the context in which Foucault issued his often quoted dictum that *"hermeneutics and semiology are two ferocious enemies."*[10] What is not often mentioned in discussions of Foucault is that here the task of hermeneutics is affirmed while that of semiology is criticized. In the context of his remarks at Royaumont, Foucault views "semiology" as the investigation of signs which remains at the level of the structural transformations within language while "believing in the absolute existence of signs." To hermeneutics, on the other hand, he assigns all inquiry into what these signs might signify, i.e., their "meaning," and in so doing he subordinates the absolute existence of signs to the infinite task of interpretation. We need not, at this point, become embroiled in the controversies over if and when Foucault renounced his approval of the hermeneutic enterprise. All we require for our present purposes is to make explicit Nietzsche's inclusion, with Freud and Marx, at the forefront of the contemporary French scene. As will become apparent in what follows, the French approach to interpretation is completely infused with genealogical, psychoanalytic and Marxist motifs, an infusion so pervasive that it often becomes impossible to differentiate between the influences of this "unholy trinity."

The other two themes, the reflection on the nature of language and the dissolution of man, are both central motifs of the structuralist movement that became prominent in France concomitant with the renewed interest in Nietzsche. However, these two themes are not the exclusive concern of the structuralists: both are raised in Foucault's *The Order of Things,* a work in which he explicitly refuses to accept the structuralist label.[11] In this text, Nietzsche figures prominently as the precursor of the *epistēmē* of the twentieth century, the *epistēmē* that erupted with the question of language as "an enigmatic multiplicity that must be mastered."[12] For Foucault, it was "Nietzsche the philologist" who first connected "the philosophical task with a radical reflection upon language,"[13] and insofar as the question of language is still the single most important question confronting the contemporary *epistēmē,* Foucault traces the roots of this *epistēmē* back to Nietzsche.

In much the same way, Foucault discovers in Nietzsche the first attempt at the dissolution of man:

> Perhaps we should see the first attempt at this uprooting of Anthropology—to which, no doubt, contemporary thought is dedicated—in the Nietzschean experience: by means of a philological critique, by means of a certain form of biologism, Nietzsche rediscovered the point at which man and God belong to one another, at which the death of the second is synonymous with the disappearance of the first, and at which the promise of the superman signifies first and foremost the imminence of the death of man.[14]

When speaking of the "disappearance" or the "death" of "man," Foucault means something quite specific: "man" functions in this context as a technical term, the name for a certain conceptual determination of human being. In other words, "man" names for Foucault that "strange empirico-transcendental doublet," the analysis of which takes place at the transcendental levels of the biological and historico-cultural conditions which make empirical knowledge possible. "Man" thus names that conceptual foundation which serves to center the increasingly disorganized representations of the classical *epistēmē* and which, as such, comes to be the privileged object of philosophical anthropology.[15] The passage quoted above, relating Nietzsche to the uprooting of anthropology, follows by one page a reference to Kant's formulation of anthropology as the foundation of philosophy. In the *Critique of Pure Reason,* Kant discussed the three questions with which human reason is interested: What can I know? What must I do? What am I permitted to hope?[16] In his *Introduction to Logic,* we find these three perennial philosophical questions referred to a fourth: What is man? Of these four questions, Kant remarks:

> The first question is answered by *Metaphysics,* the second by *Morals,* the third by *Religion,* and the fourth by *Anthropology.* In reality, however, all these might be reckoned under anthropology, since the first three questions refer to the last.[17]

Following a move first made by Heidegger in his interpretation of Kant, Foucault locates within this reckoning the birth of the discipline of philosophical anthropology.[18] These references to Nietzsche and to Kant appear in a section entitled "The Anthropological Sleep," and it is clear that Foucault sees Nietzsche waking the modern *epistēmē* from its anthropological slumber in much the same way that Kant saw himself awakened from his own dogmatic slumber by Hume.[19] Only by understanding Foucault's talk of "man" as designating a foundational concept of Kantian anthropology can we make sense of his saying that "man is a recent invention, a figure not yet two centuries old."[20]

While this foundational concept has been privileged in the discourse of the human sciences since Kant, Foucault foresees the end of man's reign as such a foundation. He locates the announcement of this end in Nietzsche's doctrine of the *Übermensch,* for the *Übermensch* will overcome nihilism only by overcoming humanity. This point is crucial for understanding Foucault's situating Nietzsche at the beginning of the end of man. For Foucault, Nietzsche offers us a philosophy of the future, and that future will belong not to man but to the *Übermensch.* The *Übermensch* thus makes his appearance in Nietzsche together with the "last man": both are introduced for the first time in Zarathustra's "Prologue."[21] This last man is literally the last of "man," and Foucault interprets the *Übermensch* as something which breaks with the tradition of metaphysical humanism. With this in mind, we can understand the significance of Foucault's final reference to Nietzsche in *The Order of Things,* where he couples Nietzsche's death of God with the death of man. Viewing Foucault's "death of man" in Nietzschean terminology, we find the death of man to be the death of the "last man," the death of the murderer of God. Foucault here recalls that in *Thus Spoke Zarathustra* ("The Ugliest Man"), God is reported to have died of pity upon encountering the last man, and he writes:

> Rather than the death of God—or, rather, in the wake of that death and in profound correlation with it—what Nietzsche's thought heralds is the end of his murderer; it

is the explosion of man's face in laughter, and the return of masks; it is the scattering of the profound stream of time by which he felt himself carried along and whose pressure he suspected in the very being of things; it is the identity of the Return of the Same with the absolute dispersion of man.[22]

Foucault applauds Nietzsche's announcement of the disappearance of man as the standard-bearer of an all-too-serious anthropocentrism for opening the postmodern *epistēmē*, one that will no longer view man as the privileged center of representational thinking and discourse. The conclusion of Foucault's archaeological project in *The Order of Things* is thus inscribed within Nietzsche's eternal recurrence of the same, as Nietzsche's dispersion of man accompanies the return of the project of a unification of language. Whereas the classical *epistēmē* had unified language around the function of representation, the modern *epistēmē* construed language as a disorganized fund to be utilized by the human subject for the purposes of meaningful expression. The human subject, "man," was formed to combat the dispersion of language, and with this dispersion of man returns the problem of language as a multiplicity to be mastered. In other words, with the dissolution of "man" as a foundational concept, the question of the "being" and "unity" of language is once again posed. The past three decades of French philosophy can to a large extent be viewed as an inquiry into the implications for the "human sciences" of the return of this question.

Our point in the preceding discussion has not been to defend Foucault's account of the crisis of the human sciences, nor to appraise the relative strengths and weaknesses of his reading of Nietzsche. It has been, rather, to set the scene for the proliferation of Nietzsche interpretations that grew in the same intellectual environment as did the structuralist project. We have chosen Foucault, therefore, not because he was a good representative of the structuralist method nor because he made a significant contribution to Nietzsche scholarship in France. Instead, Foucault has been chosen precisely because he was neither a structuralist nor a Nietzsche scholar. Yet he nevertheless recognizes and indicates Nietzsche's significance for French interpretation theory. In Foucault's focus on the reflection on language, on the new status of the sign as always already interpreted, on the problematic status of the subject, and in his linking these three foci to Nietzsche, we get a preliminary glance at how the French approach to Nietzsche interpretation differs from that of Heidegger.

The "Question of Style": Post-Structural Readings of Nietzsche

While it is impossible to categorize the proliferation of French Nietzsche interpretation in the late sixties and seventies as adhering to a single "central" view of his philosophy, we will orient our examination around the "question of style" as one question with which many of these interpretations are concerned. By the "question of style" I mean the relation between the content of Nietzsche's thinking and the manner in which this content is set forth, and under this somewhat generic term can be subsumed a number of important questions addressed in contemporary French theories of interpretation. The "question of style" as a focal point in the interpretation of Nietzsche's text was first raised explicitly by Bernard Pautrat in *Versions du soleil,*[23] and operates as well in Foucault's citing Nietzsche as the first to engage in the philosophical task of a "radical reflection upon language,"[24] in Derrida's raising the question of writing (*"c'est la question du style comme question de l'écriture"*[25]), and in Lacoue-Labarthe's "question of the text": "Without [Nietzsche], the 'question' of the text would never have erupted, at least in the precise form that it has taken today."[26]

In addressing the question of style, these interpreters attend to the *way* that Nietzsche writes as much as to what he is writing. Taking as their point of departure the Nietzschean insight into the inseparable unity of philosophical form and content (see, for example, *WP,* 818: "One is an artist at the cost of regarding that which all non-artists call 'form' as content, as 'the thing in itself.' " See also *WP,* 817, 828; *D,* 268), these interpreters bring to light a wealth of Nietzschean themes hitherto overlooked by many of his most careful and comprehensive commentators.[27] By means of an attentiveness to his theory and use of language, rhetoric, philology, metaphor, myth, and the strategic use of different literary genre (aphorism, polemic, narrative, autobiography, essay, treatise, poem, dithyramb, letter, note, etc.), Nietzsche's French interpreters explore a range of new interpretive possibilities. Although we cannot examine here all of these interpretive possibilities, it may be instructive to summarize briefly the works of Deleuze, Granier, Pautrat and Rey before examining in somewhat greater detail an analysis from Sarah Kofman, to give a sense for the sorts of interpretations that a focus on the question of style can generate. At the outset, however, we must acknowledge explicitly what each of these interpreters acknowledges implicitly: that when interpreting Nietzsche, the question of style is always a question of style*s*. And let us also note in passing a point we will return to in the next chapter, namely, that this question of multiple styles raises the question of how to distinguish better from worse styles, i.e., the question of avoiding an unmitigated interpretive relativism.

Gilles Deleuze, in *Nietzsche et la philosophie,* directs himself against what he regards as a misguided attempt to strike a compromise between the Hegelian dialectic and Nietzsche's genealogy. Whereas Hegel's thinking is always guided by the movement toward some unifying synthesis, Nietzsche, in contrast, is seen to affirm multiplicity and rejoice in diversity.[28] Deleuze thus comes to view the entirety of Nietzsche's corpus as a polemical response to the Hegelian dialectic: "To the famous positivity of the negative Nietzsche opposes his own discovery: the negativity of the positive."[29] Focusing on the qualitative difference in Nietzsche between active and reactive forces rather than the merely quantitative distinction between amounts of power, Deleuze argues that the *Übermensch's* mastery is derived from her or his ability to *actively* negate the slave's reactive forces, even though the latter may often be quantitatively greater. In other words, whereas the slave moves from the negative premise ("you are other and evil") to the positive judgment ("therefore I am good"), the master works from the positive differentiation of self ("I am good") to the negative corollary ("you are other and bad"). There is, according to Deleuze, a qualitative difference at the origin of force, and it is the task of the genealogist to attend to this differential and genetic element of force which Nietzsche calls "will to power."[30] Thus, whereas in the Hegelian dialectic of master and slave, the reactive negation of the other has as its consequence the affirmation of self, Nietzsche reverses this situation: the master's active self-affirmation is accompanied by and results in a negation of the slave's reactive force. By tracing the interplay of affirmation and negation in Nietzsche's typology of active (artistic, noble, legislative) and reactive (*Ressentiment*, bad conscience, the ascetic ideal) force, Deleuze concludes that the *Übermensch*, Nietzsche's metaphor for the affirmation of multiplicity and difference as such, is offered in response to the conception of human being as a synthesized unity provided by the Hegelian dialectic.

Jean Granier, in his six-hundred-plus-page study *Le problème de la Vérité dans la philosophie de Nietzsche,* draws on the hermeneutical insights of Heidegger and Ricoeur as he explores the relationship between Being and thinking in Nietzsche's text. According to Granier, "will to power" designates the manner in which Nietzsche sees "the essence of Being as Being-interpreted [*l'essence de l'Etre comme Etre-interprété*]."[31] Insofar as Being is always already interpreted, Granier sees Nietzsche avoiding the apparent antinomy between the relativity of knowledge and the absoluteness of Being. For Granier, relativism and absolutism are two complementary poles of one and the same ontological operation: the will to power as knowledge. Granier locates the relativistic pole, which he calls "vital pragmatism," in Nietzsche's perspectivism and his view of truth as a useful and necessary error. The absolutist pole Granier calls "intellectual" or "philological probity." This probity demands absolute respect for the text of Being and commands us "*to do justice to nature,* to reveal things as they are in their own being."[32] It is within this essential paradox of the will to power as creative, perspectival pragmatism, and as respectful of and truthful to Being, that Granier locates Nietzsche's "revolutionary" contribution to the philosophical treatment of the problem of truth. He suggests that Nietzsche, insofar as he is able to avoid both a relativistic and a dogmatic view of knowledge, may best be viewed as presenting a "meta-philosophical" account of interpretation. This is to say, in addition to the first-order interpretations of Nietzschean perspectivism, there is a second-order interpretation of the phenomenon of interpretation itself. This second-order interpretation of interpretation is put forward in a meta-language which can be evaluated neither in terms of the ideals of the interpreter (relativism), nor in terms of its absolute correspondence with "the facts" (dogmatism). Rather, this interpretation of interpretation, remaining true to the "duplicity of Being" (i.e., the identity Being = Being-interpreted), seeks to explain the phenomenon of interpretation in a way that will disqualify neither of the complementary poles whose presence is required if the truth is to be.[33]

Bernard Pautrat, in *Versions du soleil,* offers an "oriented description" of Nietzsche's text that seeks to provide a "new version" of Nietzsche's philosophy, taking as its point of departure Nietzsche's theory of language and metaphor. This description is oriented around two axes:

> on the one hand, once recognizing that Nietzsche's thought cannot exceed the limits established for it by natural language in connection with Western metaphysics (with Platonism), we must take an exact inventory of these limits, indicating the complete metaphoricity of language, unfolding all the rhetoric within—this will be the task of a theory of signs of which Nietzsche's writings, as early as *The Birth of Tragedy,* convey the insistent mark; but, on the other hand, it would suffice to awaken the metaphorical power of language in general for "the work of Nietzsche" to be marked by a different exposition, [thereby] liberating style, figures, that labor of writing not reducible to the simple transmission of a philosophical sense.[34]

Around these two axes, Pautrat organizes an examination of the family of solar metaphors in Nietzsche's text, setting them up in relation to two other philosophical "heliologies": Plato and Hegel. Whereas Plato's system is guided by the sun as ideal and Hegel's system is directed toward the complete illumination which only the sun can provide, Pautrat sees Nietzsche's heliology avoiding the heliologocentrism of these two sun-worshipers. This is to say, in Nietzsche's solar system the emphasis is placed not on the center, the sun, but on the circulation which surrounds it, the eternal return of light and darkness. Both midday and midnight play a role in Nietzsche's thinking and the appearance of light is always accompanied by shadows. By focusing on the fluidity with which Nietzsche uses language, appropriating concepts when necessary and then discarding or forgetting them when no longer useful, Pautrat examines Nietzsche's theories of metaphor and language and the ways he uses these theories as concrete manifestations of Nietzsche's theoretical insight into the world as a play of becoming.

Jean-Michel Rey, in *L'enjeu des signes,* defines his task in the following way:

> To diagonally traverse the Nietzschean "text": to read it beyond any thematic slicing up [*découpage*] so as to lay bare the signifying process [*le procès signifiant*] of a new [*inédite,* unedited] "philosophical" *writing,* the multiple play of a scene that raises itself in the space of *the after-the-fact* [*l'après-coup*]: [. . .] Not a commentary, whose economy would be the effacement of such a proceeding, but a sinuous and repetitive *reading* that attempts to indicate the major moment of the text, the "sign": the movement which inscribes its raising *at the same time as* its dismantling, the excess which it cannot maintain, the stakes which it secretly puts forward.[35]

Rey argues that Nietzsche's deconstruction of metaphysics is effected by means of his genealogical deconstruction of various philosophical concepts. In Nietzsche's hands, these concepts are revealed as merely a convention of signs [*Zeichen-Konvention*] that he transforms into a "theater of metaphors." In Nietzsche's text, Rey finds the traditional emphasis on the semiological relation of signifier and signified transformed into a genealogical relation between signifiers (metaphors) and the unconscious impulses of which they are both product and symptom. In his interpretation, Rey draws heavily on certain Freudian notions to help explicate the dynamics of Nietzsche's genealogical findings and in so doing, he attempts to demonstrate that these notions are themselves already inscribed in the Nietzschean text. In both Freud and Nietzsche, Rey locates a "logic of the signifier" which frustrates the hope for security sought in an enduring and self-identical signified.[36] Instead, both genealogy and psychoanalysis result in a transformation of the signified itself, giving it over to interpretation in the position of the signifier, thus committing each method to a process of interminable de-ciphering.

Before focusing on Sarah Kofman's interpretation, a comment on the four texts summarized above is in order. Although all four interpretations deal with the question of style, there is an important difference between the readings of Granier and Deleuze and those of Rey and Pautrat. This difference has to do with the degree of emphasis placed on the question of style in these readings and is, as such, linked to the influence of Jacques Derrida. While both Deleuze and Granier raise the question of Nietzsche's style during the course of their interpretations, this theme nonetheless remains somewhat peripheral to their central concerns (in Deleuze's case, the contrast between Nietzsche and Hegel, and in Granier's, the suggestion that Nietzsche provides a meta-philosophy of interpretation). In the texts of Pautrat and Rey, on the other hand, the question of style is central to their reading of Nietzsche. Both Pautrat and Rey, it should be noted, studied with Derrida and their readings reflect this fact, as both make frequent use of Derridean terminology and deconstructive techniques. Not coincidentally, both of these texts appeared shortly after Derrida offered a seminar at the École Normale Supérieure, in the winter of 1969–70, devoted to a theory of philosophical discourse with a particular emphasis on the status of metaphor in philosophy. Pautrat was himself a participant in this seminar and a footnote in his text reveals that a draft of *Versions du soleil* was written during that time.[37] The relation between Derrida's work and this new generation of Nietzsche interpreters is significant for understanding the sorts of interpretations they have provided, and we shall have occasion to address this relation again in the context of our examination of Derrida's reading of Nietzsche.

The final interpreter we will examine, Sarah Kofman, was also a participant in Derrida's seminar, and a first version of her text *Nietzsche et la métaphore* was presented to that assembly. As with Pautrat and Rey, the question of Nietzsche's literary style is a major theme in Kofman's reading. In addition, Kofman's text offers several examples of the sorts of genealogical deconstructions that a focus on style can generate. For these reasons, rather than merely summarizing her text, we will examine in some detail Kofman's discussion of Nietzsche's architectural metaphors. This examination will show his stylistic transformation of metaphors to be a significant aspect of the Nietzschean text. If a focus on metaphorical transformation can display new and heretofore unrecognized insights into Nietzsche's text, this will be of consequence both for deciding what sorts of approaches to adopt in reading this text, as well as for judging the success of those approaches which, implicitly or explicitly, disregard Nietzsche's use of metaphor while telling us definitively what Nietzsche "means."

In *Nietzsche et la métaphore*, Kofman attempts to show that Nietzsche's use of metaphors is not merely rhetorical, but "strategic." This is to say, Nietzsche's metaphors are not mere extravagances or stylistic literary devices devoid of philosophical import. Rather, the way Nietzsche uses metaphors reinforces one of the major themes in his philosophy: the affirmation of the play of becoming. Kofman points out that Nietzsche situates metaphor at the origin of language and truth. Concepts are, in his view, simply congealed metaphors, figurative descriptions whose metaphorical nature has been forgotten. In forgetting the metaphoricity at the origin of concepts, their figurative sense comes to be taken literally. This petrification of the concept as literal description of "reality" ultimately gives rise to the illusion of truth as eternal and unchanging, and Kofman sees this view of truth as fixed and universal as one of the hallmarks of a philosophical tradition that Nietzsche endeavors to deconstruct.[38]

Taking the tendency of metaphors to solidify into concepts as one of Nietzsche's basic insights, Kofman suggests we avoid focusing on any single Nietzschean metaphor as privileged, fundamental, or foundational. Conscious of the inherent danger in language of restricting the fluidity and mobility of sense ($\mu\varepsilon\tau\alpha\phi o\rho\acute{\alpha}$ = *Übertragung* = transference), Kofman emphasizes the Nietzschean strategy of refraining from an enduring commitment to any one particular metaphorical expression. Even the metaphor of "metaphor," so prevalent in Nietzsche's early writings, comes to be discarded and, Kofman argues, is later reappropriated as "perspective" or "interpretation" or "text."[39] This strategy reveals Nietzsche's desire to free culture of its dogmatic tendency towards one-dimensional thinking. In other words, whereas Nietzsche will eventually place an explicit value on pluridimensional thinking, on seeing the world from a multiplicity of perspectives and with more and different eyes (see *GM*, III, 12; also *GS*, 78, 374), this value has been exhibited throughout his writings in the way he shifts from metaphor to metaphor.

Kofman supports her thesis with a careful examination of the transformations in Nietzsche's architectural metaphors. Architecture, Nietzsche writes, "is a kind of rhetoric of power in forms" (*TI*, "Skirmishes of an Untimely Man," 11: "*Architektur ist eine Art Macht-Beredsamkeit in Formen,* [. . .]"), and throughout his writings Kofman sees Nietzsche turning to architecture for metaphors of culture, especially as a description of the epistemological edifice which a particular cultural system erects. Availing himself of such figures as the beehive, the tower, the medieval fortress, the Egyptian pyramid, the Roman columbarium, and the spider's web, Nietzsche performs a genealogical operation on the various models of knowledge that human beings have provided themselves, thereby deconstructing, as it were, the epistemological constructions that they have hitherto endeavored to erect. Nietzsche's point in such a genealogical deconstruction is not, for Kofman, so much to provide a critique of these architectural products as it is to decipher the good or bad taste of the architects who have constructed them. With these architectural metaphors, Kofman sees Nietzsche attending to the architectural phenomenon as a symptom of an underlying malady or health. By examining the edifice as a representation of the architect's ideal, Nietzsche the genealogist thus seeks to isolate and decipher the healthy or sick instincts that appear at the *archē*.

Kofman begins with the metaphor of the beehive as the first construction representing the conceptual edifice. The beehive, she notes, is a traditional metaphor for describing serious, bustling and purposive labor.[40] For Nietzsche, the beehive, as a geometrical architectural ensemble, symbolizes the systematic ordering of concepts and, as such, the hive appears as a metaphor for the scientific edifice. Kofman points out, however, that at this stage, the epistemological edifice is not yet marked by the disjunction of knowledge and life: the hive "is destined to inscribe the emblem of scientific labor in life, to bar the opposition of the speculative and the practical, of spirit and instinct."[41] At this level, what Nietzsche called "the false opposition of the *vita practica* and *contemplativa*" has not yet appeared (*KGW*, IV, 1: 6[17]; *SSW*, 193).

While the perfection of the hive is revealed through the instinctual ease with which it is constructed, the value bestowed upon this edifice does not result from a disinterested judgment. The value of the hive/science is symptomatic of an "initial indigence," a lack which motivates its construction while masking that motivation. This indigence is revealed in its necessity: just as the bee, if it is to survive, must construct the cells of the hive in order to deposit its honey, so too science must construct a formal edifice into which will fit the fruits of its labor. Kofman makes explicit Nietzsche's parodic intent in drawing the analogy between the activity of an insect and scientific labor, a labor that seeks to reduce the world to its own measurements. She quotes the following:

> It has been rightly said: "Where your treasure is, there will your heart be also"; our treasure is where the beehives of our knowledge are. We are constantly on the way to them, being by nature winged creatures and honey-gatherers of the spirit; there is one thing alone we really care about from the heart—something "to bring home." (*GM*, Pr., 1)

According to Kofman, Nietzsche draws the conclusion that, far from accurately mirroring or adequately explaining the world, science merely makes the presumptuous mistake of taking its own structure to be that of the world, i.e., it mistakes its own metaphors for essences. Science reveals itself to be an instance of the type of weakness which cannot recognize itself to be a perspective without perishing from that recognition. Science itself, like those "objective scholars" who work under its auspices, lacks the instinctual strength to impose its own valuations upon the world. Instead, it seeks protection in a system and nourishment from a truth whose concealed metaphorical origins reside in itself. At the level of the hive/science, Nietzsche objects not so much to the presumptuousness of science as to the self-deterrence residing at its origin. That is, science detours individuals from themselves, turning their gaze away from their originary, metaphorical power, out toward a truth lodged in the edifice that this metaphorical power itself constructed:

> We are unknown to ourselves, we men of knowledge: and with good reason. We have never sought ourselves—how could it happen that we should ever *find* ourselves? (*GM*, Pr., 1)

Whereas the hive primarily conveys the nourishing aspect of the scientific edifice, it does not adequately symbolize the protection that science offers. This leads Nietzsche, according to Kofman, to the first strategic transformation of the architectural metaphor: the hive becomes a tower or medieval fortress. This transformation reveals both the protection that science offers its adherents and the subordination of these adherents to the project of science as an end in itself: like a medieval fortress, the scientific edifice protects its inhabitants from external dangers and these inhabitants, for their part, live so as to provide for the well-being of the fortress. Nietzsche writes of science that

> it is always building new, higher stories and shoring up, cleaning and renovating the old cells; above all, it takes pains to fill up this monstrously towering framework and to arrange therein the entire empirical world, which is to say, the anthropomorphic world. Whereas the man of action binds his life to reason and its concepts so that he will not be swept away and lost, the scientific investigator builds his hut right next to the tower of science so that he will be able to work on it and to find shelter for himself beneath those bulwarks which presently exist. And he requires shelter, for there are frightful powers which continuously break in upon him, powers which oppose scientific "truth" with completely different kinds of "truths" which bear on their shields the most varied sorts of emblems. (*OTL*, 2)

In distinguishing the "active" uses of concepts and reason (the "man of action") in order to *live* (to "not be swept away and lost"), from the scientific investigator's subordinating himself to these already-existing concepts for the purpose of mere self-preservation, the genealogist discovers, within the transformation from hive to fortress, that the supreme danger to the fortress' inhabitants is life itself as the play of becoming and appearance. Kofman writes:

Man needs to barricade himself, to isolate himself, to protect his constructions from the violence that might be directed against them by other powers "with more brilliant emblems" [*puissances "aux enseignes plus éclatantes"*]. Defenses taken against the lie, myth, art, against all that overtly proclaim the cult of appearance, of surface, of fiction, that dare to avow their perspective as such: [. . .][42]

In occluding the play of illusion and becoming which is life, the tower of science is for Kofman's Nietzsche a veritable tower of Babel; science creates an artificial language and superimposes this language upon the natural play of the world. While the human species is preserved through the creation of this rigid and regular structure, this preservation is achieved at the expense of separating humans from the living world. Kofman comments: "the rigidity of the construction mimics that of a skeleton: it is only by being always already dead in life that man can survive."[43] This link between death and the rigidity of the scientific edifice becomes apparent in Nietzsche's next transformation, as the tower and fortress give way to the Egyptian pyramid and Roman columbarium.

The metaphor of the pyramid adds the idea of hierarchization to the image of the upward-striving tower of knowledge: each object is now assigned a determinate place in the conceptual edifice. The pyramidal order is, for Kofman, "the metaphor of the intelligible world of essences," organized in a geometrical fashion, and "functioning as models and norms."[44] She quotes the following:

> something is possible in the realm of these schemata which could never be achieved with the vivid first impressions: the construction of a pyramidal order according to castes and degrees, the creation of a new world of laws, privileges, subordinations, and clearly marked boundaries—a new world, one which now confronts that other vivid world of first impressions as more solid, more universal, better known, and more human than the immediately perceived world, and thus as the regulative and imperative world. (*OTL*, 1)

At issue in the transformation from tower to pyramid is not the *creation* of a *new* world, but the ordination of this new world as *regulative* and *imperative*. The authority of the pyramid thus rests on a fixed and rigid conceptual order, and within the pyramid are placed only those impressions which have been "captured and stamped by means of concepts, then killed, skinned, and as concept mummified and preserved" (*KGW*, III, 4: 19[228]; *P*, 149; *MA*, VI, p. 57).

From the pyramidal order of knowledge as the tomb of impressions mummified and preserved as concepts, Nietzsche passes quickly to the metaphor of the Roman columbarium. This subtle shift in imagery is made because "mummification implies that the sensible figure of the dead still remains: the pyramid is a noble tomb; life even in its impoverished form, is still present there."[45] The columbarium, on the other hand, conserves only the incendiary remains of the deceased, in much the same way that the concept comes to be viewed by Nietzsche as "merely the *residue of a metaphor*" (*OTL*, 1). With the metaphor of the columbarium, Nietzsche thus makes explicit that all connections between life and the inhabitants of this edifice have been severed.

While one would expect, as its creators surely do, that such an edifice, constructed as it apparently is with a mathematical rigor that leaves nothing to chance, would be extraordinarily strong, Kofman's Nietzsche discerns that precisely the reverse is the case. What is accepted here as a firm foundation is revealed as merely a congealed metaphor arising from a singular perspective. Just as chance played a role in the adoption of this foundation, another throw of the dice could just as easily stand the edifice on its head. In this "conceptual crap game [*Würfelspiels der Begriffe*]" (*OTL,* 1), the stability of the edifice endures only so long as its practitioners continue to abide by the rules. And the fates of these practitioners are, in effect, interred in the columbarium no less than the conceptual residue of their previous creations. Kofman quotes the following:

> Just as the Romans and Etruscans cut up the heavens with rigid mathematical lines and confined a god within each of the spaces thereby delimited, as with a *templum,* so every people has a similarly mathematically divided conceptual heaven above themselves and henceforth thinks that truth demands that every conceptual god be sought only within *his own* sphere. Here one may certainly admire man as a mighty genius of construction, who succeeds in piling up an infinitely complicated dome of concepts upon an unstable foundation, and, as it were, on running water. Of course, in order to be supported by such a foundation, his construction must be like one constructed of spider's webs: delicate enough to be carried along by the waves, strong enough not to be blown apart by every wind. (*OTL,* 1)

In this passage, Kofman locates Nietzsche's final strategic transformation: from columbarium to spider's web. Nietzsche views the columbarium to be, as it were, a *floating* crap game, a mighty conceptual edifice erected on a foundation of "running water." All that is required to topple such an edifice is another throw of the dice or change of perspective. Insofar as the edifice endures only so long as the faith in its foundational perspective persists, its practitioners and adherents alike are interred in the columbarium, like a spider caught in its own web along with its prey:

> because it is made from the same stuff as those whom it should shelter and protect, because it dissimulates their death and the death of all life, the columbarium is metamorphosized into the work of a spider.[46]

For Kofman, the spider's web appears as Nietzsche's most frequent metaphor for philosophical, scientific and theological system-building, and with this metaphor Nietzsche reveals his judgment as to the harmfulness of such an activity. The spider is a veritable vampire who is nourished only by feeding off the living: through the deceptive attraction of its web, the spider survives on the blood of those flies who have been lured into this web, only to find themselves therein trapped. The concepts which the spiders create are only a "phantom" or "simulacrum of life," which can hold sway only so long as the anthropomorphic web of which they are a part remains intact.[47] As such, Nietzsche exposes these concepts as symptoms of the indigence of their arachnoid creators. The spider's web thus appears to Kofman's Nietzsche as a narcissistic illusion: its proud and joyful apprehension of "objective knowledge" (connaissance) reveals itself to be merely the pleasure of the spider's recognition (reconnaissance) of the "objectivity" of a world which it has created itself.[48]

Unlike many of Nietzsche's metaphors, however, the spider continues to appear throughout his writings as a symbol of the activities of science, theology and philosophy. In the Philosophenbuch, Nietzsche speaks of the scientific knowledge of the laws of nature as representations determined by our viewing the world in relations of space, time, succession and number, and he writes that "we produce these representations in and from ourselves with the same necessity with which the spider spins" (OTL, 1). In Thus Spoke Zarathustra, he alludes to the trinity as a black triangle on the back of a tarantula, and he speaks of the priest's spirit of revenge as the tarantula's poison ("On the Tarantulas"). And in The Antichrist, we find reference to Kant as a "fatal spider" (A, 11) along with a word-play linking Spinoza with the spider—"die Spinne" (A, 17; see also BGE, 5). In each of these allusions to the spider, what is criticized are not the constructions that result from this arachnoid activity. Rather, what is scrutinized are the inhibiting consequences that follow from the spider's dogmatic postulation of its constructions as adequately corresponding to the world as a play of becoming. In other words, the spider's construction of a web of beliefs that is held to describe accurately the play of becoming has the poisonous consequence of precluding those who become entangled within this web from engaging further in creative activity.

Kofman concludes her discussion of Nietzsche's spider metaphor by linking it to his critique of God. The spider metaphor allows Nietzsche to demystify and ridicule divine teleology: "if God is the architect of the world, it is only in his being the supreme spider."[49] Of the Christian God at the hands of the metaphysicians, Nietzsche writes:

> Even the palest of the pale have still been able to master him: our honorable metaphysicians, those concept-albinos. These have spun their web around him so long that, hypnotized by their movements, he himself became a spider, a metaphysician. Thenceforward he spun the world again out of himself—sub specie spinozae—thenceforward he transformed himself into something ever paler and less substantial, became an "ideal", became "pure spirit", became "absolutum", became "thing in itself". . . . Decay of a God: God became a "thing in itself" . . . (A, 17)

Kofman suggests that Nietzsche's entire strategic transformation from beehive to spider's web has been guided by his desire to make explicit the nihilistic will that has animated the history of Western thinking as a progression away from life and the world of sensible becoming toward the abstract intelligible world of static essences. What philosophy since Parmenides has in each case endeavored to achieve is the conversion of life and becoming into "bloodless abstractions" and "conceptual mummies" surrounded by a web of formulas (cf. *PTAG*, 10; *TI*, " 'Reason' in Philosophy," 1). In the transformation of the world of the senses into an "ideal world" by means of the ossification of metaphors into concepts, Nietzsche deciphers a nihilistic, decadent will masked behind all the metaphysical finery. Under genealogical scrutiny, the creation of this well-ordered "ideal world" emerges as a decadent affirmation of the products of creative activity, accompanied by the denigration of the active process within the world of sensible becoming which has produced these creations. Because the intellect was unable to manage the world of the senses, it created for itself another world: the orderly, well-behaved and well-regulated world of intelligible essences. Viewed genealogically, the history of philosophy appears as a history of the successful seduction of human beings by this well-ordered and well-regulated "ideal world." These philosophers, like the companions of Ulysses, stop up their ears to avoid hearing the siren's music of life. Kofman closes her discussion with this Nietzschean allusion, quoting the following from the section of *The Gay Science* (372) in which the reference to Ulysses appears:

> [. . .] *ideas* are worse seductresses than our senses, for all their cold and anemic appearance, and not even in spite of this appearance: they have always lived on the "blood" of the philosopher, they always consumed his senses and even, if you will believe us, his "heart." These old philosophers were heartless: philosophizing was always a kind of philosophical vampirism. [. . .] Don't you sense a long concealed vampire in the background who begins with the senses and in the end is left with, and leaves, mere bones, mere clatter? I mean categories, formulas, *words* (for, forgive me, what *then remains* of Spinoza, *amor intellectualis dei*, is mere clatter, nothing more. What is *amor*, what *deus*, if there is not a drop of blood in them? . . .) In sum: all philosophical idealism to date was something like a disease, unless it was, as it was in Plato's case, the caution of an over-rich and dangerous health, the fear of *overpowerful* senses, the cleverness of a clever Socratic.—Perhaps we moderns are merely not healthy enough *to be in need of* Plato's idealism?[50]

Kofman's examination of architectural metaphors is just one of many such discussions in *Nietzsche et la métaphore*. Among the other "families" of metaphor examined are those drawn from the languages of art[51] and the senses,[52] the inversion of Plato's cave and sun metaphors in *Zarathustra*, Nietzsche's uprooting of Descartes' "tree of knowledge" and the utilization of various figures from Greek mythology.[53] In each case, Kofman shows that Nietzsche's style of writing, the *way* in which he utilizes metaphor, provides an important clue for understanding what is at issue in his philosophy. In so doing, Kofman claims that Nietzsche does not so much create new metaphors as "rehabilitate" those metaphors which the tradition has already adopted. This is to say, Nietzsche's strategy is to reiterate the habitual metaphors of the tradition in a way that brings their conceptual insufficiencies to light.[54] This reiteration of metaphor emerges in Kofman's text as a concrete illustration of the praxis of the Nietzschean transvaluation: within his strategic rehabilitation of the tradition's metaphors, the values implicit in these traditional metaphors are *re*valued. Nietzsche's use of metaphor itself exemplifies this transvaluation insofar as the use of metaphor within philosophical discourse had been *de*valued. By focusing on Nietzsche's use of metaphor, Kofman demonstrates that the appearance of metaphor in Nietzsche's text is not gratuitous; rather, Nietzsche's proliferation of metaphor is directed toward liberating human beings' metaphorical instinct for creative play, freeing humans for the play of perspectives in those domains (art, myth, illusion, dream) devalued by the nihilistic and decadent will of the scientific spirit of seriousness.

In contradistinction to an interpretive strategy like that of Heidegger, which strives to isolate what is "essential" in Nietzsche's thought, Kofman avoids speaking of what Nietzsche's metaphors "really mean" or what his images "essentially" represent in favor of suggesting that we can re-read Nietzsche's text from the perspective of its strategic metaphorical transformations. In so doing, she implies that had Nietzsche had an "essential thought" to express, he would have chosen a style of philosophical discourse more conducive to the task of its unambiguous expression. There is thus something of significance to discern from the manner in which Nietzsche's writing style differs from the style of a Spinoza or a Leibniz, a Kant or a Descartes. Unlike Descartes, for example, whose method seeks the metaphysical roots out of which the tree of philosophical truth grows, Kofman sees Nietzsche providing us with an "*arbre fantastique*":

> it is the best paradigm of the new philosopher, affirmer of life in all its forms, multiplying and displacing its perspectives without reference to any absolute and definitive center.[55]

Rather than seeking the sturdy roots of the Cartesian tree so as to legitimate its fruits, Nietzsche prefers to play among the branches of this fantastic tree, tasting all the varied fruits which it brings forth. This fantastic tree is life itself, and it has many offshoots which bear many different kinds of fruit. If Nietzsche the genealogist seeks to discern the origins of these fruits, therefore, it is not with the intention of justifying them; rather, genealogy seeks to discern the quality of the soil, healthy or diseased, which nurtures these fruits, so as to discover why some are ripe and others rotten.

In cultivating such a fantastic tree, Nietzsche's writing runs the risk of being misunderstood. For Kofman, Nietzsche not only accepts this risk; he *wills* it:[56] he claims being misunderstood as a title of honor (see *GS*, 371). His aphorisms, the fruit borne of his fantastic tree, are offered only to those who have the ears for them. His is an aristocratic style, forsaking the goal of communicating with all in favor of communicating only with those few who know how his text should be read, the disciples of Dionysus (cf. *EH, "Why I Write Such Good Books").* Only these readers will be able to follow Nietzsche's "dance with the pen," and they alone will be able to accept the invitation to dance which his aphorisms offer. These readers will elevate reading to the level of an art (cf. *GM,* Pr., 8) and "on every metaphor will ride to every truth" (*Z,* "The Return Home"; see also *EH,* Z3); they will recognize the aphorism as the "writing itself of the will to power," a writing which cancels all the traditional literary oppositions (form/ content, surface/depth, play/seriousness, spontaneity/reflection).[57] *Nietzsche et la métaphore* concludes on this note, suggesting that the ability to dance among aphorisms is another of Nietzsche's principles of selection which distinguish those of noble instincts from the *profanum vulgus.*

Kofman's interpretation, which persuasively displays the way Nietzsche uses metaphor to express his most important philosophical insights, is a masterful example of the sort of interpretation that can be produced by attending to the question of style. Moreover, like Pautrat and Rey, Kofman's interpretation draws heavily from the work of Derrida. In all three interpretations, we find a focus on some aspect of Nietzsche's style of philosophical discourse informed by insights drawn from semiology and psychoanalysis and opened by the Derridean critique of logocentrism. Examining these interpretations has displayed some of the heretofore masked riches that can be mined from the Nietzschean text. These readings do not assert that they have found the "truth" of Nietzsche nor do they claim to present the "totality of Nietzsche's text" in a way that will render superfluous any further interpretive production. They disavow the totalizing function of the activity of reading, and seek instead to contribute to the expansion of Nietzsche's text by promoting a proliferation of interpretations which the Nietzschean text, rich in ambiguity and stylistic mastery, prescribes. By moving beyond the artificial limitations of classical Nietzsche scholarship, centered as it was around the canonical major themes (eternal recurrence, *Übermensch,* will to power, etc.), they open Nietzsche's text to new interpretive possibilities, and our examination of them helps to further specify the setting in which Derrida's reading of Nietzsche first appeared. While Derrida credits these three interpreters, along with Philippe Lacoue-Labarthe, with demarcating the interpretive space into which he inserts his reading of Nietzsche in *Spurs,*[58] there is one important theme that he finds lacking in their interpretations: a critical confrontation with the reading of Heidegger. Although these three interpretations do not completely ignore the Heideggerian reading, Derrida finds that this reading is not given its just due, and it is in part toward inscribing the Heideggerian reading into the space opened up by the question of style that Derrida's reading of Nietzsche is directed. To this reading we must now turn.

Chapter 4

Derrida: Nietzsche Contra Heidegger

No doubt that Nietzsche called for an active forgetting of Being: it would not have the metaphysical form imputed to it by Heidegger.
                                                    —Jacques Derrida, "The Ends of Man"

[M]ethods, one must repeat ten times, are *the essential, as well as being the most difficult, as well as being that which has habit and laziness against it the longest.*
                                                    —*The Antichrist,* 59

In the preceding chapter, we merely observed several readings offered by Nietzsche's French interpreters and inspired by the question of style. We must now turn our attention more specifically to questions of method that animate these readings. To do so leads directly to Jacques Derrida, who has emerged as the leading spokesperson for the interpretive "method" known as deconstruction, and for whose philosophical project Nietzsche's significance is readily apparent to any reader familiar with the texts of these two thinkers. While he has refrained from offering a comprehensive commentary on Nietzsche's thought, Derrida often avails himself of Nietzschean motifs, and Nietzsche is either named or implicated in virtually every work to which Derrida has appended his signature. The pervasiveness of Nietzsche's inscription in the Derridean text is marked by a footnote subsequently added to his interview with J.-L. Houdebine and G. Scarpetta entitled "Positions." In the context of this footnote on historicism and truth, Derrida notes that "Nietzsche's name was not pronounced" during the interview, and he adds that "on what we are speaking about at this very moment, as on everything else, Nietzsche is for me, as you know, a very important reference."[1] Elsewhere, he is more specific as to the ways the Nietzschean text functions as an "important reference." In *Of Grammatology,* he credits Nietzsche with contributing "a great deal to the liberation of the signifier from its dependence or derivation with respect to the logos and the related concept of truth or the primary signified, in whatever sense that is understood [by his] radicalizing of the concepts of *interpretation, perspective, evaluation, difference*[. . . .]"[2] And in *Margins of Philosophy,* in the context of locating the sources of Valéry, he provides the following list of themes to look for in Nietzsche: "the systematic mistrust as concerns the entirety of metaphysics, the formal vision of philosophical discourse, the concept of the philosopher-artist, the rhetorical and philological questions put to the history of philosophy, the suspiciousness concerning the values of truth ('a well applied convention'), of meaning and of Being, of 'meaning of Being,' the attention to the economic phenomena of force and of difference of forces, etc."[3]

While his references to Nietzsche are not always affirmative, more often than not Derrida allies himself with Nietzsche in his attempt to deconstruct the logocentric tendencies of metaphysical thinking. More specifically, Nietzsche frequently makes his appearance in the Derridean text as an alternative to the nostalgic longing for full presence that Derrida locates at the core of Western metaphysics.[4] In his earliest "text" where offering an interpretation of Nietzsche is his overt concern, I think we can see again the Derridean strategy of providing Nietzsche as such an alternative. This text is *Spurs: Nietzsche's Styles,* and I will orient the examination of this text to show that *Spurs* is Derrida's attempt, on a number of levels which remain to be specified, to provide an alternative to the interpretations of Nietzsche hitherto offered and, in particular, an alternative to the Heideggerian interpretation examined in the first chapter. The nature of this alternative, however, is far from transparent, as Derrida's interpretation is not offered as either replacement or refutation of these earlier interpretations. Instead, it provides a *supplement* to these earlier readings and, as with other Derridean questions of supplementarity, this supplement both depends upon and exceeds what it supplements. Derrida's interpretation functions in terms of how it differs from these other interpretations. As a result, there can be no question of a simple and straightforward choice, for example, between Derrida's reading and Heidegger's. We have already noted Heidegger's importance for the Derridean project, and that importance remains even here, where Derrida's reading of Nietzsche is in *apparent* opposition to the reading of Heidegger. The semblance of this "opposition" abates somewhat when we recognize that Derrida's strategy in his discussion of Nietzsche's styles is two-fold. While he wants to make it clear that the question of style exceeds the Heideggerian reading, he at the same time wants to make it no less clear to his French compatriots that things are not so simple with Heidegger, and that the Heideggerian defense of presence remains a "profound" and "powerful" problematic for interpretation.[5] In discussing *Spurs,* therefore, we will try to keep the text situated between these two motifs, for there is a sense in which *Spurs* offers us another example of philosophical "undecidability," this time with respect to the adequacy of the Heideggerian reading of Nietzsche, and specifically to the success of Heidegger's attempt to include Nietzsche within the history of Western metaphysics while extricating himself from that same history. In the course of this discussion, we will highlight several methodological implications of Derrida's interpretation and, as in the case of our previous discussions, we will for the most part defer critically appraising these implications until we have finished our explication of Derrida's text.

The discussion in *Spurs* can be viewed as structured around three questions addressed to Nietzsche's writing, each unfolded as a critical foil with which

Derrida will joust with Heidegger. These three questions are the question of the text, the question of *propre*,[6] and the question of style. In raising the first question, Derrida focuses on Nietzsche's conception of woman and he uses this focus to raise the question of truth in Nietzsche's text. In so doing, the Heideggerian reading, among others, is implicitly chastised for its lack of attention to the position of woman, a lack which betokens an inadequate conception of the intricacies of the Nietzschean text and repeats the phallogocentric tradition's failure to consider questions concerning women as warranting serious reflection. From here, Derrida proceeds to consider Nietzsche's place within the metaphysical tradition. In doing so, he explicitly marks his departure from Heidegger's situating Nietzsche within that tradition as its last great representative by transmuting the Heideggerian-metaphysical question of Being into the Nietzschean-axiological question of *propre*. Last, we find the discussion of Nietzsche's forgotten umbrella. Here, Derrida most directly addresses the question of Nietzsche's styles, both as they pertain to Nietzsche's text and to the question of the text in general, as well as to the problematics of interpretation. This discussion, which issues a challenge to what Derrida calls "hermeneutics," can be read as supplementing his earlier critical discussion of the "Heideggerian hope" in the essay "Différance."[7] While the individual lines of these three discussions are intricately interwoven into a complex network that Derrida "admits" is "cryptic and parodying" (*Spurs*, p. 137; but note that even in this "admission," Derrida suggests that he, like any writer, might be lying), we shall try initially to focus on each individually, relating them when appropriate to remarks not framed within the margins of *Spurs*.

Following a citation from Nietzsche's correspondence whose significance is only gradually revealed, Derrida's text opens in the following way:

> The title of this lecture was to have been the *question of style*.
> However—it is woman who will be my subject. (*Spurs*, pp. 35–37)

In what follows this opening, two reasons emerge for Derrida's taking woman as his subject. First, because the accepted interpretations of Nietzsche's view of woman exhibit a profound lack of attention to the question of Nietzsche's styles and the economy of his text. And second, because the characteristics that Derrida finds Nietzsche attributing to woman are, to a large extent, the same attributes that he uses to characterize truth.

Traditionally, two sorts of interpretive strategy have been applied to Nietzsche's numerous comments about woman. The first views Nietzsche as a misogynist, often explaining away his apparently hostile remarks against women as a sublimated reaction against his having been raised by a domineering mother in a household composed of his mother, grandmother, sister and two maiden aunts. The second either ignores his remarks, as, for example, Heidegger does, or merely takes note of them and then disregards them as being unworthy of Nietzsche's talents and/or of no philosophical interest.[8] Derrida accepts neither of these alternatives and the grounds for their unacceptability come to the surface as his discussion unfolds. Briefly stated, he rejects the former alternative because it fails to account for the heterogeneity of Nietzsche's text, while the latter alternative is dismissed both for repeating the phallogocentric tradition's refusal to consider questions concerning women and for being an inadequate interpretive strategy. This is to say, the interpreter is faced with the demand of interpreting the *whole* text and not just those aspects of it that he or she finds important or valuable. In fact, as Derrida will attempt to show, the question of woman is extremely significant in Nietzsche's text, and his transposition of woman and truth is directed toward bringing this significance to the fore.

Much of the first half of Derrida's text appears as a running commentary on various Nietzschean remarks on "woman." These remarks are loosely woven around five themes: woman's distance, her veils, her skepticism, her adornments, and her simulation. The first theme unfolds from a reading of Section 60 of *The Gay Science,* entitled *"Women and their effect in the Distance,"* which concludes with the following lines:

> But still! But still! my noble enthusiast, there is also in the most beautiful sailing ship so much noise and bustling, and alas, so much petty, pitiable bustling. The enchantment and the most powerful effect of woman is, to use the language of philosophers, an effect at a distance, an *actio in distans:* there belongs thereto, however, primarily and above all—*distance!*

From this passage, quoted in full in *Spurs,* Derrida locates woman's first position in Nietzsche's text: she seduces from a distance. This first theme is quickly linked with the second: woman's veiled movement. Woman takes effect at a distance from behind a movement of veils because there is no essence of woman, because woman's essence is to avert herself from herself. Woman is thus self-distancing, a distantiation from self; perhaps she is *"distance* itself."

> Perhaps woman—a non-identity, a non-figure, a simulacrum—is distance's very chasm, the out-distancing of distance, the interval's cadence, distance itself, if we could still say such a thing, distance *itself.* The far is furthered. One is forced to appeal here to the Heideggerian use of the word *Entfernung:* at once divergence, distance and the distantiation of distance, the deferment of the distant, the de-ferment, it is in fact the annihilation (*Ent*) which constitutes the distant itself, the veiled enigma of proximity. (*Spurs,* pp. 49–51)

This veiled movement, effective at a distance, resembles the movement of life itself, and Derrida quotes the following "rarely quoted fragment" which reveals "the complicity, rather than the unity, between woman, life, seduction, modesty—all the veiled and veiling effects" (*Spurs,* p. 51):

for ungodly activity does not furnish us with the beautiful all, or all at once! I mean to say that the world is overfull of beautiful things, but it is nevertheless poor, very poor, in beautiful things. But perhaps this is the greatest charm of life: it puts a golden-embroidered veil of lovely potentialities over itself, promising, resisting, modest, mocking, sympathetic, seductive. Yes, life is a woman! (*GS*, 339)

To the themes of distance and veils are quickly added woman's skills at adornment and dissimulation. The skill at adornment, veiling oneself with all sorts of finery, and skillful simulation, "the great art of the lie," the art of masking, are the artist's skills *par excellence*. Derrida quotes:

Finally women. If we consider the whole history of women, are they not obliged first of all, and above all, to be actresses? If we listen to doctors who have hypnotized women, or finally, if we love them—and let ourselves be "hypnotized" by them,— what is always divulged thereby? That they "give themselves airs," even when they— give themselves. Woman is so artistic. [*Dass sie "sich geben," selbst noch, wenn sie—sich geben. Das Weib ist so artistisch.*] (*GS*, 361)

Woman's artistry here appears as the thread Derrida has sought to weave through the web of Nietzsche's remarks on woman's veiled and distant movements, her skill at self-adornment, and her masking and dissimulating behavior. The significance of this thread emerges in the fifth of Nietzsche's themes, woman's skepticism, which leads the Derridean discourse to the question of woman and truth. Derrida quotes:

I fear that women who have grown old are more skeptical in the secret recesses of their hearts than any of the men; they believe in the superficiality of existence as in its essence, and all virtue and profundity is to them only the disguising of this "truth," the very desirable disguising of a *pudendum*—an affair, therefore, of decency and modesty, and nothing more! (*GS*, 64)

The truth of "truth," of the "truth" of philosophy and religion, is that it is only a surface, that this "truth" is only a veil. Woman "knows" this, as her artistry reveals, and in this sense, she is *more truthful* than man. Derrida writes that, for Nietzsche,

There is no such thing as the truth of woman, but it is because of that abyssal divergence of the truth, because that untruth is "truth." Woman is but one name for that untruth of truth. [. . .] if woman *is* truth, *she* at least knows that there is no truth, that truth has no place here and that no one has a place for truth. And she is woman precisely because she does not believe in truth itself, because she does not believe in what she is, in what she is believed to be, in what she thus is not. (*Spurs*, pp. 51–53)

What is, for Derrida, significant about the relation Nietzsche establishes between woman and truth is woman's lack of concern for the truth: truth is superfluous to woman. And precisely because of this lack of concern with truth, woman frustrates all man's attempts to capture her. Man, still believing in the truth, believes he can possess woman, just as the dogmatic philosopher believes he can possess the truth. The irony of Nietzsche's style thus reveals that, insofar as woman no longer believes *in* truth, she herself stands as an allegorical figure *of* the truth:

> Supposing truth to be a woman—what? Is the suspicion not well-founded that all philosophers, when they have been dogmatists, have had little understanding of woman? That the gruesome earnestness, the clumsy importunity with which they have been in the habit of approaching truth have been inept and improper means for winning a wench. Certainly she has not let herself be won—and today every kind of dogmatism stands sad and discouraged. *If* it continues to stand at all! (*BGE*, Pr.)

Truth, like a woman, will not be pinned down: she allows no one to possess her. But while woman-truth is not to be found, it is nevertheless impossible for the man-philosopher to resist looking for her.

Leaving the specific claims of Derrida's interpretation of Nietzsche on woman, let us turn for a moment to the question of style. In the preceding summary, Derrida highlights two of the spurs of Nietzsche's styles. First, the ironic strategy of Nietzsche's using the sexual question, the "problem of the sexes," to raise the question of the relation between philosophy and truth. Woman, insofar as she is unconcerned with the truth, frustrates man's hope for conquest just as the truth, through its veiling and dissimulating movement, frustrates the dogmatic philosopher: "the credulous and dogmatic philosopher, who *believes* in the truth that is woman, who believes in truth just as he believes in woman, this philosopher has understood nothing" (*Spurs*, p. 53).

The second spur is what Derrida calls "the heterogeneity of Nietzsche's text." Given Nietzsche's refusal to posit an "essential truth" of woman, Derrida suggests that the interpreter refrain from searching for a systematic unity underlying the various positions of woman which surface in Nietzsche's heterogeneous text. Following this suggestion, Derrida locates in Nietzsche three types of statements on woman. First, there are the statements of the credulous man, the dogmatic philosopher who despises woman as "falsehood." Second, there is the persecution of woman in the name of the masked artist. Here, the woman is despised as the "figure or potentate of truth; [. . .] she either identifies with truth, or else continues to play with it at a distance as if it were a fetish, manipulating it, even as she refuses to believe in it, to her own advantages" (*Spurs*, p. 97). To these two reactive negations of woman, a third, positive statement is added: "woman is recognized and affirmed as an affirmative power, a dissimulatress, an artist, a dionysiac. And no longer is it man who affirms her. She affirms herself, in and of herself, in man" (*Spurs,* p. 97).[9]

Into this discussion of Nietzsche's eulogy/indictment of woman (eulogizing the artist-histrion's affirmative dissimulation and indicting the artist-hysteric's reactive dissimulation), Derrida introduces the "syntax" of castration. While alluding to Lacan,[10] the introduction of the castration motif appears as a strategic passageway toward Derrida's confrontation with Heidegger's reading of Nietzsche. "Castration," like "woman," emerges as an allegory of "truth." Whereas man believes in both castration and truth, woman suspends her belief in these two male fantasies. Within this double suspension, she is free to exert her own mastery and dominion through a dissimulating play with man's belief in castration/truth. In Nietzsche's text, however, woman's relation to castration, like her relation to truth, is far from univocal. In feigning belief and masterfully playing with man's fear of castration, woman is herself threatened, in her attempt to gain dominion, by a tendency to become like man, which is to say, she is threatened by self-castration.[11] Derrida thus restates Nietzsche's three positions on woman, this time availing himself of the syntax of castration:

> He was, he dreaded this castrated woman.
> He was, he dreaded this castrating woman.
> He was, he loved this affirming woman. (*Spurs,* p. 101)

The strangeness of Derrida's discourse on castration, very briefly sketched above, is lessened somewhat when we consider the reasons for its introduction. As always, with Derrida, these reasons are strategic, and in a move typical of his deconstructive readings of the history of philosophy, he draws our attention to what has been *excluded* or *suppressed* in the formulation of the argument. The attempt to locate castration in Nietzsche's text leads him to "a certain Heideggerian landscape." That landscape, examined in detail in the first chapter,[12] is Heidegger's reading of Nietzsche's "History of an Error" in *Twilight of the Idols.* Derrida notes that in the second epoch of his history of the idea of the "true world," Nietzsche has emphasized only the words "*sie wird Weib,*" "*it becomes woman.*" Moreover, Derrida discovers that in his careful treatment of this (hi)story, Heidegger has abandoned woman: all of the elements of Nietzsche's story are analyzed with the single exception of the idea's becoming woman. These two observations lead Derrida to take a closer look at this "inscription of woman" which the Heideggerian reading has suppressed. He cautions, however, that his examination does not proceed counter to Heidegger's; instead, he seeks to play with the excess of the Heideggerian reading and to deconstruct that reading by means of its skirting the question of woman (cf. *Spurs,* p. 85).

Derrida begins his attempt to decipher this inscription of woman by noting that the becoming-woman of the idea has been anticipated by Nietzsche in the pages of *Twilight of the Idols* that precede the "History of an Error." He cites the following aphorisms from "Maxims and Arrows":

16. *Among women.*—"Truth? Oh you don't know the truth! Is it not an assault on all our *pudeurs?*"—

27. Women are considered deep—why? because one can never discover a bottom to them. Women are not even shallow.

29. "How much the conscience formerly had to bite on! what good teeth it had!—And today? what is lacking?"—A dentist's question.

These remarks may well reveal that *"sie wird Weib"* has a context; it is not mere verbiage, and it deserves recognition. To ignore this phrase thus indicates an inadequate appreciation of the intricacy and economy of Nietzsche's text. Far from ignoring this phrase, the entirety of Derrida's reading of the "History of an Error" unfolds out of these three words as it focuses on the passage from the first to the second epoch. The inaugural moment of the idea is, for Derrida, the identity of philosophy and truth: "I, Plato, *am* the truth." The second moment marks a "progress of the idea," and the idea is transformed from the truth to a "form of truth's self-presentation" (*Spurs,* p. 87). This "progress" is important, for the idea now has a history: in the first moment, the idea was Platonic, eternal; in the second moment the idea has *become* something else, it has *"become woman."* Derrida comments on this event:

Plato can no more say "I am the truth." For here, the philosopher is no longer the truth. Severed from himself, he has been severed from the truth. Whether he himself has been exiled, or whether it is because he has permitted the idea's exile, he can now only follow its trace. At this moment, history begins, the stories begin. Distance—woman—averts truth—the philosopher, and bestows the idea. And the idea withdraws, becomes transcendent, inaccessible, seductive. It beckons from afar. Its veils float in the distance. The dream of death begins. It is woman. (*Spurs,* pp. 87–89. Translation altered slightly.)

Thus, far from being superfluous, *"sie wird Weib"* serves as shorthand to summarize the event of the idea's passage from Plato to Platonism. In this second epoch, Derrida finds all the emblems of Nietzsche's discourse on woman: the seductive distance, her veiled promise of transcendence, her inaccessibility. The history of woman-truth duly belongs to the history of this error.

As Derrida notes, however, the second epoch does not end with the idea's becoming woman. To the *"sie wird Weib"* Nietzsche adds *"sie wird christlich"* before closing the parentheses. In this conjunction of the idea's becoming woman-Christian, Derrida locates the link with the motif of castration. The link is made explicit by Nietzsche on the page immediately following the "History of an

Error." In the first paragraph of the chapter entitled "Morality as Anti-Nature," Nietzsche interprets Christianity as "castratism":

> There is a time with all passions when they are merely fatalities, when they drag their victim down with the weight of their folly—and a later, very much later time when they are wedded with the spirit, when they "spiritualize" themselves. Formerly, one made war on passion itself on account of the folly inherent in it: one conspired for its extermination—all the old moral monsters are agreed that "*il faut tuer les passions*." The most famous formula for doing this is contained in the New Testament, in the Sermon on the Mount, where, incidentally, things are by no means looked at *from a height*. There it is said, for example, with reference to sexuality, "if thy eye offend thee, pluck it out": fortunately no Christian follows this prescription. To *exterminate* the passions and desires merely in order to do away with their folly and its unpleasant consequences, this itself seems to us today merely another acute form of folly. We no longer admire dentists who *extract* teeth to stop them from hurting. . . . On the other hand, it is only fair to admit that on the soil out of which Christianity grew, the concept "*spiritualization* of passion" could not possibly be conceived. For the first church, as is well known, fought *against* the "intelligent" in favor of the "poor in spirit": how could one expect from it an intelligent war against passion?— The Church combats the passions with excision in every sense of the word: its practice, its "cure" is *castratism*. It never asks: "How can one spiritualize, beautify, deify a desire?"—it has at all times laid the emphasis of its discipline on extirpation (of sensuality, of pride, of the lust to rule, of avarice, of vengefulness).—But to attack the passions at their roots means to attack life at its roots: the practice of the Church is *hostile to life* . . .

The Church, unable to control the passions, seeks to extirpate them, like an overzealous dentist whose cure for every toothache is excision.[13] This ecclesiastical "cure" of castration is denounced by Nietzsche for being "hostile to life": whereas life seeks self-mastery, the Church seeks self-mutilation; whereas the strong-willed are "able to impose moderation on themselves, [. . .] the saint in whom God takes pleasure is the ideal castrate" (*TI*, "Morality as Anti-Nature," 2, 4). In being hostile to life, Derrida notes that the "Church is also hostile to woman who is herself life (*femina vita*)" (*Spurs*, p. 93. Translation altered. Cf. *GS*, 339). In Nietzsche's critique of the Church's castratism, Derrida thus finds new support for his claim regarding the heterogeneity of Nietzsche's text on woman. It is not woman but the Church, itself a *patriarchal* authority, that utilizes man's fear of castration for the purpose of manipulation. And woman, as the affirming artistic dissimulatress who is life itself, suffers at the hands of the Church fathers insofar as they project upon her the sources of man's castration fears.[14]

It is in the context of these remarks on woman-truth-castration that Derrida moves on to the critical confrontation with Heidegger's reading. Derrida had already noted, in introducing his reading of Nietzsche's "*sie wird Weib*" that "the

Heideggerian reading of Nietzsche [. . .] must be accounted for" and that "the arguments of Heidegger's mighty tome are much less simple than is generally admitted" (*Spurs*, p. 73). He echoes these remarks when he writes that while Heidegger's reading, insofar as it had abandoned woman, has been "idling offshore" as regards the "sexual question," things still may not be so simple.

> The conceptual significations and values which would seem to decide the stakes or means in Nietzsche's analysis of the sexual difference [. . .] are all based on what might be called a process of *propriation* (appropriation, expropriation, taking, taking possession, gift and barter, mastery, servitude, etc.). (*Spurs*, p. 109)

These remarks indicate the complexity of Derrida's strategy of deconstruction as it relates to the Heideggerian reading. In general, Derrida's deconstructive reading seeks to indicate those assumptions and motifs which a text acknowledges but must suppress in order to function. In the case at hand, rather than confront Heidegger's reading head on, Derrida seizes upon an opening within the Heideggerian reading that remains dormant in Heidegger's own thinking.[15] In so doing, he in effect allows the Heideggerian interpretation to dismantle itself. This is to say, rather than respond directly to the Heideggerian claim that Nietzsche stands as the last metaphysician, Derrida attempts to show that Heidegger's own path of escape from metaphysics operates in Nietzsche's text as well. This is done in terms of what Derrida calls the question of the *propre*.

In *Positions*, Derrida writes that "the value *propre* (propriety, propriate, appropriation, the entire family of *Eigentlichkeit, Eigen, Ereignis*) [. . .] is perhaps the most continuous and most difficult thread of Heidegger's thought."[16] In *Spurs*, he attempts to unravel this thread in the context of Nietzsche's heterogeneous text on woman. For Derrida, Nietzsche's text is animated by the "hymen's graphic," a *pharmakon* which renders the question of the *propre* (property-propriety) no longer possible. The "hymen's graphic," as Derrida explains in *Dissemination*,[17] poses the undecidable question of possession: in man's taking of the hymen and/or woman's giving of the hymen, the hymen itself is not to be possessed. No*thing* is taken and no*thing* is given. The "hymen" exists only in the undecidable between of giving and taking. This undecidability is itself contained within the double-meaning of "hymen" as both "the virginal membrane" and "marriage": hymen in the first sense *is,* as the preserver of virginity, only so long as hymen in the second sense remains unconsummated. The undecidability of the hymen, which Derrida focuses on in *Dissemination* as a guiding thread interwoven within the Mallarméan corpus, operates in the Nietzschean text as well, insofar as the appearance of woman comes about according to an "already formalizable law":

> Either, at times, woman is woman because she gives, because *she gives herself,* while the man for his part takes, possesses, indeed takes possession. Or else, at other times,

she is woman because, in giving, she is in fact *giving herself for* [*la femme en se donnant se* donne-pour], is simulating, and consequently assuring the possessive mastery for her own self. (*Spurs*, p. 109. Translation altered slightly.)

The point of this formalization, for Derrida as for Nietzsche, is that it renders the question of possession, of propriation, undecidable. In woman's gift of herself, man never *knows* whether the gift is genuine or only a simulation, he never *knows* whether he possesses the *true* woman or whether he is possessed by a veiled dissimulation. For Derrida, the undecidability of subordination/domination with respect to the woman's gift escapes both dialectics and ontology. As such, the undecidability of the question of the *propre* appears as the limit of "onto-phenomenological or semantico-hermeneutic investigation." And as stands woman, so stands truth: the undecidability of truth's giving-itself or giving-itself-for reiterates the undecidability of woman. Derrida concludes that "propriation is more powerful than the question *ti esti,* more powerful than the veil of truth or the meaning of being. [. . .] For the question of the meaning or the truth of being is not *capable* of the question of the *propre*" (*Spurs*, p. 111. Translation altered slightly.).

This limit, Derrida quickly points out is a singular one: it limits not so much an ontical or ontological region of being but poses "the very limit of being itself" (*Spurs*, p. 113). This is not to say that a reading of Nietzsche can dispense altogether with the question of being. Rather, the limit makes clear that the question of the *propre* is not derivative of the question of being. Nor should this be taken to mean that the question of the *propre* can now be approached directly, and Derrida cautions that one should not naively conclude that we can now proceed straightaway to place the metaphysical question "What is . . . ?" before the *propre*. Whereas Heidegger, perhaps more clearly than anyone else, should have recognized this limit, Derrida criticizes the Heideggerian interpretation for its refusing to allow the question of the *propre* to erupt. "Heidegger's reading subsists, throughout the near totality of its trajectory, in the hermeneutic space of the question of the truth (of being)" (*Spurs*, p. 115). Yet another reading, Derrida's own, is opened up by a "certain dehiscence" in the Heideggerian reading, and it proceeds out of that reading with "a violent yet almost internal necessity. [. . .] Each time that Heidegger refers the question of being to the question of the *propre,* of propriate, of propriation (*eigen, eignen, ereignen, Ereignis* especially) the dehiscence bursts forth anew" (*Spurs*, pp. 115–117).

For Derrida, this irruption does not mark a rupture in Heidegger's thought, for already in *Being and Time* the opposition of authenticity (*Eigentlichkeit*) and inauthenticity (*Uneigentlichkeit*) was organizing the existential analytic of Da-sein. Yet the permanency of a certain valuation of the *propre/Eigentlichkeit* in Heidegger's thought is "regularly disoriented by an oblique movement which inscribes truth in the process of propriation" (*Spurs*, p. 117). Derrida takes Heidegger's reading of Nietzsche as an instance of just such a disorientation. By asserting a certain value to a "genuine" apprehension of Being, Heidegger develops the opposition between metaphysics and non-metaphysics. And insofar as Nietzsche forgets Being, he lacks this *propre* relation and stands condemned as a metaphysician. Yet, according to Derrida, the oppositional structure itself is limited by the question of the *propre:* "If the form of opposition and the oppositional structure are themselves metaphysical, then the relation of metaphysics to its other can no longer be one of opposition" (*Spurs*, pp. 117–119).

This was all known to Heidegger, and the limitation of Being even appears in his interpretation of Nietzsche. Derrida quotes from the last chapter of Heidegger's *Nietzsche* while inserting the following remarks:

> [. . .] a proposition of the type *"Das Sein selbst sich anfänglich ereignet"* [. . .] gives way to a proposition in which "Being" itself is reduced (*Das Ereignis er-eignet*)—gives way, but only after the intervention between them of ". . . *und so noch einmal in der eigenen Anfängnis die reine Unbedürftigkeit sich ereignen lässt, die selbst ein Abglanz ist des Anfänglichen, das als Er-eignung der Wahrheit sich ereignet."* Finally, then, once the question of production, doing, machination, the question of the *event* (which is one meaning of *Ereignis*) has been uprooted from ontology, the proper-ty or propriation of the *propre* is named as exactly that which is *propre* to nothing and no one. Truth, unveiling, illumination are no longer decided in the appropriation of the truth of Being, but are cast into its bottomless abyss as non-truth, veiling and dissimulation. The history of Being becomes a history in which no being, nothing, happens except *Ereignis'* unfathomable process. The proper-ty of the abyss (*das Eigentum des Ab-grundes*) is necessarily the abyss of proper-ty, the violence of an event which befalls without Being. (*Spurs*, p. 119; translation altered slightly. Derrida echoes Klossowski in saying, regarding Heidegger's text, that remarks such as those quoted above defy translation. On this point, at least, I am in complete agreement.)

Mightn't it be, asks Derrida, that what Nietzsche calls style's form or the non-place of woman is this abyss of truth as non-truth and propriation as a-propriation? The undecidability of the giving/taking of woman's gift of herself is itself echoed in Heidegger's own "undecidable" regarding the giving and the gift of Being in the *"es gibt Sein."*[18] No determinate gift is given in the *es gibt Sein,* any more than a determinate thing is given in the woman's gift of herself. The moral which Derrida draws from this "hymen's graphic," the moral which Heidegger was unable to draw from the Nietzschean text, is that "because they constitute the process of propriation, the *giving* and the *gift* can be construed neither in the boundaries of Being's horizons nor from the vantage point of its truth, its meaning" (*Spurs*, p. 121).[19]

Spurs concludes by returning explicitly to the question of style, a return which obliquely announces that "style" has been the topic all along: both Nietzsche's styles of writing and the styles of reading which are called for/upon in order to apprehend such a writing. The site of this return is a passage found among Nietzsche's unpublished notes from the period of *The Gay Science:*

"I have forgotten my umbrella" (*KGW*, V, 2: 12[62]: *"ich habe meinen Regenschirm vergessen"*)

What are we to make of this "text"? Derrida refuses to call it a "fragment" because the concept of fragmentarity itself contains an appeal to some totalizing complement, an appeal that is here being questioned (cf. *Spurs*, p. 125). And inasmuch as the idea of a unity underlying Nietzsche's "fragments" is central to Heidegger's privileging of *The Will to Power*,[20] this refusal again inscribes Heidegger's reading of Nietzsche into the margins of *Spurs*. For Derrida, this text is a "monument of hermeneutic somnambulism" that frustrates on many counts the project of the hermeneut. We cannot know, with certainty, either the intentions of its author or even, for that matter, the identity of that author: because of the quotation marks, the *"ich"* stands as a definite pronoun whose referent is indefinite. Is Nietzsche the author, or is this perhaps a citation from the text of another which has made its way into Nietzsche's notebook for some as yet undetermined reason? Perhaps it is something Nietzsche overheard on the street, or perhaps it is a note to himself which was to be attached to an aphorism that came not to be written. Derrida concludes: "There is no infallible way of knowing the occasion of this sample or what it could have been later grafted onto" (*Spurs*, p. 123). While the context of Nietzsche's remark perhaps could be reconstructed, the possibility persists that this text will remain in isolation. In addition, we cannot deny the possibility of its having no context at all: it might simply be a random cipher behind which is concealed no hidden meaning. We will never know *for certain* where this cipher belongs or what, if anything, was intended by it, and it is this possibility which is most disconcerting for the hermeneut. While the hermeneutic circle calls for the constitution of meaning from out of the relation of part and whole, fragment and context, the meaning of "I have forgotten my umbrella" appears to be completely transparent: all the words are familiar and can be understood in the absence of any other context; it can be translated into another language with no apparent loss of meaning. Nevertheless, in another very real sense, we simply have no idea of what this text means, and it is the possibility of this text's concealing some secret meaning that troubles hermeneutics.

The hermeneut, unsatisfied with playing on the surface of the text and discontented with remaining at the level of a contextless, transparent meaning, may seek to discover some deeper significance which lies hidden beneath the textual surface. Armed with the assurance that the text has some deeper meaning, the hermeneut is free to decode this hidden meaning in any of a number of ways. Derrida suggests a possible "psychoanalytic" decoding. "Umbrella" is a well-known psychoanalytic symbol and the act of "forgetting" is equally ripe with psychoanalytic significance. Perhaps the author of this text is lamenting the repression of his aggressive instinct (his phallus), normally carried along with one as one might bring along an umbrella. Perhaps he has just now recognized the successful completion of his castration. Significantly, Derrida recalls in the second postscript, appended after his presentation at Cerisy, that he had forgotten (like an umbrella?) Heidegger's reference to (this same Nietzschean text?) the tradition's misunderstanding of its own forgetfulness of Being.[21] In *Zur Seins-frage,* while talking about nihilism and the forgetting of Being, Heidegger comments: "Thus, in a thousand ways, has the 'forgetting of Being' been represented as if Being, figuratively speaking, were the umbrella that some philosophy professor, in his distraction, left somewhere."[22] Could this, perhaps, be a clue to deciphering the hidden significance of this text? Is the author (Nietzsche?) expressing his (unconscious?) awareness of having participated in the oblivion of Being?

Do such interpretations reveal the secret of Nietzsche's umbrella, do they successfully decode the meaning inscribed in "I have forgotten my umbrella"? Or do they instead reveal something else:

> [that] there is no end to its parodying play with meaning, grafted here and there, beyond any contextual body or finite code. It is quite possible that that unpublished piece, precisely because it is readable as a piece of writing, should remain forever secret. But not because it withholds some secret. Its secret is rather the possibility that indeed it might have no secret, that it might only be pretending to be simulating some hidden truth within its folds. Its limit is not only stipulated by its structure but is in fact intimately con-fused with it. The hermeneut cannot but be provoked and disconcerted by its play. (*Spurs,* p. 133)

This is not to say that the interpreter should give up trying to discover what the text might mean. Rather, Derrida is suggesting that the hope for a *decidable* meaning, for an end to the play of interpretation, be put out of play. Writing, like Nietzsche's woman, can give itself or it can give itself *for.* The writer can lie, can adopt a mask, can refuse to mean what she or he writes. These are always possibilities, and Derrida here uses this "umbrella" to pierce the assured horizon of the hermeneutic quest for decidability, as Nietzsche himself attempted to perforate the projects of all the *Schleiermachers* (cf. *EH,* CW3). In fact, says Derrida, "the hypothesis that the totality of Nietzsche's text, in some monstrous way, might be of the type 'I have forgotten my umbrella' cannot be denied" (*Spurs,* p. 133).

This possibility, which brings the hermeneut to despair, is for Derrida precisely the allure and fascination of reading. And it is this possibility which leads Derrida to refrain from speaking, as Heidegger does, of the "totality of Nietzsche's text" or the "truth of Nietzsche's text." There is no such thing as a "truth of Nietzsche" or a "truth of Nietzsche's text," any more than there is a truth of woman. In *Beyond Good and Evil,* Nietzsche prefaces the statement of a "few truths about 'woman as such' " with the following warning: "assuming that it is now known from the outset how very much these are after all only—*my* truths" (231). That Nietzsche emphasizes "**meine** *Wahrheiten*" as he does indicates that what follows are not "truths" at all, at least not in the sense that the tradition has understood Truth: single, decidable, univocal, eternal, immutable, universal. In effect, Nietzsche is always saying: "These are *my* truths; where are yours? These are *my* women; where are yours? This is *my* way; where is yours? For *the* truth, *the* woman, *the* way—that does not exist" (cf. *Z,* "On the Spirit of Gravity").

For Nietzsche, there are only truth*s* in the plural, and never *the* Truth. Similarly, the question of style reveals itself, for Derrida's Nietzsche, to be a question of style*s*. In *Ecce Homo,* Nietzsche declares that he is capable of a multiplicity of styles and he dispenses with "style *in itself*" as "a pure folly, mere 'idealism,' on a level with the 'beautiful in itself,' the 'good in itself,' the 'thing in itself' " (*EH,* III, 4). For Derrida, Nietzsche's availing himself of such a multiplicity of styles

> suspends the decidable opposition of true and non-true, and inaugurates the epochal regime of quotation marks which is to be enforced for every concept belonging to the system of philosophical decidability. The hermeneutic project which postulates a true sense of the text is disqualified under this regime. Reading is freed from the horizon of the meaning of being or the truth of being, liberated from the values of the production of the product or the presence of the present. (*Spurs,* p. 107. Translation altered slightly.)

Reading, in other words, is free to play. Nietzsche's multiple styles remove the logocentric imperative of the pathos of truth and replace this imperative with an invitation to play. The epoch of quotation marks points to the reader's predicament of rarely knowing with certainty "who" is writing in Nietzsche's text. Utilizing a multiplicity of masks and metaphors, Nietzsche's styles confront the reader with the undecidable question "Who is writing?" Is it the free spirit? Dionysus? Apollo? Zarathustra? the Anti-Christ? the spirit of gravity? the Wagnerian? Nietzsche? Can we even ask "Who is Nietzsche?" Are some masks identical with "Nietzsche" and others sarcastic or parodic responses of "Nietzsche"? For Derrida, "Nietzsche" himself, as a proper name, falls under the epoch of quotation marks, and it is for this reason that the Heideggerian question of the "truth of Nietzsche" or the "totality of Nietzsche's text" must be suspended.[23]

This suspension of the question of truth frees reading from the limit of hermeneutics, and Derrida's departure from the Heideggerian problematic appears nowhere more clearly than in their differing conceptions of reading. To elucidate this departure, we must first examine the way in which Derrida distinguishes his approach to reading from what he refers to as the hermeneutic project. Then we will conclude our discussion of Derrida by showing how, in at least one important sense, he subsumes Heidegger's reading within this hermeneutic project.

We have already seen how, in *Spurs,* Derrida views the hermeneutic project as a search for the true sense of the text. When queried on this point in the discussion following his presentation of "La question du style" at Cerisy, he makes explicit his departure from this project: "By *hermeneutics,* I have designated the deciphering of a meaning or of a truth shielded in a text. I have opposed this to the transforming activity of interpretation."[24] This is to say, hermeneutics seeks to discover a finished meaning or truth (a "transcendental signified") beneath the textual surface, thereby arresting the text in a certain position. For Derrida, this fixing of textual position and "settling on a thesis, meaning, or truth [is the] mistake of hermeneutics, the mistaking of hermeneutics [. . .] that the final message of 'I have forgotten my umbrella' should challenge."[25] In opposition to the hermeneutical arresting of the text, Derridean reading as a transformational activity contents itself with the infinite play of the text's surface.[26] There is no exit from the labyrinth of the text, and the move to something outside the text (a complete or finished "meaning" which informs the play of signs) is put out of play for reasons provided in *Of Grammatology:*

> the writer writes *in* a language and *in* a logic whose proper system, laws, and life his discourse by definition cannot dominate absolutely. He uses them only by letting himself, after a fashion and up to a point, be governed by the system. And the reading must always aim at a certain relationship, unperceived by the writer, between what he commands and what he does not command of the patterns of the language he uses.[27]

Because the signifying activity of the sign always, by definition, exceeds the intention of the author, reading should not merely aim at a re-production of that signifying intention. Such re-production is, however, what Derrida sees as the hermeneut's goal. By freeing the interpretive activity of reading from the constraint of re-production, of "doubling the text," the task of reading now appears as an active, creative production. And without a "transcendental signified" or an identical redoubling to serve as a(n attainable or merely regulative) telos, this productive activity is endless. This distinction between the production of Derrida's "active interpretation" and the re-production of the hermeneutical method leads him to transform the hermeneutic circle into an ellipsis. Having dispensed with the goal of deciphering a fixed meaning, the hermeneutic circle is decentered: "Repeated, the same line is no longer exactly the same, the ring no longer has exactly the same center, *the origin has played.*"[28] Freed from the constraint of a fixed point of reference, of a center (*the* truth, *the* meaning of the text), Derrida's active interpretation transforms the movement of circular revolution into a movement of elliptical evolution. While this transformation liberates reading from the search for a transcendental signified, it nevertheless evolves *in and out of the text,* and thus "cannot be executed however one wishes." What is required, says Derrida, are "protocols of reading."[29] Although these "protocols" remain to be specified, it is clear that Derrida views the methodological practices of hermeneutics as being far from satisfactory for the production of active interpretations. From this brief sketch, the point which Derrida objects to in the project of hermeneutics should be clear. If hermeneutics seeks to make *present* some meaning or truth which lies hidden behind or beneath or inside the text, then hermeneutics belongs with the logocentric metaphysics of presence which Derrida is continually attempting to deconstruct. But to many thinkers whose sympathies lie with Heidegger, it is not at all clear that this critique pertains to the Heideggerian hermeneutic. Thus, we find commentators like David Hoy willing to sacrifice Schleiermacher and Dilthey to Derridean deconstruction, while arguing that such an attack misses the mark when it comes to the hermeneutics of Heidegger or Gadamer.[30] Hoy is clearly right in claiming that recent hermeneutic theory has advanced beyond the objectivist, ethnocentric, and psychologistic assumptions of nineteenth-century hermeneutics, and he is also correct in pointing out that Heidegger and Gadamer do not share their hermeneutic predecessors' "ontological commitment to a metaphysics of presence."[31] This response, however, misses the force of the Derridean deconstruction of Heidegger. As we have already mentioned, for Derrida, things are never so simple with Heidegger: Heidegger is, in Derrida's estimation, not just another logocentric metaphysician of presence and the confrontation with Heidegger takes place at a point different from that of the Derridean deconstruction of hermeneutics in general. This point is frequently overlooked both by Derrida's deconstructionist colleagues as well as those hermeneutic thinkers who still align themselves with Heidegger. Nevertheless, on this point, Derrida is clear: "the Heideggerian problematic is the most 'profound' and 'powerful' defense of what I attempt to put into question under the rubric of the *thought of presence*."[32] Before we conclude our explication of Derrida, therefore, we must first survey the site of his deconstruction of Heidegger. This site has already appeared, to a certain extent, in our examination of *Spurs* with regard to the question of the *propre*. According to Derrida, there remains within Heidegger's immense laboring toward the destruction of metaphysics a certain noncritical privilege to the voice as the proper presence of Being. This is to say, Derrida locates in Heidegger a certain originary presence of Being in the voice, the *phonē*, accompanied by the derivative valuation of the *grammē*, the written cipher, as having fallen from this originary presence of Being. Speaking of Socrates' refusal to disengage himself from thinking, Heidegger writes "This is why he is the purest thinker of the West. This is why he wrote nothing. For he who begins to write on coming out of thought [*aus dem Denken*] will inevitably resemble those people who run to seek refuge against a strong draft. This remains the secret of an as yet hidden history: that all Western thinkers after Socrates, notwithstanding their greatness, have to be such fugitives."[33]

For Derrida, this privileging of the voice, Heidegger's "phonologism," underwrites both his privileging poetic speech and song, and his disdain for literature and writing.[34] These two points emerge quite clearly in Heidegger's meditation on thinking, where he opposes thinking as "what is spoken in poetry" or "sounded in speech" to literature as "what has been literally written down, and copied, with the intent that it be available to a reading public."[35] In "Hölderlin and the Essence of Poetry," for example, Heidegger defines poetry as "the inaugural naming [Nennen] of being and of the essence of all things—not just any speech [Sagen], but that particular kind which for the first time brings into the open all that which we then discuss and deal with in everyday language."[36] And in "Language in the Poem," Heidegger describes his task as a discussion of "the site that gathers George Trakl's poetic Saying into his poetic work[. . . .]"[37] Thus, even within Heidegger's affirmation of the poetry of Trakl, Rilke, or Hölderlin, it is not the poem as written literature that is valued but the truth (Being) which is, as it were, spoken in the poem. The written grammē remains as the silent mark which has fallen from the presence of Being as spoken.

If there is, for Derrida, a single central point of departure from the Heideggerian problematic, it is in terms of the concepts of origin and fall.[38] These concepts, which Derrida views as essentially metaphysical, function in what he calls the "central axis" of Heidegger's destruction of ontology in Being and Time: "that which separates the authentic from the inauthentic and, in the last analysis, primordial from fallen temporality."[39] Derrida's point here is important: when Heidegger writes, for example, that "factical existence 'falls' as falling from primordial, authentic temporality [die faktische Existenz 'fällt' als verfallende aus der ursprünglichen, eigentlichen Zeitlichkeit],"[40] there does seem to be a certain primacy and propriety accorded to the originary and authentic temporality prior to the fall. The concluding lines of Being and Time give further evidence that this primacy is accorded in terms of the presencing of Being: "Is there a way which leads from primordial time to the meaning of Being? Does time itself manifest itself as the horizon of Being?"[41]

This is not the only "fall" Derrida locates in Heidegger's thinking. There is also the fall of Being into its oblivion, a fall that, according to Heidegger, has itself been forgotten by metaphysics insofar as metaphysics has forgotten the ontological difference, the difference between Being and beings. In response to this forgotten fall of Being into beings, Derrida locates what he calls the "Heideggerian hope": a certain nostalgia for Being's proper name. Derrida quotes the following passage from Heidegger's "Der Spruch des Anaximander":

> The relation to the present, unfolding its order in the very essence of presence, is unique (ist eine einzige), altogether incomparable to any other relation. It belongs to the uniqueness of Being itself (Sie gehört zur Einzigkeit des Seins selbst). Therefore, in order to name what is deployed in Being (das Wesende des Seins), language would have to find a single word, the unique word (ein einziges, das einzige Wort). There we see how hazardous is every word of thought (every thoughtful word: denkende Wort) that addressed itself to Being (das dem Sein zugesprochen wird). Nevertheless what is hazarded here is not something impossible, because Being speaks everywhere and always throughout language.[42]

From citations like this, Derrida concludes that Heidegger hopes for "the alliance of speech and Being in the unique word, in the finally proper name."[43] It is in poetic discourse that the possibility for such an "alliance" is located. In his dwelling upon the nature of language as "Saying [*Sagen*]," Heidegger, in 1958, writes: "To go by the poetic experience and by the most ancient tradition of thinking, the word gives Being."[44] Long after Heidegger's "*Kehre,*"[45] he continued to maintain a phonocentric position, claiming that "the essential nature of language makes itself known to us as what is spoken,"[46] and Derrida consistently takes Heidegger to task for his phonocentric hope for the presencing of Being in the speaking of the unique word and/or the proper name.[47]

Insofar as thought, for Heidegger, seeks to express Being through the speaking of the unique word, Derrida seems justified in claiming that Heidegger's thought of Being is a thought of a transcendental signified.[48] For this reason, Derrida will object to such Heideggerian claims as his having succeeded "in arriving at Nietzsche's philosophy proper" or his "attempt to experience the truth of that word concerning the death of God."[49] Such claims indicate a hermeneutic intention foreign to the Derridean approach to reading, an intention which strives to discern the full presence of meaning and truth. Thus, whereas Heidegger writes: "Obedient to the voice of Being, thought seeks the word through which the truth of Being may be expressed,"[50] Derrida responds that "we must *affirm* [the lack of the unique word or proper name]—in the sense that Nietzsche puts affirmation into play—with a certain laughter and with a certain dance."[51] It is this laughter and this dance of Derridean affirmation that we have sought to display in the preceding examination of Nietzsche's multiple styles.

Reading Derrida Reading Heidegger Reading Nietzsche

Thus far, I have refrained from intentionally directing any critical response to the Derridean reading of Nietzsche examined in the preceding pages. A major difficulty facing the critic in this task is *deciding* on the criteria to apply to his interpretation, for he explicitly disavows the traditional criterion (i.e., "getting the text right") for judging the adequacy of an exegetical commentary. Moreover, as we will see in the final chapter, a pluralistic approach to interpretation is committed to the view that there are multiple ways to get a text "right," and it will attempt to appraise interpretations, in part, in terms of the internal standards they set for themselves and, in part, in terms of their consequences for subsequent interpretive activity. In order to evaluate his reading and inquire whether he is more successful than Heidegger in avoiding both interpretive dogmatism and relativism, we must first sharpen the distinction he draws between his own style, the method of Heidegger, and the method of what Derrida labels "hermeneutics." In so doing, the risks of each interpretive approach will come to the fore.

As has been noted already, Derrida's main objection to the hermeneutic method is that he sees as its goal the *re*-production or doubling of the text. The problem with this method is that it is merely preservative and not productive: assured that the text contains some meaning that transcends the play of signs, the hermeneutic method seeks first to ascertain and then to protect this transcendent meaning. The basic mistake of this procedure, which Derrida calls "commentary," is the move to something, the "meaning," which transcends the text: *"The security with which commentary considers the self-identity of the text, the confidence with which it carves out its contours, goes hand in hand with the tranquil assurance that leaps over the text toward its preserved content, in the direction of a pure signified."*[52] The "axial proposition" of Derrida's method of active interpretation, however, asserts that *"there is nothing outside the text [il n'y a pas de hors-texte]."*[53] This indicates that Derrida's "critical reading" seeks to *produce* the "signifying structures" of writing which are themselves a part of the text and not outside it.

> To produce this signifying structure obviously cannot consist of reproducing by the effaced and respectful doubling of commentary, the conscious, voluntary, intentional relationship that the writer institutes in his exchanges with the history to which he belongs thanks to the element of language. This moment of doubling commentary should no doubt have its place in a critical reading. To recognize and respect all its classical exigencies is not easy and requires all the instruments of traditional criticism. Without this recognition and this respect, critical production would risk almost anything. But this indispensable guardrail has always only *protected,* it has never *opened,* a reading.
> Yet if reading must not be content with doubling the text, it cannot legitimately transgress the text toward something other than it, toward a referent (a reality that is metaphysical, historical, psychobiographical, etc.) or toward a signified outside the text whose content could take place, could have taken place outside of language, that is to say, in the sense that we give here to that word, outside of writing in general.[54]

We see here how Derrida marks off his own style of reading from the exegetical commentary that he takes to be the result of hermeneutics. It must be pointed out again, however, that Derrida does not here completely reject the task of hermeneutics, nor is hermeneutics *just* an exegetical doubling and re-enacting in one way or another of the original creative activity of the author which gave birth to the text. Nevertheless, our first task is to consider whether or not this is an accurate portrayal of the hermeneutic method. Is it the case that, as Derrida writes, the clear perception of meaning, the "comprehension of the sign in and of itself, in its immediate materiality as a sign, if I may so call it, is only the first moment but also the indispensable condition of all hermeneutics and of any claim to transition from the sign to the signified"?[55] While this is an extremely narrow conception of the hermeneutic project, there does seem to be a significant strain within the hermeneutic tradition of which this appears to be an accurate character-ization; for example, the hermeneutics of Schleiermacher, whose task was "to understand the text at first as well as and then even better than its author."[56] Or the hermeneutics of Emilio Betti, who argues for the edifying consequences of accurately apprehending the objectivations of superior minds:

> The gain we derive for our own education and self-development from great works of art is one thing; another is the realization that within the cosmos of objectivations of mind we can find meaning-contents which we acknowledge to be superior to our subjectivity and which we approach through understanding—not so much out of our own strength, but through being raised by them.[57]

From such remarks, it does appear that the hermeneutic method of Schleiermacher or Betti views the "first moment" and "indispensable condition" of its task to be the transition from the sign to the signified in their project of deciphering the "objective meaning" of a text. And insofar as the adequacy of interpretation is judged in terms of the degree to which it accurately reproduces this "objective meaning," determined as it is by the author's original intention, this methodology can be viewed, as Derrida suggests, as guided in its first moment by the goal of "doubling the text."[58] Even Gadamer, whose hermeneutic avoids many of the problems faced by the rigid methodologies of Schleiermacher or Betti, claims that "all reproduction [of art, music or poetry] is primarily interpretation and seeks, as such, to be correct."[59] While Gadamer admits that "the sense of a text in general reaches far beyond what its author originally intended," he nevertheless remains committed to correctness as the goal of interpretation and takes the move from the sign to the signified as the indispensable condition of hermeneutics: "the task of understanding is concerned in the first place with the meaning of the text itself."[60]

Whereas Derrida admits that his reading "must be intrinsic and remain within the text,"[61] he rejects the admittedly unattainable goals of correctness of reproduction or identity of redoubling. Such goals continue to adhere to categories of the metaphysics of presence insofar as they view the task of reading to be a *re*-production of a/the "meaning," understood as something which is somehow *present* in the text. As such, Derrida regards these goals as merely "preservative" and insufficient for "opening" a reading. Yet when judged according to these traditional standards, Derrida's "productive reading" appears to transgress the limits of the text insofar as these limits have been prescribed by the conception of meaning as presence. This need not entail, however, that "productive reading" does, indeed, "leave the text." Instead, such a judgment may reveal only the insufficiency of these standards for evaluating the merits of "productive reading," as this reading views "meaning" not as *present in* the text but as *produced through* the activity of reading the text. If we return, for a moment, to Nietzsche's "dance with the pen," we may perhaps gain an insight into the sort of evaluative schema that could fit this "productive reading." If Derridean readers attempt to follow this dance, their aim is not to mimic the dancer's steps, gesture for gesture. Good dancers do not merely repeat the steps that they might find in an instruction manual or choreographer's notebook; rather, accomplished dancers embellish and enhance the basic movements with their own style and artistry. Similarly, active interpreters do not merely repeat the thought processes of the author; instead, they take the text as a guide within which they are free to create new movements and textual patterns. In this sense Derrida can claim that reading is never finished yet remains within the text, for there is no end to the possible supplementation of the dance's choreography.

While we can clearly discern the differences between Derrida's view of reading and the method he attributes to traditional hermeneutics, the differences between Derrida's and Heidegger's methods are more subtle. Regarding their respective readings of Nietzsche's text, I would suggest that one way to view these differences is in terms of the respective methodological tasks of deconstruction in the case of Derrida, and overcoming in the case of Heidegger. Heidegger, for his part, reads Nietzsche for the purpose of overcoming: seeking the recovery of Being from its oblivion at the hands of the metaphysicians, Heidegger reads the history of philosophy in general with the intention of "overcoming" the metaphysical oblivion of Being. Nietzsche, insofar as he is a part of this tradition which has forgotten Being, thus falls prey to this totalizing reading. Derrida draws the term "*déconstruction*" from his own interpretation of Heidegger. When asked about the genesis of the term, Derrida comments:

> When I made use of this word, I had the sense of translating two words from Heidegger at a point where I needed them in the context. These two words are *Destruktion*, which Heidegger uses, explaining that *Destruktion* is not a destruction but precisely a destructuring that dismantles the structural layers in the system, and so on. The other word is *Abbau*, which has a similar meaning: to take apart an edifice in order to see how it is constituted or deconstituted.[62]

Unlike Heidegger's *Destruktion*, however, Derridean *déconstruction* does not seek the overcoming of metaphysics; rather, convinced of the inescapable closure of metaphysical thinking, deconstructive reading seeks instead to circumvent the border between what is within the philosophical tradition as a metaphysics of presence, and what is external to that tradition. By displaying those marginal concepts that the tradition both authorizes and excludes, a deconstructive reading inhabits the closed field of metaphysical discourse without at the same time confirming that field. Instead, it allows a text to dismantle itself by bringing forth the internal inconsistencies and implicit significations which lie concealed within the textual network. While sympathetic to the Heideggerian project, Derrida is explicit in distancing his own method from Heidegger's attempt to escape onto-theology: "Here or there I have used the word *déconstruction*, which has nothing to do with destruction. That is to say, it is simply a question of (and this is a necessity of criticism in the classical sense of the word) being alert to the implications, to the historical sedimentations of the language which we use—and that is not destruction."[63]

> To "deconstruct" philosophy, thus, would be to think—in the most faithful, interior way—the structured genealogy of philosophy's concepts, but at the same time to determine—from a certain exterior that is unqualifiable or unnameable by philosophy—what this history has been able to dissimulate or forbid, making itself into a history by means of this somewhere motivated repression.[64]

The respective consequences of the deconstructive and Heideggerian readings of Nietzsche reflect this difference in intent. Calling upon the language of the *propre*, this difference reflects the qualitative shift from *ap*propriation to *ex*propriation. The *Oxford English Dictionary* defines "appropriation" as "taking as one's own or to one's own use," while "expropriation" is defined as "the action of depriving (a person) of property; deprivation; an instance of this." This distinction bears on these two readings of Nietzsche: whereas Derrida's reading clearly appropriates Nietzsche's text and puts it to its own use, the Heideggerian reading tends to expropriate or dispossess Nietzsche's thought by reading into it an "essential truth" which does not appear to fit with this text.[65] One might say, in this regard, that whereas the hermeneutics of Betti or Schleiermacher leads to exegesis, Heidegger's hermeneutic results in *eisegesis,* reading out of the text (*Aus-lesen*) only what it has itself already read into the text (*Hinein-lesen*). Returning to Schleiermacher's formula, however, there is a sense in which Heidegger's reading appears to be grounded on the assumption that he knows Nietzsche better than Nietzsche knew himself. It is this thought which strikes the reader when confronting Heidegger's assertion of the essential truth of Nietzsche's word "God is dead" or his providing the definitive answer to the question "Who is Nietzsche's Zarathustra?" Armed with the conviction that he knows Nietzsche's "one and only thought," the doctrine "which is left unsaid in what he says," Heidegger is thus freed from attending to many of the specific claims of the Nietzschean text. This tendency of Heidegger's reading is apparent to even his most staunch defenders. Thus Gadamer, for example, while for the most part willing to defend Heidegger's Nietzsche interpretation, nevertheless can write that "all in all, Heidegger's attempt to think through the history of philosophy exhibits the violence of a thinker who is driven by his own questions and who seeks to recognize himself in everything."[66] Elsewhere, Gadamer responds to Karl Löwith's criticism of Heidegger's hermeneutic method with the claim that Löwith "does not see that the violence done by many of Heidegger's interpretations by no means follows from this theory of understanding."[67] While Gadamer regards Heidegger's "productive misuse of the texts" as betraying "something more like a lack of hermeneutical awareness," at issue in the present discussion is precisely the textual "distortions" which result from Heidegger's *eisegetical, expropriative reading.*

Returning again to the metaphor of dance, we can express the difference between Derrida's interpretation and Heidegger's in the following way: the deconstructive dance is improvisational, its movement is "abstract," offering variations on the "original" choreography, often transformed to such an extent that the audience finds it difficult to recognize what dance is being performed. Yet, for all its strangeness, when this deconstructive dance is performed well, the reader gets the sense that this new version *fits,* that there are interpretive links, however obscure or oblique, to the "original" dance that is being enacted. Still, readers are often hard pressed to justify their conclusions concerning the performance's fitness, and even the most sympathetic readers may be uncomfortable without a firmer support for their judgment as to whether or not a performance fits. Heidegger, on the other hand, frequently appears to be dancing to his own tune, paying little more than lip service to the "original" steps of the dance he is performing. Even when the Heideggerian performance resembles its original, the discerning reader will notice that this performance is overdetermined by a telos, the recovery of Being, which does not fit Nietzsche's "dance with the pen."

For some, deconstructive reading poses a danger for interpretation inasmuch as traditional ways of determining when the transformational activity of reading becomes a metamorphosis are no longer accepted in deconstructive interpretation. Derrida will maintain that the intertextual network can never be completely severed and that, because of the disseminating logic of citationality and the "iterability of the mark," the transformations never break their ties with the "original."[68] Nevertheless, the interpretive critic is left with the task of delineating this transformational activity of reading *as interpretive.* Derrida himself acknowledges the difficulty of this task. In a "candid" admission that much work still needs to be done, he writes, referring to the texts of Marxism:

> These texts are not to be read according to a hermeneutical or exegetical method which would seek out a finished signified beneath a textual surface. Reading is transformational. [. . .] But this transformation cannot be executed however one wishes. It requires protocols of reading. Why not say it bluntly: I have not yet found any that satisfy me.[69]

It is not clear that such protocols *can* be specified, or that they are desirable, from within the deconstructionist program. In an essay entitled(?) "TITLE (to be specified),"[70] Derrida addresses the question of what is entailed in the specification of a title. In the course of this essay, certain restrictions on the play of interpretation appear to result from this specification. Would similar restrictions not result if the protocols of reading ever come to be specified? One suspects that the deconstructionists feel they would. Could protocols be specified in such a way that they would not inevitably lead to a restriction of the free play of interpretation? As yet, the deconstructionists have refrained from specifying such protocols, and the deconstructive *différance* would seem to preclude such an eventuality. Until such protocols can be specified which satisfy their desire to open the text to the play of interpretation without, at the same time, allowing these interpretations to be "executed however one wishes," deconstructive reading will continue to run the risk of which Nietzsche himself was well aware: *"the text finally disappeared under the interpretation"* (*BGE*, 38).[71] While this outcome may not be all that undesirable for deconstructionists who willingly affirm the risks of interpretation, the critical response which their transformational approach to interpretation has elicited from more traditional interpretive methodologists makes clear that such an outcome is considered by many to be quite undesirable.

In concluding the second part of this study, it appears that we have returned to the initial point of departure: the difficulty of avoiding both dogmatism and relativism in interpretation. Our examination of the Heideggerian and deconstructive readings of Nietzsche reveals a new inscription of the hermeneutic dilemma: whereas the Heideggerian reading tends to dogmatically overdetermine the Nietzschean text, thereby expropriating Nietzsche's thought as a discourse on the meaning and truth of Being, the deconstructive reading, in its fondness for indeterminacy and undecidability, appears to more traditional interpreters to exhibit a relativistic tendency toward "underdetermining" that same text, thereby walking that fine line between use and abuse, and making problematic any judgment as to the lack of fit-ness of certain interpretations. While there is clearly much of value in these deconstructive readings, in their opening up new terrain in the Nietzschean text by focusing as they do on the questions of language, style, and rhetoric, there is no less danger of losing Nietzsche's text beneath these disseminating, transformational interpretations than there was of losing the text within the Heideggerian project of overcoming the metaphysical oblivion of Being. In Part Three, we will explore whether Nietzsche's text itself can help us in avoiding both the Heideggerian tendency toward overdetermination and the deconstructive tendency toward underdetermination.

Part 3
Nietzsche

Chapter 5

Language, Metaphor, Rhetoric

Perhaps universal history is but the history of several metaphors.
—Borges

Der Philosoph in den Netzen der Sprache *eingefangen.*
—Nietzsche

As noted in Chapter Three, Michel Foucault cites Nietzsche's "radical reflection upon language" as, in part, initiating the modern epoch.[1] While one need not accept this characterization of modernity, Foucault brings to the fore an important aspect of Nietzsche's thought to which, until quite recently, little attention has been given. While many of Nietzsche's commentators have acknowledged his early work on rhetoric and language as a professor of classical philology at the University of Basel (1869–1879), few have related Nietzsche's early insights into the nature of language to the work of his so-called "mature" period.[2] More often than not, Nietzsche's break with the academic world of classical philology is taken to indicate a significant turn in the Nietzschean project, dividing his earlier, strictly "scholarly" pursuits from his more "philosophically" significant later work as the revaluer of values and philosopher of the *Übermensch* and the eternal recurrence. This strict division between the "young" and the "mature" Nietzsche needs to be brought into question, as several of Nietzsche's early views on language, while no longer pursued as a specific topic of inquiry, reappear throughout the entirety of his writings.[3] Moreover, his views on language inform many of his later positions, insofar as several of Nietzsche's criticisms of the traditional problems of metaphysics and epistemology appear as consequences of some of his earliest insights into the nature of language and metaphor. This is not to say that there is a uniformity to Nietzsche's corpus, nor do I want to imply that Nietzsche's thought did not evolve, that his analyses did not become more sophisticated, or that he did not change certain of his views (for example, concerning the value of philology or the concept of the Dionysian, as we will see in the following chapter). But acknowledging the evolution of Nietzsche's philosophical project should not blind us to the continuity that exists in Nietzsche's thought concerning certain issues and, in particular, to the continuity of his views on the tropological, normative and semiotic implications of language. This conception of language, as we shall see, is essential for understanding some of Nietzsche's more vitriolic and polemical counterdoctrines to the traditional philosophical quest for knowledge and truth.

123

Before beginning our examination of Nietzsche, let me digress for a moment to discuss my use of Nietzsche's unpublished writings in this and the subsequent chapters of this study. Neither the comments collected in the *Philosophenbuch* nor those collected as *The Will to Power* were published by Nietzsche, and these texts do not have the same status within the Nietzsche canon as do the published texts. Nevertheless, I have found it helpful to draw on these writings for several reasons. First, because several passages from the unpublished works (for example, the essay "On Truth and Lies in an Extramoral Sense") have received so much critical attention that it seems to me that, whether or not Nietzsche published them, they have *de facto* become part of the Nietzsche canon. Second, because many of the unpublished notes reflect Nietzsche's thought-experiments and, as such, do provide alternative perspectives that he considered seriously even if he decided ultimately not to publish them or simply never got around to publishing them. And third, as I develop certain Nietzschean suggestions concerning interpretation, I intend to go beyond anything Nietzsche himself did with these remarks. He did not formally attend to the task of developing an interpretive method, but I will argue that some of his comments, whether published or not, can assist us in carrying out that task. I do not believe that the unpublished notes I cite disclose the "truth" behind Nietzsche's published works, as Heidegger appears to have thought. Nor do I depend in any way on the "argument" developed in those works—the *Philosophenbuch* and *The Will to Power*—attributed to Nietzsche but in fact "constructed" by his literary executors. Since the appearance of the Colli and Montinari *Kritische Gesamtausgabe,* the philological evidence clearly shows the order of the notes in these books as published not to be of Nietzsche's design. These works, therefore, should have no privileged place in the Nietzsche canon other than as a part of Nietzsche's unpublished *Nachlass.* But while the order of the notes in these texts may not have been Nietzsche's, the notes themselves nevertheless were penned by Nietzsche and, as a result, I believe that they can supplement several themes that emerge in the published works, and they can be used in the development not of *Nietzsche's* but of a *Nietzschean* approach to interpretation.

From the outset, Nietzsche directs his explorations into the nature of language toward demystifying the philosophical pretensions of truth and knowledge, as our quest for knowledge reveals itself to be grounded on the "fundamental human drive [. . .] toward the formation of metaphor [*Trieb zur Metapherbildung*]" (*MA,* VI, p. 88; *KGW,* III, 2: p. 381; *OTL,* 2). This is to say, human knowledge is possible only by means of language and, in Nietzsche's view, language reveals itself to be founded on human beings' capacity for the creation of metaphor. At the center of Nietzsche's position is his critique of the philosophical faith in concepts and the representational nature of language. Whereas philosophy had traditionally conceived knowledge to be a mirroring of reality with the aid of concepts (words) as representations (*Vorstellungen*) of that reality, Nietzsche argues that "the intellect unfolds its principal powers in dissimulation [*Verstel-*

lung]" (*MA*, VI, p. 76; *KGW*, III, 2: p. 370; *OTL*, 1). The primary example of this dissimulation is the process of naming; philosophy itself, says Nietzsche, begins with the legislation of nomenclature (cf. *PTAG*, 3: "*ein Namengeben ist mit [Philosophie] verbunden.*"). This process of naming gives rise to *concepts*, seen as the consequence of an artificial process of differentiation, classification, and designation (cf. *KGW*, III, 3: 3[15]: "*Ein* gemerktes *Symbol ist immer ein Begriff: man begreift, was man bezeichnen und unterscheiden kann.*"). In naming, what is at best similar is designated as identical by virtue of bestowing upon what is similar the *same name* (see *KGW*, III, 4: 30[30]; *PHT*, 47). It is in this sense that "knowledge" appears as the rapid classification and categorization of things that are similar to each other (*MA*, VI, p. 49; *KGW*, III, 4: 19[179]; *P*, 131), and that the formation of concepts is the equation of things which are not equal. Language is thus not an instrument of representation, for there is ultimately nothing to be represented:

all presence is a *two-fold representation:* first as *image*, then as *image* of the *image*.
   Life is the incessant procreation of this double representation: [. . .] The empirical world only *appears* and *becomes*. (*KGW*, III, 3: 7[175]: *alles Vorhandene ist in* doppelter *Weise* Vorstellung: *einmal als* Bild, *dann als* Bild *des* Bildes. Leben *ist jenes unablässige Erzeugen dieser doppelten Vorstellungen:* [. . .] *Die empirische Welt* erscheint *nur, und* wird.)
   In becoming, the representative nature of the thing shows itself: it *gives* nothing, it *is* nothing, everything becomes, i.e., is representation [*es giebt nichts, es* ist *nichts, alles wird, d.h. ist Vorstellung*]. (*KGW*, III, 3: 7[203])

This is to say, for Nietzsche language is merely a sum of concepts which are themselves the artistic imposition of an image or hieroglyphic sign upon other images (see *KGW*, III, 3: 8[41]). There is no originary presence at the inception of language; instead, at the origin of language stands the primal force (*Urkraft*) of the artist whose creative power is recognized in the primal process (*Urprozess*) of world-production as an infinite regress of images: "*ein Bild des Bildes des Bildes*" (*KGW*, III, 3: 7[175]).

Situated within this nominalistic view of knowledge, couched as it is in Scho-penhauerian terminology, lies *metaphor,* which for Nietzsche "means to treat something as *identical* which has been recognized as similar in one point" (*KGW*, III, 4: 19[249]). This definition displays one of Nietzsche's two most frequent uses of "metaphor" in his early writings: the identification, through words, of things which are not the same. Nietzsche's other primary use of metaphor is drawn from his reading of Aristotle's *Poetics:* "a metaphor is the carrying over [*Uebertragung*] of a word whose usual meaning is something else, either from the genus to the species, from the species to the genus, from species to species, or according to proportion" (*Rh*, p. 317; *ET*, p. 55).[4] However, Nietzsche goes beyond Aristotle's restriction of metaphor to a *linguistic* "carrying over," and comes to regard any transference from one sphere to another (e.g., physical to spiritual, literal to figurative, audible to visual, subject to object, etc.) as an instance of metaphor. This second use of metaphor is clearly exhibited in his coming to view the concepts with which knowledge operates as the result of a three-stage metaphorical translation: "To begin with, a nerve stimulus is transferred [*übertragen*] into an image: first metaphor. The image, in turn is imitated in a sound: second metaphor" (*MA*, VI, p. 79; *KGW*, III, 2: p. 373; *OTL*, 1). And from this sound (i.e., the word) comes the concept: third metaphor (see *MA*, VI, p. 21; *KGW*, III, 4: 19[67]; *P*, 55). In this series of metaphorical translations (nerve impulse—image—sound/word—concept), Nietzsche isolates an expressive transference through four experiential spheres: physiology, intellect, acoustics-linguistics, and abstraction. Each is marked by a selective, creative carrying over from one "language" to another and, as such, Nietzsche wants to rule out any question of establishing a "proper relation" or literal translation between spheres:

> between two absolutely different spheres, as between subject and object, there is no causality, no correctness, no expression, but at most an *aesthetic* relation: I mean, a suggestive transference, a stammering translation into a completely foreign language. For which there is required, in any case, a freely inventive intermediate sphere and mediating force. (*MA*, VI, p. 85; *KGW*, III, 2: p. 378; *OTL*, 1)

In this "inventive intermediate sphere" the human capacity for metaphor-formation operates and, as a result of this "mediating force," the claims of "knowledge" become a completely human affair.

Because of the obtrusiveness of this metaphorical capacity, Nietzsche views the conclusions which the human knowledge-drive (*Erkenntnisstrieb*) derives from concepts to be thoroughly anthropomorphic (see *P*, 41, 64, 77, 78, 80; *PCP*, 171, 174; *PTAG*, 11; *OTL*, passim). To take just one example, consider the following discussion of the origin of "Being":

> The concept of Being! As if this concept did not indicate the most miserable empirical origin already in the etymology of the word. For *esse* at bottom means "to breath": if man uses it of all other things, then he transfers the conviction that he himself breathes and lives by means of a metaphor, that is, by means of something illogical to other things and conceives of their existence as a breathing according to human analogy. Now the original meaning of the word soon becomes effaced; so much however still remains that man conceives of the existence of other things according to the analogy of his own existence, therefore anthropomorphically, and in any case by means of an illogical transference. (*PTAG*, 11)

For Nietzsche, a concept is thus revealed to be merely "the *residue of a metaphor*," merely a word which is abstracted and generalized and "simultaneously has to fit countless more or less similar cases" (*MA*, VI, pp. 83, 81; *KGW*, III, 2: pp. 376,

373–374; *OTL*, 1). As such, while we believe and behave as if the concept were something factual, it is revealed by Nietzsche to have been

> constructed through a process of ignoring all individual features. We presuppose that nature behaves in accordance with such a concept. But in this case, first nature and then the concept are anthropomorphic. The *omitting* of what is individual provides us with the concept, and with this our knowledge begins: in *categorizing* [*Rubriziren*], in the establishment of *classes*. But the essence of things does not correspond to this: it is a process of knowledge which does not touch upon the essence of things. (*MA*, VI, p. 58; *KGW*, III, 4: 19[236]; *P*, 150)

In this scheme, the hope for knowledge as the *adequatio intellectus et rei*, for language as accurately representing reality, is completely dashed, for even at the level of so-called "pure perception" metaphors are already operating (see *MA*, VI, p. 85, p. 54; *KGW*, III, 2: p. 378, III, 4: 19[217]; *OTL*, 1, *P*, 144). In the context of these remarks, we find Nietzsche's famous definition of truth:

> What then is truth? A mobile army of metaphors, metonymies, and anthropomorphisms—in short, a sum of human relations which have been poetically and rhetorically enhanced, transposed, and embellished, and which after long use seem fixed, canonical and binding to a people: truths are illusions which we have forgotten are illusions; metaphors which are worn out and without sensuous power, coins which have lost their picture and now matter only as metal, no longer as coin. (*MA*, VI, p. 81; *KGW*, III, 2: pp. 374–375; *OTL*, 1)

Far from corresponding to reality, what we take as truth is a thorough-going anthropomorphism, the application of the usual, conventional metaphors. Only by forgetting their metaphorical beginnings and congealing the metaphor into a "concept" are truth and knowledge possible. Nietzsche's point, however, is not to indict the forgetting of metaphor so much as to restrain the philosopher's arrogant claims to knowledge.

> *Imitation* is the opposite of *knowing*, to the extent that knowing certainly does not want to admit any transference, but wishes instead to cling to the impression without metaphor and apart from the consequences. The impression is petrified for this purpose; it is captured and stamped by means of concepts. Then it is killed, skinned, mummified, and preserved as a concept.
> But there is no "real" expression and *no real knowing apart from metaphor*. Yet deception on this point remains, i.e., the *belief* in a *truth* of sense impressions. The most accustomed metaphors, the usual ones, now pass for truths and as standards for measuring the rarer ones. The only intrinsic difference here is the difference between custom and novelty, frequency and rarity.
> *Knowing* is nothing but working with the favorite metaphors, an imitation [*Nachahmen*] which is no longer felt to be an imitation. Naturally, therefore, it cannot penetrate to the realm of truth[. . . .] (*MA*, VI, p. 57; *KGW*, III, 4: 19[228]; *P*, 149)

Throughout these notes, we find numerous references to the misconception of language as adequately expressing some "natural" relationship between words and things as well as the view that knowledge "involves the *identification of things which are not the same,* of things which are only similar" (*MA,* VI, p. 58; *KGW,* III, 4: 19[236]; *P,* 150). In so doing, we see exhibited a strategy to which Nietzsche returns again and again throughout his writings, namely, the focus on some mistaken belief so as to bring to the fore the genealogy of this belief, that is, to raise the question "Why did such a belief arise?" In the case of these erroneous claims to "knowledge," the motivating force for these errors is what Nietzsche calls the "pathos of truth." This pathos of truth strives for fixity, for static conceptual points of reference around which to organize a systematic body of beliefs. The truth comes to be fixed and generalized by means of concepts and is, as some*thing* static, capable of being possessed: "philosophy and religion as a longing for *property*" (*KGW,* III, 4: 29[224]; *PHT,* 60). While Nietzsche acknowledges that a certain amount of security is to be gained as a consequence of the possession of such fixed and certain truths, this security is attained at the expense of denigrating human creative power:

> Only by forgetting this primitive world of metaphor, only by means of the petrification and coagulation of a mass of images which originally streamed from the primal faculty of human imagination like a fiery liquid, only in the invincible faith that *this* sun, *this* window, *this* table is a truth in itself, in short, only by forgetting that he himself is an *artistically creating* subject, does man live with any repose, security, and consistency. (*MA,* VI, p. 84; *KGW,* III, 2: p. 377; *OTL,* 1)

This is to say, while Nietzsche acknowledges the necessity of truth, the necessity of forgetting the creative, metaphorical origin of concepts, he nevertheless objects to the certainty of these "truths" as the primary criterion upon which to judge their value. Nietzsche views philosophy as having come to be dominated by an unbridled "knowledge-drive which *judges* more and more according to the degree of certainty," whereas he argues that "the only criterion which counts for us is the aesthetic criterion" (*MA,* VI, p. 13; *KGW,* III, 4: 19[37]; *P,* 41).[5] Ultimately, to accept the certainty of truth as a criterion of value is, for Nietzsche, to judge truth on moral grounds. In his view, "truth makes its appearance as a social necessity" (*MA,* VI, p. 38; *KGW,* III, 4: 19[175]; *P,* 91), and the conception of truth as certainty has arisen as a consequence of human beings entering into a community. The harmony of such a community requires these "truths" as "uniformly valid and binding designations" (*MA,* VI, p. 78; *KGW,* III, 2: p. 371; *OTL,* 1). Without such uniform, obligatory designations, the community cannot function in that we suffer "from the malady of words and mistrust any feeling of our own that has not yet been stamped with words" (*H,* 10). The liar, in this context, is thus one who abuses or fails to adhere to the "linguistic conventions." But at a deeper level, the level of truths and lies in an *extra*-moral sense, truths are themselves "lies," they are "illusions which we have forgotten are illusions," and to be truthful is merely "to lie according to a fixed convention" (*MA*, VI, pp. 81–82; *KGW*, III, 2: p. 375; *OTL*, 1). It is at this level that Nietzsche's inquiry seeks to operate, and within this context he seeks to replace the criterion of certainty with one drawn from aesthetics: "the beauty and grandeur of an interpretation of the world [*einer Weltconstruction*] (alias philosophy) is what is now decisive for its value, i.e., it is judged as *art*" (*MA*, VI, p. 18; *KGW*, III, 4: 19[47]; *P*, 49). This choice of aesthetic criteria is, for Nietzsche, one of necessity, for the criteria by which to judge correctness or certainty are not available to human beings:

> the correct perception—which would mean the adequate expression of the object in a subject—as a contradictory impossibility: for between two absolutely different spheres, as between subject and object, there is no causality, no correctness, no expression: there is, at most an *aesthetic* relation. (*MA*, VI, p. 85; *KGW*, III, 2: p. 378; *OTL*, 1)

From his views of language as providing no information about things as they are in themselves, and of truth as forgotten, congealed metaphors, Nietzsche argues that questions of epistemology are more appropriately seen as questions of rhetoric. Inasmuch as epistemology (and philosophy in general) proceeds by means of language, and language is essentially rhetorical (persuasive, seductive), all questions regarding language and, *ipso facto*, regarding philosophy are questions of rhetoric. Nietzsche asserts that "the deepest philosophical knowledge lies ready-made in language" (*MA*, V, p. 467, from a fragment entitled "On the Origin of Language") and concludes that "words are the seducers of philosophers: they struggle in the nets of language" (*KGW*, IV, 1: 6[39]; *SSW*, 199). This ready-made knowledge which lies in language never captures the "full essence of things." Rather,

> with respect to their meanings, all words are in themselves and from the beginning tropes. Instead of that which truly takes place, they present a sound image, which fades away in time: language never expresses something completely, but displays only a feature which appears outstanding to it. (*Rh*, p. 299; *ET*, p. 23; see also *KGW*, III, 3: 8[72])

Human beings' creative, aesthetic powers are thus present at the origin of language and from language we can derive no more knowledge than we have already incorporated into it:

> The full essence of things will never be grasped. Our utterances by no means wait until our perception and experience have provided us with a many-sided, somehow respectable knowledge of things; they result immediately when the impulse is perceived. Instead of the thing, the sensation takes in only a feature. That is the *first*

viewpoint: *language is rhetoric,* because it wishes to convey only a *doxa,* not an *epistēmē.* (*Rh,* p. 298; *ET,* p. 23)

Ironically borrowing here from Plato's own rhetoric, we find Nietzsche attempting to deconstruct the authority which post-Platonic epistemology has endeavored to attain. Because language is a human creation which expresses only anthropomorphic relations, all the results drawn from linguistic use are, on Plato's own criteria from the "Divided Line," merely opinions, illusions, *doxa,* and not knowledge (*epistēmē*) at all. For all his hostility toward rhetoric,[6] because he spoke and wrote with language, even Plato himself is condemned by Nietzsche to the realm of rhetoric.

Nietzsche's move away from the representational model of language and toward a rhetorical model thus has a two-fold consequence: it both limits the authority of epistemology while at the same time broadening the scope of rhetorical inquiry. Tropes are no longer viewed, as they had been in classical discussions of rhetoric, as having a simply ornamental value which is derivative upon a standard drawn from proper, literal usage.[7] Instead, Nietzsche's *Rhetorik* posits the trope as the paradigmatic case of linguistic usage:

> tropes are not just occasionally added to words but constitute their most proper nature. It makes no sense to speak of a "proper meaning" which is carried over only in special cases. There is just as little distinction between actual words and tropes as there is between ordinary *speech* [*regelrechten* Rede] and the so-called *rhetorical figures.* What is usually called speech is actually all figuration. (*Rh,* p. 300; *ET,* p. 25)

This tropological view of language appears throughout Nietzsche's early writings, and we can locate in these notes numerous examples of the sort of rhetorical analysis that he advocates.[8] Taking just one of these examples, we shall briefly look at some of his references to the role of *metonymy* in language.

Metonymy, metaphor, and synecdoche are the three tropes emphasized by Nietzsche in his rhetoric lectures. While the extensions of these three basic tropes frequently overlap, Nietzsche principally defines metonymy as the "substitution of cause and effect" (*Rh,* p. 299; *ET,* p. 25).[9] The primary manifestation of such a substitution is the confusion of an entity with its consequences. This metonymic substitution is essential for the processes of abstraction and concept-formation (see *KGW,* III, 4: 19[204]). In the *Rhetorik,* he singles out the transition from *eide* to *ideai* in Plato as instructive, for "here metonymy, the substitution of cause and effect, is complete" (*Rh,* p. 319; *ET,* p. 59). This is to say, in Plato we find complete the attribution of the characteristics of the effect (the *eide,* the shape or form of that which appears) to the *ideai* or ideal forms as cause. This Platonic substitution is by no means an isolated instance; rather, Nietzsche locates metonymy, the "false inference" from effect to cause, at the essence of *all* synthetic judgment: "A synthetic judgment describes a thing according to its consequences, i.e., *essence* and *consequences* become *identified,* i.e., a *metonymy"* (*MA,* VI, p. 59; *KGW,* III, 4: 19[242]; *P,* 152). Metonymy thus resides at the center of all synthetic definitions, for in defining something (Nietzsche uses as an example: "The pencil is an elongated body."), we inevitably incorporate anthropomorphic relations, and relations of any sort "can never be the essence, but only consequences of this essence" (*MA,* VI, p. 59; *KGW,* III, 4: 19[242]; *P,* 152). He concludes that it is of the nature of definitions to involve a *"false equation,"* and that to employ any synthetic inference

> presupposes the popular metaphysics, i.e., the metaphysics which regards effects as causes.
>
> The concept "pencil" is confused with the "thing" pencil. The "is" of a synthetic judgment is false, it includes a transference: two different spheres, between which there can never be an equation, are placed next to each other. (*MA,* VI, p. 59; *KGW,* III, 4: 19[242]; *P,* 152)

Throughout Nietzsche's discussion of rhetoric in the early writings, one can find numerous instances of this sort of analysis. While the objects analyzed may differ, the strategy operating within these analyses remains the same. Nietzsche consistently attempts to demystify the authority that has been bestowed on language through a strategic deconstruction of the traditional rhetorical distinction between figurative and literal language. By showing that all language is by its nature figurative, Nietzsche does not merely intend to invert the traditional view of the primacy of the literal and the derivative status of the figurative. Rather, his attempt to reveal the literal/figurative distinction as an illusion is directed toward shaking the security of the linguistic foundations upon which philosophy since its inception has been built.[10] This is to say, Nietzsche regards the *construction* of the philosophical systems of the past (Plato, Aristotle, Descartes, Kant, et al.) to be grounded on an unquestioned faith in the primacy of the literal, and shaking this faith will be a first step toward dismantling these systematic constructions. In this sense, Nietzsche's rhetorical critique may be understood as a *de*-construction. Throughout Nietzsche's discussion of the philosophical tradition, he utilizes metaphors from architecture to characterize philosophical systems as a sort of construction (*Bauen*). As we saw in our earlier discussion of Sarah Kofman's *Nietzsche et la métaphore,* this appears nowhere more clearly than in "On Truth and Lies in an Extramoral Sense," where he views man as a "genius of construction [*Baugenie*]" while tracing the evolution of the epistemologists' "conceptual edifice [*Bau der Begriffe*]" through such figures as the beehive, the tower, the medieval fortress, the Egyptian pyramid, the Roman columbarium, and the spider's web. In his project of transvaluing all values, the first step will be to trace these epistemological constructions back to their origins, that is, to genealogically decipher their source in a strong or weak will to power. In the context of the present discussion, Nietzsche's critique of philosophical language thus takes the form of a *de*-construction, an *Ab-bau* of these systems, a dismantling or undoing of their epistemological constructions by tracing them back to their metaphorical or rhetorical roots.[11] The success of the Nietzschean *de*-construction will not allow the philosopher to escape from within the nets of language, however; but facilitating such an escape was never his intention. Rather, by revealing the hope of a literal designation and an adequate, natural relation between words and things to be unrealizable, Nietzsche directs himself toward the critical task of demonstrating that philosophers *do not know* what they think they "know." We must recognize, however, that this critical task is by no means restricted to Nietzsche's early writings. Again and again, he returns to the task of demystifying the epistemological pretensions of philosophy,[12] as we shall now see.

In his early account of language, we find Nietzsche experimenting with four themes which recur in various ways throughout his writings. These four themes are all loosely woven around his deconstruction of many of our claims about what we think we know about the world. The first two themes are critical—Nietzsche's rejection of two of the traditional doctrines of epistemology: the correspondence theory of truth and the referential theory of meaning. The criticisms of these two doctrines are grounded on two of Nietzsche's basic insights: the view of language as a human creation which remains essentially separate from "reality," and the view of the world as a process of becoming. While he dispenses with a strictly rhetorical account of knowledge in giving expression to these four themes in his later works, their expression continues to focus, to a large extent, on the phenomenon of language. This is to say, while he no longer resorts primarily to the rhetorical terminology of "metaphor" and "tropes," Nietzsche continues to discuss the epistemological illusions inherent in words and grammar. By focusing on this recurrent experimentation with linguistic phenomena, we will be able to trace the genealogy of Nietzsche's *perspectival* account of knowledge back to his earliest rhetorical insights.

As we saw above, an essential aspect of Nietzsche's early nominalistic critique of knowledge is the triple metaphorical transference from nerve impulse to image to word to concept. Each stage in this series marks a translation from one experiential sphere to another: physiological—intellectual—acoustic-linguistic—abstract. While he no longer refers explicitly to these "translations" as "metaphorical" transferences, this series continues to inform Nietzsche's thinking. To cite just two examples:

> Words are acoustical signs [*Tonzeichen*] for concepts; concepts, however, are more or less definite image signs [*Bildzeichen*] for often recurring and associating sensations, for groups of sensations. (*BGE*, 268)

> First *images*—to explain how images arise in the spirit. Then *words*, applied to images.

Finally *concepts,* possible only when there are words—the collecting together of many images in something nonvisible but audible (words). (*WP,* 506)

As he did earlier, Nietzsche continues to use this genetic analysis of concepts in order to dismantle two reigning epistemological illusions: the referential theory of meaning and the correspondence theory of truth. The former asserts that language, by virtue of its powers of representation, stands in some sort of privileged relation (*adequatio*) to an extralinguistic referent or meaning ("reality"), while the latter designates as "truth" that which stands in such a relation of adequation or correspondence to reality. While Nietzsche often blurs the distinction between these two theories, we find frequent objections to them both throughout his later writings.

Taking the referential theory first, Nietzsche continues to assert that language, by its nature an anthropomorphic creation, cannot provide us with "correct" information about that which lies "outside" language. In other words, there is an unbridgeable gap between "words" and "things" (see *Z,* "The Convalescent," 2). What one does with language is create another world, a world which misleads us "into imagining things as being simpler than they are, separate from one another, indivisible, each existing in and for itself" (*WS,* 11). It is not language which is mistaken, but rather the belief that, with language, one possesses knowledge of the world: "The maker of language was not so modest as to believe that he was only giving things designations, he conceived rather that with words he was expressing supreme knowledge of things" (*HAH,* 11). Nietzsche concludes that we must understand our means of expression as "mere semiotics [*blosse Semiotik*]" and thus, "the demand for an adequate mode of expression is senseless" (*WP,* 625). Because language expresses a merely anthropomorphic relationship, it is pointless to inquire as to the referential accuracy of the description of the designated object outside of its relationship with the designator.[13]

At this point, we can see how Nietzsche's discussion of reference merges with his critique of truth as correspondence, for to speak of an objective referent outside of the relationship with that which refers to it is to speak of an "in-itself." And this "in-itself" is, for Nietzsche, presupposed by a correspondence theory of truth: "The concept 'truth' is nonsensical. The entire domain of 'true-false' applies only to relations, not to an 'in-itself' " (*WP,* 625). For truth as correspondence to be of any value for us, we would have to know what the thing was in-itself, so that we could determine whether or not our linguistic representation adequately corresponded to it. But we are not privy to such knowledge: we simply lack the organs to make such determinations regarding the realm of the in-itself (see *GS,* 354). Lacking such organs, what we are left with is language: a "process of abbreviation" (*BGE,* 268), "conceptual mummies" (*TI,* " 'Reason' in Philosophy," 1) and "petrified words" (*D,* 47). And inasmuch as language determines thought, inasmuch as *"we cease to think when we refuse to do so under the constraint of language*" (*WP*, 522; see also *BGE*, 20), our intellect cannot but miscarry in its attempt to give birth to knowledge and truth.

An example of such a miscarriage is revealed in Nietzsche's critique of logic. Logic commits many of the same mistakes which Nietzsche had previously attributed to language. Originally intended as a "means of facilitation" and "not as truth" (*WP*, 538), logic arose as an aid to communication:

> That *communication* is necessary, and that for there to be communication something has to be firm, simplified, capable of precision (above all in the *identical* case . . .). For it to be communicable, however, it must be experienced as *adapted*, as "*recognizable.*" The material of the senses adapted by the understanding, reduced to rough outlines, made similar, subsumed under related matters. Thus the fuzziness and chaos of sense impressions are, as it were, *logicized*. (*WP*, 569)

This creation of "identical cases" is analogous to what Nietzsche had earlier spoken of as the "making equal what is unequal" that stands at the origin of language (see *MA*, VI, p. 58; *KGW*, III, 4: 19[236]; *P*, 150). Thus logic, like language, is essentially falsification: "the will to *logical truth* can be carried through only after a fundamental *falsification* of all events is assumed. [. . .] logic does *not* spring from the will to truth" (*WP*, 512). It is thus "owing to a requirement of logic" that "thingness" is invented, because "logic handles only formulas for what remains the same" (*WP*, 558, 517). Logic must in each case presuppose the "thing," "being," the logician's "self-identical 'A.' " But the question remains to be asked: "Are the axioms of logic adequate to reality or are they a means and measure for us to *create* reality, the concept 'reality' for ourselves?" (*WP*, 516). Nietzsche's judgment as to the adequation of logic repeats his judgment regarding language: "Logic is the attempt *to comprehend the actual world by means of a scheme of being posited by ourselves; more correctly, to make it formulatable and calculable for us* . . ." (*WP*, 516). Logic, like language, "depends on presuppositions with which nothing in the real world corresponds" (*HAH*, 11), and its propositions contain "no *criterion* of truth" but posit "an *imperative* concerning that which *should* count as true" (*WP*, 516). What both logic and language, as instruments of man's desire for knowledge, presuppose are conditions which are completely lacking in the actual world: fixity, enduring constancy, stasis, identity; in a word, Being. Thus, at the bottom of Nietzsche's criticism of logic, as well as his rejections of the correspondence theory and referential theory stands one of Nietzsche's basic tenets: "*Knowledge* and *becoming* exclude one another" (*WP*, 517).

Because the world, for Nietzsche, is marked by the complete absence of stasis or fixity, and because knowledge and language both require as their basic presupposition a notion of static identity over time, the conclusions which our intellectual faculties draw from the world can be nothing other than illusory. In his early writings, Nietzsche spoke of knowledge as working with petrified concepts and congealed metaphors which, while necessary, could not in principle accurately capture the world as a Heraclitean flux or process of continual becoming. In his later works, he continues to adhere to this judgment. The means of expression that language has at its disposal are "useless for expressing becoming" and "we posit a crude world of stability, of 'things,' etc." only as a consequence of "our inevitable need to preserve ourselves" (WP, 715). Insofar as "the character of the world in a state of becoming is incapable of formulation," there is needed a fictitious world of "subject," "substance," "reason," "being," "truth"; that is, an ordered, simplified, falsified, artificially distinguished world that is "known" (see WP, 517). It is this falsified world of "conceptual mummies" that occupies the philosophers:

> Philosophy, as I alone still admit, as the universal form of history, as the attempt to somehow describe and abbreviate in signs Heraclitean becoming (as if *translated* and mummified in a type of apparent Being [*Sein*]). (KGW, VII, 3: 36[27])

While philosophers believe that their conceptual knowledge provides them with essential definitions of the world as it is in-itself, nothing could be more mistaken, inasmuch as "all concepts in which an entire process is semiotically concentrated [*ein ganzer Prozess semiotisch zusammenfasst*] elude definition: only that which has no history is definable" (GM, II, 13). And for Nietzsche, insofar as all aspects of the world are engaged in the eternal process of becoming, all our words and concepts will be such semiotic concentrations. The philosophers' world of conceptual knowledge is therefore a consequence of their inattention to becoming or their "lack of historical sense." This "lack of historical sense, their hatred of even the idea of becoming, their Egyptianism" is one of the central "idiosyncrasies" of philosophers. As a consequence of their philosophical Egyptianism

> they think they are doing a thing *honor* when they dehistoricize it, *sub specie aeterni,*—when they make a mummy of it. All that philosophers have handled for millennia have been conceptual mummies; nothing actual has escaped from their hands alive. (TI, " 'Reason' in Philosophy," 1)

This "dehistoricizing" (*enthistorisiren*), which results from our linguistic inability to express becoming, is essential to all our claims to knowledge and is, in part, why Nietzsche continues to claim, throughout his writings, that all our "knowledge," all our "truth," is "false."

Nietzsche does not content himself, however, with merely asserting that all our knowledge is false. Rather, he endeavors to explain, to a certain extent, how such a state of affairs could have arisen. In his early writings, he spoke of knowledge as an anthropomorphic translation of the actual world into terms which humans can understand. In his later works, Nietzsche still maintains this position, inasmuch as he continues to view knowledge as operating by means of language as a human creation imposed on the world of becoming. In particular, the apparent grounds for this view center on two features of Nietzsche's characterization of knowledge: first, the claim that consciousness and language, which together give rise to the various claims of knowledge, are "surface phenomena"; and second, that knowledge amounts to little more than a translation of what is strange and novel into what is old and familiar.

Demonstrating the superficiality of consciousness is a consistent theme in Nietzsche's later writings, and this view comes to be articulated in terms of the relation between thinking and language ("we *think only* in the form of language—" [*WP*, 522]), and the social origin of both consciousness and language. In a note from the Winter 1883–84, Nietzsche outlines his task:

> It must be shown to what extent everything conscious remains on *the surface:* how an action and the image of an action *differ*, how *little* one knows of what *precedes* an action: how fantastic are our feelings of "freedom of will," "cause and effect": how thoughts are only images, how words are only signs: the inexplicability of every action: the superficiality of all praise and blame: *how essential* **fiction** [**Erfindung**] and **imagination** [**Einbildung**] are in which we dwell consciously: how all our words refer to fictions (our affects, also) and how the bond between man and man depends on the transmission and elaboration of these fictions: [. . .] (*WP*, 676; *KGW*, VII, 1: 24[16])

Nietzsche's clearest statement of the outcome of his investigation into the superficiality of consciousness appears in Section 354 of *The Gay Science*. In this section, Nietzsche views consciousness as being, for the most part, a "superfluous" mirror of our life which develops in proportion to human beings' capacity and need for communication: "consciousness is really only a net of communication between human beings—it is only as such that it had to develop: a solitary human being who lived like a beast of prey would not have needed it." Consciousness thus does not belong to our individual existence but is, rather, a consequence of our "social or herd nature." Conscious thinking is, therefore, only a small part of our cognitive life, "the most superficial and worst part" which "*takes the form of words, which is to say signs of communication.*" This harsh judgment against consciousness is the consequence of Nietzsche's view that only what is "average" and "common" in a person can be communicated: "Fundamentally, all our actions are altogether incomparably personal, unique, and infinitely individual, there is no doubt of that; but as soon as we translate them into consciousness, *they no longer seem to be.*" The value of consciousness is strictly instrumental: as a member of a social community (the "herd"), we must disclose ourselves to other members of the community. To make such a self-disclosure, we must become self-conscious, which amounts to making what is individual and unique about our experience "average" and capable of being communicated. This conclusion Nietzsche calls the essence of phenomenalism and perspectivism as I understand them: owing to the nature of *animal consciousness*, the world of which we can become conscious is only a surface- and sign-world, a more common, a meaner world [*nur eine Oberflächen- und Zeichenwelt ist, eine verallgemeinerte, eine vergemeinerte Welt*],—whatever *becomes* conscious becomes by the same token shallow, thin, relatively stupid, general, sign, herd-signal: all becoming-conscious involves a great and thorough corruption, falsification, reduction to superficialities, and generalization.

This conclusion, which echoes Nietzsche's criticism of language itself, appears again in the second feature of his characterization of knowledge: the view of knowledge as a sort of "pigeon-holing," a *Rubrizieren*: knowledge as a reduction/ translation of what is strange (in)to what is familiar ("*was bekannt ist, ist erkannt*" [*GS*, 355]). Nietzsche asks "What do they want when they want 'knowledge' [*Erkenntniss*]?" And he answers: "Nothing more than this: something strange is to be reduced to something *familiar* [*etwas* Bekanntes]" (*GS*, 355). With this play on words (*bekannt/erkannt/Erkenntniss/Bekanntes*), Nietzsche reinforces his earlier criticisms of language, knowledge, and consciousness. Language, insofar as it functions through designating as the *same* things that are only similar, is essentially reductive. Furthermore, consciousness and knowledge, insofar as they are possible only in and through language, are equally reductive. Both operate by means of incorporating what is new into a systematic framework of familiar categories:

> In *our* thought, the *essential feature* is fitting new material into old schemas (= Procrustes' bed), *making* equal what is new. (*WP*, 499)

> *Explanation* [*Erklärung*]: that is the expression of a new thing by means of the signs of things already known. (*KGW*, VII, 3: 34[249])

We saw above, in our examination of Section 354 of *The Gay Science*, Nietzsche's criticism of the linguistic reductionism at the origin of consciousness. In the following section of *The Gay Science*, we find Nietzsche criticizing this same reductionism at the origin of knowledge:

> isn't our need for knowledge precisely this need for the familiar, the will to uncover under everything strange, unusual, and questionable something that no longer disturbs us? Is it not the *instinct of fear* that bids us to know? And is the jubilation of those who attain knowledge not the jubilation over the restoration of a sense of security? (*GS*, 355; see also *D*, 26)

By tracing the genealogy of knowledge back to a desire for security, Nietzsche links this critique with the previous criticism of consciousness, in that the security which follows from the reduction of the strange and questionable to the familiar is again a sign of the herd. Not strong enough to confront a world of novelty, one seeks to translate all that is new into the conventional wisdom of the community of which one is a part and through which one is nurtured and preserved. Such translating is an essential function of language, and Nietzsche's judgment regarding the linguistic reductionism at the origin of consciousness and language is the same:

> We no longer have a sufficiently high estimate of ourselves when we communicate. Our true experiences are not at all garrulous. [. . .] In all talk there lies a grain of contempt. Language, it seems, was invented only for what is average, medium, communicable. With language, the speaker immediately *vulgarizes* himself. (*TI*, "Skirmishes of an Untimely Man," 26)

In the preceding pages, we have seen how Nietzsche's reflections on language function as an essential component of his later thinking. Insofar as language is a mere semiotic, a simplified, falsified, human-created sign-system, and insofar as all thinking is possible only in and through the means provided by language, Nietzsche regards the "knowledge" and "truth" derived from language as failing to do the job which they are thought to perform. Thus, Nietzsche concludes that "knowledge" is merely a collection of perspectival illusions which, while necessary for the preservation of the human species, stands as a function not of truth but of *power*. This conclusion is summarized in the following note of Spring 1888:

> *On epistemology: merely empirical:*
> There exists neither "spirit," nor reason, nor thinking, nor consciousness, nor soul, nor will, nor truth: all are fictions that are of no use. There is no question of "subject and object," but of a particular species of animal that can prosper only through a certain relative *correctness,* above all, *regularity* of its perceptions (so that it can accumulate experience) . . .
> Knowledge works as a *tool* of power. Hence it is plain that it increases with every increase of power . . .
> The meaning of "knowledge": here, as in the case of "good" or "beautiful," the concept is to be regarded in a strict and narrow anthropomorphic and biological sense. In order for a particular species to maintain itself and increase its power, its conception of reality must comprehend enough of the calculable and constant for it to base a scheme of behavior on it. *The utility of preservation,* not some abstract-theoretical need not to be deceived, stands as the motive behind the development of the organs of knowledge . . . they develop in such a way that their observations suffice for our preservation. In other words: the measure of the desire for knowledge depends upon the measure to which the *will to power* grows in a species: a species grasps a certain amount of reality *in order to become master of it, in order to press it into service.*
> the mechanistic concept of *motion* is already a translation of the original process into the *sign language of sight and touch.*
> the concept "atom," the distinction between the "seat of a driving force and the force itself," is a *sign-language derived from our logical-psychical world.*

We cannot change our means of expression at will: it is possible to understand to what extent they are merely semiotic.

The demand for an *adequate mode of expression* is *senseless:* it is of the essence of a language, a means of expression, to express a mere relationship . . . The concept "truth" is *contradictory* . . . The entire domain of "true"[-]"false" applies only to relations, not to an in-itself" . . . *Nonsense:* there is no "essence-in-itself," it is relations that constitute an essence, just as there can be no "knowledge-in-itself." . . . (*KGW,* VIII, 3: 14[122]; *WP,* 480, 625. All ellipses and emphasis are Nietzsche's.)

To close our examination of Nietzsche's account of language, we will investigate what is perhaps Nietzsche's most sustained attempt to deconstruct a philosophical construction that he finds to be a linguistic illusion. This illusion is "[. . .] the seduction of language (and of the fundamental errors of reason that are petrified in it) which conceives and misconceives all effects as conditioned by something that causes effects, by a 'subject,' [. . .]" (*GM,* I, 13). For Nietzsche, as we have seen, words continually lead us astray, and from his investigation into the relation between language and knowledge he concludes that "a philosophical mythology lies concealed in *language* which breaks out again every moment, however careful one may be otherwise" (*WS,* 11). The belief in the subject or ego is a central figure in this mythological constellation, which finds a "firm form in the functions of language and grammar" (*WP,* 631). Nietzsche is careful to distinguish the problem of linguistic illusion with which he is concerned from the "epistemological" opposition of subject and object. These linguistic illusions, Nietzsche argues, are not the consequence of a subject's being confronted with external objects that are then misperceived or mislabeled. Thus he leaves the distinction of subject and object to "the epistemologists, who have become entangled in the snares of grammar (the metaphysics of the people)" (*GS,* 354). Instead, Nietzsche confronts the more fundamental problem of the linguistic illusion giving rise to the belief in the subject itself. This illusion, a "rude fetishism" (*TI,* " 'Reason' in Philosophy," 5), is the result of our "grammatical custom" of positing a doer in addition to the deed.

Nietzsche frequently singles out Descartes as the prime example of the philosopher seduced by this linguistic illusion. Descartes is, in effect, taken in by language:

"There is thinking: therefore there is something that thinks:" this is the upshot of all Descartes' argumentation. But this means positing as "true a priori" our belief in the concept of substance:—that when there is thought there has to be something "that thinks" is simply a formulation of our grammatical custom that adds a doer to every deed. (*WP,* 484; for Nietzsche's critique of Descartes, see also *KGW,* VII, 3: 40[16, 20, 23])

That there is an "I" which thinks, that this ego is the cause of thinking and is known as an "immediate certainty," begs all the metaphysical questions which it

was supposed to have answered (see *BGE*, 16). Far from arriving at an Archimed-
ean point of foundational knowledge that will serve to ground the construction of
Descartes' metaphysical system, the Cartesian belief in the ego as an "immediate
certainty" is nothing but an inference "according to the grammatical habit: 'There
is an activity; every activity requires an agent, consequently —' " (*BGE*, 17).
The subject as an underlying substratum behind action is thus viewed by Nietzsche
to be the consequence of an "eternal grammatical blunder" (*D*, 120).[14] Nietzsche
likens the belief in the subject to the artificial separation of lightning from its
flash, taking the latter for an action, an operation of an underlying neutral
substratum (the subject) called "lightning." He concludes: "But there is no such
substratum; there is no 'being' behind doing, effecting, becoming; 'the doer' is
merely a fiction added to the deed—the deed is everything" (*GM*, I, 13).

The addition of this substratum, as we have seen, is a consequence of our
inability to comprehend the processes of becoming: we set up a word at the
horizon of our knowledge, at the point where our ignorance begins (see *WP*,
482). But in each case of naming, the "thing" named and the "word" itself remain
mere designations that bring us no closer to the "truth." Nietzsche thus continues
to assert, regarding all the epistemological claims drawn from our linguistically
informed thinking, that "we have not got away from the habit into which our
senses and language seduce us. Subject, object, a doer added to the doing, the
doing separated from that which it does: let us not forget that this is mere semiotics
and nothing real" (*WP*, 634).

While we have focused on Nietzsche's de-construction of the subject/ego as a
consequence of the philosopher's entanglement within the nets of language, this
is by no means an isolated example of his strategy of linguistically dismantling
what he views to be a philosophical *construction*. In fact, at one level of analysis,
Nietzsche sees all of the metaphysicians' and epistemologists' "articles of faith"
to be "grammatical blunders." Selecting just a few of the more noteworthy
examples, we find the following:

"thinking": "Thinking," as epistemologists conceive it, simply does not
occur; it is a quite arbitrary fiction, arrived at by selecting one
element from the process and eliminating all the rest, an artificial arrangement for the purpose of intelligibility. (*WP*, 477;
cf. *WP*, 501)

"thing": A "thing" is the sum of its effects, synthetically united by a
concept or image. (*WP*, 551; cf. *WP*, 634) Linguistic means of
expression are useless for expressing "becoming"; it accords
with our inevitable need to preserve ourselves to posit a crude
world of stability, of "things," etc. (*WP*, 715)

"will": Willing seems to me to be above all something *complicated*,
something that is a unit only as a word—and it is precisely in

this one word that the popular prejudice lurks, which has defeated the always inadequate caution of philosophers. (*BGE*, 19; cf. *WP*, 46)

"motion":   Motion is a word, motion is not a cause. (*KGW*, VIII, 3: 14[98]; cf. *WP*, 634, 635)

"cause and effect":   There are neither causes nor effects. Linguistically, we do not know how to rid ourselves of them. (*WP*, 551; cf. *TI*, "The Four Great Errors," 1, 2, 3)

"natural law":   "Regularity" in succession is only a metaphorical expression, *as if* a rule were being followed here; not a fact. In the same way "conformity with a law." (*WP*, 632; cf. *WP*, 634)

"soul":   For, formerly, one believed in "the soul" as one believed in grammar and the grammatical subject: one said "I" is the condition, "think" is the predicate and conditioned—thinking is an activity to which thought *must* supply a subject as cause. (*BGE*, 54)

From this collection of remarks, we can see that Nietzsche's task as the revaluer of all values involves an extended critique of the philosophical articles of faith which are derived from our linguistic situation. In fact, there is evidence that this strategy of linguistic de-construction makes up an essential aspect of the Nietzschean transvaluation:[15]

Language belongs in its origin to the age of the most rudimentary form of psychology: we find ourselves in the midst of a rude fetishism when we call to mind the basic presuppositions of the metaphysics of language [*der Sprach-Metaphysik*]—which is to say, of *reason*. It is *this* which sees everywhere deed and doer; this which believes in will as cause in general; this which believes in the "ego," in the ego as being, in the ego as substance, and which *projects* its belief in the ego-substance on to all things—only thus does it *create* the concept "thing". . . . Being is everywhere thought in, *foisted on*, as cause; it is only from the conception "ego" that there follows, derivatively, the concept "Being". . . . At the beginning stands the great fateful error that the will is something which *produces an effect*—that will is a *faculty*. . . . Today we know it is merely a word. . . . (*TI*, " 'Reason' in Philosophy," 5)

This passage, which reveals "reason," "will," "cause," "effect," "ego," "Being," "substance," and "thing" to be mere words, mere linguistic "fetishes" which correspond to "nothing real," makes clear that the dismantling of metaphysical language will be a necessary task if a transvaluation of values is to be accomplished. Insofar as "we really ought to free ourselves from the seduction of words!" (*BGE*, 16), the overcoming of the metaphysical and substantive presuppositions of language is intimately linked to another of Nietzsche's requirements for the task of transvaluation: the death of God.

It is no more than a moral prejudice that truth is worth more than a mere appearance; [. . .] Indeed, what forces us at all to suppose that there is an essential opposition of "true" and "false?" Is it not sufficient to assume degrees of apparentness and, as it were, lighter and darker shadows and shades of appearance—different *valeurs* to use the language of painters? Why couldn't the world *that concerns us*—be a fiction? And if somebody asked, "but to a fiction there surely belongs an author?"—couldn't one answer simply: *why?* Doesn't this "belongs" perhaps belong to the fiction, too? Is it not permitted to be a bit ironical about the subject no less than the predicate and object? Shouldn't philosophers be permitted to rise above faith in grammar? All due respect for governesses—but hasn't the time come for philosophy to renounce the faith of governesses? (*BGE,* 34)

God, the ultimate foundation of those values requiring revaluation, is revealed to be linguistically derived: God appears as the doer who is added to the deed of the world, the great author to whom philosophers faithfully attribute responsibility for the creation of the cosmological text that we call "world." And so long as we all continue to believe in grammar, in the metaphysical and epistemological presuppositions concealed within language which lead us to attach substantive agents to actions, we will continue to believe in God. This is the thought underlying Nietzsche's cryptic remark in *Twilight* that he "fear[s] we are not getting rid of God because we still believe in grammar" (" 'Reason' in Philosophy," 5). Just as God must die for the *Übermensch* to live and prosper by means of a transvaluation of all values, so too must we suspend our faith in the authority of language if a transvaluation is to be possible.

We shall conclude the examination of Nietzsche's conception of language with his raising this question of authority, of author(ity) and text. This rejection of all authorial/authoritarian privilege as well as the conception of language on which it is based are integral to Nietzsche's interpretive method. Our first task in elaborating this method must be an examination of the two component moments that delineate the boundaries within which Nietzschean interpretation operates. Before proceeding with this task, however, let me raise what would seem to be an obvious question concerning the preceding discussion, namely, what is the status of Nietzsche's own language? Does he simply provide another metaphorical, anthropomorphic expression in his account of the metaphorical nature of language?[16] And if so, what do his metaphors offer that the metaphors of the tradition ("correspondence," "reference," "truth") do not? It seems to me that Nietzsche cannot claim any authority for his language, that is, he cannot privilege his own language by claiming to provide a meta-linguistic (and therefore non-metaphorical) description of philosophical language. Moreover, on a number of occasions, he freely admits that his own discourse is likewise imprisoned within metaphor and interpretation. This is to say, Nietzsche explicitly acknowledges, for example, that "Dionysus" is a "myth," that the "eternal recurrence" is a *"thought of a possibility"* (*KGW,* V, 2: 11[203]), that *"Übermensch"* is a "metaphor" (*WP,* 866), and that the "will to power" is only an interpretation (*BGE,*

22). In making such admissions, Nietzsche reaffirms the conclusions of his analysis of language. This reaffirmation has a positive, therapeutic consequence, however, for in refusing to sanction his own discussion as a "true" or "correct" description of "reality," Nietzsche suggests that a transvaluation of values will be accompanied by a recognition of the universal scope of the activity of interpretation. That is to say, inasmuch as we have no access to "reality" other than through the interpretations and metaphors we impose from our perspectivally-determined situation (see *WP*, 600), the hope for an "accurate" or "true" description of this "reality" must be given up. Nietzsche's critique of philosophical language has been directed toward precisely this end, for in freeing the activity of interpretation from the dogmatic, life-negating constraints of divine and linguistic authority, Nietzsche's deconstruction of epistemology *opens* the text of becoming to an unending, pluralistic play of interpretation. To appraise the contribution which this pluralistic approach might make to the contemporary dialogue concerning hermeneutics and theories of interpretation, we will need to examine what is entailed by Nietzsche's replacing "truth" with "affirmation of life" as the standard according to which interpretations are judged. Before undertaking this examination, we must first clarify the two themes that guide Nietzsche's interpretive practices.

Chapter 6

Perspectivism, Philology, Truth

Speaking seriously, there are good reasons why all philosophical dogmatizing, however solemn and definitive its airs used to be, may nevertheless have been no more than a noble childishness and tyronism. And perhaps the time is at hand when it will be comprehended again and again how little used to be sufficient to furnish the cornerstone for such sublime and unconditional philosophers' edifices as the dogmatists have built so far,—any old popular superstition from time immemorial (like the soul superstition which, in the form of the subject and ego superstition, has not even yet ceased to do mischief), some play on words perhaps, a seduction by grammar, or an audacious generalization of very narrow, very personal, very human, all-too-human facts.
—Beyond Good and Evil, Pr.

It is not for nothing that I have been a philologist, perhaps I am a philologist still [. . .] for philology is that venerable art which demands of its votaries one thing above all: to go aside, to take time, to become still, to become slow—it is a goldsmith's art and connoisseurship of the word *which has nothing but delicate, cautious work to do and achieves nothing if it does not achieve it* lento. *But for precisely this reason it is more necessary than ever today, by precisely this means does it entice and enchant us the most, in the midst of an age of "work," that is to say, of hurry, of indecent and perspiring haste, which wants to "get everything done" at once, including every old or new book:—this art does not so easily get anything done, it teaches to read* well, *that is to say, to read slowly, deeply, looking cautiously before and aft, with reservations, with doors left open, with delicate eyes and fingers[. . . .]*
—Daybreak, Pr., 5

The omnipresent references to both the processes and products of interpretation make it tempting to view Nietzsche as a precursor of modern hermeneutics.[1] However, the difficulties involved in a systematic exposition of Nietzsche's conception of interpretation are considerable, insofar as he refrained from providing anything even approximating a set of methodological guidelines for judging between competing interpretations. In an effort to organize his varied remarks on interpretation, we shall focus on two themes articulated in various ways throughout the entirety of his writings. These themes are perspectivism and philology and, as our examination unfolds, each will appear to place certain demands on the process of interpretation. These demands give rise to differing conceptions of "truth," and Nietzsche's apparent inconsistency regarding the status of "truth"

144

will emerge in part as a consequence of the methodological antinomy of perspectivism and philology. Moreover, the tension between these two interpretive themes will be shown to anticipate the competing tendencies toward relativism and dogmatism that plague modern hermeneutics. In examining these two themes, we will question whether we must view the opposition between perspectivism and philology as one that confronts the interpreter with the task of reducing or subordinating one theme to the other in order to remove the apparent contradiction within Nietzsche's thinking which their mutual affirmation seems to entail.

Stated in its most concise form, perspectivism is the Nietzschean doctrine that asserts there are no uninterpreted "facts" or "truth." Before we can elaborate on the specific claims of this doctrine, however, warnings against two possible misunderstandings of what is to follow are in order. The first has to do with the scope of the Nietzschean doctrine of perspectivism. It is not uncommon to find Nietzsche's doctrine of perspectivism criticized for being paradoxical, nihilistic, or even solipsistic.[2] These judgments arise from a common misunderstanding of perspectivism, namely that perspectivism is put forth as an ontological position. It is a basic presupposition of the following investigation that Nietzsche's remarks concerning perspectives delineate a position whose domain is "epistemic" rather than "ontological." This is not to say, however, that perspectivism is offered as an epistem*ological* position in the restricted sense of providing a "*theory* of knowledge" rather than a "theory of being." Instead, the designation as "epistemic" means to imply that the perspectival account concerns what we can "know" and not what there "is." In other words, Nietzsche's perspectival account does not provide a theory at all; it is a rhetorical strategy[3] that offers an alternative to the traditional epistemological conception of knowledge as the possession of some stable, eternal "entities," whether these be considered "truths," "facts," "meanings," "propositions," or whatever. As we shall see, Nietzsche views these "entities" as beyond the limits of human comprehension, and, whether or not they exist (a question Nietzsche regards as an "idle hypothesis" [see *WP*, 560]), he concludes that we are surely incapable of "knowing" them.

The second caveat concerns the relationship between "perspective" ("*Perspektive*") and "interpretation" ("*Auslegung*," "*Interpretation*," "*Ausdeutung*") in Nietzsche's writings. Although commentators frequently regard these terms as synonymous and Nietzsche himself at times remarks that the doctrine of perspectivism defines everything as interpretation, this hasty identification of perspective and interpretation seems to me to be unfortunate. To help clarify this confusion, I will distinguish between the two terms in the following way: an interpretation emerges in the act of organizing, in one way or another, a collection of diverse perspectives. Thus, whereas our perspectives are, in a certain sense which remains to be specified, "determined" and outside our control, the *form* which we give to these perspectives, the interpretation which we as will to power construct with them, is not. On a certain level, this distinction will reveal itself to be merely heuristic, inasmuch as perspectives never "exist" outside of some form-giving interpretive matrix and this interpretive matrix is always already perspectivally conditioned. Nevertheless, the utility of this distinction will become clear as our examination of Nietzsche unfolds.

In part, my thesis is that in providing a description of what and how we can "know," perspectivism offers an alternative to traditional epistemology. That is to say, Nietzsche puts forward the doctrine of perspectivism as an "empirical" conclusion regarding human finitude: because human beings are situated bodily at a particular point in space, time, and history, their capacity for knowledge is inevitably limited. Being so situated, human beings are not capable of the "objective," "disinterested" observation of "reality" demanded by the traditional account of knowledge. Rather, there are only evaluations made from a particular perspective (see *WP,* 259, 567). Nietzsche distinguishes three basic types of perspective, each placing certain limits on what human beings can know, and we can classify these types under the headings "physiological," "instinctual," and "socio-historical."

The most pervasive perspectives in the Nietzschean account are those of physiology. In this group, one can classify those perspectives determined by our sensory apparatus in particular and human physiology in general. For Nietzsche, there is no escape from the perspectives which our physiology imposes on us, and these perspectives must be considered in any adequate account of what we can know. In *Daybreak,* in a paragraph entitled "In Prison," Nietzsche writes:

> My eyes, however strong or weak they may be, can see only a certain distance, and it is within the space encompassed by this distance that I live and move, the line of this horizon constitutes my immediate fate, in great things and small, from which I cannot escape. Around every being there is described a similar concentric circle, which has a mid-point and is peculiar to him. Our ears enclose us within a comparable circle, and so does our sense of touch. Now, it is by these horizons, within which each of us encloses his senses as if behind prison walls, that we *measure* the world, we say that this is near and that far, this is big and that small, this is hard and that soft: this measuring we call sensation—and it is all of it an error! According to the average quantity of experiences and excitations possible to us at any particular point of time one measures one's life as being short or long, poor or rich, full or empty: and according to the average human life one measures that of all other creatures— all of it an error! If our eyes were a hundredfold sharper, man would appear to us tremendously tall; it is possible, indeed, to imagine organs by virtue of which he would be felt as immeasurable. On the other hand, organs could be so constituted that whole solar systems were viewed contracted and packed together like a single cell: and to beings of an opposite constitution a cell of the human body could present itself, in motion, construction and harmony, as a solar system. The habits of our senses have woven us into lies and deception of sensation: these again are the basis of all our judgments and "knowledge"—there is absolutely no escape, no backway or bypath into the *real world!* We sit within our net, we spiders, and whatever we may catch in it, we can catch nothing at all except that which allows itself to be caught in precisely *our* net. (*D,* 117)

Elsewhere, he writes regarding the evaluative nature of sense perception that "we have senses for only a selection of perceptions—those with which we have to concern ourselves in order to preserve ourselves. *Consciousness is present only to the extent that consciousness is useful.* It cannot be doubted that all sense perceptions are permeated with *value judgments*" (*WP*, 505). Because "perception" (*Wahrnehmen*) is essentially a "taking-as-true" (*als-Wahr-nehmen*), we cannot escape the evaluative dimension through some recourse to physiology. Nor can we divorce our more explicitly "evaluative" judgments from our physiological limitations, as Nietzsche makes clear in *The Gay Science* when, in speaking of the changes in taste regarding questions of aesthetics or morality, he writes that "aesthetic and moral judgments are among these 'subtle nuances' of the *physis*" (*GS*, 39). The consequence of this interpretation for the traditional account of knowledge is clear:

> Never to be able to see into things out of any other eyes but *these*? And what uncountable kinds of beings may there not be whose organs are better equipped for knowledge! What will mankind have come to know at the end of all their knowledge?—their organs! And that perhaps means: the impossibility of knowledge! (*D*, 483)

Our apprehension of the world, because it is restricted by our physiological and sensory capabilities, can provide us with nothing other than very limited perspectives on the world. The conclusion Nietzsche draws from his various expressions of physiological perspectivism vis-à-vis the status of knowledge remains the same: we simply lack any organ for "knowledge" or "truth" about the "world" (see *GS*, 354).

In addition to these unavoidable physiological perspectives, what we can know is also conditioned by a collection of impulses which can be loosely grouped as "instinctual." In this grouping, we can situate Nietzsche's remarks on drives, needs, and affects as well as the instincts proper, insofar as these impulses all play a role in determining what we "know." For Nietzsche, all our judgments have a prehistory in our "instincts, likes, dislikes, experiences and lack of experiences" (*GS*, 335). Whereas knowledge had been traditionally opposed to the instinctual impulses, Nietzsche views knowledge as "actually nothing but a *certain behavior of the instincts toward one another*" (*GS*, 333). Ultimately, this "certain behavior" is the struggle for mastery: each instinct has its own perspective which it seeks to establish as a norm for conceptual judgment. Nietzsche writes:

> It is our needs *that interpret the world;* our drives and their For and Against. Every drive is a kind of lust to rule; each one has its perspective that it would like to compel all the other drives to accept as a norm. (*WP*, 481)

At the center of this instinctual *bellum omnium contra omnes* stands the instinct for self-preservation. Cognizant of the existential conditions necessary for preservation, our instincts adopt a perspective on the world that will facilitate our preservation:

> Our empirical world would be determined by the instincts of self-preservation even as regards the limits of its knowledge: we would regard as true, good, valuable that which serves the preservation of the species . . . (*WP*, 583A)

In Nietzsche's account of what we can know, there appears yet a third class of perspectives—the "socio-historical." These are the perspectives determined by the individual's personal history as well as the general socio-historical context in which the individual is situated. This is to say, the scope of what we can "know" is limited by our own individual experiences along with the historically conditioned and socially accepted standards of what is to count as "true" or "real." For Nietzsche, what one has experienced conditions what one can understand: "Ultimately, nobody can get more out of things, including books, than he already knows. For what one lacks access to from experience one will have no ear" (*EH*, III, 1; cf. *EH*, I, 1; *D*, 119). Because our experiences are ultimately individual and unique, our knowledge of the world must reflect this inevitable limitation: "I believe that everyone must have his own individual opinion concerning everything about which an opinion is possible, because he himself is an individual, unique thing, which adopts towards all other things a new attitude which has never been adopted before" (*HAH*, 286). Thus, "even under the hands of the greatest painter-thinkers, there arise only pictures and miniatures *out of one* life, namely their own life—and indeed nothing else is even possible" (*AOM*, 19). We are, in Nietzsche's view, "always in our own company" and can see and hear only what we have eyes and ears for: "Whatever in nature and in history is of my own kind, speaks to me, spurs me on, and comforts me —: the rest I do not hear or forget right away" (*GS*, 166).

The uniqueness of our perspective is not asserted at the expense of historical and social influences, however. Rather, these socio-historical factors reinforce Nietzsche's conclusion: "You are still burdened with those estimates of things that have their origin in the passions and loves of former centuries" (*GS*, 57). In the preceding chapter, we saw that Nietzsche emphasized the philosopher's "idiosyncratic" lack of historical sense and inattention to becoming as it related to the conceptual mummifications of language (cf. *TI*, " 'Reason' in Philosophy," 1). The lack of historical sense has a similar consequence with respect to the philosopher's faith in eternal and unchanging truths, as Nietzsche counters that only historically limited perspectives are possible:

> *Family failing of philosophers.*—All philosophers have the common failing of starting out from man as he is now and thinking they can reach their goal through an analysis of him. They involuntarily think of "man" as an *aeterna veritas*, as something that remains constant in the midst of all flux, as a sure measure of things. Everything the

philosopher has declared about man is, however, at bottom no more than a testimony as to the man of a *very limited* period of time. Lack of historical sense is the family failing of all philosophers; many, without being aware of it, even take the most recent manifestation of man, such as has arisen under the impress of certain religions, even certain political events, as the fixed form from which one has to start out. They will not learn that man has become, that the faculty of knowledge has become; while some of them would have it that the whole world is spun out of this faculty of knowledge.—Now, everything *essential* in the development of mankind took place in primeval times, long before the 4,000 years we more or less know about; during these years mankind may well not have altered very much. But the philosopher here sees "instincts" in man as he now is and assumes that these belong to the unalterable facts of mankind, and to that extent could provide a key to the understanding of the world in general: the whole of teleology is constructed by speaking of the man of the last four millennia as of an *eternal* man towards whom all things in the world have had a natural relationship from the time he began. But everything has become: there are *no eternal facts,* just as there are no absolute truths.— Consequently what is needed from now on is *historical* philosophizing, and with it the virtue of modesty. (*HAH,* 2)

This is to say, not only are there no fixed and stable truths to extract from the process of becoming, but the observer, by virtue of being situated within this process, must adopt a limited and historically circumscribed perspective on the process itself. What philosophers have called human "instincts" are themselves just these valuating structures, historically sedimented and incorporated into "man" as a part of his "essence."

From this brief typology, we can see how perspectivism arises in part in response to the overly simplistic concept of knowledge that has animated the philosophical tradition. In this typological analysis, moreover, three basic characteristics of perspectives in general are revealed: perspectives are inevitable, indispensable, and "false." Because of our physiological, instinctual, and historical limitations, we cannot avoid adopting a particular and, to a certain extent, idiosyncratic perspective on the world:

How far the perspective character of existence extends or indeed whether existence has any other character than this; whether existence without interpretation, without "sense," does not become "nonsense"; whether, on the other hand, all existence is not essentially actively engaged in *interpretation* [*ob, andrerseits, nicht alles Dasein essentiell ein* auslegendes *Dasein ist*]—that cannot be decided even by the most industrious and most scrupulously conscientious analysis and self-examination of the intellect; for in the course of this analysis the human intellect cannot avoid seeing itself in its own perspectives, and *only* in these. We cannot look around our own corner: it is a hopeless curiosity that wants to know what other kinds of intellects and perspectives there *might* be[. . . .] (*GS,* 374)

In addition to noting the inevitability of perspectives, Nietzsche goes on to point out their indispensability. Perspectives are what make the world manageable, and the perspectives adopted are viewed as necessary for preservation. Yet a perspective's indispensability will not serve as a criterion for the truth of that perspective. Regarding the perspective of the ego, Nietzsche comments that "[h]owever habitual and indispensable this fiction may have become by now,— *that* alone proves nothing against its imaginary origin: a belief can be a condition of life and *nonetheless* be *false*" (*WP,* 483). While the possible falsity of a necessary perspective leads the dogmatic philosopher to nihilistic despair, Nietzsche accepts and affirms the necessity of falsity in the cheerful spirit of the *gaya scienza:*

> The falseness of a judgment is for us not necessarily an objection to a judgment; in this respect our new language may sound strangest. The question is to what extent it is life-promoting, life-preserving, species-preserving, perhaps even species-cultivating. And we are fundamentally inclined to claim that the falsest judgments (which include the synthetic judgments a priori) are the most indispensable for us; that without accepting the fictions of logic, without measuring reality against the purely invented world of the unconditional and self-identical, without a constant falsification of the world by means of numbers, man could not live—that renouncing false judgments would mean renouncing life and a denial of life. To recognize untruth as a condition of life—that certainly means resisting accustomed value feelings in a dangerous way; and a philosophy that risks this would by that token alone place itself beyond good and evil. (*BGE,* 4; cf. *WP,* 602)

By subordinating the question of a perspective's being "true" or "false" to that of its "value for life" as the criterion upon which perspectival evaluations are to be judged, the way is cleared for Nietzsche to put the perspectival doctrine to work in the project of the transvaluation of values.

Within the project of transvaluing previous values, perspectivism functions in two important ways. The first of these is critical: the perspectival account of knowledge is used to deconstruct the traditionally privileged objects of epistemology. This is to say, the justification for Nietzsche's critique of "fact," "truth," "meaning," "reality," etc., follows from his insights into the perspectival character of knowledge. Throughout the Nietzschean text, one finds statements denying the existence of these privileged epistemic objects: "[. . .] there is no 'truth' " (*WP,* 616), "There are no facts [. . .]" (*WP,* 604), "Is meaning not necessarily relative meaning and perspective?" (*WP,* 590), "There is no 'reality' [. . .]" (*GS,* 57). Upon examination, one notes that such remarks recur in similar contexts. In each case, what is rejected is the *privileged* epistemic status accorded to these objects, their "givenness."[4] And in each case, the grounds for rejecting the privileged status of the "given" epistemic object is the pervasiveness of perspective and interpretation, that is, perspectives and interpretation are already at work prior to the judgment that something is a "fact" or a "truth" or a "meaning" or "real."

Looking first at Nietzsche's denial of "facts," we find the following remark:

Against positivism, which halts at phenomena—"There are only *facts*"—I would say: No, facts are precisely what there is not, only interpretations. We cannot establish any fact "in itself": perhaps it is folly to want to do such a thing. (*WP*, 481)

The folly involved in speaking of a "fact-in-itself" is that the designation of something as a "fact" already involves an imposition of value, that is, an evaluation from a particular perspective—an interpretation: "There are no 'facts-in-themselves,' *for a sense must always be projected into them before they can be facts*" (*WP*, 556). To label something as a "fact" is to group together in relative isolation a set of perspectives taken from the "continuous stream" of becoming (see *WS*, 11). As such, facts are not given but invented. In a section from *Daybreak* entitled "*Facta! Yes, Facta Ficta!*" ("*Facts! Yes, Invented Facts!*"), Nietzsche makes this point explicit with respect to historical "facts":

A historian has to do, not with what actually happened, but only with events supposed to have happened: for only the latter have *produced an effect*. Likewise only with supposed heroes. His theme, so-called world history, is opinions about supposed actions and their supposed motives, which in turn give rise to further opinions and actions, the reality of which is however at once vaporised again and produces an *effect* only as vapor—a continual generation and pregnancy of phantoms over the impenetrable mist of unfathomable reality. All historians speak of things which have never existed except in imagination. (*D*, 307)

Nietzsche reiterates this judgment with respect to both "meaning" and "reality." What we call "reality" is physiologically determined by our sensory apparatus directed by the perspectives of our needs:

One should not understand this *compulsion* to construct concepts, species, forms, purposes, laws—"a world of identical cases"—as if they enabled us to fix the *real world* [*wahre Welt*]; but as a compulsion to arrange a world for ourselves in which our existence is made possible:—we thereby create a world which is calculable, simplified, comprehensive, etc., for us.

This same compulsion exists in the *sense activities* that support reason,—by simplification, coarsening, emphasizing, and elaborating, upon which all "recognition," all ability to make oneself intelligible rests. Our *needs* have made our senses so precise that the "same apparent world" always reappears and has thus acquired the semblance of *reality*. (*WP*, 521)

Thus, the attribution of "reality" to something is merely another human contribution to the world of becoming which, if we are to accept the traditional grounds for such an attribution, appears unjustifiable. To the "sober realists" whose "love of 'reality' " has led them to proclaim that "the world really is as it appears," Nietzsche writes:

Every feeling and sensation contains a piece of this old love; and some fantasy, some prejudice, some unreason, some ignorance, some fear, and ever so much else has contributed to it. That mountain there! That cloud there! What is "real" in that? Subtract the phantasm and every human *contribution* from it, my sober friends! If you *can!* If you can forget your descent, your past, your training—all of your humanity and animality. There is no "reality" for us—not for you either, my sober friends[. . . .] (*GS*, 57)

In a similar fashion, "meaning" appears as an anthropomorphic contribution, an artificial limit imposed upon the world so as to make it more manageable. In the *Nachlass,* we find the following "definition" of perspectivism: "In so far as the word 'knowledge' has any meaning, the world is knowable; but it is *interpretable* otherwise, it has no meaning behind it, but countless meanings.— 'Perspectivism' " (*WP*, 481). The quest for a univocal meaning is another of the dogmatic philosopher's pipedreams, for there is no meaning in the in-itself. Rather, "meaning" is one of the values we interpret into things ("*in die Dinge hinein interpretirt*" [*WP*, 590]). As such, all meaning is relative and perspectival, which for Nietzsche is to say nothing more than that it is a manifestation of will to power as the creative force of interpretive imposition (see *WP*, 589, 590).

In the background of Nietzsche's critique of "meaning," "reality," and "fact" stands "truth," for the "will to truth" and faith in the "true world" have led to the imposition of these other values upon becoming. "Truth" is the epistemic designation of ultimate privilege, the highest sanction to be bestowed upon a belief. Having been baptized "True," a belief is no longer subject to question, revision, or reinterpretation. Not surprisingly, therefore, a deconstruction of "Truth" which returns it to the field of interpretive play is of paramount importance in Nietzsche's perspectival account. In *On The Genealogy of Morals,* Nietzsche concludes his polemic against the ascetic ideal with the raising of a "*new problem*": that of the *value* of truth. The concluding sections of the *Genealogy* reveal that Nietzsche has been attacking not so much the particular truths affirmed by the ascetic ideal as the privileged status, the "overestimation," of the value of truth itself (*GM*, III, 25). The constraint of asceticism results from the "*faith in the ascetic ideal itself* [. . .]—it is the faith in a *metaphysical* value, the absolute value of *truth*" (*GM*, III, 24). Against this faith the polemic of the *Genealogy* has rallied, and Nietzsche defines his future task with the following proclamation: "The will to truth requires a critique—let us define our own task—the value of truth must for once be experimentally *called into question*" (*GM*, III, 24).

Upon questioning, the will to truth reveals itself to be a sign of weakness, a drive in search of necessary conditions for the preservation of a *decadent* will to power: "The will to truth is a *making* firm, a *making* true and durable, an abolition of the false character of things, a reinterpretation of it into beings" (*WP*, 552). In the *Nachlass,* we find the following lexical excursion regarding "perception": "What then is 'perception'? *Taking*-something-*as-true:* Saying yes to something"

(*KGW*, VII, 3: 34[132]: "*Was ist denn 'wahrnehmen'*? *Etwas*-als-wahr-nehmen: *Ja sagen zu Etwas.*"). What is privileged as "truth" is for Nietzsche a name for "*the kind of error* without which a certain species of life could not live" (*WP*, 493). In his view of truth as an error necessary for a certain species' preservation, we can clearly see the link between Nietzsche's denial of the privileged status of truth and the doctrine of perspectivism:

> That the *value of the world* lies in our interpretation (— that other interpretations than merely human ones are perhaps somewhere possible —); that previous interpretations have been perspective valuations by virtue of which we can survive in life, i.e., in the will to power, for the growth of power; that every *elevation of man* brings with it the overcoming of narrower interpretations; that every strengthening and increase of power opens up new perspectives and means believing in new horizons—this idea permeates my writings. The world *with which we are concerned* is false, i.e., is not a fact but a fable and approximation on the basis of a meager sum of observations; it is "in flux," as something in a state of becoming, as a falsehood always changing but never getting near the truth: for—there is no "truth." (*WP*, 616)

This link is crucial in terms of understanding an important ambiguity regarding Nietzsche's position vis-à-vis truth. This ambiguity concerns Nietzsche's denial of truth while at the same time proclaiming a multiplicity of truths. To understand this ambiguity in a way that does not fall victim to the charge of self-reference, one must attend to the rhetorical strategies that guide Nietzsche's introduction of "truth" into his texts. Sometimes "truth" designates for Nietzsche the privileged object of epistemology (the ascetic faith in absolute Truth) and sometimes it designates a perspective necessary for survival. Nietzsche often uses the latter designation so as to demystify the former: "There are many kinds of eyes. Even the sphinx has eyes—and consequently there are many kinds of 'truths,' and consequently there is no truth" (*WP*, 540).

One should not assume from such remarks, however, that Nietzsche is asserting a hard and fast opposition between the epistemologist's use of "truth" and his own use of "perspective" as an individual "truth" necessary for self-preservation. In the end, all of these "truths" are themselves only perspectives. To understand Nietzsche's distinction between Truth and truths as well as his view of the "falsity" of both truths and perspectives, one must attend to the strategic use of the traditional epistemological concept of "Truth" within Nietzsche's effort to deconstruct this concept. When Nietzsche speaks of Truth in the singular, he is referring to the Platonic-Kantian tradition's view of Truth as a single, univocal, eternal, immutable relation of correspondence. Thus, in saying that "perspectives are necessarily false," Nietzsche indicates that if we retain the epistemological criteria of truth as adequate correspondence (*adequatio*), we must conclude that everything we apprehend perspectivally (i.e., *all* our "knowledge") is *false according to these epistemological criteria.* Nietzsche's strategy in proclaiming the falsity of perspectives is clear: he wants us to reject the traditional epistemolog-ical conception of truth, and he makes this point by confronting the epistemologist with the following paradox: if we accept the epistemological standard of truth, then we must provisionally assert that all these "truths" are erroneous: " 'Truth': this, according to my way of thinking, does not necessarily denote the antithesis of error, but in the most fundamental cases only the posture of various errors in relation to one another" (*WP*, 535).

The same rhetorical strategy operates in his claim that a multiplicity of truths leads to the conclusion that there is no Truth: the assertion of a multiplicity of truth*s* effectively deconstructs the epistemological standard of truth as single and univocal. Whereas Nietzsche wants ultimately to remove the *ideal* of truth from his perspectival account (cf. *CW*, Epilogue: "The concepts 'true' and 'untrue' have, it seems to me, no meaning in optics. —"), he continues to confront those believers in Truth with the paradoxes of " 'truths' but no Truth" and the " 'falsity' of truths/perspectives" in an effort to awaken them from their dogmatic slumber to the joys of creative, interpretive play:

> "Truth" is therefore not something there, that might be found or discovered—but something *that must be created* and that gives a name to a *process*, or rather to a will to overcome that has in itself no end—introducing truth, as a *processus in infinitum*, an *active determining—not* a becoming-conscious of something [that] is "in itself" firm and determined. It is a word for the "will to power". (*WP*, 552)

There is an opposition at the heart of Nietzsche's doctrine of perspectivism, but it is not the opposition between truth and perspective. Rather, Nietzsche strives to develop the opposition between the weak, decadent will to power's acceptance of the "given" *as true,* and the strong, masterful will to power's interpretive creativity. The strategic development of this opposition appears in each of the Nietzschean deconstructions just examined. In each case, the privi-leged status of the given epistemic object is revealed to rest upon an already effected interpretation. For Nietzsche, what things are like before our interpretive appropriation, i.e., what things are like *in themselves,* is an "idle hypothesis" insofar as it presupposes that interpretation and perspective are not essential (see *WP*, 560):

> A "thing-in-itself" just as perverse as a "sense-in-itself," a "meaning-in-itself." There are no "facts-in-themselves," *for a sense must always be projected into them before there can be "facts."*
> The question "what is that?" is an *imposition of meaning [Sinn-Setzung]* from some other viewpoint. "Essence," the "essential nature," is something perspectival and already presupposes a multiplicity. At the bottom of it there always lies "what is that for *me?*" (for us, for all that lives, etc.) (*WP*, 556)

This is to say, there is no "in-itself" that is *given* to disinterested appropriation, as the dogmatic Platonic-Kantian-Christian metaphysical and epistemological tradition has presupposed. Rather, there are only perspectivally informed interpretations of limited scope and value.

This conclusion leads us to the second, *affirmative* function of perspectivism within the Nietzschean project. Removing the privileged status of the given ("truth," the "in-itself"), clears the way for the creative play of interpretation. Whereas truth stood as a limit which discouraged individuals from moving beyond its borders, the absence of truth's limitations invites us to explore new domains of creative possibilities. It is toward opening these interpretive possibilities that Nietzsche traces the genealogy of the "true world" to a consequence of the inability to create within the flux of becoming:

> Man seeks "the truth": a world that is not self-contradictory, not deceptive, does not change, a *true* world—a world in which one does not suffer; contradiction, deception, change—causes of suffering! He does not doubt that a world as it ought to be exists; he would like to seek out the road to it. [. . .]
>
> The belief that the world as it ought to be *is*, really exists, is a belief of the unproductive who do *not desire to create a world* as it ought to be. They posit it as already available, they seek ways and means of reaching it.—"Will to *truth*"—*as the impotence of the will to create. (WP, 585A)*

For Nietzsche, the dogmatic "will to truth" and "desire for certainty" are harmful and symptoms of decadence; they rob existence of the "marvelous uncertainty and rich ambiguity" (*GS*, 2) which permit the production of fresh interpretations. He confesses to a "profound aversion to reposing once and for all in any one total view of the world [. . . and refuses] to be deprived of the stimulus of the enigmatic" (*WP*, 470). The doctrine of perspectivism is directed in part toward restoring the stimulating enigma and ambiguity of existence. The world holds no single, univocal truth, and our cognitive methods should reflect this situation (cf. *WP*, 600). An aphorism from *The Wanderer and His Shadow* affirms the value of adopting different perspectives in the following way:

> *Saying Two Ways.*—It is good to express a thing consecutively in two ways and thus give to it a right and left foot. Truth can indeed stand on one leg; but with two she will walk and travel around [*wird sie gehen und herumkommen*]. (*WS*, 13)

The restoration of the world's enigmatic character and the ability to wield a multiplicity of perspectives when confronting this enigma are affirmed by Nietzsche to be signs of strength, as his discussion of the *positive* consequences of nihilism makes clear. The presupposition of the hypothesis of nihilism is

> That there is no truth, that there is no absolute nature of things nor a "thing-in-itself"

— this, too, is merely nihilism, and *even the most extreme* [nihilism]. It places the value of things precisely in the lack of any reality corresponding to these values and in their being merely a symptom of strength on the part of the value-positers, a simplification for the *sake of life.* (*WP*, 13)

Because values and the capacity for changes in values are both symptoms or signs of the level of power of those positing the values, nihilism stands as a "partly destructive, partly ironic" ideal of the highest degree of powerfulness and the over-richest life (*WP*, 14). Insofar as all belief is a mere *"holding-for-true [Für-wahr-halten]*,"

The most extreme form of nihilism would be the view that *every* belief, every holding-for-true, is necessarily false: *because there simply is no* **true world.** Thus: a *perspectival appearance* whose origin lies in us (in so far as we continually *need* a narrower, abbreviated, simplified world).

— that it is the **measure of strength** to what extent we can admit to ourselves, without perishing, the *semblance [Scheinbarkeit]*, the necessity of lies.

To this extent, nihilism, as the **denial** *of a truthful world, of being, might be a divine way of thinking:—*(*WP*, 15)

As such, Nietzsche concludes that "[i]t is a measure of the degree of *strength of will* to what extent one can do without *meaning* in things, to what extent one can endure to live in a meaningless world *because one organizes a small portion of it oneself*" (*WP*, 585A).

It is in the context of this affirmation of the value of a multiplicity of perspectives and the creative interpretive possibilities this multiplicity entails that the optical metaphor, Nietzsche's most pervasive perspectival metaphor, comes forth most clearly. His call for the multiplication of perspectives is a call for optical experimentalism, for viewing the world with as many eyes as possible: "Problem: *to see* things *as they are! Means:* to be able to see them from a hundred eyes, from *many* persons" (*KGW*, V, 2: 11[65]). Of *The Birth of Tragedy*, Nietzsche writes that its task was *"to look at science under the optics of the artist, but at art under that of life. . . ."* (*BT*, SC2). The multiplicity and creativity of optical experimentalism is esteemed for not prematurely foreclosing life's "rich ambiguity," and the results of this optical experimentation are judged according to whether they creatively enhance or impoverish this ambiguity which *is* life. Against the fixed and limited methods directed by the will to truth, Nietzsche calls for a new ideal: "intellectual nomadism" (*AOM*, 211).[5] As thinkers, we are, as it were, adventurers "in the midst of the ocean of becoming" (*D*, 314), and because no *single* method is sufficient for knowledge of becoming,

We have to tackle things experimentally, now angry with them and now kind, and be successively just, passionate and cold with them. One person addresses things as a policeman, a second as a father-confessor, a third as an inquisitive wanderer.

Something can be wrung from them now with sympathy, now with force; reverence for their secrets will take one person forwards, indiscretion and roguishness in revealing their secrets will do the same for another. We investigators are, like all conquerors, discoverers, seafarers, adventurers, of an audacious morality and must reconcile ourselves to being considered on the whole evil. (*D*, 432)

The ability to multiply and experiment with a plurality of perspectives thus opposes the philosophical dogmatism which endeavors to acquire *one* set of "truths" for all situations and events of life (cf. *HAH*, 618). About philosophical dogmatism, Nietzsche remarks that perhaps the time has come to comprehend

how little used to be sufficient to furnish the cornerstone for such sublime and unconditional philosophers' edifices as the dogmatists have built so far,—any old popular superstition from time immemorial (like the soul superstition which, in the form of the subject and ego superstition, has not even yet ceased to do mischief), some play on words perhaps, a seduction by grammar, or an audacious generalization of very narrow, very personal, very human, all-too-human facts. (*BGE*, Pr.)

The error which the dogmatist makes is not so much substantive, in that he arrives at the wrong truth, but *methodological,* in that he denies perspective, "the basic condition of all life" (*BGE*, Pr.). This same methodological error of dogmatically narrowing perspective and proclaiming one perspective as "true" while denying the legitimacy of all others is the focus of Nietzsche's critique of both morality (see *BGE*, 188) and Christianity (see *A*, 9). In each case, Nietzsche views the narrowing of perspective and the refusal to experiment with optics as a sign of weakness: "[t]he greater the impulse toward unity, the more firmly may one conclude that weakness is present; the greater the impulse towards variety, differentiation, inner decay, the more force is present" (*WP*, 655). If there is a criterion by which to judge perspectives, it is not their "truth" or "falsity" insofar as, for Nietzsche, "the concepts 'true' and 'untrue' have [. . .] no meaning in optics" (*CW*, Epilogue). As ways of seeing, morality and Christianity are "disease(s) of the eye [. . .] immune to reasons and refutations" (*CW*, Epilogue). But while immune to refutation, they are not immune from critique; and the grounds for the Nietzschean critique is their denial of perspectival multiplicity and their impoverishment of will to power as interpretive force which this denial reflects: "that every *elevation of man* brings with it the overcoming of narrower interpretations; that every strengthening and increase of power opens up new perspectives and means believing in new horizons—this idea permeates my writings" (*WP*, 616).

While Nietzsche remarks that "[e]very thinker paints his world in fewer colors than *are actually there*" (*D*, 426), he advises that we must nevertheless resist

the ridiculous immodesty that would be involved in decreeing from our corner that perspectives are permitted only from this corner. Rather has the world become "infinite" for us all over again, inasmuch as we cannot reject the possibility that *it may include infinite interpretations*. (*GS,* 374)

Once again, the criterion of multiplicity comes forth: insofar as there is "no limit to the ways in which the world can be interpreted, [. . .] the plurality of interpretations [is] a sign of strength" (*WP,* 600).

The immediate consequence of affirming a multiplicity of perspectives is a transvaluation of the "concept" of "objectivity." For Nietzsche, the "myth" of objectivity, of objects that "paint or photograph themselves by their own activity on a purely passive medium," is an illusion (*H,* 6). He continues: "But it is only a superstition to say that the picture given to such a man by the object really shows the truth of things." The objective apprehension of truth is not only a myth, however; it is a "bad" myth, for one forgets that the moment of apprehension is a *creative* moment, a moment of spontaneous artistic "composition." To overcome the inhibiting consequences of this bad myth, Nietzsche creates a new myth of "objectivity." Objectivity will no longer be understood

as "contemplation without interest" (which is a nonsensical absurdity), but as the ability *to control* one's Pro and Con and to dispose of them, so that one knows how to employ a variety of perspectives and affective interpretations in the service of knowledge. (*GM,* III, 12)

Accepting the inherent limitation of each individual, perspectival optic, if we are to salvage the myth of objectivity at all it will be retained only in the form of a heuristic ideal, as a call for a "panoptics":

There is *only* a perspective seeing, *only* a perspective "knowing"; and the *more* affects we allow to speak about one thing, the *more* eyes, different eyes, we can use to observe one thing, the more complete will our "concept" of this thing, our "objectivity," be. (*GM,* III, 12)

In opposition to the Kantian "disinterested spectator" as the paradigm of objective judgment, Nietzsche posits Argos (see *AOM,* 223), the hundred-eyed monster who has mastered his pro and con and raised himself to "justice" (*Gerechtigkeit*). As a "genius of justice," the master of interpretation "sets every thing in the best light and observes it carefully from all sides" (*HAH,* 636). This interpretive genius of justice has learned "to grasp the sense of perspective in every value judgment" (*HAH,* Pr., 6) and refuses to restrict its proliferative play. The call to this future "objectivity" thus calls us to combat the injustices perpetrated in the name of Truth that permeate objectivity's checkered past.

You shall learn to grasp the *necessary* injustice in every For and Against, injustice as inseparable from life, life itself as *conditioned* by the sense of perspective and its injustice. You shall above all see with your own eyes where injustice is always at its greatest: where life has developed at its smallest, narrowest, neediest, most incipient and yet cannot avoid taking *itself* as the goal and measure of things and for the sake of its own preservation secretly and meanly and ceaselessly crumbling away and calling into question the higher, greater, richer—you shall see with your own eyes the problem of *order of rank,* and how power and right and spaciousness of perspective grow into the heights together. (*HAH,* Pr., 6)

With this problem of the "order of rank," we return to one of the caveats which prefaced this discussion of perspectivism, namely, the relation between perspective and interpretation. Involved in the process of interpretation is the establishment of an order of rank amongst the multiplicity of competing perspectives. This order of rank gives *form* to the chaos of a potentially infinite number of possible perspectives, and the value of an interpretation is decided on the grounds of the order of rank so imposed and the life-enhancing or life-negating interests that such an imposition reflects for the individual or group who imposes this order. In the *Nachlass,* Nietzsche expresses this point with the help of the following musical metaphor: "*Things touch our chords, but we make a melody out of them*" (*KGW,* V, 1: 6[440]). This capacity to create order where none exists, to legislate the anarchy of one's competing and contradictory perspectives, "[t]o become master of the chaos one is; to compel one's chaos to become form [. . .]" is what Nietzsche calls the "grand style [*grosse Stil*]" (*WP,* 842). And as such, the "grand style" is intimately linked with "grand politics [*grosse Politik*]," conceived as *self*-legislation (Selbst-*Gesetzgebung*), as self-mastery over "the greatest multiplicity of drives, in the relatively greatest strength that can be endured" (*WP,* 966). It is Nietzsche's hope that the transvaluation will result in a new type of person, a type possessed of grand style and politics, who will view themself as an artist views her or his material; who will represent the antithetical character of existence most strongly and courageously; who will allow themselves the greatest multiplicity of contradictory perspectives, while maintaining the formative power of self-dominion and the ability to discipline themselves to wholeness (see e.g., *TI,* "Skirmishes," 49; *WP,* 899, 900, 933, 957, 960, 972, 976).

Nietzsche's metaphor for this new type of person, this grand stylist and grand politician who has mastered the problem of the order of rank is *Dionysus.* It must be remembered that the concept of the Dionysian is transformed in the progression of Nietzsche's thinking, and here I am alluding to the appearance of Dionysus in Nietzsche's later works. In the early works, especially *The Birth of Tragedy,* the Dionysian, as the world of chaos and frenzied rapture, is opposed to the Apollonian world of order, image, and dreams. In the works from *Zarathustra* onward, the Apollonian impulse to order is incorporated into Nietzsche's conception of Dionysus, which no longer opposes Apollo but is now opposed to the Pauline interpretation of the Christ: "Have I been understood?—*Dionysus versus the Crucified*" (*EH,* IV, 9). The Christian imposition of an order of rank *hostile* to life negates our ambiguous and contrary world by affirming a "better," "simpler," less threatening "true" world "beyond" this one. Dionysus, as the grand stylist and grand politician, as Nietzsche's image of *controlled* superabundance, affirms the rich ambiguity and contrariety of the world through his imposition of a life-enhancing order of rank. Dionysus, eternally in danger of being torn to pieces by his own tremendous multiplicity of perspectives, returns eternally to wholeness through his mastering this multiplicity. In our concluding chapter, we will examine this Dionysian self-legislation which gives form to an ever-increasing multiplicity of perspectives, and the role it plays in Nietzsche's judgment regarding the value of interpretive pluralism. First, however, we must examine Nietzsche's view of philology, for his remarks on philology appear to contradict several of the conclusions drawn in the preceding discussion of perspectivism.

Although Nietzsche's early work in philology as a professor at the University of Basel (1869–1879) is often acknowledged, little notice has been taken by Nietzsche's English- and German-speaking commentators of the appearance of philological concerns in his later works.[6] On careful reading, however, one discovers references to philology throughout his writings. Tracing the history of these remarks on philology, three discernible positions emerge. In his earliest works, Nietzsche praises the discipline of philology and the work of certain philologists. In the years following the publication of *The Birth of Tragedy* (1872) and until the mid 1880s, his view changes considerably. During this period, he is extremely critical of what he views to be the narrow-minded, secure, and superfluous world of academic philology. And in his final years, as evidenced by the prefaces of 1885–86 appended to the re-publication of his earlier texts (*BT, HAH, HAH* Bd. II [*AOM* and *WS*], *D, GS,*) as well as the texts and notes that followed 1885, a third *transvalued* conception of philology appears. This transvalued conception of philology as "the art of reading well" will play an important part in the interpretive approach that will be generated from the Nietzschean text. Before we can confront what Nietzsche means by philology as the art of reading well, however, we shall first examine his two earlier positions on philology.

Nietzsche entered the world of classical philology highly recommended. Friedrich Ritschl, his professor at Bonn and Leipzig and one of the foremost philologists of his day, wrote of Nietzsche that "he will one day stand in the front rank of German philology"[7] and, with Ritschl's help, Nietzsche secured an academic appointment at Basel. While the majority of Nietzsche's teaching and writing during this period would today fall under the heading of "classics,"[8] Nietzsche also engaged in reflection upon the methodological practices of philology. Moreover, it would not be inappropriate to view Nietzsche's methodological reflections as "hermeneutical," insofar as there had not yet developed the rigorous separation of the objects examined in philology and those pursued in hermeneutics. In this respect, much of Nietzsche's reflection on philological methodology falls under the modern conception of hermeneutics.[9] In fact, in his earliest lectures, he uses the term "hermeneutics" in reference to an aspect of the philological method. Philology, he writes, concerns itself with methods for *understanding* and *judgment* of what has been transmitted." *"Criticism"* involves the methods that *evaluate* the processes of transmission, while *"hermeneutics"* is concerned with methods for *understanding* those things which have been transmitted (see *MA*, Vol. II, "Einleitung in das Studium der classischen Philologie," pp. 348–349: *"Die Methode, etwas Ueberliefertes zu* verstehen *und zu* beurtheilen. [. . .] Kritik *betrifft die* Ueberlieferung, Hermeneutik *das* Ueberlieferte.")*. Nietzsche's use of this terminology is not so surprising when one realizes that as a philologist, he was familiar with the work of Friedrich August Wolf, one of the important philological forerunners of modern hermeneutics in response to whose work Schleiermacher's earliest hermeneutic formulations first arose.[10] While he does make reference to "hermeneutics," "philology" remains the general designation that he applies to the discipline whose task is to achieve an understanding of the past, and in what follows we will see that much of what contemporary philosophers incorporate within the scope of hermeneutics is of a piece with Nietzsche's conception of philology.

In his inaugural address at Basel ("Homer and Classical Philology"), Nietzsche speaks of philology, the "science of antiquity [*Wissenschaft um das Alterthum*]," as an aggregate of scientific activities: part history, part natural science, part aesthetics:

> history, insofar as it endeavors to comprehend the manifestations of the individualities of peoples in ever new images, and the prevailing law in the disappearance of phenomena; natural science, insofar as it strives to fathom the deepest instinct of man, that of speech [*Sprachinstinkt*]; aesthetics, finally, because from various antiquities at our disposal it endeavors to pick out the so-called "classical" antiquity, with the view and pretension of excavating the ideal world buried under it, and to hold up to the present the mirror of the classical and everlasting standards. (*KGW*, II, 1: pp. 249–250)

Because of its heterogeneous nature, philology as a discipline suffers from the lack of a rigorous method (*"strenge Methode"*) characteristic of other scientific disciplines. We thus find Nietzsche criticizing a number of methodological alternatives adopted by philologists which, in his view, miss the central aim of philology. For example, the overzealous erudition of the "philological 'moles,' the animals that practice dust-eating *ex professo,* and that grub up and eat for the eleventh time what they have already eaten ten times before" (*KGW*, II, 1: pp. 250–251). Related to these harmless bookworms are those philologists embroiled in a sort of "cult of personality." Lost within the labyrinth of ancient texts, they devote their time to isolating the essential personality traits of the "author," in order to make a name for themselves in the profession by discovering the "true" author of some text, or by conclusively refuting the "false" attribution of a text to someone else.[11] Nietzsche also criticizes the conception of philology as an apology for or a valorisation of antiquity. He regards the former as an attempt to project the values of the present back into the past, thereby making antiquity less alien (see *KGW*, IV, 1: 3[52]; *WPh*, 15), while the latter wrongly glorifies the past as a consequence of a profound dissatisfaction with the present (see *KGW*, IV, 1: 3[4], 5[55, 87], 7[6]; *WPh*, 26–29).

Each of these methodological alternatives misses the rightful task of philology, which is "to understand our own age by means of antiquity" (*KGW*, IV, 1: 3[62]; *WPh*, 7). Philology, as the "messenger of the Gods," has as its goal neither the scholarly, disinterested appropriation of the past nor the willful creation of that past. Instead, philology should seek to promote an attitude that will facilitate our being receptive to the wisdom of antiquity (see *KGW*, II, 1: pp. 267–268). To the diligent philologists who continue to "swoop down on Homer in the mistaken belief that something of him can be obtained by force," Nietzsche advises that "antiquity speaks to us when it feels a desire to do so, not when we do" (*KGW*, IV, 1: 3[56]; *WPh*, 88). From the beginning, Nietzsche rejects the majority of work produced by philologists: "In short, ninety-nine philologists out of a hundred *should* not be philologists at all" (*KGW*, IV, 1: 3[20]; *WPh*, 2). Yet there remains an important and difficult task for the philologist to perform: to understand antiquity from the point of view of the present while at the same time understanding the present from the point of view of antiquity. This paradoxical task, which Nietzsche calls "the antinomy of philology" (*KGW*, IV, 1: 3[62]; *WPh*, 7), leads him to view the genuine philologist as a "peculiar centaur" striving for an impossible synthesis of past and present (*KGW*, II, 1: p. 253). Insofar as most philologists are found to be more or less content to immerse themselves in the past, Nietzsche finds the appropriate mixture of antiquarian erudition and contemporary cultural critique all-too-often lacking. The future philologists, for Nietzsche, "must be skeptical in regard to our entire culture" (*KGW*, IV, 1: 5[55]; *WPh*, 26), and they will interrogate the past from this perspective, seeking in antiquity the genealogy of "our modern wrongheadedness [*Verkehrtheit*]" (*KGW*, IV, 1: 3[52]; *WPh*, 15). Because "there are no disinterested philologists" (*KGW*, IV, 1: 3[62]; *WPh*, 7), it is only with an understanding of the past and the present and of him- or herself as an *interested* observer of them both that the philologist will be able to take his or her rightful place as cultural critic and "educator of educators" (*KGW*, IV, 1: 7[7]; *WPh*, 46).

Nietzsche began his academic career hoping to advance this new understanding of philology: "People in general think that philology is at an end—while I believe that it has not yet begun" (*KGW*, IV, 1: 3[70]). Soon after, however, he lost much of his optimism for the future of his chosen profession. Following the appearance of *The Birth of Tragedy,* a work Nietzsche hoped would serve as a model of the new philology and which was almost universally rejected in philological circles, he relinquished any expectation of rescuing philology from the philologists. While he later came to view his being a philologist as an "eccentricity

[*Exzentrizität*]" and experiment "*outside* [his] center [ausserhalb *[s]eines Zentrum*]" (Letter to C. Fuchs, Dec. 14, 1887), Nietzsche's second position on philology, in the years following *The Birth of Tragedy*, is marked by a movement away from the academic world and an increasing hostility toward the labors of philological academicians. In their effort to make philology into an objective science, Nietzsche judges the philologists to have made themselves into little more than glorified editors seeking rigorous methods for the restoration and purification of the texts of antiquity. Such methods do allow the philologists to achieve their goal: "the simple desire to understand what the author says" (*HAH*, 270). But this goal, the one-sided desire of philology as "the art of reading rightly [*die Kunst des richtigen Lesens*]" (*HAH*, 270), comes to be rejected by Nietzsche insofar as it fails to account for the rich ambiguity and multiplicity of textual meanings. Blinded by the desire to clearly understand what the text wants to say, the philologists fail to suspect what Nietzsche calls the text's "*double* sense" (see *HAH*, 8). This suspicion of a "double sense" leads Nietzsche to his third position, in which he articulates a transvalued concept of philology. The task of the philologists is no longer to promote the "art of reading rightly"; rather, the philologists must teach instead "the art of reading *well* [*die Kunst gut zu lesen*]" (*A*, 52).

In addition to the contrast with the dogmatic and restrictive tendency of philology as "reading rightly," Nietzsche's return in his later writings to philology as the "art of reading well" yields an apparent safeguard against the relativistic tendency of his perspectival account of knowledge. In advocating that one learn to read well, Nietzsche proffers a notion of textual *autonomy,* insofar as the reader is cautioned to *respect* the text and remain open to that which the text presents. We thus find Nietzsche concluding his preface to *Daybreak* with the following warning: "My patient friends, this book desires for itself only perfect readers and philologists: *learn* to read me well!" This warning is preceded by an explanation of what it means to read well, in which philology's new task emerges as the promotion of a certain *style* of reading, one that proceeds *lento* and with *delicatesse:*

It is not for nothing that I have been a philologist, perhaps I am a philologist still, that is to say, a teacher of slow reading:—in the end I also write slowly. Nowadays it is not only my habit, it is also to my taste—a malicious taste, perhaps?—no longer to write anything which does not reduce to despair every sort of man who is "in a hurry". For philology is that venerable art which demands of its votaries one thing above all: to go aside, to take time, to become still, to become slow—it is a goldsmith's art and connoisseurship of the *word* which has nothing but delicate, cautious work to do and achieves nothing if it does not achieve it *lento*. But for precisely this reason it is more necessary than ever today, by precisely this means does it entice and enchant us the most, in the midst of an age of "work", that is to say, of hurry, of indecent and perspiring haste, which wants to "get everything done" at once, including every old or new book:—this art does not easily get anything done, it teaches to read *well*, that is to say, to read slowly, deeply, looking cautiously before and aft, with reservations, with doors left open, with delicate eyes and fingers[. . . .] (*D*, Pr., 5)

The philologist as the teacher of slow reading is the teacher of reading as rumination (*Wiederkäuen*) upon the text (see *GM*, Pr., 8): not content merely to read the words, one must *decipher* what is read, one must continue to think while reading and reflect critically on what one reads (see *FEI*, Pr.).

The value of this "art of reading well" appears most clearly when Nietzsche contrasts it to its opposite tendency, the "bad philology" or "lack of philology" that he observes among Christian theologians. The worst readers, says Nietzsche, are "those who act like plundering soldiers" (*AOM*, 137). "In order to apply their profound interpretations, they frequently first adjust the text in a way that will facilitate this, or in other words, they *corrupt* it" (*WS*, 17). To lack philology, in this context, is to be unable "to read off a text as a text without interposing an interpretation" (*WP*, 479). In *The Antichrist*, Nietzsche notes the theologians' "*incapacity for philology*":

> Philology is to be understood here in a very wide sense as the art of reading well— of being able to read off a fact *without* falsifying it by interpretation, *without* losing caution, patience, subtlety in the desire for understanding. Philology as *ephexis* [undecisiveness] in interpretation. (*A*, 52)

As the art of reading well, philology's task is thus to guard against what we might call "teleological" interpretation, that is, interpretations rigidly predetermined and controlled by the desire to understand something for a specific purpose as, for example, the priests have hitherto interpreted the world in ways that insure their own claims to power. By inscribing philology within the margins of the Greek *ephexis*, the root of the phenomenological *epochē*, Nietzsche makes clear that the philologist, in order to read well, must refrain from moving too quickly and must attempt to control his or her interests while letting the text speak for itself. The philologist, in other words, must strive to keep the question of interpretation open, for "*there is no sole saving interpretation*" (Letter to C. Fuchs, Aug. 26, 1888).[12]

For Nietzsche, the primary example of the Christian theologians' incapacity for philology is the text of the New Testament itself:

> To have glued this New Testament, a kind of rococo of taste in every respect, to the Old Testament to make *one* book as the "Bible," as "the book in itself": that is perhaps the greatest audacity and "sin against the spirit" that literary Europe has on its conscience. (*BGE*, 52)

In superimposing the New Testament upon the Old Testament, Nietzsche finds in Christian philology a veritable manual of *bad* philology:

The philology of Christianity.—How little Christianity educates the sense of honesty and justice can be gauged fairly well from the character of its scholars' writings: they present their conjectures as boldly as if they were dogmas and are rarely in any honest perplexity over the interpretation of a passage in the Bible. Again and again they say "I am right, for it is written —" and then follows an interpretation of such impudent arbitrariness that a philologist who hears it is caught between rage and laughter and asks himself: is it possible? Is this honorable? Is it even decent?—How much dishonesty in this matter is still practiced in Protestant pulpits, how grossly the preacher exploits the advantage that no one is going to interrupt him here, how the Bible is pummelled and punched and the *art of reading badly* is in all due form imparted to the people: only he who never goes to church or never goes anywhere else will underestimate that. But after all, what can one expect from the effects of a religion which in the centuries of its foundation perpetrated that unheard-of philological farce concerning the Old Testament: I mean the attempt to pull the Old Testament from under the feet of the Jews with the assertion it contained nothing but Christian teaching and *belonged* to the Christians as the true people of Israel, the Jews being only usurpers. And then there followed a fury of interpretation and construction that cannot possibly be associated with a good conscience: however much Jewish scholars protested, the Old Testament was supposed to speak of Christ and only of Christ, and especially of his Cross; whenever a piece of wood, a rod, a ladder, a twig, a tree, a willow, a staff is mentioned, it is supposed to be a prophetic allusion to the wood of the Cross; even the erection of the one-horned beast and the brazen serpent, even Moses spreading his arms in prayer, *even* the spits on which the Passover lamb was roasted—allusions to the Cross and as it were preludes to it! Has anyone who asserted this ever believed it? Consider that the church did not shrink from enriching the text of the Septuagint (e.g., in Psalm 96, verse 10) so as afterwards to employ the smuggled-in passage in the sense of Christian prophecy. For they were conducting a *war* and paid more heed to their opponents than to the need to stay honest. (*D*, 84)

In this passage, Nietzsche introduces two criteria into philology: honesty (*Redlichkeit*) and justice (*Gerechtigkeit*). And it is clear that what the philologist must be honest and just towards is the *text*. In the above passage, the New Testament scholars are faulted for their dishonesty and injustice toward the text of the Old Testament. The application of philological honesty and justice is not, however, limited by Nietzsche to the narrow concept of the text as written document or book. Rather, in his transvalued notion of philology, the world becomes a text that Nietzsche exhorts us to read well (see, for example, *HAH*, 8, where Nietzsche discusses what is needed for metaphysicians to apply the philological method established for books to "the writing of nature [*die Schrift der Natur*]"). All the while, moreover, the philological demands of honesty and justice require that we keep the text *separate* from its interpretation. In one of Nietzsche's final notebooks, from Spring, 1888, we find the following remark: "The *lack of philology:* one continually confuses the exegesis with the *text*—and what an 'exegesis'!" (*KGW*, VIII, 3: 15[82]: *"Der* Mangel an Philologie: *man verwechselt beständig die Erklärung mit dem* Text—*und was für eine 'Erklär-*

ung'!"). Only through this transvalued sense of philological diligence, directed by a sense of honesty and justice that precludes the overly enthusiastic assertion of any one interpretation as *the* correct one, will we be able to avoid the fate of all bad philology, that fate in which the text finally disappears under the interpretation (see *BGE,* 38).

This demand for honesty and justice raises a problem, however, for it would appear that Nietzsche is positing some *thing,* the "text," which exists in itself independent of the interpretations of it. Such a view would, however, be inconsistent with the perspectival account of knowledge discussed above, which precluded any move toward positing an entity outside of the interpretive matrix. This inconsistency is most explicit when we compare the differing conceptions of truth to which perspectivism and philology apparently give rise. As we have already noted, perspectivism entails that "there is no truth." "Truth" appears in the perspectival account as *"provisional assumptions"* (*WP,* 497), "prejudices" (*BGE,* 5), "the posture of various errors in relation to one another" (*WP,* 535), valuations which express "conditions of preservation and growth" (*WP,* 507), etc. Philology, on the other hand, in calling for our "being able to read off a fact *without* falsifying it by interpretation" (*A,* 52) or demanding that we "be able to read off a text as a text without interposing an interpretation" (*WP,* 479), would seem to entail that there is some text or some truth which is subsequently falsified through the interpretive act.

It is precisely this question of the relation between text and interpretation that has appeared as a focal point of disagreement between two of the French readings of Nietzsche examined in Chapter Three, and a brief summary of the disagreement between Jean Granier and Sarah Kofman over how to interpret this relation will help clarify what is at issue in Nietzsche's affirmation of both philology and perspectivism. Granier, in *Le problème de la Vérité dans la philosophie de Nietzsche,* subordinates Nietzsche's "perspectivistic phenomenalism" to the rigorous philological probity which demands "absolute respect for the text." Focusing on those Nietzschean passages which appear to assert the independence of the text (e.g., *A,* 52; *WP,* 479; *KGW,* V, 2: 11[65]), Granier argues that Nietzsche's affirmation of philology as the art of reading well is a call to overcome our perspectival falsifications and read through these illusions to the originary text of Being:

> The rules of true philology require us to sacrifice interest and utility to the demands of a textual understanding which would restore, to the extent that it is possible, the original signification [*la signification primitive*]. [. . .] For the most noble and courageous spirits, one voice speaks louder than the voice of their own vital interests, and this voice commands them *to do justice to nature,* to reveal things as they are in their own being.[13]

Granier views Nietzsche's solution to the antinomy of perspectivism and philology as grounded in the Nietzschean intuition that *"Being is interpreted-Being* [*l'Etre comme l'Etre-interprété*]."[14] As such, Nietzsche's approach to textual interpretation emerges as a "radical ontological problematic,"[15] and Nietzsche's rigorous philological method proposes the *epochē* of our anthropomorphic perspectives in order to facilitate our reading the primordial "text" of interpreted-Being honestly and justly:

> The passion for knowledge is the manifestation of that intransigent intellectual probity which forbids us to interpret Being as a function of our needs and wishes, that is, in an anthropomorphic manner, and which commands us to have absolute respect for the "text."[16]

Sarah Kofman offers a critical alternative to Granier's reading in her review of his book, republished as an appendix to *Nietzsche et la métaphore*. In this review, Kofman criticizes Granier's "ontologization" of Nietzsche for remaining within the Heideggerian problematic of the question of Being. In his ontological interpretation, Granier fails to attend to the axiological and genealogical dimension of Nietzsche's thinking which underlies his renunciation of the language of Being. In opposition to Granier's antinomy of perspectivism and philology, Kofman suggests that we locate in Nietzsche a two-tiered interpretive analysis. Whereas the task of philology, for Granier's Nietzsche, is to decipher Being as that which *constitutes* perspectival interpretations, Kofman's Nietzsche views "Being" itself as a text constituted *by* the primary interpretations of the spontaneous instinctual evaluations which need to make life intelligible.[17] Kofman thus views philology as genealogical: its task is not, pace Granier, to decipher Being as the ground of interpretations; rather, the philological task of reading well is "to decipher, behind all the secondary interpretations, the initial interpretations which are symptomatic of a type of evaluating will."[18] Kofman rejects the notion that there is an "absolute text" to which we can refer in order to judge the truth of interpretations, and she concludes that, for Nietzsche, "the text without interpretation is no longer a text [*Le texte sans interprétation n'est plus un texte*]."[19] Philology is, therefore, honest and just not because it maintains an "absolute respect" for the text, but because it presents its interpretations *as* interpretations.[20]

The disagreement between Granier and Kofman as to how to interpret the relation between interpretation and text focuses our attention on a crucial point in Nietzsche's approach to interpretation. Insofar as the doctrine of philology does appear, at times, to posit a(n admittedly oblique) border between text and interpretation, reconciling this doctrine with Nietzsche's perspectival account may face considerable difficulties. In the concluding chapter, we will examine whether a Nietzschean pluralistic approach can avoid these difficulties. The solution to this problem will give rise to a transvalued notion of *text* to accompany Nietzsche's transvalued conception of philology. That is to say, whereas Nietzsche's early conception of philology as a discipline which seeks to establish a rigorous exegetical method (*"strengen Erklärungskunst"*) does appear incompatible with the perspectival denial of truth, the transvalued conception of philology as the art of reading well does not stand primarily in opposition to the doctrine of perspectivism, but opposes itself instead to *bad* philological method. Thus, the transvalued text which is to be read well, while distinct from any *particular* interpretation, itself remains *nothing other than interpretation*. This is to say, while no single interpretation will be coextensive with the text, nor will any one interpretation "get the text right", our only access to the text, our only means of apprehending it, will be through an act of interpretation. We shall see that this transvalued conception of the text as itself interpretation does not exclude the possibility of adjudicating between conflicting interpretations. It does, however, suspend adjudication based on the criterion of correctness or accuracy of reproduction of some originary, univocal meaning. Instead, it proposes "genealogical" criteria which themselves derive from the demands of both philology and perspectivism, and which give rise to an approach to interpretation that I have chosen to call "interpretive pluralism." The opposition between perspectivism and philology thus does not face the interpreter with the methodological demand of choosing one or the other; rather, perspectivism and philology emerge as the *limits* between which Nietzsche's pluralistic approach to interpretation plays.

Chapter 7

Genealogy, Interpretation, Text

The most valuable insights are the last to be discovered, but the most valuable insights are methods.

—*The Antichrist,* 13

Mise-en-scène

This final chapter sets for itself the task of elaborating some of the methodological implications for a theory of interpretation suggested by the Nietzschean text. Before we proceed with this task, a brief survey of the terrain already covered in this exposition is in order. In Parts One and Two, we examined two of the leading contemporary interpretive styles as exhibited in their respective readings of Nietzsche's text. For the Heideggerian hermeneutic, Nietzsche's text appeared as an occasion for philosophizing: Heidegger puts his reading forward in the context of a totalizing interpretation of the history of Western metaphysics as the oblivion of Being, and he comes to view Nietzsche's thinking as the culminating expression of this metaphysical forgetfulness of Being. In Part One, it appeared that Heidegger's method suffers from what Nietzsche called a "lack of philology": in his hermeneutic-dogmatic assertion of having discovered the true meaning of Nietzsche's thinking, Heidegger corrupts the Nietzschean text, and unjustifiably limits the rich and playful ambiguity of Nietzsche's writing. For the French post-structuralists, on the other hand, Nietzsche's text is also an occasion, but an occasion for play rather than totalization. Within the intertextual network of Nietzsche's critique of logocentrism and onto-theology, they freely play with the Nietzschean text, developing Nietzsche's deconstructive motifs in conjunction with those of his companions in proto-deconstruction: Marx and Freud. While perhaps more in keeping with the spirit of Nietzsche's text than the Heideggerian interpretation, the deconstructive readings appeared to run the risk of losing the Nietzschean text within their proliferative play. Part Two concluded by suggesting that we view the debate between the Heideggerian and deconstructive readings of Nietzsche as a reinscription of the hermeneutic dilemma of interpretive dogmatism and relativism. The deconstructionists criticize the Heideggerian reading for its claim to have deciphered the "essential truth" of Nietzsche's text in its interpretation of this text as the culmination of the metaphysical oblivion of Being. The more traditional Heideggerian interpreters, on the other hand, object to the deconstructionists' refusal to specify the "protocols" of their readings,

169

perceiving the consequence of this refusal to be an unmitigated relativism that sanctions any and all interpretations.

In the exposition of Nietzsche heretofore undertaken in Part Three, tendencies toward each of these interpretive extremes have surfaced. In Chapter Five, we examined Nietzsche's deconstruction of linguistic authority. In denying the possibility of correctly reproducing the world of becoming in language, Nietzsche critiqued both the correspondence theory of truth and the referential theory of meaning in a way that opened the fields of traditional epistemological inquiry to the creative play of interpretation. Language emerged not as a tool for the mirroring of reality, but as an anthropomorphic creation through which human beings delineate their relatively idiosyncratic relationships with each other and with "nature." This conception of language was found to operate in the two competing interpretive motifs examined in the preceding chapter. On the one hand, we find Nietzsche's doctrine of perspectivism, which asserts that our access to the world of becoming is restricted to fragmented profiles and horizons determined by our physiological, instinctual and socio-historical limitations. This relativistic impulse is countermanded by Nietzsche's call for philology, the "art of reading well," which demands that we avoid the willful corruption and violation of the text through the imposition of "overly enthusiastic" and unjustifiable interpretations. Whereas perspectival interpretation seems to allow for an un-bounded play of creative textual appropriation, philological interpretation seems to call for methodological rigor and meticulous attention to the text itself. In claiming that there is nothing other than interpretation (perspectivism) while at the same time calling for an apprehension of the text without falsifying it by interpretation (philology), Nietzsche appears to anticipate the contemporary her-meneutic dilemma of relativism and dogmatism.

We must now consider whether Nietzsche's two conflicting interpretive tenden-cies can be understood in a way that avoids the undesirable consequences of both dogmatic and unmitigated relativistic approaches to interpretation. A helpful suggestion in this matter can be drawn from Derrida's discussion of the two "interpretations of interpretation" in "Structure, Sign, and Play in the Discourse of the Human Sciences." Derrida writes of the two interpretations that

> The one seeks to decipher, dreams of deciphering a truth or an origin which escapes play and the order of the sign, and which lives the necessity of interpretation as an exile [while the other calls for] the joyous affirmation of the play of the world and the innocence of becoming, the affirmation of a world of signs without fault, without truth, and without origin which is offered to an active interpretation.[1]

For Derrida, neither of these two interpretations of interpretation can be reduced without remainder to a form of its other, as the irreducible difference between them is what makes interpretation possible. Nor can we simply choose one mode of interpretation and dispense with the other, as good interpretive practice requires both attentiveness to textual detail and creativity of engagement with the text. While Derrida designates the former interpretation as "Rousseauistic" and the latter as "Nietzschean," the preceding discussion of philology and perspectivism locates both interpretations of interpretation in Nietzsche's text.[2] Nevertheless, this Derridean insight into the "undecidability" of the two interpretations of interpretation can be employed to demonstrate the advantages of a pluralistic approach to interpretation.

By "undecidability," I take Derrida to mean that the "logic" of the two interpretations of interpretation is not the binary logic of exclusive disjunction (either . . . or . . .): we are not faced with a disjunctive choice between either rigorous textual attentiveness or playful creativity. Nor is an interpretive method faced with the demand of arriving at a synthesis or *Aufhebung* of these two competing interpretive tendencies, in which the conflict between them is overcome in a higher unity. Rather, a pluralistic approach will refrain from making either choice and will play between these two interpretive styles, *at once* serious *and* playful, attentive *and* creative. We find such a pluralistic approach in Nietzsche's text itself in the method he calls *genealogical* analysis. As an analytic method for deciphering the values of certain ideals in terms of the health/strength or disease/weakness of the will to power that posits them as ideal, genealogy seeks to uncover the significance of the affirmation of certain values within social praxis. To do so, it must both examine these values in the historical/textual context in which they emerge and question the interpretive privileging of these values by suggesting other interpretive perspectives. Nietzschean genealogy isolates what is determined to be good or true and asks, for example, who gains by this determination, whose strength is increased, whose power expanded? In so doing, genealogy can be viewed as a methodological interstice between perspectivism and philology insofar as it demands *both* playful appropriation of *and* meticulous attention to the developmental history of contemporary values. Operating under the demands of both perspectivism and philology, Nietzsche's genealogical method plays between these competing demands in a way that modifies each within their mutual affirmation while refusing to posit any synthetic unity at the level of a universal method. The first step in explicating this pluralistic approach to interpretation is to examine Nietzsche's method of genealogical inquiry as an example of the *praxis* of interpretive pluralism. In particular, this examination will show the way Nietzschean genealogy, without appealing to the criteria of interpretive "truth" or "correctness," can both attend to the text *and* allow for a plurality of interpretations. In so doing, it will display genealogy as an interpretive practice which, because it retains a standard by which to judge between competing interpretations, can accept multiple and conflicting interpretations without succumbing to an unmitigated relativism in which it relinquishes the ability to judge some interpretations as better than others.

Genealogy

For the **overcoming** *of the previous ideals (philosopher, artist, saint), a* history
of origins [Entstehungs-Geschichte] *is necessary.*
—*KGW*, VII, 1: 16[14]

As a Nietzschean method of analysis, genealogy is by no means limited to the
genealogy of morality and the ascetic ideal found in his text of 1886 entitled *On
the Genealogy of Morals*. Instead, a careful reading of Nietzsche's writing reveals
numerous examples of genealogical analysis in his examination of various phenomena. In a few pages of *The Gay Science,* for instance, we find Nietzsche
inquiring into the origins of morality, scholars, religion, consciousness and
knowledge (*GS*, 345–355), and as early as the notes for the never completed
"Untimely Meditation" *We Philologists* (1875), he wrote of the right attitude in
the examination of antiquity as a search for the origins of "contemporary wrongheadedness" (see *KGW*, IV, 1: 3[52]).
    In these genealogical inquiries into the origins of contemporary values and
beliefs, Nietzsche is by no means seeking an origin that might serve as their
foundation.[3] In fact, he explicitly distinguishes his genealogical method from the
misguided glorification of origins that he finds exhibited in the observations of
historians (see, e.g., *TI*, "Maxims and Arrows," 24; *WS*, 3). He regards this
glorification of origins as a "metaphysical after-shoot [*metaphysische Nachtrieb*]"
of the historical contemplation that "makes us believe that what stands in the
beginning of all things is also what is most valuable and essential" (*WS*, 3). This
quest for the origin as the true locus of significance and value is quite different
from Nietzsche's genealogical inquiry. In a section from *Daybreak* entitled "Order
of Rank," Nietzsche distinguishes four sorts of thinkers and, in so doing, he
makes clear the difference in value between the historical *quest* for the origin as
a path to salvation, and the genealogical *questioning* of the origin as a moment
of critique:

> There are, first of all, superficial thinkers [*oberflächliche Denker*]; secondly, deep
> thinkers [*tiefe Denker*]—those who go down into the depths of a thing; thirdly,
> thorough thinkers [*gründliche Denker*], who thoroughly explore the grounds of a
> thing—which is worth very much more than merely going down into its depths!—
> finally, those who stick their heads into the swamp: which ought not to be a sign
> either of depth or thoroughness! They are the dear departed underground [*Unter-
> gründlichen*]. (*D*, 446)

These "underground thinkers" are not genealogists, for in their search for "the
origin of things, they always believed they would discover something of incalculable significance [*Bedeutung*] for all later action and judgment, [. . .] they always

presupposed, indeed, that the *salvation* of man must depend on *insight into the origin of things"* (*D,* 44).

What the foundational inquiry into origins fails to recognize is what Nietzsche sometimes refers to as the "psychological" aspect of genealogy.[4] This is to say, genealogical analysis seeks not only the origins of modern convictions but also the reasons and justifications which the proponents of these convictions have given in asserting their hegemony. For example, regarding the errors of metaphysics, Nietzsche remarks that mere recognition of these errors *as* errors is not sufficient for overcoming them. In addition, a *"retrogressive movement [rückläufige Bewegung]* is necessary: [one] must comprehend the historical as well as the psychological justification in such representations [. . .]"* (*HAH,* 20). The same requirement holds for epistemological errors: "What I noticed was rather that no epistemological skepticism or dogmatism had ever risen free from ulterior motives,—that it has a value of the second rank as soon as one has considered *what* it was that *compelled* the adoption of this position" (*WP,* 410). In pursuing a genealogical inquiry into the history of origins, Nietzsche produces something quite different from a simple history of particular systems of belief (see *GS,* 345). Instead, this inquiry discovers "the *hidden* history of philosophy, the psychology of its great names" (*EH,* Pr., 3), that is, the hidden *values for life* at work behind the explicit affirmation of certain values as ideals. Nietzsche's call for *psycho*-genealogical inquiry is thus a call to reflect upon what was ultimately willed in the positing of certain values as valuable. It is in this sense that psychology will be the "queen of the sciences [and] path to the fundamental problems" (*BGE,* 23). If it is to discern the worth of these originary values, psychology must "descend into the depths" and investigate the morphology and development of the will to power as manifested in those values which have been posited. In this way, *"psychological genesis"* will discover what these ideals "genuinely mean" (*KGW,* VIII, 1: 7[35]), not in the epistemological sense of uncovering the true referent or the accurate representation of a state of affairs, but rather in the psycho-genealogical sense of deciphering the significance which these ideals hold as a symptom of the health or disease of the will to power that has posited them *as ideal.*

This view of psychology makes clear that the aim of the genealogical search for origins is not the discernment of truth but the deciphering of value. Genealogy thus functions in the Nietzschean text primarily as a method of deconstructive critique to uncover the significance of the affirmation of certain values within social praxis rather than as a tool for the acquisition of knowledge or the discovery of true descriptions regarding states of affairs. In other words, genealogical inquiry involves a critical re-reading and re-interpretation of the history of various phenomena from the perspective of the values inscribed *at their origin,* in an attempt to trace the evolution of the re-inscription of these values through the course of their historical development. My recourse here to the metaphors of reading and inscriptions are carefully chosen, but the allusion in this case is not so much to Derridean deconstruction as to Nietzschean genealogy itself. In the preface to *On the Genealogy of Morals,* Nietzsche writes that the color gray is vital for a genealogist of morals: *"gray,* that is, what is documented, what can actually be confirmed and has actually existed, in short the entire long hieroglyphic record, so hard to decipher, of the moral past of mankind" (*GM,* Pr., 7). In the context of a discussion of genealogy, "gray" is a metaphor serving a twofold function. First, it alludes to language and thus recalls Nietzsche's critique of language as an imperfect tool for the acquisition of knowledge. Given the metaphorical and anthropomorphic origin of concepts, the genealogist must be attentive to the implicit values which have been fixed within (linguistic) concepts. Rather than accepting these concepts as a gift from the tradition, Nietzsche advises that "what is needed above all is an absolute skepticism toward all inherited concepts" (*WP,* 409). In addition to the allusion to language, "gray" implicates the process of interpretation itself. What is gray is neither black nor white, neither true nor false; gray is *in between* and it is within the realm of the gray that the interpretive play of values will unfold.

Returning now to the question of truth, it is clear that *the* Truth is not the aim of genealogical inquiry. The "will to truth" is itself to be "investigated psychologically" (*WP,* 583C). In part, the task of Nietzsche's *Genealogy* was to undertake this investigation, as "the value of truth must for once be experimentally *called into question"* (*GM,* III, 24; see also *GM,* Pr., 6). The *Genealogy* itself is an example of the psychological investigation called for in *The Will to Power* (583C) and *Beyond Good and Evil* (23): it descends into the depths of morality and the ascetic ideal to genealogically uncover the morphology of decadent will to power that manifests itself there as the "will to truth." Because assessing the value of the will to power, as "the force that forms, simplifies, shapes, invents," is more significant for genealogical interpretation than ascertaining the "truth" of what is formed, simplified, etc. (see *WP,* 602, 605), Nietzsche's *Genealogy of Morals* concerns itself with the life-negating origins and consequences of the ascetic ideal, its *Woher* and *Wohin,* rather than with an inquiry into the "truth" of that ideal.

In descending to the psychological depths of morality and the ascetic ideal, the *Genealogy* exhibits the critical function of all genealogical inquiry. As the work of "subterranean" explorers, genealogy both mines and undermines (see *D,* Pr., 1). In seeking out the origins of contemporary cultural convictions and assessing the value for life of those convictions, Nietzsche resorts again and again to genealogical analysis as a critical tool. Insofar as values can only be assessed as interpretations (manifestations of will to power) and not as "truth," Nietzsche regards genealogical critique to be sufficient for "definitive refutation":

In former times, one sought to prove that there is no God—today one indicates how the belief that there is a God could *arise* and how this belief acquired its weight and importance: a counterproof that there is no God thereby becomes superfluous.— When in former times one had refuted the "proofs of the existence of God" put forward, there always remained the doubt whether better proofs might not be adduced than those just refuted: in those days atheists did not know how to make a clean sweep. (*D*, 95)

The genealogical criteria for assessing these values which are sufficient for making such a clean sweep are expressed in various forms in Nietzsche's text, but at bottom these criteria always confront the values under scrutiny with the same question: do these values lead to the ascent or decline of life? Drawing again from his semiotic insight into language, Nietzsche regards the history which is genealogically re-read as possessing value only as a sign-language of decay or growth: "Judgments, value judgments concerning life, for or against, can in the last resort never be true: they possess value only as symptoms, they come into consideration only as symptoms,—[. . .]" (*TI*, "The Problem of Socrates," 2). Morality itself is "merely sign-language, merely symptomatology." Insofar as "*there are no moral facts*, [. . .] morality is only an interpretation of certain phenomena, more precisely a *mis*-interpretation" that refers to nothing real (*TI*, "The Improvers of Mankind," 1). Nevertheless, "as *semiotics* it remains of incalculable value" to the careful genealogist, whose interpretive skills and sensitivity facilitate the deciphering of a morality as a sign of the decadent instincts of those who adhere to its precepts.

   Morality is not, however, the only realm criticized for the life-negating character of its originary impulses. Nietzsche prides himself on his subtle sense of smell in being able to sniff out the decadent instincts of religious, philosophical, and aesthetic values as well (see, e.g., *EH*, I, 1). Within the perspective of genealogical critique, Nietzsche bases his conclusions regarding the assessment of value in each case on his re-reading of contemporary manifestations of will to power in terms of their position vis-à-vis the various forms in which he expresses this fundamental genealogical distinction: ascension/decline, health/decadence, enhancement/impoverishment, superabundance/lack, overflowing/hunger, strength/ weakness, etc. The pervasiveness of Nietzsche's application of this genealogical distinction is evidenced in passages like the following:

morality: In the narrower sphere of so-called moral values one cannot find a greater contrast than that between a *master morality* and the morality of *Christian* value concepts: [. . . master morality is] the sign language of what has turned out well, of *ascending* life, of the will to power as the principle of life. Master morality *affirms* as instinctively as Christian morality *negates* [. . .] The former gives to things out of its own abundance—it transfigures, it beautifies the world and *makes it more rational*—the latter impoverishes, pales and makes uglier the value of things, it *negates* the world. (*CW*, Epilogue)

philosophy: In some it is their deprivations that philosophize; in others, their riches and strengths. (*GS*, Pr., 2)

aesthetics: Regarding all aesthetic values I now avail myself of this main distinction: I ask in every instance, "is it hunger or superabundance that has
here become creative?" (*GS*, 370)

religion: To say it again, this depressive and contagious instinct thwarts those
instincts bent on preserving and enhancing the value of life: both as
a *multiplier* of misery and as a *conservator* of everything miserable it
is one of the chief instruments for the advancement of decadence—
pity persuades to nothingness: . . . One does not say "nothingness":
one says "the Beyond"; or "God"; or "*true* life"; [. . .] This innocent
rhetoric from the domain of religio-moral idiosyncrasy at once appears
much less innocent when one grasps *which* tendency is here draping
the mantle of sublime words about itself: the tendency *hostile to life*.
(*A*, 7)

What the application of this distinction points to, and what will be most
significant for a pluralistic approach to interpretation, is that correctness or truth
does not serve as the standard by which interpretations are to be judged. For
example, although the moral interpretation of the world is false, its falsity is not
the grounds upon which Nietzsche criticizes it: "The falseness of a judgment is
for us not necessarily an objection to a judgment; in this respect our new language
may sound strangest" (*BGE*, 4). Rather, morality is criticized to the extent that
it affirms values which are hostile to life. But there is, as Nietzsche writes, no
correlation between falsity and the hostility to life: our falsest judgments may
indeed be those most indispensable for the enhancement of life. If the true/false
or correct/incorrect oppositions will not serve as a standard for assessing an
interpretation's value for or against life, then what will provide such a standard?
In the following interpretation, I propose an answer to this question which takes
up Nietzsche's enhancement/impoverishment opposition and views it from the
perspective of *style*.

Here we return to the "question of style" so prevalent in the deconstructive
readings of Nietzsche examined in Part Two, but we return to it in a way that
brings out the double-genitive nature of the "question of style." This is to say,
there is an ambiguity inherent in the Nietzschean question of style, as this question
addresses both the question of Nietzsche's *styles* of philosophizing in relation to
what is expressed in that philosophizing, as well as the question of style itself as
a theme in the Nietzschean project and the adjudicatory function that it plays in
the Nietzschean transvaluation. Whereas the French readings of Nietzsche were
shown to focus on the former question of Nietzsche's styles of philosophizing,
the latter question of style is here being raised as a factor to consider in judging
between competing interpretations. In raising this question of style in the context
of Nietzsche's genealogical method, I do not intend to suggest that genealogy
should be understood *only* in terms of the critical distinction it provides with
respect to *styles* of interpretation. Clearly, there is more to Nietzsche's genealogi-

cal deconstruction of the moral and Christian interpretations than the stylistic criterion alone can indicate. Instead, I am attempting to draw attention to the wider applications of the *methodological* insights which I find exemplified in Nietzschean genealogy. This is to say, if a "stylistic" opposition can be shown to operate in Nietzsche's text as a standard according to which interpretations can be judged, and if this standard can be applied in a manner similar to his genealogical opposition of affirmation and negation of life, this may facilitate the application of Nietzsche's *method* for the ranking of interpretations beyond its restriction to the somewhat hyperbolic terminology of ascension and decline of life.[5]

In a section from *The Gay Science* entitled "One Thing is Necessary," Nietzsche begins: "To 'give style' to one's character—a great and rare art:" (*GS*, 290). In this context, style is not simply an aesthetic category, and in affirming the necessity of giving style to one's character, Nietzsche is not merely advocating some sort of aestheticism.[6] We find a hint to what is meant here by "style" in *The Case of Wagner*, where Nietzsche refers to style as a "higher lawfulness [*höhere Gesetzlichkeit*]" (*CW*, 8). When we incorporate this conception of "higher lawfulness" into the distinction of ascension and decline, we arrive at a possible standard: decline comes forth as a decadent style and ascent appears as the grand style. In the context of discussing Wagner as a "perfect" form of decadent style, Nietzsche writes:

> For the present I merely dwell on the question of *style*—What is the sign of every *literary* decadence? That life no longer dwells in the whole. The word becomes sovereign and leaps out of the sentence, the sentence reaches out and obscures the meaning of the page, the page gains life at the expense of the whole—the whole is no longer a whole. But this is the simile of every style of decadence: [. . .] (*CW*, 7)

This decadent style, for Nietzsche, is "furthest of all from one thing, and that is the *grand style*" (Letter to C. Fuchs, Winter, 1884–85). In opposing decadent to grand style, Nietzsche makes clear that there is no "style in itself" (see *EH*, III, 4), and the mere imposition of an ordering principle on one's chaos of contradictory drives is not sufficient for the attribution of value. Rather, a "higher lawfulness" and "order of rank" is imposed from a certain perspective which Nietzsche's genealogical analysis seeks to decipher as life-enhancing or life-negating. Thus, decadent style appears as the imposition of a lawfulness ultimately leading to the dissolution of the whole and the impoverishment of life, while the lawfulness of the grand style imposes a form upon chaos that results in a disciplining to wholeness and the enhancement of life (cf. *A*, 59). The grand stylist, as a master of self-legislation, is able to control "the greatest multiplicity of drives" (*WP*, 966) through the imposition of a life-enhancing order of rank upon these drives. "Grand health [*grosse Gesundheit*]" is another of Nietzsche's names for the imposition of such a life-enhancing order of rank, and we find genealogical analysis at the stylistic level directed toward deciphering the orders of rank which are imposed in various interpretations, and ascertaining whether the imposition of these orders of rank reflects the ascending life of grand health and style, or the declining life of decadent style.

We can see this stylistic distinction functioning in Nietzsche's text in his assessment of the different values of the Roman and Christian appropriations of the past. In the previous chapter, we examined the bad philological method exhibited by Christian theologians in their appropriating the Old Testament and re-inscribing its message in their own style in the New Testament. Of this appropriation Nietzsche writes that it is "perhaps the greatest audacity and 'sin against the spirit' that literary Europe has on its conscience" (*BGE*, 52). He goes on to criticize the authors of the New Testament for having enacted a "huge philological farce concerning the Old Testament," by which he refers to the "attempt to tear the Old Testament from the hands of the Jews under the pretext that it contained only Christian doctrines and *belonged* to the Christians" (*D*, 84). Reading these passages tempts one to view Nietzsche as criticizing the Christian re-interpretation of the Old Testament on the grounds that it no longer accurately represents the "meaning" or "truth" of the Old Testament. Such a view, however, becomes problematic when one compares Nietzsche's passages on the Christian appropriation of the Old Testament with the following passage which, on the surface, appears to describe an analogous interpretative process, the Roman poets' translation of the Greek classics:

> *Translations.*—The degree of the historical sense of any age may be inferred from the manner in which this age makes *translations* and tries to absorb former ages and books. In the age of Corneille and even of the Revolution, the French took possession of Roman antiquity in a way for which we would no longer have courage enough— thanks to our more highly developed historical sense. And Roman antiquity itself: how forcibly and at the same time how naively it took hold of everything good and lofty of Greek antiquity, which was more ancient! How they translated things into the Roman present! How deliberately and recklessly they brushed the dust off the wings of the butterfly that is called moment! Thus Horace now and then translated Alcaeus or Archilochus; and Propertius did the same with Callimachus and Philetas (poets of the same rank as Theocritus, if we *may* judge). What was it to them that the real creator had experienced this and that and had written the signs of it into his poem!—as poets, they had no sympathy for the antiquarian inquisitiveness that precedes the historical sense; as poets, they had no time for all those very personal things and names and whatever might be considered the costume and mask of a city, a coast, or a century: quickly, they replace it with what was contemporary and Roman. They seem to ask us: "Should we not make new for ourselves what is old and find ourselves in it? Should we not have the right to breathe our own soul into this dead body? For it is dead after all; how ugly is everything dead!"—They did not know the delights of the historical sense; what was past and alien was an embarrassment for them; and being Romans, they saw it as an incentive for a Roman conquest—not only did one omit what was historical; one also added allusions to the present and,

above all, struck out the name of the poet and replaced it with one's own—not with any sense of theft but with the very best conscience of the *imperium Romanum*. (*GS*, 83)

Translation is here described as a form of conquest, as adding allusions to the present, as striking out the author's name and replacing it with one's own. Do these characteristics not apply to the New Testament authors' relation to the Old Testament? Does the Roman re-translation of the Greek poets not parallel the Christian re-inscription of the Old Testament? In each case, what Nietzsche describes is the creative appropriation of a precursor text which is altered to fit into a subsequent cultural context. Judged merely at the level of creative appropriation, there seems to be little to distinguish between the Roman and Christian re-inscriptions. And yet, whereas the Christian appropriation is described as a "huge philological farce," Nietzsche clearly admires what resulted from the Roman appropriation of Greek antiquity. In *The Antichrist,* Nietzsche is critical of the historical falsification which resulted from the "ecclesiastical interpretation of history," an interpretation oblivious to the demands of integrity *in historicis* (*A,* 26). Yet in the passage above, Nietzsche praises the Romans precisely for this lack of historical sense.

The different values ascribed to these two re-translations indicate that the creativity of appropriation alone is not sufficient for assessing the worth of an interpretation. Nor is the correctness of interpretive reproduction the grounds for assessing the relative merits of each interpretive style, as neither the Christians nor the Romans accurately reproduce the precursor text's meaning. Instead, the different values that Nietzsche attributes to these two re-translations can be traced to *genealogical* considerations. This is to say, the normative distinction Nietzsche draws between the Roman and Christian appropriations can be viewed as a consequence of the different interpretive styles that he finds operating within them. The Romans, themselves a noble culture in the grand style, are justified in Nietzsche's view in re-translating the texts of another noble culture, that of Greek antiquity, into their own present (cf. *A,* 59). The Christians, whose re-translation was guided by the decayed instincts and decadent style of the priests, are not justified in their re-creation, and the consequence of their art of "bad reading" is a book of which Nietzsche writes that "one does well to put on gloves when reading" (*A,* 46). It is this difference in interpretive style (grand vs. decadent), betokening a fundamental genealogical difference (life-enhancement vs. life-negation), that permits Nietzsche to affirm the Roman omission of historical sense while criticizing the Christian interpretation for the same omission.

The contrast between Nietzsche's evaluation of the Roman and Christian styles of textual appropriation is instructive as an example of a way to judge interpretations without appealing to the criterion of correctness of meaning or accuracy of reproduction. Employing the criteria of enhancement and impoverishment of life, Nietzschean genealogy avoids the dogmatic assertion of a "correct" interpretation, while at the same time avoiding an unmitigated relativism in which all interpretations are regarded as having equal value. In so doing, genealogy occupies a space between the interpretive demands of both philological attention and perspectival creativity. Within genealogical analysis, neither philological nor perspectival considerations alone are sufficient, and Nietzsche refrains from assessing the value of an interpretation solely in terms of either the degree of textual attentiveness which it exhibits (as evidenced by his affirmation of the Romans' inattention), or the creativity which is instantiated in its production (as indicated by his criticism of the Christians' creative production of the New Testament).

By adjudicating interpretive activity in terms of value (grand style—life-enhancement vs. decadent style—life-negation) rather than correctness, the interpretive praxis of Nietzschean genealogy operates within the *undecidability* of perspectivism and philology, drawing insights from each without exclusively affirming either. Recall here Nietzsche's remark on the importance of the color "gray" for the genealogist (*GM*, Pr., 7). The "gray" is what is "documented," and when Nietzsche genealogically deciphers the "entire long hieroglyphic record [. . .] of the moral past of mankind," he does attend to these "documents." In responding to what these "gray" documents "present," however, Nietzsche refuses to determine univocally their "meanings," while acknowledging both that his response comes from a particular perspective and that other perspectives are possible. In other words, he acknowledges that the "events" in the moral past of mankind are *ambiguous* and that the "meanings" which are to be "found" in these events are a function of the perspective from which they are examined. Thus, in attending to these moral texts from the perspective of the Dionysian and the transvaluation of values, these texts signify the negation of life and stand as an obstacle to the furthering of *this* perspective. Viewed from another perspective, for example, the perspective of "slave morality," these texts reveal themselves as "valuable," indeed they are necessary insofar as the slave moralists could not survive without them. Genealogical analysis refuses to posit a single interpretation as "correct" for all life, yet does not hesitate to judge certain interpretations as lacking in value for certain lives. In refraining from positing its conclusions as the "essential" meanings of the texts it deciphers which are "true" for all possible perspectives, Nietzschean genealogy provides us with a model of interpretive pluralism. It offers interpretations which proclaim themselves *as* interpretations; it avoids determining the text to which it responds as having a "single," "true" meaning; and it nevertheless retains a "standard" by which to judge between and rank the interpretations that do arise from the multiplicity of perspectives which it permits to be brought to the text. The remainder of this study will elaborate some of the implications for interpretation suggested by this interpretive approach.

Interpretive Pluralism

The same text allows countless interpretations: there is no "correct" interpretation.

—*KGW*, VIII, 1: 1[120]

How far the perspective character of existence extends or indeed whether existence has any other character than this; whether existence without interpretation, without "sense," does not become "nonsense"; whether, on the other hand, all existence [Dasein] is not essentially an interpreting *existence [auslegendes Dasein]—[. . .] I should think that today we are at least far from the ridiculous immodesty that would be involved in decreeing from our corner that perspectives are permitted only from this corner. Rather has the world become "infinite" for us all over again, inasmuch as we cannot reject the possibility that* it may include infinite interpretations.

—*The Gay Science*, 374

The assumption that guides this study has been that the basic problem facing an approach to interpretation is to avoid dogmatism while retaining a way to judge between competing interpretations. In the preceding section, Nietzsche's genealogical method was explicated in terms of its successfully avoiding this problem, insofar as his affirmation of perspectivism within the philological project of textual attention precluded any dogmatic assertion of a "truth" or "correct" interpretation, while it retained a standard (affirmation vs. negation of life) which could be used to adjudicate the multiplicity of interpretations occasioned by perspectivism. What remains is to elaborate in greater detail how a pluralistic approach that takes Nietzsche's thinking as its point of departure can contribute to solving this interpretive problem.

Before we begin, let me here return to an issue raised at the end of the Introduction and make a few remarks about my "use" of Nietzsche's text as an occasion for confronting some of the basic issues in the methodology of interpretation, and my employment of this reading as both an interpretation *of* Nietzsche's text and as itself an illustration of the praxis of interpretive pluralism. First, we must note that Nietzsche himself did not address explicitly the *methodological* implications of a pluralistic approach to interpretation. Nevertheless, in my reading of Nietzsche, which, it must be admitted, is at the same time the writing of Nietzsche's text as this text appears in the pages of this study, I find a number of points pertinent to many of the issues at the forefront of contemporary discussions of interpretive methods. Although the pluralistic method developed in the following pages is my construction, I will continue to refer frequently to Nietzsche's "texts." These references are not made in an appeal for validation, however; rather, I am both acknowledging my debt to his thinking as well as attempting to show that within these texts can be found a contribution to the contemporary debate over methods of interpretation.

Such references, moreover, should not be taken as my attempt to specify the "essential meaning" of Nietzsche's text, and the interpretation of that text which emerges in this study is not a "better" reading of Nietzsche than some of the other readings examined earlier, if by "better" is meant "more *correct*" or "more *comprehensive.*" Such criteria for assessing the merits of an interpretation presuppose what the pluralistic approach to interpretation denies, namely, that we should view interpretation as a "totalizing" activity that should be judged in terms of how much of the "original" text it "captures" within it or subsumes under the thematic structures which the interpretation imposes on the text. Instead, my interpretation attempts to instantiate the values affirmed within interpretive pluralism in seeking to *open* the Nietzschean text to a *new* reading, thereby revealing within this text new insights which can give rise to further interpretation. In so doing, this interpretation does not intend to display itself in a way that precludes or preempts other interpretations. Rather, it seeks to show that by bringing a new perspective to the Nietzschean text (i.e., viewing this text from the perspective of the methodology of interpretation), a new interpretation can be provided which, although it may differ from other, more traditional readings of Nietzsche, can nevertheless be shown to *fit* this text.

Two basic principles guide a Nietzschean interpretive pluralism. The first is that nothing exceeds the scope of interpretive activity. If there is a single, "foundational" presupposition in Nietzsche's philosophizing, it is the universalization of the scope of the interpretive process. This insight, which is reflected in his conception of language as anthropomorphic and metaphorical as well as his view of the perspectival character of all existence, is brought to bear upon all those fields of inquiry which were thought to escape the interpretive character of existence. One by one, they are each revealed to be nothing other than interpretation: metaphysics is only a "bad interpretation," (*KGW*, VII, 1: 6[1]), morality is "an *exegesis*, a way of interpretation" (*WP*, 254, 258), physics (*BGE*, 14), religion (*GS*, 353), reason (*WP*, 522): all appear in Nietzsche's text as modes of interpretation. Similarly, the privileged objects of these fields of inquiry are themselves revealed to be "merely" interpretations. We find Nietzsche deciphering the interpretive character of all "events" (*KGW*, VIII, 1: 1[115]), "facts" (*WP*, 481), "meanings" (*WP*, 604), "truths" (*WP*, 616), "necessity" (*WP*, 552), "beings" (*WP*, 715), "consciousness" (*WP*, 477). This comprehensive list reveals that there are no privileged objects that can escape the field of interpretive activity, nor is there anything that can bring the process of interpretation to a close.

Before moving to the second basic principle of interpretive pluralism, let us pause for a moment to consider a frequent objection to this Nietzschean insight, one which seeks to reduce Nietzsche's position to a version of the Liar's paradox. The objection runs something like this: "if everything is interpretation, then 'will to power,' '*Übermensch*,' and all of the other major themes in Nietzsche's philosophy are themselves only interpretations. Nietzsche thus provides us with no *ultimate* standard for judging the truth of *his* interpretations, and therefore we are free to reject the interpretations he provides." Such an objection, however, begs the question against Nietzsche in an important sense, for while we must grant that one is free to reject his interpretations, one cannot base this rejection, as is often done, upon the grounds that Nietzsche's philosophy fails to satisfy some standard ("truth," "the facts," "reality") whose legitimacy as a standard he explicitly criticizes. Thus, to accuse his interpretations of not being "true" is simply to accuse them of being precisely what he claims they are—*interpretations*, and not truths, facts, or anything else that purports to be an unambiguous representation of reality. On this point, Nietzsche is perhaps more consistent than many of his commentators have supposed.[7] This is to say, Nietzsche explicitly acknowledges that "Dionysus" is a "myth," that "*Übermensch*" is a "metaphor" (*WP*, 866) and that "will to power" is only an interpretation. Dwelling on this last point for a moment, the consistency of Nietzsche's text in regard to the universal scope of interpretation comes into view, and Nietzsche's response to this objection emerges as a re-affirmation of his position on the universal scope of interpretation. In a section from *Beyond Good and Evil,* Nietzsche concludes one of the many passages in which everything is revealed to be a form of will to power with the following remark: "Supposing that this is also only interpretation—and you will be eager enough to make this objection?—well, so much the better" (*BGE*, 22). In affirming the possibility that will to power is itself "only" an interpretation, Nietzsche makes the only response to this objection which his position permits. In other words, advocating a position which calls for multiple interpretations precludes Nietzsche's offering his interpretations as universally true and dogmatically binding on all interpreters. This response, however, is quite revealing in terms of disclosing how Nietzsche conceives will to power. If, on the one hand, the "*world is will to power—and nothing besides!*" (*WP*, 1067), and if, on the other hand, the world displays the universality of interpretation, then we can conclude that "will to power" is Nietzsche's name for the activity of interpretation. This is to say, what Nietzsche names "will to power" is *his* interpretation of the activity of interpretation, at once *an* interpretation and the *process* of interpretation itself. Nietzsche in fact says as much in *On the Genealogy of Morals:* if the will to power is ignored, "one overlooks the essential priority of the spontaneous, aggressive, expansive, form-giving forces that give new interpretations and directions" (*GM,* II, 12). In the same section, we also find the following remark:

> whatever exists, having somehow come into being [*irgendwie Zu-Stande-Gekommenes*], is again and again reinterpreted to new ends, taken over, transformed, and redirected by some power superior to it; all events in the organic world are a *subduing, becoming master,* and all subduing and becoming master involves a fresh interpretation, an adaptation through which any previous "meaning" and "purpose" are necessarily obscured or even obliterated.

Thus "will to power" operates through the interpretive imposition of meaning and is in Nietzsche's view nothing other than a name for the active process of interpretation itself. Rather than subjecting himself to self-refutation, Nietzsche further strengthens his claim to the universal scope of interpretive activity by acknowledging "will to power" as an interpretation *and* as a name for the interpretive process.

We can now move to the second basic principle of interpretive pluralism, which calls for the proliferation of competing interpretive perspectives. This call for the proliferation of interpretations reiterates many of the points discussed in the previous chapter, where we examined Nietzsche's use of the optical metaphor and his affirmation of the multiplicity of perspectives. In the remainder of this chapter, we shall develop the methodological consequences that this principle of proliferation[8] entails for the process of textual interpretation. At this point, we must recall the distinction made in the previous chapter between perspective and interpretation. While they are intimately connected, there is a difference between the multiplication of perspectives and the proliferation of interpretations. Interpretation, as we saw, is the ordering of a chaotic aggregate of perspectival viewpoints into meaningful wholes. Thus, the multiplication of perspectives facilitates the proliferation of interpretation: one brings new points of view to what is to be interpreted and these new points of view (perspectives) occasion new bestowals of meaning (interpretations). Because, as Nietzsche puts it, there are "no eternal horizons or perspectives" (*GS,* 143), the way should be opened for our interpretations to reflect our individual differences. This affirmation of difference(s) is made possible through experimenting with a variety of perspectives and actively creating new interpretations that avoid the overly hasty and unjust circumscription of the text's (world's) rich ambiguity and pluridimensionality. We find ourselves in a situation in which interpretive experimentalism is both necessary and desirable: necessary because the more we experiment with other perspectives and impose alternative interpretations, the greater will be the riches commandeered from the text/world's infinite reserve; and desirable because it is through our willingness to experiment with new perspectives that we avoid stagnation (cf. *GS,* 143) and show our individuality as accomplices in the co-creation of sense. Interpretive pluralism thus affirms the value of adopting a multiplicity of perspectives from which a plurality of interpretations can be generated, and it rejects the privileging of any single perspective or interpretation as the correct one. At one point, Nietzsche considers how Beethoven might respond to a masterful interpretation of one of his compositions, and he has Beethoven utter the following reply:

Well, well! That is neither I nor not-I, but some third thing—it seems to me, too, something right, if not just *the right thing* [*etwas Rechtes, wenn es gleich nicht* das Rechte *ist*]. But you must know yourselves what to do, as in any case it is you who have to listen—(*AOM,* 126)

The case would be the same with regard to any "object" of interpretation: there may be many "right" interpretations—Nietzsche suggests there may be an *infinite* number insofar as there are an infinite number of possible perspectives to adopt in viewing the text—but not *the* right one, that is, no *one* of these interpretations can be asserted as "correct" for all possible perspectives, all possible interpreters, and all possible ends.[9]

It is within the context of this rejection of the privileging of any single interpretation as "the correct interpretation" that we locate a Nietzschean deconstruction of author(ity). In Chapter Five, we examined Nietzsche's "death of God" in the context of his critique of the authority of language. God appeared as the author of the cosmological text (*"die Schrift der Natur"*), whose author(ity) as the source of meaning and purpose had to be deconstructed in order to make way for the *Übermensch's* transvaluation and re-interpretation of this great text of Nature. In the present context, we find an analogous deconstruction of literary author(ity), as Nietzsche rejects the traditionally privileged positioning of the author as a locus of textual signification for being an unjustifiable and unwarranted limitation on the activity of interpretation.

Given his views of the metaphorical, creative and ambiguous nature of language and the unavoidability of perspectival appropriation, one should not be surprised to find in Nietzsche's text a suspicion regarding the privileges of literary author-(ity). "A poet," Nietzsche writes, "is absolutely not an authority for the meaning of his verse" (Letter to C. Fuchs, Aug. 26, 1888; see also *GS*, 369). As early as his inaugural lecture at Basel, Nietzsche was critical of the cult of personality which had come into fashion in academic circles. This cult of personality runs the danger of losing the text in its efforts to discover the author's identity and tie this identity back into the text as a standard for discerning the textual meaning. This attitude, which in Nietzsche's view reached its zenith in the philological debates over the "Homer question," fails to grasp the critical insight that "Homer" as the composer of the *Iliad* and the *Odyssey* is an *"aesthetic* judgment" (*HCP* in *KGW*, II, 1: p. 263). For Nietzsche, whether or not there was *one* individual, Homer, who stands as the creative originator of these two texts should not be the focus of interpretation, and thus the biographical data as to what "Homer" was like and what meanings "he" intended by these texts becomes an inquiry of little value.

In addition to being of little value, the identification of the author and his or her text often proves detrimental to the text's reception (see *AOM,* 153). If a book is good, according to Nietzsche, it is worth more than the personality or biography of its author, and the personalization of the text, i.e., viewing it as a text by a particular individual with particular intentions, desires, etc., inhibits the text's ability to communicate (see, e.g., *AOM,* 156, *HAH,* 197). To combat the temptation to confuse the author's biography with his or her work, Nietzsche advises that we make a strict separation between the two. Once the text has been written, it lives a life of its own (see *HAH,* 208, entitled "The Book Almost

Become Human"). While Nietzsche anticipates psychoanalytic criticism in suggesting that we treat philosophical texts as their authors' "personal confessions, [. . .] a kind of involuntary and unconscious memoir" (*BGE*, 6), there is no interpretive imperative to treat texts this way. In bringing the text into the public domain, the author relinquishes all authority over what it is to mean: "When his work opens its mouth, the author must shut his" (*AOM*, 140). The text is free to confront different readers who are themselves free to adopt a multiplicity of perspectives on it. In the *Nachlass*, Nietzsche concludes a fragment entitled *"Travelbook on the way to reading [Reisebuch unterwegs zu lesen]"* with the following remark: "The preface is the author's right; the reader's is— the postface [*Die Vorrede ist des Autors Recht; des Lesers aber—die Nachrede*]" (*KGW*, IV, 2: 23[196]). Interpretation operates within this "postface," and in his affirmation of the *activity* of interpretation, Nietzsche expresses an antipathy toward any factor which tends to inhibit this activity and limit its proliferative play. His deconstruction of author(ity) is thus a deconstruction of authorial/authoritarian privilege insofar as Nietzsche wants to give to the author no special position, either as source or ultimate arbiter, in the determination of textual meaning.

With the refusal to accord to the author a privileged position within this interpretive space, and with the pluralistic deconstruction of all author(itarian) restrictions on the activity of interpretation, the principle of proliferation emerges as a meta-interpretive standard by which to judge between competing *methods* of interpretation. This is to say, a method of interpretation is acceptable if it does not put an end to the proliferating play of the activity of interpretation itself, and a method is to be criticized if it restricts the possibility of imposing alternative interpretations. Nietzsche's text expresses such a meta-interpretive principle within the terminology of enhancement and impoverishment of life: those methods which restrict the multiplication of perspectives and the proliferative play of interpretation result in interpretations which are hostile to life. Insofar as the denial of perspective is the denial of "the basic condition of all life" (*BGE*, Pr.), we find "the old philologist" Nietzsche unable to avoid identifying "bad modes of interpretation" (*BGE*, 22). In each case, the grounds for identifying a mode of interpretation as "bad" is that it leads to a narrowing of the variety of possible interpretations and the negation of life (see, e.g., *WP*, 616). This narrowing of possible points of view or "denying of perspective" is the essential characteristic of all dogmatism, and insofar as "every such *exaggeration* of a *single* viewpoint is in itself already a sign of sickness" (*WP*, 1020), it is, in part, on account of this interpretive dogmatism that Nietzsche rejects both the moral and ecclesiastical modes of interpretation. In *On the Genealogy of Morals,* the methods of both moral and ecclesiastical interpretation are revealed to be grounded in the ascetic ideal and its absolute faith in the universal value of truth (*GM*, III, passim). In this context we find one of Nietzsche's clearest statements of the methodological procedures of interpretive dogmatism:

The ascetic ideal has a *goal*—this goal is so universal that all the other interests of human existence seem, when compared with it, petty and narrow; it interprets epochs, nations, and men inexorably with a view to this one goal; it permits no other interpretation, no other goal; it rejects, denies, affirms, and sanctions solely from the point of view of *its* interpretation—(*GM*, III, 23)

In opposition to this dogmatic interpretive style, Nietzsche calls for a new species of philosopher who will be called "*experimenter [Versucher]*" (*BGE*, 42).[10] While these "philosophers of the future" will be friends of "truth,"

they will certainly not be dogmatists. It must offend their pride, also their taste, if their truth is supposed to be a truth for everyman—which has so far been the secret wish and hidden meaning of all dogmatic aspirations. (*BGE*, 43)

This is to say, these philosophers of the future will employ a mode of interpretation which resists what Nietzsche calls the "tyranny of the true," the desire to posit their truths alone as existing (see *D*, 507). This method of interpretation will instead acknowledge that "truth" does not exist as an absolute *in* things; rather, if truth exists at all, it will exist as a function of the relationships between "objects" of interpretation and the interpretive perspectives brought to those "objects" (see *KGW*, V, 1: 6[441]). As such, a good interpretive method will recognize that there is "no limit to the ways in which the world can be interpreted [*unendliche Ausdeutbarkeit der Welt*]" (*WP*, 600). It is this recognition of the limitless interpretive possibilities that both precludes any dogmatic interpretive approach and sanctions a pluralistic approach to interpretation.

Although adopting a pluralistic approach cannot rule out a priori the possibility that any particular interpretation *can* be shown to fit the text, it does not entail that all interpretations are of equal worth. This is the point where interpretive pluralism circumvents the forced choice between absolute textual fidelity and unbridled textual violation, and distinguishes itself from the sort of empty relativism which asserts that in the absence of a "correct" interpretation, *all* other interpretations are *equally* justified. We already indicated Nietzsche's distancing of his pluralistic position from the sort of relativism that cannot judge between competing interpretations in our examination of the adjudicatory function that style served in his genealogical approach. In emphasizing a conception of stylistic mastery as the ability to attend to the text while bringing to it a variety of perspectives, interpretive pluralism rejects "totalization" as the primary goal of interpretive activity. In calling for a plurality of interpretations, this approach affirms those readings that enhance the play of signification offered by the text, insofar as these readings reveal new aspects of the text and submit these new aspects to the further play of interpretation. In its affirmation of these readings, the meta-interpretive principle of proliferation reveals its usefulness as a standard of judgment: interpretations which enhance the text insofar as they open the text to further interpretive activity are "better" than those interpretations which aim to preclude the imposition of alternative interpretations by presenting themselves as the "truth" or the "essential meaning" or the "totality" of the text. In applying this standard, however, interpretive pluralism does not sanction the claim that "totalizing" interpretations are "wrong," any more than it authorizes the claim that readings which open the text are "right." Rather, it affirms the value of keeping the activity of interpretation open, and in calling for a plurality of interpretations, this approach does "justice"[11] to the pluridimensionality and plurivocity of the text, whether that text be a literary work, a historical event, a social practice, or the world.

   Returning to Nietzsche's text, we find this meta-interpretive standard, which opens the text to a proliferation of interpretations while bracketing the question of "correctness" or "incorrectness," at work both in his affirmation of the endless interpretability of the world, and in his rejection of dogmatism insofar as its assertion of "the Truth" seeks to put an end to the *activity* of interpretation. This standard operates as well in those qualities which, arising from the demands of both perspectivism and philology, Nietzsche affirms as signs of a good interpretive style. In his denial of a single correct interpretation as the telos which should guide interpretive activity, Nietzsche's approach to interpretation is *opened* to the play of perspective. To countermand the hegemony of any particular, narrowly circumscribed viewpoint, Nietzsche advocates an "adventurous" (*GS,* 324) and "inventive" (*GS,* 143) style. By bringing a variety of perspectives to the text, the interpreter takes risks insofar as the encounter with the text is a reciprocal questioning of both text and interpreter. The text is questioned in the light of these various perspectives and is thereby opened up to new insights and new meanings. At the same time, the questioner becomes the questioned: do these perspectives work with the text, can they be used to master the text, or does the text exceed the perspectives and escape this attempt at conquest? If so, what does this say about the value of these perspectives, what does the abortive attempt at mastery entail with respect to the legitimacy and utility of adopting such perspectives and what does it tell us about the style of the one who has adopted them?

   To answer these questions demands that we be attentive to the perspectives of the text itself, and here we return to the methodological consequences of Nietzsche's transvalued view of philology as the "art of reading well." The philologist, as the teacher of the *lento* (*D,* Pr., 5) and the art of reading as rumination [*Wiederkäuen*] (*GM,* Pr., 8), teaches a style of reading that is "cautious," (*D,* Pr., 5), "honest" (*A,* Pr.), and "just" (*GS,* 289). This style of reading is in control of its perspectives and refrains from the overly enthusiastic interpretations which do the text an injustice, either by selectively focusing on certain aspects of the text while ignoring others, or by rigidly imposing a single meaning on the rich ambiguity of the text and forcing the text to conform to this meaning. Philology, Nietzsche tells us, teaches its adherents the leisurely art and expertise of goldsmithing applied to words (*D*, Pr., 5). Like the goldsmiths, who know the limits of their material and yet can forge this raw material into ever-new and creative forms, so too the philologists know the limits of the text; they know when interpretation becomes violation and corruption and yet they can still work and rework the text, forging ever-novel and creative meanings "between the lines" (see *FEI*, Pr.). Within this view of the philologist as goldsmith, a transvalued and "extra-moral" notion of interpretive "responsibility" emerges. "Responsibility," as the *ability to respond*, serves as a practical guide to insure that the interpretations imposed remain connected with the text. That is to say, the interpretive "responsibility" of the philological goldsmith, while not providing a rigid system of rules to follow, nevertheless acknowledges that its forging of meaning must respond to and fit with the text. As such, this forging will be both supple and delicate, generously bringing its own perspectives to the text and animating the text with these new perspectives, while remaining subtle and cautious in its working creatively *with* what the text contributes to the interpretive process. It is in the tension between these two tendencies, between the adventurous, conquering impulse of creativity and invention, and the delicate, cautious impulse of honesty and justice, that Nietzsche situates the processes of interpretation. The sign of "good" style in interpretation will be the mastery of both these impulses while maintaining this tension, as Nietzsche makes clear when he affirms the new concept of "objectivity" in interpretation. This new "objectivity" will not resurrect the object of interpretation as a thing-in-itself that the activity of interpretation seeks to represent faithfully. Rather, it will acknowledge that all seeing and knowing is perspectival, while affirming the value of seeing with more and different eyes, and will be understood "as the ability *to control* one's Pro and Con and [. . .] employ a *variety* of perspectives and affective interpretations" in *responding* to the text (cf. *GM*, III, 12).

In setting forth this new "objectivity" as befitting the task of interpretation, Nietzsche subscribes to the demands of both perspectivism and philology, for the attainment of this new "objectivity" requires mastery of the creative multiplication of perspectives as well as a rigorous attentiveness to the text being interpreted. We are encouraged to increase the perspectives from which we view the text, but in such a way that we remain in control over these perspectives and use only those perspectives which can be made to *fit* with the text. We will not be able to determine *in principle* or before the fact whether or not a perspective can be made to fit. Rather, its fitness will have to be decided *in practice*, in terms of the strength and value of the interpretation(s) that can be generated from it.

A point needs to be made here regarding my use of the language of "fitting" rather than "appropriation," and the distinction this draws between an interpretation's *fitting with* the text and its being *appropriate to* the text. We have already seen, while examining the Derridean critique of Heidegger's nostalgia for a return to the *propre*, some of the problems implicit in the language of appropriation. In Nietzsche's approach to interpretation, there is also a suspicion regarding the language of appropriation insofar as it connotes certain demands of morality and conventionality. In the case of Nietzsche's own genealogical interpretations, for example, one might hesitate to say that they were *appropriate*. Certainly, in the context in which they appeared, Nietzsche's critiques of Christianity and morality were not received as appropriate responses to their respective texts, nor were they intended to be appropriate. In fact, Nietzsche's calling his work "untimely [*unzeitgemässe*]," for example, in the *Untimely Meditations* or in his "Skirmishes of an Untimely Man" in *Twilight of the Idols*, brings to the fore the lack of propriety of Nietzsche's interpretations. To be "timely," for Nietzsche, is to be appropriate to one's time, and inasmuch as he views the present times to be decadent, Nietzsche regards untimeliness and inappropriateness as a sign of distinction. While his interpretations fail to adhere to the accepted standards of propriety, they can nevertheless be shown to "fit" with the texts that he examines. The language of "fitting" thus avoids much of the implicit moralizing and conventionalism that often seems to accompany the language of "appropriation" as it is employed in discussions of interpretive methodology. It also avoids the notion of possession communicated by the language of appropriation,[12] and because it connotes a relation of working-with rather than taking-possession-of, I have chosen to speak of interpretive "fitness" rather than "propriety" in this explication of a pluralistic approach.

Keeping this distinction in mind, we must now examine whether Nietzsche's pluralistic approach to interpretation, poised as it is between the demands of both perspectivism and philology, can avoid the hermeneutical dilemma, whether expressed in the form of dogmatism vs. relativism or the related form of objectivism vs. subjectivism in interpretation.[13] I think this dilemma can be avoided successfully in either form by means of a strategic deconstruction of the opposition in which the dilemma is posed. This is to say, by deconstructing the binary (either/or) relation that animates the dilemma and showing this opposition to be illusory, the critical validity that the dilemma was felt to possess is annulled. A prime example of this strategy appears in *Twilight of the Idols*, when Nietzsche deconstructs the opposition between the true world and the apparent world. In the final stage of this deconstruction, Nietzsche writes:

> 6. The true world we have abolished: what world then remains? the apparent one perhaps? . . . But no! *with the true world we have also abolished the apparent one!* (*TI*, "How the 'True World' Finally Became a Fable")

We have abolished the apparent world because it has come to be defined as "apparent" only in terms of its opposition to the "true" world. Without the "true world" to serve as a standard, the designation as "apparent" is rendered meaningless. That is to say, the traditional (de)valuation of "appearance" is wholly dependent on its being the negation of that which the tradition has affirmed as "truth." Without a "true world" whose standards it fails to satisfy, there can be no *apparent* world either; there is only *a* world, neither true nor apparent, or *multiple* worlds, subject to multiple interpretations. By deciphering one pole of the binary opposition (the "true world") to be an illusion, the opposition itself loses its critical force.[14]

Applying this strategy to the hermeneutic dilemma, we can see how the Nietzschean approach can avoid that dilemma's noxious consequences. Clearly, there is no problem checking the dogmatic or objectivistic side: in calling for the utilization of a multiplicity of perspectives and a proliferation of competing interpretations, interpretive pluralism explicitly rejects the dogmatic assertion of a "correct" interpretation or "objective" meaning (*the* Truth). However, in advocating a multiplicity of perspectives which are necessarily individual, this approach would appear to leave itself open to the charges of being relativistic or subjectivistic. While an interpretive pluralist would, at one level, have to accept these charges, he or she would do so only after having applied to them Nietzsche's deconstructive strategy, so as to rob them of the critical force which his or her critics would intend.[15] This is to say, relativism is a "genuine" problem only when it is compared to a judgment made according to some absolute, dogmatic standard. When not operating from within a context framed by the false disjunction "either one truth/meaning or every interpretation is as good as every other interpretation," the charge of relativism loses its critical force and no longer appears to be the crime against Reason that philosophers have often thought it to be. Likewise, regarding subjectivism, the subject as the center of judgments is criticized only in terms of its failing to satisfy the standards of objectivity. If one denies, as Nietzsche does, the subject/object schema (see, e.g., *GS*, 346), if both "subject" and "object" are themselves interpretations (*WP*, 481), then the critical force of "subjectivism" is obviated. When Nietzsche writes, for example, that "one may not ask: 'who then interprets?' " (*WP*, 556), it is because such a question already mislocates the interpretive process. Likewise, one may not ask "what then is interpreted?" Interpretation is not grounded in either the subject or object; it exists in the *between,* in the space which separates them.[16] And the attempt to focus the interpretive process in the direction of either the subject or the object will only serve to obscure the dynamics of this process.

It is precisely to avoid this falsely framed context that we have chosen to speak, as did Nietzsche, of perspectival *multiplicity* and interpretive *pluralism,* for "relativism" has come to be so tainted by this false disjunction ("one truth or anything goes") within the discursive practices of philosophy that it is virtually unrecoverable. The pluralistic approach to interpretation can thus respond to the text as an occasion for creative play, but in such a way that it refrains from positing any endpoint to the interpretive process while at the same time refusing to sanction all those interpretations which do arise as equally meritorious. In Nietzsche's case, this was accomplished by means of replacing the criteria of truth and falsity of interpretation with the criteria of healthy and decadent styles of interpretations. Those interpretations which are healthy, i.e., those interpretations which enhance the creative and procreative impulse of life (the "will to power") are justifiable, while those decadent interpretations which impoverish the will to power are illegitimate. The point of the examination of Nietzsche's discussion of the adjudicatory function of style was not to weigh the relative merits and liabilities of health or life-enhancement as a criterion for the adjudication of competing interpretations. Rather, it has been to show that by adopting such a criterion, Nietzsche can avoid the dilemma of choosing between dogmatism and relativism in his approach to interpretation. Insofar as health or life-enhancement is a situation-specific and variable standard (cf. *GS,* 120: "there is no health-in-itself"), there can be no single correct interpretation which will enhance life or promote health for all interpreters and for all times. While we might all affirm health as a standard, what we each regard as healthy will be determined as a function of the perspectives from which we are operating. Nietzsche thus can affirm health as a standard without thereby specifying a universally applicable criterion for what is to count as healthy or life-enhancing. In so doing, Nietzsche allows for a proliferation of acceptable interpretations (thereby avoiding the dogmatic assertion of a single "correct" interpretation), while retaining a standard by which to distinguish "better" from "worse" interpretations (thus avoiding an empty relativism in which all interpretations are of equal value).

It is important to note that, in resorting to the language of life-enhancement and life-negation or healthy and decadent will to power, Nietzsche appears himself to be offering another privileged binary opposition. I would suggest, however, that his binary is in one way significantly different from the traditional binary oppositions like good/evil or truth/error that he genealogically dismantles. Nietzsche remained to some extent caught in the metaphysical snares of grammar and the oppositional structures inherent in language, and he may not have been able to follow completely his own call to "free ourselves from the seductions of words" (*BGE,* 16). Yet his analysis does suggest a way to avoid these binary structures. One can interpret healthy and decadent will to power in a non-oppositional sense in terms of viewing "health and disease" or "enhancement and negation" as two poles of a single monistic continuum which is will to power. Such an interpretation does not posit two mutually exclusive alternatives which call for some choice, as is the case with the classical binary oppositions that Nietzsche rejects. Where the classical oppositions focus on standards that are absolute (good or evil, truth or error), Nietzsche's opposition (affirmation *and* negation of life) is expressed in terms of the normative limits of an open-ended continuum of will to power which admits only of "degrees of gradation" (see *GS,* 112). We can only move closer to or further from health or life-enhancement. We cannot attain health or life-enhancement *absolutely.* In fact, the idea of *"absolute* health" or *"absolute* enhancement of life," like the concept of "the highest integer," may be incoherent. To speak as Nietzsche does in terms of a continuum places emphasis on the process of moving toward one's goal rather than the endpoint of absolutely attaining it. This transvalues the notion of a choice between opposites, as one's place along the continuum is to be appraised not in terms of an absolute position but in terms of the degree to which one's place manifests an *active* imposition of creative force. Nietzsche indicates such an interpretation when he speaks of the will to power as the procreative force which *is* life. This will to power can be increased or decreased, strengthened or weakened, but there is no binary opposition involved: there is only will to power.[17]

If we accept the general structure of Nietzsche's position and, in a way which Nietzsche himself suggests, determine "will to power" as the activity of interpretation itself, we can draw the following methodological conclusions: a pluralistic approach sanctions the proliferation of interpretations and, in so doing, it refrains from positing any universal criteriology for judging the "validity" or "veracity" of the interpretations which arise. Instead, it suggests a meta-interpretive standard that seeks to insure that interpretations present themselves *as* interpretations, always partial and subject to revision, in a way that refrains from foreclosing the activity of interpretation. In affirming the openness of interpretation, however, interpretive pluralism does not disregard the text. Rather, it situates textual response-ability within the activity of interpretation itself. That is to say, it is the task of the interpretation added to the text to demonstrate how it appears to *fit* with the text. Leaving this question of the text and textual fitness open for the moment, we can summarize the pluralistic guidelines suggested by Nietzsche's text as follows: interpretive pluralism affirms those interpretations which acknowledge the demands of philological attentiveness (i.e., they show themselves to fit with the text) *and* further enhance our capacity for creative interpretation, and this approach is critical of those interpretations which fail to attend to these basic philological considerations (they fail to show their textual fitness) and/or which limit the play of future interpretive activity.

In concluding this discussion, let me return to a metaphor Nietzsche provides as a clue for understanding how a balance can be achieved between the philological rigor that accounts for the unfitness of some interpretations, and the perspectivism that allows for the proliferation of a multiplicity of interpretations. In *Human, All-Too-Human* (278), Nietzsche discusses the metaphor of the dance. Dancing, he writes, is not merely the mechanical following of a pattern of steps. Rather, the dancer must possess both strength and flexibility. He or she must follow the basic pattern of steps, but in following the pattern, the dance is created anew, in as fluid and as beautiful a form as the dancer is capable of creating. Similarly, a good interpretation is not merely the rigorous appropriation of the meaning contained within the text. Rather, it is an interpretation that maintains control over a multiplicity of perspectives, and that is determined both by the text to which the interpreter responds and by what the interpreter brings to the text in conjunction with his or her capacity to create. A textual interpretation will be as strong and as supple, as creative and as fitting as the interpreter is him- or herself. It is in this sense that, as Nietzsche writes, we can get no more out of texts than what we bring to them (see *EH*, III, 1). As a choreographed history, Nietzschean genealogy demonstrates that we need not choose between the dogmatic assertion of one meaning and the relativistic acceptance of any meaning. Instead, the activity of interpretation must play between these two alternatives, whose only functions are to mark the end of the play. Interpretive pluralism recognizes these two alternatives as the limits between which the play of interpretation must unfold, and for this reason it situates itself in the *between* linking methodological rigor and creative apprehension.

The Question of the Text

> *How can we know the dancer from the dance?*
> —Yeats, "Among School Children"

> *This is a text without end [ein* Text ohne Ende*] for thinkers [. . . .]*
> —*Assorted Opinions and Maxims,* 212

One final question remains to be addressed before we can close this examination of Nietzsche's pluralistic approach to interpretation, namely, what becomes of the text within the proliferating play of interpretive pluralism? We previewed the answer to this question at the conclusion of Chapter Six, where we suggested that Nietzsche's transvaluation of philology brings with it a transvalued concept of the text. In this concluding section, I will indicate how we might understand this transvalued text.

In both his explicit comments and implicit assumptions regarding texts and textuality, we find Nietzsche anticipating many of the central problems at the forefront of contemporary debates over the question of textuality. Philippe Lacoue-Labarthe observes that without Nietzsche, "the 'question' of the text would never have erupted, at least in the precise form that it has taken today."[18] In particular, we find Nietzsche anticipating the "precise form" of the contemporary question of textuality in two important ways. The first is his broadening the extension of the metaphor of textuality. In universalizing the scope of interpretation to the point where nothing escapes the field of interpretive activity, Nietzsche broadens the extension of the textual metaphor beyond the confines of literature and the printed or spoken word. We thus find Nietzsche speaking of such "things" as Greek history, morality, and *homo natura* as texts. Moreover, in speaking of these texts, Nietzsche makes clear that their existence as texts is not the existence of static, completed objects. Rather, as texts, they are "palimpsests" which undergo a continual process of re-writing (see *H,* 3). Our task in reading these texts, for example, in the case of the text of *homo natura,* is thus

> to become master over the many vain and overly enthusiastic interpretations and connotations that have so far been scrawled and painted over that eternal basic text [*ewigen Grundtext*] of *homo natura;* [. . .] (*BGE,* 230)

The status of the text as palimpsest brings us to the second way that Nietzsche anticipates the contemporary question of textuality. The irreducible tension in Nietzsche between the perspectival and philological aspects of interpretation gives rise to a tension in his conception of the text itself, as we saw at the conclusion of Chapter Six, where this tension was located at the center of the disagreement between Sarah Kofman's and Jean Granier's readings of Nietzsche. Philology seems to imply that the text exists as an object for interpretive activity to which this activity has certain obligations (honesty, justice, attentiveness, fidelity, etc.), while perspectivism seems to preclude any conception of the text as an independent object which exists in itself apart from the activity of interpretation. To resolve this irreducible opposition is to provide an answer to the question of the relationship between texts and interpretations, and Nietzsche suggests such an answer by means of what I have called his transvalued conception of the text.

In Nietzsche's transvaluation of the text, he suggests a *practical* rather than an *ontological* solution to the question of the text.[19] This is to say, Nietzsche does not concern himself with answering the question of the ontological status of texts. Instead, he provides a conception of the text that will work in the context of the praxis of interpretive pluralism. Questions of ontology, in the case of the text as elsewhere in Nietzsche's philosophizing, are viewed to be superfluous insofar as they exceed the limits of finite human comprehension within the domain of a universalized field of interpretation. In other words, questions of ontology are for Nietzsche ultimately questions regarding the way things are in themselves apart from the activity of interpretation. Insofar as human understanding is limited to this interpretive domain, all ontological speculation is, therefore, an "*idle hypothesis.*" Nietzsche writes:

> That things possess a *constitution in themselves* quite apart from interpretation and subjectivity [*Interpretation und Subjektivität*] is *a quite idle hypothesis:* it presupposes that *interpreting and being-subjective* [*Interpretiren und Subjektivsein*] are *not* essential, that a thing freed from all relationships would still be a thing. (*WP*, 560)

The consequences of this position for the question of textuality are clear: there is no "text-in-itself" apart from the activity of interpretation, and a text freed from all interpretive relationships would no longer be a text. While this tells us only what a text is *not* (i.e., it is not any*thing* other than interpretation), Nietzsche refuses to specify what a text *is,* insofar as the posing of the question "what is a text?" already stands as an *imposition* of meaning in predetermining an answer within an ontological framework (cf. *WP*, 556). Nietzsche does suggest, however, an alternative way to answer the ontological question "what is . . . ":

> A thing would be defined once all beings [*Wesen*] had asked "what is that?" and had answered their question. Supposing one single being, with its own relationships and

perspectives for all things, were missing: then the thing would not yet be "defined."
(*WP, 556*)

Insofar as "things" exist only in relations, the "definition" of a "thing" must account for the multiplicity of possible relationships in which it may be found. Applying this view to the question of textuality, Nietzsche's transvalued conception of the text suggests the following: the "text" is not an independently existing object but the heuristic aggregate of all possible interpretations which can be imposed on it. This is to say, a text is distinct from any *particular* interpretation, but it *is* nothing other than a product of interpretive activity. The text and its interpretations exist only in a relationship of *reciprocal* creation: the "text" is fabricated from the totality of possible interpretations which themselves emerge in response to the text. As a consequence, there can be no single totalizing interpretation which completely masters the "essential meaning" or "truth" of the text; no one interpretation will exactly replicate the text, nor will any one interpretation get the text "exactly right," for it is the "nature" of the text as an infinite reservoir of possible signification to exceed all attempts at totalization.

It is with this sort of view of textuality that Nietzsche can speak of the text as a palimpsest, at once written and subject to continual revision (re-vision = to see again). He can thus conclude that texts, like truths, are not discovered but created (see *WP, 552*), and they are created by means of the reciprocal interpenetration of text and interpretation. Regarding the text of Greek history, Nietzsche writes that "their familiar history is a polished mirror, always reflecting something that is not in the mirror itself" (*AOM, 218*). What is reflected in the text is thus our own interpretive style as it is determined by what we respond to in the text. In answering Yeats' famous question "How can we know the dancer from the dance?" Nietzsche would joyfully affirm that we can't know the dancer from the dance, nor can we rigidly differentiate the interpretation from the text. In its performance, the dancer *is* the dance, and in the activity of interpretation, the interpretation *is* the text. But just as the same dance will be performed differently by different dancers, the same text will be incarnated differently by different interpretations. This conclusion, it must be emphasized, is one of *practical* value and not ontological definition. Given the rich ambiguity of the text/world, given the multiplicity of possible interpretations of the text/world, and given the absence of a universally applicable criteriology for appraising such an infinite multiplicity of possible interpretations, no conception other than the reciprocal "determination" and interpenetration of text and interpretation will account for the necessity of interpretive pluralism while retaining a method for assessing the relative strengths and weaknesses of these competing interpretations.

By way of concluding this exposition, I will discuss one last Nietzschean metaphor, that of the labyrinth. This metaphor frequently appears in Nietzsche's discussions of textuality and interpretation, and these appearances suggest that the labyrinth is a basic Nietzschean image for the structure of the text. In this regard, we find Nietzsche making references to his own texts as labyrinths: *Thus Spoke Zarathustra* is described as a "labyrinth of daring knowledge" (*EH*, III, 3), while his *Untimely Meditations* are seen as a labyrinth in which readers risk becoming entrapped (*KGW*, VII, 3: 37[5]). Because of the labyrinthine structure of his texts, Nietzsche lists strength, courage and a "predestination for the labyrinth" among the traits which his "rightful readers" must possess (*A*, Pr.). This is to say, armed with the knowledge that a labyrinth can also be a goldmine, these readers will have both the courage to enter the textual labyrinth and the strength to commandeer what is to be found therein (see *KGW*, VII, 3: 37[5]). The image of the labyrinth is not restricted to texts in the narrow sense, however, and just as Nietzsche extended the metaphor of the text beyond the domain of literature, we find a concomitant extension of the image of the labyrinth as Nietzsche uncovers the labyrinthine nature of such texts as the modern soul (*CW*, Pr.), past cultures (*BGE*, 224), existence (*GS*, 322), and life (*BGE*, 29).

The image of the labyrinth is accompanied in Nietzsche's writings by another image, that of Dionysus. As the dancing god and grand stylist, Dionysus is the master of the labyrinthine text. Within the extensive literature dealing with Nietzsche's conception of the Dionysian, little attention has been paid to the relation between Dionysus and the labyrinth as an allegory of his conception of textual interpretation. I will close my discussion of Nietzsche by suggesting an interpretation of this Dionysian allegory.

For Nietzsche, Dionysus' fate is to undergo the eternal recurrence of self-dispersion and return to wholeness (see *WP*, 1052). This is also, as I have attempted to show, the fate of interpretation within the labyrinth of the text. Just as Dionysus risks becoming fragmented in losing his way within the labyrinth, the interpreter risks fracturing the text through adopting a multiplicity of perspectives and experimenting with alternative interpretations. Through self-mastery, however, Dionysus always returns to wholeness with an increased level of strength, and through stylistic mastery, the masterful interpreter is rewarded with an increased understanding of the rich ambiguity of the textual labyrinth. In putting forth this image of the Dionysian mastery of the labyrinth, Nietzsche in effect confronts the interpreter with a challenge to see how far into the textual labyrinth one can go without losing one's way and becoming hopelessly entangled within its complex maze of possible interpretations. Returning to Nietzsche's myth, we discover that Dionysus does not escape from the labyrinth unassisted. As a labyrinthian man, Dionysus "never seeks the truth but always only his Ariadne" (*KGW*, VII, 1: 4[55]). Ariadne, who provides the thread by means of which Dionysus makes his escape from the labyrinth, is the answer to the Dionysian suffering that risks irretrievable fragmentation in his wandering within the labyrinth (see *EH*, Z8). If Dionysus is Nietzsche's image of the intrepid multiplier of perspectives, might not Ariadne's thread be the thread of philological rigor that insures that these perspectives follow the walls of the labyrinthine text? Just as Dionysus can master the labyrinth only with the assistance of Ariadne's thread, so too the multiplication of perspectives can be used to master the text only with the assistance of philological attention. For Nietzsche, a union between Dionysus and Ariadne is required in order to escape from the labyrinth. In the same way, I have attempted to show that a union of perspectivism and philology, as limiting alternatives between which interpretation must play, offers a means of escape from the hermeneutic dilemma, and that we can make such an escape within the praxis of interpretive pluralism.

Notes

Introduction

1. See, for example, Martin Heidegger, "The Way Back into the Ground of Metaphysics," translated by Walter Kaufmann in *Existentialism from Dostoevsky to Sartre* (New York: New American Library, 1975), pp. 265–279. Heidegger's last published work, *On Time and Being,* translated by Joan Stambaugh (New York: Harper and Row, Publishers, Inc., 1972) addresses this issue as well. See especially the essay "The End of Philosophy and the Task of Thinking," which opens with a call for the "transformation" of metaphysical thinking (p. 55).

2. See, for example, Richard Rorty, *Philosophy and the Mirror of Nature* (Princeton: Princeton University Press, 1979), especially Chapter Eight.

3. For a more detailed review of the history of contemporary hermeneutics, the reader is referred to the following discussions: Wilhelm Dilthey, "The Development of Hermeneutics," in *Dilthey: Selected Writings,* translated and edited by H. P. Rickman (Cambridge: Cambridge University Press, 1976); Richard E. Palmer, *Hermeneutics* (Evanston: Northwestern University Press, 1969); Paul Ricoeur, "The Task of Hermeneutics," translated by John B. Thompson in *Hermeneutics and the Human Sciences* (Cambridge: Cambridge University Press, 1981). See also the editorial introduction (where many of the points discussed in this chapter are developed in greater detail) and texts collected in *The Hermeneutic Tradition: From Ast to Ricoeur,* edited by Gayle L. Ormiston and Alan D. Schrift (Albany: State University of New York Press, 1990).

4. The opening sentence of Schleiermacher's Outline for the 1819 Lectures on Hermeneutics reads: "At present there is no general hermeneutics as the art of understanding but only a variety of specialized hermeneutics." Friedrich D. E. Schleiermacher, *Hermeneutics: The Handwritten Manuscripts,* edited by Heinz Kimmerle and translated by James Duke and Jack Forstman (Missoula, Mont.: Scholars Press, 1977), p. 95.

5. Schleiermacher, *Hermeneutics,* p. 112; see also pp. 64, 69.

6. Schleiermacher, *Hermeneutics,* p. 64.

7. Dilthey, *Selected Writings,* p. 261.

8. Dilthey, *Selected Writings,* p. 256.

9. Dilthey, *Selected Writings,* p. 260. Translation altered slightly.

10. Dilthey, *Selected Writings,* p. 207.

11. Dilthey, *Selected Writings,* p. 208. Translation altered slightly.

12. Martin Heidegger, *Being and Time,* translated by John Macquarrie and Edward Robinson (London: SCM Press, Ltd., 1962), p. 62.

13. Heidegger, *Being and Time,* p. 487.

14. For a more detailed explication of the disagreements between these camps, see David C. Hoy, *The Critical Circle* (Berkeley: University of California Press, 1978).

15. Hans-Georg Gadamer, *Truth and Method*, Second Edition, translated and edited by Garrett Barden and John Cumming (London: Sheed and Ward, Ltd., 1975), p. 350.

16. Gadamer, *Truth and Method*, p. xi.

17. See Hans-Georg Gadamer, *Philosophical Hermeneutics*, translated and edited by David E. Linge (Berkeley: University of California Press, 1976), p. 28; see also *Truth and Method*, p. 263.

18. Gadamer, *Truth and Method*, p. 421.

19. Gadamer, *Truth and Method*, pp. 431–432.

20. Emilio Betti, *Hermeneutics as the General Methodology of the Geisteswissenschaften*, translated by Josef Bleicher in Ormiston and Schrift, eds. *The Hermeneutic Tradition*, pp. 177–178, 182–183.

21. Betti, p. 187.

22. E.D. Hirsch, Jr., *Validity in Interpretation* (New Haven: Yale University Press, 1967), p. 242.

23. Hirsch, p. 164.

24. Hirsch, p. 25.

25. Betti, p. 164.

26. For the specifics of this debate see Jürgen Habermas, "The Hermeneutic Claim to Universality," translated by Josef Bleicher in *The Hermeneutic Tradition*, pp. 245–272; and Hans-Georg Gadamer's response in "On the Scope and Function of Hermeneutical Reflection," translated by G. B. Hess and Richard E. Palmer in *Philosophical Hermeneutics*, pp. 18–43.

27. It is interesting to note that, in part, Gadamer's response takes the form of accusing *Habermas* of *dogmatism:* "The concept of reflection and bringing to awareness that Habermas employs (admittedly from his sociological interest) appears to me, then, to be itself encumbered with dogmatism, and indeed, to be a misinterpretation of reflection" (*Philosophical Hermeneutics*, pp. 34–35).

28. See Jacques Derrida, *Positions*, translated by Alan Bass (Chicago: University of Chicago Press, 1981), p. 63. See also the various texts and commentaries on the differences between Gadamer's and Derrida's approaches to interpretation in *Dialogue and Deconstruction: The Gadamer-Derrida Encounter*, edited by Diane P. Michelfelder and Richard E. Palmer (Albany: State University of New York Press, 1989).

29. Jean-Paul Sartre, *What is Literature?* translated by Bernard Frechtman and reprinted as *Literature and Existentialism* (Secaucus, N.J.: Citadel Press, Inc., 1972), p. 46.

Chapter 1: Heidegger Reading Nietzsche

1. Quoted in Bernd Magnus, *Heidegger's Metahistory of Philosophy: Amor Fati, Being and Truth* (The Hague: Martinus Nijhoff, 1970), p. 80.

2. Martin Heidegger, *Platons Lehre von der Wahrheit* (Bern: Francke Verlag, 1947), p. 5: *"Die 'Lehre' eines Denkers ist das in seinem Sagen Ungesagte."*

3. Martin Heidegger, *Nietzsche. Volume One: The Will to Power as Art*, translated by David F. Krell (San Francisco: Harper and Row, Publishers, Inc., 1979), pp. 8–9. This text is a translation of Heidegger's *Nietzsche*, Band I (Pfullingen: Verlag Günther Neske, 1961), pp. 11–254. Hereafter, references to this translation will be cited in the text as *"N I"* followed by the page numbers.

4. Martin Heidegger, *What is Called Thinking?* translated by J. Glenn Gray (New York: Harper and Row, Publishers, Inc., 1968), p. 73. Hereafter, references to this work will be cited in the text as *"WCT"* followed by the page number.

5. Karl Jaspers, *Nietzsche: An Introduction to the Understanding of his Philosophical Activity,* translated by Charles F. Wallraff and Frederick J. Schmitz (Tucson: University of Arizona Press, 1965), p. 5.

6. Bernd Magnus, "Nietzsche's Philosophy in 1888: *The Will to Power* and the *Übermensch*," *The Journal of the History of Philosophy*, Vol. 24, No. 1 (January 1986), pp. 79–98. For my own position on the status of the *Nachlass*, see my remarks at the beginning of Chapter Five below, p. 124.

7. This latter alternative, in fact, may often be the case. This interpretation is useful for understanding the relation between Nietzsche's published account of the eternal recurrence and the various "cosmological proofs" of the eternal recurrence found in his notebooks. Regarding the problematic status of Nietzsche's attempts at a cosmological proof, see Magnus, *Heidegger's Metahistory of Philosophy*, pp. 9–26, and Arthur C. Danto, *Nietzsche as Philosopher* (New York: Columbia University Press, 1980), pp. 203–213.

8. William J. Richardson, S.J., *Heidegger: Through Phenomenology to Thought* (The Hague: Martinus Nijhoff, 1963), p. 22.

9. This tendency toward *expropriation* appears most clearly in Heidegger's discussion of the primordial understanding of truth (*alētheia*) as unconcealment. When confronted with philological evidence that already in Homer *alētheia* had the sense of "correctness," Heidegger in effect responded that *even the Greeks* did not understand what they knew about *alētheia:*

    > Opening is named with *alētheia*, unconcealment, but not thought as such. The natural concept of truth does not mean unconcealment, not in the philosophy of the Greeks either. It is often and justifiably pointed out that the word *alēthes* is already used by Homer only in the *verba dicendi*, in statement and thus in the sense of correctness and reliability, not in the sense of unconcealment. But this reference means only that neither the poets nor everyday language usage, not even philosophy see themselves confronted with the task of asking how truth, that is, the correctness of statements, is granted only in the element of the opening of presence. (*On Time and Being*, p. 70)

10. The link between Nietzsche's *ephexis* and the phenomenological *epochē* will be picked up in Chapter Six; see pp. 164, 220 note 12.

11. We must examine, for example, whether Heidegger's reading will fall prey to the same criticism Nietzsche makes of the New Testament theologians' "insertion" of Christ into the Old Testament in *Daybreak*, 84, discussed below, pp. 164–166.

12. This reductive appeal to a thinker's one thought is a classical philological theme. Friedrich Ast, in his *Grundlinien der Grammatik, Hermeneutik und Kritik* (Landshut: 1808), says that the key to understanding a Platonic dialogue is to understand it in terms of that "one idea [woven] through all dialogues, constituting the soul of the Platonic dialogues, [which] in every individual text appears in a different representation, viewed from a different perspective" (Section 88). Selections from Ast's *Grundlinien* have been translated by Dora van Vranken and appear in Ormiston and Schrift, eds., *The Hermeneutic Tradition: From Ast to Ricoeur*, pp. 39–56.

13. Martin Heidegger, *Nietzsche* Band I, p. 475. *"Nietzsche gehört zu den wesentlichen Denkern. Mit dem Namen 'Denker' benennen wir jene Gezeichneten unter den Menschen, die einen einzigen Gedanken—und diesen immer 'über' das Seiende im Ganzen—zu denken bestimmt sind. Jeder Denker denkt nur einen einzigen Gedanken."* As we shall see, to think this thought about *"beings as a whole"* is not to think the thought of the *Seinsfrage*, the thought about the

Being of beings. For Heidegger, Nietzsche *begins* to think the *Seinsfrage* when he thinks the will to power *as* the eternal recurrence of the same. However, insofar as Nietzsche fails to distinguish between the question of the Being of beings and the question of beings as a whole, he is still, according to Heidegger, thinking "metaphysically."

14. Martin Heidegger, *Nietzsche. Volume Four: Nihilism*, translated by Frank A. Capuzzi and edited by David F. Krell (San Francisco: Harper and Row, Publishers, Inc., 1982), pp. 9–10 (translation modified). This text is a translation of Heidegger's *Nietzsche*, Band II (Pfullingen: Verlag Günther Neske, 1961); the quote appears on p. 40.

15. Martin Heidegger, "Nietzsche's Word: 'God is Dead,' " translated by William Lovitt in *The Question Concerning Technology and Other Essays* (New York: Harper and Row, Publishers, Inc., 1977), pp. 54–55. Heidegger's essay originally appeared as "Nietzsches Wort: 'Gott ist tot,' " in *Holzwege*. Hereafter, references to the Lovitt translation will be cited in the text as "*NW*" followed by the page number.

16. Martin Heidegger, *Identity and Difference*, translated by Joan Stambaugh (New York: Harper and Row, Publishers, Inc., 1969), p. 59.

17. Martin Heidegger, "Wer ist Nietzsches Zarathustra?" written in 1953 and first published in *Vorträge und Aufsätze*, Teil I (Pfullingen: Verlag Günther Neske, 1954), pp. 97–122. Translation by Bernd Magnus first appeared in *Review of Metaphysics*, Vol. XX (March 1967) and was later reprinted in *The New Nietzsche*, edited by David B. Allison (New York: Dell Publishing Co., Inc., 1977), pp. 64–79. Hereafter, references to this essay will be cited as "*NZ*" followed by the page number in the Allison edition.

18. "Essence" is the traditional translation for the German noun "*Wesen*" and, in what follows, I will for the most part render Heidegger's "*Wesen*" by "essence." However, Heidegger packs much more into "*Wesen*" than can be accurately rendered by the traditional concept of essence as "whatness." In fact, it is a central theme in Heidegger's philosophy to show that *Wesen* does not simply mean *what* something is, but means also the way in which something endures as what it is. In "The Question Concerning Technology," he writes that "*Wesen* understood as a verb is the same as *währen* [to last or endure]" (Martin Heidegger, *The Question Concerning Technology*, p. 30). Elsewhere, Heidegger writes that "the *substantive* '*Wesen*' did not originally mean 'whatness,' *quidditas*, but enduring as presence [*Währen als Gegenwart*]" (Martin Heidegger, *An Introduction to Metaphysics*, translated by Ralph Manheim [Garden City, N.Y.: Doubleday and Company, Inc., 1961], p. 59). In the present discussion, readers of Heidegger must keep in mind both senses of *Wesen*, as "essence" ("whatness") and as "coming-to-presence" (*Anwesen*), if they are to understand his discussion of the essence of nihilism in Nietzsche as the event ("coming-to-presence") of the highest values devaluing themselves.

19. Heidegger, *Being and Time*, p. 67.

20. These points are elaborated in Heidegger's *Nietzsche*, Band II, pp. 421–436 and 450–454, a translation of which can be found in Heidegger, *The End of Philosophy*, translated by Joan Stambaugh (New York: Harper and Row, Publishers, Inc., 1973), pp. 19–32 and 46–49.

21. The value of art over truth plays a central role in Heidegger's reading of Nietzsche and we will return to this theme in discussing Heidegger's interpretation of Nietzsche's overturning of Platonism. See pp. 49–52.

22. Heidegger notes, in this regard, that Nietzsche unravels the riddle of the eternal recurrence while standing under the gateway named "Moment" (cf. Z, "On the Vision and the Riddle").

23. Heidegger appeals to this note at several crucial points in his Nietzsche interpretation as evidence of Nietzsche's remaining committed to a metaphysical project. The most significant appeal comes in the final section ("Nietzsche's Fundamental Metaphysical Position") of *Nietzsche. Volume Two: The Eternal Recurrence of the Same*, edited and translated by David F. Krell

(New York: Harper and Row, Publishers, Inc., 1984), pp. 201–202. In addition, see its appearance in *N* I, p. 19, and *Nietzsche. Volume Three: The Will to Power as Knowledge and Metaphysics,* edited by David F. Krell and translated by Joan Stambaugh, David F. Krell, and Frank A. Capuzzi (New York: Harper and Row, Publishers, Inc., 1987), pp. 156, 213, and 245.

24. *"Der Wille zur Macht als Kunst,"* in *Nietzsche,* Band I, pp. 11–254. For translation, see note 3.

25. This image is suggested by David F. Krell in his analysis of Heidegger's lecture in *N* I, p. 232.

26. Heidegger might just as well have claimed that "art is *more true* than the truth." For by "the truth" Nietzsche only (and always) means the "true world" of Platonic metaphysics and Christian morality. It is in this sense that, for Nietzsche, "the truth" is an error, for the Platonic-Christian "true world" does not exist. Art, therefore, is more true than the supersensuous "true world" in that it brings into unconcealment the createdness of beings as configurations of will to power. In Heidegger's discussion, he does not at this point develop the idea that, for Nietzsche, "art is *more true* than 'the truth.'" However, this development seems quite in keeping with the progression of his thought, and in this regard he could have availed himself of numerous passages in Nietzsche's early *Nachlass* in which Nietzsche attempted to work out the relation between art, truth, and knowledge. To cite one such passage which might supplement Heidegger's point, Nietzsche writes *"The truthfulness of art:* it alone is now honest" (*KGW,* III, 4: 19[105]). Nietzsche's point here is that art, unlike the quest for truth along the path of a theory of knowledge, is able to recognize its necessarily illusory character in that its "raw material" is itself appearance (*Schein*). Although Nietzsche had not at this time (1872) formulated the theme of will to power, the appreciation of the "truth" of art is a theme that persists through the entirety of his corpus.

27. Krell is, I think, correct to translate *Rausch* as "rapture" rather than intoxication or frenzy, as Nietzsche's translators have done. See his brief explanation in the translator's note in *N* I, p. 92.

28. Heidegger uses the term "Platonism" and not Plato: by "Platonism," he refers to the tradition's dominant interpretation of the Platonic texts and in particular, to the tradition's interpretation of Plato's theory of knowledge, an interpretation which Nietzsche for the most part follows. To speak of Plato would require a detailed examination of these texts, a task from which Heidegger refrains in these lectures.

29. This section also occupies a central place in Derrida's critique of Heidegger's Nietzsche interpretation, discussed in Chapter Four, pp. 101–103.

Chapter 2: Nietzsche's Psycho-Genealogy: A Ludic Alternative to Heidegger

1. Heidegger, *Nietzsche,* Band I, p. 475. See *Nietzsche. Volume Three: The Will to Power as Knowledge and as Metaphysics,* p. 4.

2. See the extended discussion of *pharmakon* in Jacques Derrida, *Dissemination,* translated by Barbara Johnson (Chicago: University of Chicago Press, 1981) pp. 63–171.

3. Derrida, *Dissemination,* p. 70.

4. This basic movement, which exceeds conceptual binarism, can be seen to operate in many of Derrida's terms, e.g., "trace," "supplement," *"différance,"* "hymen," "reserve," "archi-writing." See, in this regard, Jacques Derrida, *Positions,* pp. 42–43.

5. We can only note here another related way that Platonism-nihilism functions as a *pharmakon*. This concerns Nietzsche's ambivalent judgment of the value of nihilism in the *Genealogy of Morals:* although he emphasizes the poisonous effect of Platonic nihilism on the noble cultures of the Greeks, he does not ignore the remedy this same nihilism provided for those slavish followers who adopted the ascetic ideal as their own.

6. See, in this regard, Heidegger's extended interpretation of *WP*, 12 as Nietzsche's recounting of nihilism as the history of the West in *Nietzsche. Volume Four: Nihilism*, pp. 24–57. Although Heidegger acknowledges the various forms in which nihilism appears in Nietzsche's text, his overdetermination of value-creation as an exclusively metaphysical act precludes his taking seriously Nietzsche's remarks on nihilism's potentially active, affirmative character.

7. Heidegger, *Nietzsche. Volume Four: Nihilism*, p. 16.

8. Martin Heidegger, "Letter on Humanism," translated by Frank A. Capuzzi in *Basic Writings,* edited by David F. Krell (New York: Harper and Row, Publishers, Inc., 1977), p. 196.

9. Eugen Fink, *Nietzsches Philosophie* (Stuttgart: W. Kohlhammer Verlag, 1960), p. 13.

10. Fink, p. 41.

11. Fink, p. 188.

12. Fink, p. 188.

13. Sarah Kofman focuses on Heraclitus in her criticism of Heidegger in "Nietzsche and the Obscurity of Heraclitus," translated by Françoise Lionnet-McCumber in *Diacritics,* Vol. 17, No. 3 (Fall 1987), pp. 39–55. She argues that Heidegger misses the strategic value of obscurity: both Heraclitus and Nietzsche are intentionally obscure in order to frustrate their overly hasty appropriation by those readers/listeners unprepared to understand them. Interestingly, Kofman concludes her discussion by raising the same charge of bad philology against Heidegger that guides this chapter: "The confrontation and the debate of [Nietzsche and Heidegger] on Heraclitus shows at any rate that it is not easy to reduce Nietzsche to a metaphysician. It is precisely in order to carry out this operation and to shake off the ghost which haunts him that I suspect Heidegger did not always use an honest, straightforward, and rigorous philological approach in his reading of Nietzsche" (p. 54).

14. This distinction is suggested by Lawrence M. Hinman, "Nietzsche's Philosophy of Play," *Philosophy Today* (Summer 1974), pp. 118–119.

15. Bernd Magnus argues persuasively for this sort of interpretation of the eternal recurrence in *Nietzsche's Existential Imperative* (Bloomington: Indiana University Press, 1978).

16. Alexander Nehamas addresses this point in his excellent study *Nietzsche: Life as Literature* (Cambridge: Harvard University Press, 1985), Chapter Five, esp. pp. 142–152. See also Magnus's discussion in *Nietzsche's Existential Imperative*, pp. 72–88.

17. A similar interpretation of the eternal recurrence as, among other things, a "principle of selection," is suggested by Gilles Deleuze in *Nietzsche and Philosophy*, translated by Hugh Tomlinson (New York: Columbia University Press, 1983), pp. 68–71.

Chapter 3: The French Scene

1. Georges Bataille, *Sur Nietzsche* (Paris: Gallimard, 1945).

2. Gilles Deleuze, *Nietzsche et la philosophie* (Paris: Presses Universitaires de France, 1962). English translation: *Nietzsche and Philosophy*. We should note that Deleuze himself, in *Différence et répétition* (Paris: Presses Universitaires de France, 1968), credits two essays by Pierre Klossowski for "renovating or reviving the interpretation of Nietzsche" (pp. 81–82). These

essays are "Nietzsche, le polythéisme et la parodie," first presented in 1957 and published in *Un si funeste désir* (Paris: NRF, 1963), pp. 185–228, and "Oubli et anamnèse dans l'expérience vécue de l'éternel retour du Même," presented at the Royaumont Conference on Nietzsche in 1964 and published, along with the other addresses and discussions, in *Nietzsche: Cahiers du Royaumont, Philosophie* No. VI (Paris: Éditions de Minuit, 1967), pp. 227–235.

3. Jean Granier, *Le problème de la Vérité dans la philosophie de Nietzsche* (Paris: Éditions du Seuil, 1966); Maurice Blanchot, *L'Entretien infini* (Paris: Gallimard, 1969); Pierre Klossowski, *Nietzsche et le cercle vicieux* (Paris: Mercure de France, 1969) [Klossowski also translated Heidegger's two-volume *Nietzsche* for publication by Gallimard in 1971]; Jean-Michel Rey, *L'enjeu des signes. Lecture de Nietzsche* (Paris: Éditions du Seuil, 1971); Bernard Pautrat, *Versions du soleil. Figures et système de Nietzsche* (Paris: Éditions du Seuil, 1971); Pierre Boudot, *L'ontologie de Nietzsche* (Paris: Presses Universitaires de France, 1971); Sarah Kofman, *Nietzsche et la métaphore* (Paris: Payot, 1972); Paul Valadier, *Nietzsche et la critique du christianisme* (Paris: Éditions du Cerf, 1974).

4. See, for example, *Bulletin de la Société française de philosophie*, No. 4 (Oct.–Dec. 1969), on "Nietzsche et ses interprètes"; *Poétique*, Vol. V (1971) on "Rhétorique et philosophie"; *Revue Philosophique*, No. 3 (1971) on "Nietzsche"; *Critique*, No. 313 (1973) on "Lectures de Nietzsche."

5. Over 800 pages of presentations and subsequent discussions from this conference were published in two volumes as *Nietzsche aujourd'hui* (Paris: Union Générale D'Éditions, 1973). In addition to many of the authors cited in note 3 above, papers were presented at Cerisy by E. Biser, E. Blondel, E. Clémens, G. Deleuze, J. Delhomme, J. Derrida, E. Fink, L. Flam, E. Gaède, D. Grlic, Ph. Lacoue-Labarthe, K. Löwith, J.-F. Lyotard, J. Maurel, J.-L. Nancy, N. Palma, R. Roos, J.-N. Vuarnet, and H. Wismann.

6. Derrida, *Positions*, p. 9.

7. *Nietzsche: Cahiers du Royaumont*, pp. 183–200. An English translation by Alan D. Schrift appears in *Transforming the Hermeneutic Context: From Nietzsche to Nancy*, edited by Gayle L. Ormiston and Alan D. Schrift (Albany: State University of New York Press, 1990), pp. 59–67.

8. A similar view is advanced by Paul Ricoeur. See *Freud and Philosophy: An Essay on Interpretation*, translated by Denis Savage (New Haven: Yale University Press, 1970), pp. 32–35; see also "The Critique of Religion," in *The Philosophy of Paul Ricoeur* (Boston: Beacon Press, 1978), pp. 213–222.

9. Michel Foucault, *Nietzsche: Cahiers du Royaumont*, p. 189; *Transforming the Hermeneutic Context*, p. 64.

10. Foucault, *Nietzsche: Cahiers du Royaumont*, p. 192; *Transforming the Hermeneutic Context*, p. 67.

11. See, for example, the following remark which Foucault included in his foreword to the English edition of *The Order of Things* (New York: Random House, Inc., 1973), p. xiv: "In France, certain half-witted 'commentators' persist in labelling me a 'structuralist.' I have been unable to get it into their tiny minds that I have used none of the methods, concepts, or key terms that characterize structural analysis."

12. Foucault, *The Order of Things*, p. 305.

13. Foucault, *The Order of Things*, p. 305.

14. Foucault, *The Order of Things*, p. 342. Gilles Deleuze comments on Foucault's coupling the disappearance of man with the death of God in "On the Death of Man and Superman," in *Foucault*, translated by Seán Hand (Minneapolis: University of Minnesota Press, 1988), pp. 124–132; see also the discussion on pp. 87–93. These remarks should be compared with Deleuze

and Félix Guattari's comments on the death of God and the death of the Oedipal father in *Anti-Oedipus*, translated by Robert Hurley, Mark Seem and Helen R. Lane (Minneapolis: University of Minnesota Press, 1983), pp. 106ff.

15. See Foucault, *The Order of Things*, pp. 312–313.

16. Immanuel Kant, *Critique of Pure Reason*, A 805f, B 833f.

17. Immanuel Kant, *Kant's Introduction to Logic*, translated by T. K. Abbott (New York: Philosophical Library, 1963), p. 15.

18. See Martin Heidegger, *Kant and the Problem of Metaphysics*, translated by James S. Churchill (Bloomington: Indiana University Press, 1962), pp. 213–215. Whether or not Foucault was led to this view by his reading of Heidegger is an open question. Nevertheless, it should be noted that Foucault, like Derrida, was profoundly influenced by Heidegger. In an interview granted shortly before his death, Foucault remarked that "Heidegger has always been for me the essential philosopher. [. . .] My entire philosophical development has been determined by my reading of Heidegger. But I recognize that it is Nietzsche who supplanted him. I do not know Heidegger sufficiently well. I am not really familiar with *Being and Time* or the things recently edited. My knowledge of Nietzsche is much better than what I know of Heidegger; it remains nonetheless that they are the two fundamental experiences I have had" (*Les Nouvelles*, June 28, 1984, p. 40; this interview has been translated by Thomas Levin and Isabelle Lorenz as "The Return of Morality," in Michel Foucault, *Politics, Philosophy, Culture: Interviews and Other Writings 1977–1984*, edited by Lawrence D. Kritzman [New York: Routledge, Chapman, and Hall, 1988], pp. 242–254). Foucault goes on to credit Heidegger for initiating his own understanding of Nietzsche, and he explains his "failure" to write on these two authors in the following way: "[Although] I have never written on Heidegger, and I have written only a brief article on Nietzsche, they are, however, the authors whom I have most read. I believe it is important to have a small number of authors with whom one thinks, with whom one works, but on whom one does not write. I will perhaps write on them one day, but at that moment they will no longer be instruments of thought for me" (*Les Nouvelles*, p. 40). How Heidegger may have functioned as an "instrument of Foucauldian thought" is an issue that, with the exception of Deleuze (see the final few pages of his *Foucault*, especially pp. 108–113), has not yet been addressed by either Foucault's or Heidegger's commentators.

19. See Immanuel Kant's Introduction to the *Prolegomena to Any Future Metaphysics*.

20. Foucault, *The Order of Things*, p. xxiii; see also pp. 308, 386–387. Kant's *Logic* was first published in 1800.

21. Cf. the following: "The antithesis of the *Übermensch* is the *last man:* I created him conjointly with the former" (*KGW*, VII, 1: 4[171]).

22. Foucault, *The Order of Things*, p. 385.

23. Pautrat, *Versions du soleil*, pp. 36–39.

24. See Foucault, *The Order of Things*, p. 305.

25. Jacques Derrida, "La question du style," in *Nietzsche aujourd'hui*, Vol. I, p. 270.

26. Philippe Lacoue-Labarthe, *"La Dissimulation,"* in *Nietzsche aujourd'hui*, Vol. II, p. 12.

27. This is particularly true in the case of Nietzsche's first American commentators, most of whom either apologize for what they see as Nietzsche's stylistic excesses, or attempt to separate Nietzsche's philosophical merit from his stylistic mastery. Arthur C. Danto exemplifies the former attitude: "If one takes the trouble to eke his philosophy out, to chart the changes in signification that his words sustain in their shiftings from context to context and back, then Nietzsche emerges almost as a systematic as well as an original and analytic thinker. This task, however, is not a simple one. His thoughts are diffused through many loosely structured

volumes, and his individual statements seem too clever and topical to sustain serious philosophical scrutiny" (*Nietzsche as Philosopher*, p. 13). Walter Kaufmann, on the other hand, adopts the latter strategy when he claims that, in writing a book on Nietzsche, "I had been reacting against the view that Nietzsche was primarily a great stylist, and the burden of my book had been to show that he was a great thinker" (*Nietzsche: Philosopher, Psychologist, Antichrist* [Princeton: Princeton University Press, 1974], p. viii). In the past few years, there have been several notable exceptions to this inattention to style on the part of Nietzsche's English-speaking commentators. In particular, the question of style is central to Alexander Nehamas's *Nietzsche: Life as Literature;* Bernd Magnus's recent focus on what he refers to as the self-consuming or self-deconstructing quality of Nietzsche's major themes (especially perspectivism, eternal recurrence and *Übermensch;* see "Self-Consuming Concepts," in *International Studies in Philosophy*, Vol. XXI, No. 2 [1989], pp. 63–71); Allan Megill's *Prophets of Extremity: Nietzsche, Heidegger, Foucault, Derrida* (Berkeley: University of California Press, 1985); and Gary Shapiro's *Nietzschean Narratives* (Bloomington: Indiana University Press, 1989).

28. See Deleuze, *Nietzsche and Philosophy*, p. 197.

29. Deleuze, *Nietzsche and Philosophy*, p. 180.

30. Deleuze, *Nietzsche and Philosophy*, p. 50.

31. Granier, *Le problème de la Vérité dans la philosophie de Nietzsche*, p. 463.

32. Granier, p. 325.

33. Granier, pp. 604–609. We will return to this un-Nietzschean formulation in Chapter Six, when we have occasion to examine Sarah Kofman's critique of what she views as Granier's residual Heideggerianism.

34. Pautrat, *Versions du soleil*, p. 9.

35. Rey, *L'enjeu des signes*, p. 7.

36. See Rey, p. 214.

37. Pautrat, *Versions du soleil*, p. 10.

38. This view of metaphor as the forgotten origin of truth is a basic theme in Nietzsche's early writings that were titled the *Philosophenbuch* by his early editors (*MA*, VI, pp. 3–119). Included in these notes is the unpublished essay "On Truth and Lies in an Extramoral Sense," where truth is defined as "A mobile army of metaphors, metonymies, and anthropomorphisms[, . . .] which after long use seem fixed, canonical and binding to a people: truths are illusions which we have forgotten are illusions; metaphors which are worn out and without sensuous power [. . .]" (*OTL*, 1). The importance of this and other themes found in the *Philosophenbuch* will be examined at length in Chapter Five.

39. Cf. Kofman, *Nietzsche et la métaphore*, pp. 29, 121.

40. Kofman, p. 91. (Rickels, p. 91.) Kofman's discussion of architectural metaphors has been translated by Peter T. Connor and Mira Kamdar in *Looking After Nietzsche*, edited by Laurence A. Rickels (Albany: State University of New York Press, 1990). References to this translation will follow parenthetically the French page reference. In her discussion of the beehive, Kofman focuses on the *edifice* of the hive as an architectural structure, and her conclusions regarding the creators of the hive follow from the genealogical deconstruction of this edifice. For this reason the "beehive" is considered as an architectural rather than an instinctual or entymological metaphor. Similarly, she focuses on the *web* of the spider as an *architectural* structure and derives from this edifice her conclusions regarding the harmfulness of the spider's architectural activity.

41. Kofman, p. 91. (Rickels, p. 91.)

42. Kofman, pp. 94–95. (Rickels, p. 93.)

43. Kofman, p. 96. (Rickels, p. 94.)

44. Kofman, p. 97. (Rickels, p. 95.)

45. Kofman, pp. 97–98. (Rickels, p. 95.)

46. Kofman, p. 101. (Rickels, p. 97.)

47. Kofman, p. 102. (Rickels, p. 98.)

48. Kofman, p. 103. (Rickels, p. 98.)

49. Kofman, p. 103. (Rickels, p. 98.)

50. Although here he affirms Plato's idealism as a healthy response to his (Plato's) overpowerful senses, Nietzsche takes a different view of Plato in, for example, *Twilight of the Idols*: "Plato is a coward in the face of reality,—consequently he flees into the ideal;" (*TI*, "What I Owe the Ancients," 2). Situating Nietzsche's "praise" of Platonic idealism in the context of his many critical remarks from this same period (1887–88) against idealism (see, e.g., *CW*, Epilogue; *EH*, II, 2; *EH*, III, 4; *WP*, 16), the positive reference to Plato in *The Gay Science* appears to function not as an affirmation of Plato's "idealism," but as a critique of the "moderns," whose senses have decayed to such an extent that the positing of ideals is no longer necessary.

51. For example, Nietzsche's use of musical ("*Things touch our chords, but we make a melody out of them*" [*KGW*, V, 1: 6[440]]), theatrical (historical reflection as "the work of a dramatist" [*H*, 6]), and painterly ("We have given things a new color; we go on painting them continually" [*GS*, 152]) images.

52. For example, the eye as metaphor for perceptual knowledge (e.g., *GM*, III, 12), the ear as metaphor for understanding (e.g., *EH*, III, 1), the nose as metaphor for the capacity to discern decadence (e.g., *EH*, I, 1), taste as metaphor for the power to impose and assess value (e.g., *PTAG*, 3).

53. For Kofman's discussion of these metaphors, see pp. 149–163.

54. See Kofman, pp. 89, 171.

55. Kofman, p. 162. The reference to Descartes's tree metaphor is from the preface to *Principles of Philosophy*. Kofman discovers Nietzsche's "*arbre fantastique*" in *The Gay Science* (371):

> [. . .] we ourselves keep growing, keep changing, we shed our old bark, we shed our skins every spring, we keep becoming younger, fuller of future, taller, stronger, we push our roots ever more powerfully into the depths—into evil—while at the same time we embrace the heavens ever more lovingly, more broadly, imbibing their light ever more thirstily with all our twigs and leaves. Like trees we grow—this is hard to understand, as is all of life—not in one place only, but everywhere, not in one direction but equally upward and outward and inward and downward; our energy is at work simultaneously in the trunk, branches and roots; we are no longer free to do only one particular thing, to *be* one particular thing.

Kofman's distinction between Nietzsche's *arbre fantastique* and the Cartesian tree of philosophical truth anticipates the methodological distinction of the rhizomatic and the arborescent drawn by Gilles Deleuze and Félix Guattari in *Rhizome* and *Mille Plateaux*. See, for example, "Rhizome," translated by Paul Patton in *I&C*, No. 8 (Spring 1981), pp. 52–62. A different version of this essay appears as the Introduction to *A Thousand Plateaus*, translated by Brian Massumi (Minneapolis: University of Minnesota Press, 1987); see pp. 6–18.

56. Kofman, p. 163.

57. Kofman, p. 167.

58. Translated by Barbara Harlow (Chicago: University of Chicago Press, 1979). This "text" is a revised version of the paper Derrida presented at the Colloque de Cerisy in 1972 entitled "La question du style" (*Nietzsche aujourd'hui*, Vol. I, pp. 235–287). Hereafter, references to the Harlow translation will appear in the text as "*Spurs*" followed by the page number.

Chapter 4: Derrida: Nietzsche Contra Heidegger

1. Derrida, *Positions*, p. 105.

2. Jacques Derrida, *Of Grammatology*, translated by Gayatri C. Spivak (Baltimore: Johns Hopkins University Press, 1974), p. 19.

3. Jacques Derrida, *Margins of Philosophy*, translated by Alan Bass (Chicago: University of Chicago Press, 1982), p. 305.

4. See, for example, the contrast drawn between Nietzsche and Rousseau in *Of Grammatology*, and the related contrast between Levi-Strauss and Nietzsche in "Structure, Sign and Play in the Discourse of the Human Sciences," in *Writing and Difference*, translated by Alan Bass (Chicago: University of Chicago Press, 1978).

5. Cf. Derrida, *Positions*, p. 55.

6. In what follows, I have chosen to leave "*propre*" untranslated. While Derrida's translators most frequently render *propre* as "proper-ty," this translation tends to overdetermine the multivalence that, for Derrida, is essential to the concept of the *propre*. Amongst the connotations which are always hovering around Derrida's use of *propre* are proper, own, same, self-same, property, appropriate, suitable, good, correct, appropriation, propriety. For similar reasons, Heidegger's "*Ereignis*" will also remain untranslated.

7. Jacques Derrida, "Différance," in *Margins of Philosophy*, p. 27.

8. Perhaps the best example of this latter view is Walter Kaufmann, who, as an apologist for Nietzsche, writes: "Nietzsche's writings contain many all-too-human judgments—especially about women—but these are philosophically irrelevant; . . . Nietzsche's prejudices about women need not greatly concern the philosopher" (*Nietzsche: Philosopher, Psychologist, Antichrist*, p. 84). For a discussion of Nietzsche's early positive reception by German feminism, see R. Hinton Thomas, *Nietzsche in German politics and society, 1890–1918* (Manchester: Manchester University Press, 1983), pp. 80–95.

9. This third, affirmative woman is discussed by Elizabeth Berg in her review of Sarah Kofman, *L'Enigma de la femme* (Paris: Éditions Galilée, 1980) [English translation: *The Enigma of Woman: Woman in Freud's Writings*, translated by Catherine Porter (Ithaca: Cornell University Press, 1985)], Luce Irigaray, *Speculum de l'autre femme* (Paris: Éditions de Minuit, 1974) [English translation: *Speculum of the Other Woman*, translated by Gillian C. Gill (Ithaca: Cornell University Press, 1985)], and *Amante marine de Friedrich Nietzsche* (Paris: Éditions de Minuit, 1980). See "The Third Woman," in *Diacritics*, Vol. 12 (Summer 1982), pp. 11–20.

10. In *Spurs*, Derrida mentions Lacan only once. He returned to the question of woman as a figure of castration and truth in his interpretation of Lacan's seminar on Poe's *The Purloined Letter*. See "Le Facteur de la Vérité," first published in *Poétique* 21 (1975) and translated by Alan Bass in *The Post Card: From Socrates to Freud and Beyond* (Chicago: University of Chicago Press, 1987), pp. 411–496.

210 Notes

11. This, as Derrida notes, is the reason behind Nietzsche's indictment of nineteenth-century feminism. Cf. *Spurs*, pp. 103ff.

12. See pp. 47–49.

13. This reference to dental excision, along with the earlier reference to the "dentist's question" concerning the "bite of conscience," recalls the extract from Nietzsche's letter to Malwida von Meysenbug (November 7, 1872) with which Derrida opens *Spurs*. In this letter, Nietzsche discusses the forthcoming visit of "Wagner mit Frau" and their intention to meet with a dentist to whom Nietzsche owes a debt of thanks.

14. A similar point has been made by several feminist critics in response to a "church" of more recent origin: psychoanalysis. See, for example, Suzanne Gearhart's "The Scene of Psychoanalysis: The Unanswered Questions of Dora," in *In Dora's Case: Freud—Hysteria—Feminism*, edited by Charles Bernheimer and Claire Kahane (New York: Columbia University Press, 1985), pp. 105–127. Gearhart points out that "Freud's strategy with Dora—that of turning her rational indictment against her father back against her—was precisely that adopted by Freud toward the feminists' indictment of a masculine bias of psychoanalysis" (p. 109). Using the Lacanian mechanism of countertransference, Gearhart and others suggest that Freud frequently adopts this strategy in situations where his own neurotic fears risk being disclosed.

15. Elsewhere, Derrida confronts the Heideggerian reading more directly, particularly in response to Heidegger's "simply" situating Nietzsche within the history of metaphysics. In addition to the epigraphs to this and the first three chapters, we can here cite one more instance:

    > Nietzsche, Freud, and Heidegger, for example, worked within the inherited concepts of metaphysics. Since these concepts are not elements or atoms, and since they are taken from a syntax and a system, every particular borrowing brings along with it the whole of metaphysics. This is what allows these destroyers to destroy each other reciprocally—for example, Heidegger regarding Nietzsche, with as much lucidity and rigor as bad faith and misconstruction, as the last metaphysician, the last "Platonist." One could do the same for Heidegger himself, for Freud, or for a number of others. And today no exercise is more widespread. (*Writing and Difference*, pp. 281–282; see also *Of Grammatology*, pp. 19–20, 287; "The Ends of Man," in *Margins*, p. 136.)

    More recently, Derrida has addressed Heidegger's Nietzsche in "Guter Wille zur Macht (II): Die Unterschriften interpretieren (Nietzsche/Heidegger)," in *Text und Interpretation*, edited by Philippe Forget (Munich: Wilhelm Fink Verlag, 1984), pp. 62–77. An English translation of this essay by Diane P. Michelfelder and Richard E. Palmer entitled "Interpreting Signatures (Nietzsche/Heidegger): Two Questions" appears in Michelfelder and Palmer, eds., *Dialogue and Deconstruction: The Gadamer-Derrida Encounter*, pp. 58–71.

16. Derrida, *Positions*, p. 54. The *propre* is also the focal point of Derrida's critique of Heidegger in "*Ousia* and *Grammē*: Note on a Note from *Being and Time*," in *Margins*, pp. 29–67, and it is at issue as well in Derrida's attempt to initiate a correspondence between Heidegger and Freud in the essay "To Speculate—on 'Freud,' " in *The Post Card*, esp. pp. 356–368.

17. The logic of the hymen is developed by Derrida in "The Double Session," in *Dissemination*, pp. 173–285, especially pp. 208–214. Derrida elaborates on some of these points in an interview in which he responds to questions regarding "feminism" and the "non-place of woman." See "Choreographies," translated by Christie V. McDonald in *Diacritics*, Vol. 12: *Cherchez La Femme: Feminist Critique/Feminine Text* (Summer 1982), pp. 66–76.

18. See Martin Heidegger, *On Time and Being*, pp. 5–8 and passim.

19. A very different view of the *propre*, which appears to be addressed in part to Derrida's remarks, is found in Hélène Cixous's chapter titled "The Empire of the Selfsame," in Cixous and Catherine Clément's *The Newly Born Woman*, translated by Betsy Wing (Minneapolis: University of

Minnesota Press, 1986), pp. 78–83. Cixous claims that while a typically masculine economy of gift-giving is based on a desire for appropriation, it is actually erected from the fear of expropriation. Women's gift-giving, on the other hand, can not be subsumed under the "Empire of the *propre*" because history has taught women to give without any expectation of receiving something in return. Because "economy, as a law of appropriation, is a phallocentric production," Cixous claims that a woman's libidinal economy, most clearly perceived on the level of *jouissance,* will escape identification by the masculine category of property (pp. 80–82). In so doing, she implies that Derrida's undecidable question of the *propre* still retains too much of this category.

20.   See, for example, Heidegger, *Nietzsche. Volume One: The Will to Power as Art:* "What lies before us today as a book with the title *The Will to Power* contains preliminary drafts and fragmentary elaborations for that work. The outlined plan according to which these fragments are ordered, the division into four books, and the titles of those books also stem from Nietzsche himself" (p. 7).

21.   The significance of this postscript is subject to multiple readings, and Derrida's jokes concerning his having *forgotten* Heidegger's remark on the forgetting of Being should not be missed. Similarly, the first postscript plays with forgetting, recollection, and confirmation by third parties, and perhaps we should not discount the significance of the dating of the first postscript: "1.4.73"—April Fools' Day!

22.   Martin Heidegger, *The Question of Being,* translated by William Kluback and Jean T. Wilde (New York: Twayne Publishers, Inc., 1958), pp. 90–91; quoted in *Spurs,* p. 143.

23.   Derrida later notes that Heidegger opens the preface to his two-volume *Nietzsche* by placing Nietzsche's name between quotation marks. The opening sentence thus reads " *'Nietzsche'—der Name des Denkers steht als Titel für* die Sache *seines Denkens* ['Nietzsche'—the name of the thinker stands as the title for *the matter* of his thinking]." This peculiar opening is discussed by Derrida in "Interpreting Signatures," in *Dialogue and Deconstruction,* pp. 60–62. Nietzsche's "proper name" is also at issue in Derrida's other text "on" Nietzsche: *Otobiographies: The Teaching of Nietzsche and the Politics of the Proper Name,* translated by Avital Ronell in *The Ear of the Other: Otobiography, Transference, Translation,* edited by Christie V. McDonald and translated by Peggy Kamuf (New York: Schocken Books, 1985), pp. 3–38.

24.   Jacques Derrida, "La question du style," in *Nietzsche aujourd'hui* I, p. 291.

25.   Derrida, "Choreographies," p. 69. On the occasion of his own "thesis defense" (June 2, 1980), Derrida disclosed some of the reasons behind his having refused to articulate a "thesis" in many of his texts. His remarks have been published as "The time of a thesis: punctuations," translated by Kathleen McLaughlin in *Philosophy in France Today,* edited by Alan Montefiore (Cambridge: Cambridge University Press, 1983), pp. 34–50.

26.   See Derrida, *Positions,* p. 63.

27.   Derrida, *Of Grammatology,* p. 158.

28.   Derrida, "Ellipsis," in *Writing and Difference,* p. 296.

29.   Derrida, *Positions,* p. 63.

30.   See, for example, David Couzens Hoy, "Forgetting the Text: Derrida's Critique of Heidegger," in *boundary 2* (Fall 1979), pp. 223–235, esp. pp. 229–231.

31.   *Ibid.,* p. 231. Others, however, are not so willing to sacrifice Schleiermacher. See, for example, Werner Hamacher, "Hermeneutic Ellipses: Writing the Hermeneutical Circle in Schleiermacher," translated by Timothy Bahti in Ormiston and Schrift, eds., *Transforming the Hermeneutic Context: From Nietzsche to Nancy,* pp. 177–210.

32. Derrida, *Positions*, p. 55.

33. Heidegger, *What is Called Thinking?* p. 17. This translation is from Derrida's citation of this passage in *Memoires for Paul de Man*, translated by Cecile Lindsay, Jonathan Culler, and Eduardo Cadava (New York: Columbia University Press, 1986), p. 152.

34. See Derrida, *Positions*, p. 11. Christopher Norris develops the contrast between the passive hearing presupposed by phonocentrism, and the active interpretation advocated by Derrida and Nietzsche in his review of *The Ear of the Other*. See "Deconstruction against Itself: Derrida and Nietzsche," in *Diacritics*, Vol. 16, No. 4 (Winter 1986), pp. 64–65.

35. Heidegger, *What is Called Thinking?* pp. 133–134. Derrida addresses these points in a discussion critical of Heidegger's remark that "Science does not think" in *Memoires for Paul de Man*, pp. 108–111 and 151–152.

36. Martin Heidegger, "Hölderlin and the Essence of Poetry," translated by Douglas Scott in *Existence and Being* (Chicago: Henry Regnery Co., 1949), p. 307.

37. Martin Heidegger, "Language in the Poem," translated by Peter D. Hertz in *On the Way to Language* (San Francisco: Harper and Row, Publishers, Inc., 1971), p. 160.

38. See Derrida, *Positions*, p. 54. We have already seen one example of the "fall" in Chapter One, where Heidegger discovers the fall of great art into "aesthetics."

39. Derrida, *"Ousia* and *Grammē,"* in *Margins*, p. 63.

40. Heidegger, *Being and Time*, p. 486.

41. Heidegger, *Being and Time*, p. 488.

42. Quoted in Jacques Derrida, "Différance," in *Margins of Philosophy*, p. 27. "Der Spruch des Anaximander" is the final essay in Heidegger's *Holzwege* and has been translated as "The Anaximander Fragment," in *Early Greek Thinking* by David F. Krell and Frank A. Capuzzi (New York: Harper and Row, Publishers, Inc., 1975), pp. 13–58. The citation appears on p. 52. Derrida's translator has chosen to use Krell and Capuzzi's translation in *Margins*. I have changed this translation slightly to more accurately reflect Derrida's citation of the French translation of Heidegger's "Anaximander Fragment."

43. Derrida, "Différance," in *Margins of Philosophy*, p. 27.

44. Martin Heidegger, "The Nature of Language," a series of three lectures delivered in 1957–58, translated by Peter D. Hertz in *On the Way to Language*, p. 88.

45. There is still much debate among Heideggerians as to when the *"Kehre"* takes place and what significance the *Kehre* holds for the understanding of Heidegger's thinking. Gadamer characterizes the *Kehre* in the following way:

> when he began to reshape his own project so as to dissociate it completely from the Husserlian model—and it is this which we call Heidegger's *"Kehre"*—metaphysics and its greatest representatives would serve only as a backdrop against which the intentions of his own thought would attempt to display themselves through criticism. From this point on, metaphysics no longer appeared as the question of being, but rather as the real and fateful *obscuring* of the question of being: as the history of that forgetfulness-of-being which began with Greek thought and which has developed, in the course of modern thought, into the fully developed world view and mindset of calculative and technological thinking, characteristic of the present day. (Hans-Georg Gadamer, "Heidegger and the History of Philosophy," translated by Karen Campbell in *The Monist*, Vol. 64, No. 4 [October 1981], p. 437.)

If we follow the Gadamerian characterization, then most of the Derridean discussion of Heidegger and all of the Heideggerian references to poetic thinking and speaking should be situated *after* the *Kehre* and Heidegger's apparent break with the project of transcendental phenomenology.

46. Heidegger, "The Nature of Language," p. 76.

47. This is a central point in Derrida's "Interpreting Signatures," where he remarks that Heidegger's desire for a single, unique proper name leads him to gather under one name "Western metaphysics" as an assembled unity. This strategy is especially inappropriate when reading Nietzsche's text because "next to Kierkegaard, was not Nietzsche one of the few great thinkers who multiplied his names and played with signatures, identities, and masks? Who named himself more than once, with several names?" (*Text und Interpretation*, p. 72, *Dialogue and Deconstruction*, p. 67).

48. Cf. Derrida, *Of Grammatology*, p. 20. The justification for this claim is disputed by Alex Argyros in "The Warp of the World: Deconstruction and Hermeneutics," in *Diacritics*, Vol. 16, No. 3 (Fall 1986), pp. 47–55. Argyros claims that Derrida tends to read Heidegger "literally" when it comes to the "meaning of Being." He suggests that if Derrida "interpreted actively" Heidegger's remarks, a different judgment might result.

49. Martin Heidegger, *Nietzsche*, Vol. I, p. 10; "Nietzsche's Word 'God is Dead,' " p. 99.

50. Martin Heidegger, "Postscript" (1943) to "What is Metaphysics?" translated by R. F. C. Hull and Alan Crick, in *Existence and Being*, p. 391.

51. Derrida, "Différance," in *Margins of Philosophy*, p. 27.

52. Derrida, *Of Grammatology*, p. 159.

53. Derrida, *Of Grammatology*, p. 158.

54. Derrida, *Of Grammatology*, p. 158.

55. Jacques Derrida, "Cogito and the History of Madness," in *Writing and Difference*, p. 32.

56. Fr. D. E. Schleiermacher, *Hermeneutics: The Handwritten Manuscripts*, p. 112; see also pp. 64, 69.

57. Emilio Betti, *Hermeneutics as the General Methodology of the Geisteswissenschaften*, in Ormiston and Schrift, eds., *The Hermeneutic Tradition*, pp. 193–194.

58. In America, this view of hermeneutics has been championed by E. D. Hirsch, Jr.: "This book has concerned itself hitherto with establishing that interpretation does at least have a determined object of knowledge—the author's verbal meaning—and it has shown that such knowledge is in principle attainable" (*Validity in Interpretation*, p. 163).

59. Hans-Georg Gadamer, *Truth and Method*, p. xix.

60. Gadamer, *Truth and Method*, p. 335. See also, in this regard, Gadamer's various comments on the priority of a "hermeneutics of trust" over a "hermeneutics of suspicion," for example, in "Text and Interpretation," in Michelfelder and Palmer, eds., *Dialogue and Deconstruction*, pp. 21–51, and "The Hermeneutics of Suspicion," in *Hermeneutics: Questions and Prospects*, edited by Gary Shapiro and Alan Sica (Amherst: University of Massachusetts Press, 1984), pp. 54–65.

61. Derrida, *Of Grammatology*, p. 159.

62. Derrida, *The Ear of the Other*, pp. 86–87. I owe thanks to Richard Palmer for first bringing this remark to my attention.

63. Jacques Derrida, from the discussion following "Structure, Sign, and Play in the Discourse of the Human Sciences," in *The Structuralist Controversy*, edited by Richard Macksey and Eugenio Donato (Baltimore: Johns Hopkins University Press, 1970), p. 271.

64. Derrida, *Positions*, p. 6.

65. Let me here acknowledge a third style of reading, only hinted at in certain notes along the way in the preceding remarks, which rejects this distinction between appropriation and expropriation

and seeks to establish a reading outside the domain of ownership and possession. This style of reading is suggested by Cixous in her critique of the "Empire of the *propre*" (*The Newly Born Woman*, p. 80; see note 19 above), and more generally in her remarks on *écriture feminine*. It is suggested as well by Deleuze and Guattari when they call for the experimentation *with* rather than the interpretation *of* texts.

> The book is no longer a microcosm, in the classical or European manner. The book is not an image of the world, still less a signifier. It is not a noble organic totality, neither is it a unity of sense. [. . .] We no longer read, but also we no longer write, in the old way. There is no death of the book, but a different way of reading. In a book, there is nothing to understand, but much to make use of. Nothing to interpret or signify, but much to experiment with. ("Rhizome," in *I&C*, p. 67)

They speak of significance and "interpretosis" (the obsession for interpreting) as the two diseases of the earth (see Deleuze's discussion of this point in Deleuze and Claire Parnet, *Dialogues*, translated by Hugh Tomlinson and Barbara Habberjam [New York: Columbia University Press, 1987], pp. 47–51), and seek to integrate textuality into an extratextual practice.

> We will no longer ask what a book, signifier or signified means, we will no longer look for a meaning in a book; we will ask—what does it function with, in connection with what does it or doesn't it transmit intensities, into which other multiplicities are its own introduced and metamorphosed, with which other bodies without organs is its own made to converge? A book only exists by virtue of what is outside it. ("Rhizome," in *I&C*, p. 50)

> For reading a text is never a scholarly exercise in search of what is signified, still less a highly textual exercise in search of a signifier. Rather it is a productive use of the literary machine, a montage of desiring-machines, a schizoid exercise that extracts from the text its revolutionary force. (*Anti-Oedipus*, p. 106)

Like Cixous, Deleuze and Guattari suggest a textual economy that exceeds the logic of appropriation:

> Proust, though credited with being highly signifying, said that his book was like a pair of spectacles: see if they suit you, whether or not thanks to them you perceive things which you otherwise wouldn't have grasped; if not, disregard my book, look for others which suit you better. Find scraps of book, those which are of use to you or suit you. [. . .] The combinations, permutations, utilizations are never internal to the book, but depend on connections with a particular outside. Yes, take what you want. ("Rhizome," in *I&C*, pp. 67–68)

66. Gadamer, "Heidegger and the History of Philosophy," p. 444.

67. Gadamer, *Truth and Method*, Appendix IV, pp. 456–457. It must be noted that Gadamer is not always so quick to concede the excesses of Heidegger's interpretation. In fact, in his meeting with Derrida he defends Heidegger's interpretation against Derrida and the French interpreters, claiming that they could "come to believe that the experience of Being that Heidegger tried to uncover behind metaphysics is exceeded in radicality by Nietzsche's extremism" only because

> the French followers of Nietzsche have not grasped the significance of the seductive and tempting challenge of Nietzsche's thought. [. . .] Heidegger's attempt to think Being goes far beyond [Nietzsche's] disintegration of metaphysics in the thinking of values, or better yet, he goes back behind metaphysics itself without finding the satisfaction that Nietzsche found in the extreme of its self-disintegration. ("Text and Interpretation," in *Dialogue and Deconstruction*, p. 25. Translation altered slightly.)

68. See Derrida's discussion of grafting, citationality, and iterability in "Signature, Event, Context," in *Margins of Philosophy*, pp. 320–321.

69. Derrida, *Positions,* p. 63.

70. Jacques Derrida, "TITLE (to be specified)," translated by Tom Conley in *Sub-Stance,* No. 31 (1981), pp. 5–22.

71. For examples of such a disappearance, see what becomes of Nietzsche at the hands of Pautrat's Freudian reading in "*Nietzsche Méduse*" (*Nietzsche aujourd' hui* I, pp. 9–30; English translation "Nietzsche Medused" by Peter Connor in Rickels, ed., *Looking After Nietzsche,* pp. 159–173), or Lyotard's Marxist reading in "*Notes sur le Retour et le kapital*" (*Nietzsche aujourd' hui* I, pp. 141–157; English translation "Notes on the Return of Kapital," in *Semiotext(e),* Vol. III, No. 1 [1978], pp. 44–53). This criticism might not be fair, however. Keeping in mind the distinction between exegetical commentary and critical, productive reading, it is not clear that the readings of, for example, Pautrat or Lyotard, are offered as "interpretations" in the traditional sense. Rather, one gets the impression that these readings are "experimental" in the sense called for by Deleuze and Guattari, intending only to point out some similarities or intertextual connections between Nietzsche and Freud or Nietzsche and Marx. If this is the case, then evaluative criteria other than those applied when judging the legitimacy or fitness of an interpretive commentary must be sought.

Chapter 5: Language, Metaphor, Rhetoric

1. Michel Foucault, *The Order of Things,* p. 305. Samuel IJsseling echoes this claim in his discussion of Nietzsche and rhetoric (see *Rhetoric and Philosophy in Conflict,* translated by Paul Dunphy [The Hague: Martinus Nijhoff, 1976], pp. 106ff), as does Arthur C. Danto in his attempt to bring Nietzsche into dialogue with contemporary analytic philosophy (see *Nietzsche as Philosopher,* esp. pp. 11–14 and 83–87).

2. A notable exception is Daniel Breazeale; see "The Word, the World, and Nietzsche," in *Philosophical Forum,* Vol. VI, Nos. 2–3 (Winter-Spring 1975), pp. 301–320.

3. The source for many of Nietzsche's remarks on language will be the *Philosophenbuch,* a collection of Nietzsche's notes of 1872–1875. Letters from this period (see, for example, June 11, 1872 to E. Rohde; November 21, 1872 to E. Rohde; December 7, 1872 to E. Rohde; March 2, 1873 to C. von Gersdorff; March 22, 1873 to E. Rohde) make reference to a work in progress on pre-Platonic philosophy. This work was to be composed of two parts: a "historical" section, part of which appeared as "Philosophy in the Tragic Age of the Greeks," and a "theoretical" section. Some of the notes for this "theoretical" section were given the title *Philosophenbuch* by the editors of the *Musarionausgabe* (Vol. VI, pp. 1–119), and under this title were included four subdivisions: "The Last Philosopher. The Philosopher. Reflections on the Struggle between Art and Knowledge" (1872), "The Philosopher as Cultural Physician" (1873), "On Truth and Lies in an Extramoral Sense" (1873), and "The Struggle between Science and Wisdom" (1875). These notes, along with two other collections ("On the Pathos of Truth" [1872] and "Thoughts on the Meditation: Philosophy in Hard Times" [1873]) are edited and translated by Daniel Breazeale in *Philosophy and Truth* (Atlantic Highlands, N.J.: Humanities Press, 1979). To facilitate reference, citations from these works will take the following form: page reference from the *Musarionausgabe;* fragment reference, when available, from the Colli and Montinari *Kritische Gesamtausgabe;* and chapter title followed by paragraph number from the Breazeale translation.

4. Cf. Aristotle, *Poetics,* 21. Nietzsche delivered a lecture course on ancient rhetoric at the University of Basel early in the 1870s, and part of the notes for this course have been published in the *Musarionausgabe,* (Vol. V, pp. 287–319), and translated by Carole Blair in *Friedrich Nietzsche on Rhetoric and Language,* edited by Sander L. Gilman, Carole Blair, and David J.

Parent (Oxford: Oxford University Press, 1989), pp. 3–59 (hereafter referred to in this chapter as *ET*). While the Musarion editors date the construction of these notes for presentation in the summer semester, 1874, the French translators have argued that these notes were more likely written for presentation in the winter semester of 1872 (See "Rhétorique et langage," translated by Philippe Lacoue-Labarthe and Jean-Luc Nancy, *Poétique* 5 [1971], p. 101.). Although the controversy regarding the date of origin of these notes is far from resolved (for example, Samuel IJsseling [*Rhetoric and Philosophy in Conflict*, p. 107] and Joachim Goth [*Nietzsche und die Rhetorik* (Tübingen: Max Niemeyer Verlag, 1970), p. 2] subscribe to the Musarion editors dating while Paul DeMan [*Allegories of Reading* (New Haven: Yale University Press, 1979), p. 104] and Lawrence M. Hinman ["Nietzsche, Metaphor, and Truth," in *Philosophy and Phenomenological Research*, Vol. 43, No. 2, (Dec. 1982)] side with the French), it will be sufficient for the present purpose to note that either date will situate these notes as contemporaneous with the notes of the *Philosophenbuch*.

5. This is one of the major themes in *The Birth of Tragedy*, where Nietzsche first attempted to replace morality with *art* as "the truly metaphysical activity of man" (*BT*, SC5), while arguing that "it is only as an *aesthetic phenomenon* that existence and the world are eternally *justified*" (*BT*, 5, 24).

6. See, e.g., the *Gorgias* and *Phaedrus* and Nietzsche's discussions of Plato's view of rhetoric in *Rh*, pp. 289ff (*ET*, pp. 7ff), as well as his lecture notes entitled "Introduction to the Study of the Platonic Dialog," (*MA*, IV, pp. 365–443).

7. It should be noted that Nietzsche's move beyond the "ornamental" view of tropes is not wholly original. In fact, as both DeMan (*Allegories of Reading*, pp. 104–105) and the French translators of his *Rhetorik* (pp. 100–103) point out, Nietzsche borrows freely from a number of rhetorical studies which appeared in the decade prior to his lectures. Lacoue-Labarthe and Nancy, in the Introduction to their translation of the *Rhetorik*, go so far as to suggest that we view Nietzsche's lectures as a "collage" of insights which he drew from a number of current textbooks for the study of classical rhetoric, especially Richard Volkmann's *Die Rhetorik der Griechen und Romer in systematischer Übersicht dargestellt* (Berlin: Ebeling und Plahn, 1872), Friedrich Blass's *Die griechische Beredsamkeit in dem Zeitraum von Alexander bis auf Augustus* (Berlin: 1865), and Gustav Gerber's *Die Sprache als Kunst* (Bromberg: Mittler'sche Buchhandlung, 1872). For an informative discussion of Gerber's relation to Nietzsche's *Rhetorik*, see Anthonie Meijers, "Gustav Gerber und Friedrich Nietzsche," in *Nietzsche-Studien*, Band 17 (Berlin: Walter de Gruyter, 1988), pp. 369–390. See also the *Konkordanz* between Gerber's and Nietzsche's texts, edited by Meijers and Martin Stingelin in *Nietzsche-Studien*, Band 17, pp. 350–368. The links between Nietzsche and his contemporaries should not be taken as evidence that Nietzsche's work in rhetoric is wholly unoriginal. As we shall see, the originality of his discussion is located in Nietzsche's application of these rhetorical insights to a deconstruction of certain philosophical "errors."

8. For an interesting application of this type of rhetorical analysis, see Hayden White's discussion of Nietzsche in Chapter Nine of *Metahistory: The Historical Imagination in Nineteenth-Century Europe* (Baltimore: Johns Hopkins University Press, 1973), pp. 331–374. In particular, see his analysis of *On the Use and Abuse of History*, where Nietzsche's three methods of historiography (monumental, antiquarian, critical) are viewed as history conceived in the modes of metonymy, synecdoche, and irony, respectively (cf. pp. 351ff). White argues that whereas Nietzsche did not explicitly resort to such a tropological analysis in the second of his *Untimely Meditations*, he could have reinforced his "proposed antidote" to the excess of these three forms of historiography by returning to his discussion of metaphor, inasmuch as "history in the Metaphorical mode is really what is behind his defense of what he called the 'superhistorical' and 'unhistorical' points of view in the last section of 'The Use and Abuse of History' " (p. 352).

9. Kenneth Burke, in Appendix D ("Four Master Tropes") of *A Grammar of Motives* (Cleveland: The World Publishing Co., 1962), engages in an analysis that bears a striking resemblance to Nietzsche's. The four master tropes for Burke are metaphor, metonymy, synecdoche, and irony and he distinguished between their "figurative" (rhetorical) and "literal" or "realistic" usages:

> For *metaphor,* we could substitute *perspective;*
> For *metonymy,* we could substitute *reduction;*
> For *synecdoche,* we could substitute *representation;*
> For *irony,* we could substitute *dialectic.* (p. 503)

These distinctions, Burke is quick to point out, are "evanescent [. . .] for not only does the dividing line between the figurative and the literal usages shift, but also the four tropes shade into one another" (p. 503). While by no means a Nietzsche scholar, Burke was perhaps the first to comment on the connection between metaphor and perspective in Nietzsche (see his *Permanence and Change* [New York: New Republic, Inc., 1935], pp. 116–127), a connection which Sarah Kofman focuses on in *Nietzsche et la métaphore,* and which will be addressed in what follows.

10. Philippe Lacoue-Labarthe arrives at a similar conclusion in "Le détour (Nietzsche et la rhétorique)," first published in *Poétique* 5 (1971), pp. 53–76 and reprinted in *Le Sujet de la philosophie (Typographies I)* (Paris: Aubier-Flammarion, 1979), pp. 31–74. He argues that "Nietzsche seeks to confront the language of philosophy and science with the question of its pretension to truth, of its desire for a pure and simple literality,—of its proper meaning, if you will" (*Poétique* 5, p. 53). For Lacoue-Labarthe, Nietzsche only considers rhetoric in his effort to reveal the essence of language and he can locate in Nietzsche no fixed concept of rhetoric other than as the foundation of a certain linguistic usage (see p. 59). In analyzing the relation between Nietzsche's *Rhetorik* and *The Birth of Tragedy,* Lacoue-Labarthe concludes that Nietzsche's "detour" into rhetoric is ultimately directed toward the possibility of recovering the primal language of myth (see pp. 72–76).

11. Derrida himself comments on the connection between deconstruction, destructuring, and *Abbau* in *The Ear of the Other,* pp. 86–87, and *The Post Card,* p. 267. See also Rodolphe Gasché's discussion of the "conceptual filiation" of deconstruction with Heidegger's *Destruktion* and Husserl's *Abbau,* in *The Tain of the Mirror: Derrida and the Philosophy of Reflection* (Cambridge: Harvard University Press, 1986), pp. 109–120.

12. Paul DeMan has specifically focused on the role of metonymy, discussed above, as the "substitution of cause and effect," in "Nietzsche's Theory of Rhetoric," Chapter Five of *Allegories of Reading.* He views Nietzsche's deconstruction of many of the traditional philosophical oppositions (subject/object, inner world/outer world, cause/effect) in *The Will to Power* as grounded on Nietzsche's reversal of the metonymic false inferences which have animated Western metaphysical thinking since Plato. While DeMan focuses on *The Will to Power* (especially *WP,* 479), one could apply Nietzsche's discussion of metonymy to a number of other passages in his later writings. For example, one could show, without much trouble, Nietzsche's discussion in *Twilight of the Idols* of "The Four Great Errors" (the errors of "mistaking cause for consequences," of "false causality," of "imaginary causes," and of "free will") to be in each case an instance of the metonymic "false inference" from effect to cause.

13. For a recent attempt to retain a notion of reference within a metaphorical account of language, see Paul Ricoeur, *The Rule of Metaphor,* translated by Robert Czerny (Toronto: University of Toronto Press, 1977). In arguing for the autonomy of poetical and philosophical discourse, Ricoeur offers a "tensional" theory of "live metaphor" as an alternative to the view of philosophical concepts as "dead metaphors" that he finds Derrida, in "White Mythology," appropriating from Nietzsche. In this context, Ricoeur outlines a theory of "split" or "displayed reference":

the metaphorical statement is precisely the one that points out most clearly the relationship between suspended reference and displayed reference. Just as the metaphorical statement captures its sense as metaphorical midst the ruins of the literal sense, it also achieves its reference upon the ruins of what might be called (in symmetrical fashion) its literal reference. If it is true that literal sense and metaphorical sense are articulated within an interpretation, so too it is within an interpretation that a second-level reference, which is properly the metaphorical reference, is set free by means of the suspension of the first-level reference. (p. 221)

In the concluding chapter of *The Rule of Metaphor*, Ricoeur uses this theory of displayed reference to support his view that metaphorical truth, as a "re-description of reality," is found in the tension between the suspended literal reference and the displayed figurative reference of a living metaphor.

14. The similarities between Nietzsche's and Hume's critiques of substance and personal identity are noteworthy. For discussions of these similarities, see David C. Hoy, "Nietzsche, Hume, and the Genealogical Method," in *Nietzsche as Affirmative Thinker*, edited by Yirmiyahu Yovel (Dordrecht: Martinus Nijhoff, 1986), pp. 20–38, and Nicholas Davey, "Nietzsche and Hume on Self and Identity," in the *Journal of the British Society for Phenomenology*, Vol. 18, No. 1 (January 1987), pp. 14–29.

15. This is one of the central themes in Charles E. Scott's reading of Nietzsche in *The Language of Difference* (Atlantic Highlands, N.J.: Humanities Press International, Inc. 1987).

16. This question, which raises the problem of self-referentiality in Nietzsche's texts, will be discussed in some detail in Chapter Six in terms of perspectivism ("Is Nietzsche's doctrine of perspectivism itself *only* a perspective?") and in Chapter Seven in terms of the status of Nietzsche's claim that "there are only interpretations" (i.e., "Is this claim in some way privileged or is it also an interpretation?").

Chapter 6: Perspectivism, Philology, Truth

1. This view has recently been advocated by two commentators: Nicholas Davey in "Nietzsche's Aesthetics and the Question of Hermeneutic Interpretation" (*British Journal of Aesthetics*, Vol. 26, No. 4 (Autumn 1986), pp. 328–344, and Johann Figl in "Nietzsche und die philosophische Hermeneutik des 20. Jahrhunderts" (*Nietzsche-Studien*, Band 10–11 [Berlin: Walter de Gruyter, 1981–1982], pp. 408–430). In exploring the relation between Nietzsche's thought and the philosophical hermeneutics of Dilthey, Heidegger, and Gadamer, Figl concludes that "[t]he close study of Nietzsche's notes—especially those of his late period of creativity—can show that the essential tendencies which lay the foundation of philosophy as hermeneutics were already anticipated in this thinker" (p. 430). Figl undertakes this close study and develops this foundation in *Interpretation als philosophisches Prinzip: Friedrich Nietzsches universale Theorie der Auslegung im späten Nachlass* (Berlin: Walter de Gruyter, 1982). Davey, on the other hand, addresses Nietzsche's early work, building "a case for submitting Nietzsche's early aesthetics within the hermeneutic tradition and in so doing to wrest his aesthetics from the continuing but inexplicable tendency of many of his contemporary interpreters to regard his early thoughts on art as an expression of a late romantic irrationalism" (p. 340). He argues that Nietzsche's attack on aesthetic disinterestedness offers a "more radical" solution than Dilthey to the question of the objectivity of aesthetic interpretation and the hermeneutic problem of distantiation, i.e., the "gulf between the *Weltanschauungen* of interpreted and interpreter" (p. 331).

2. See, for example, Arthur Danto's discussion of perspectivism in *Nietzsche as Philosopher,* pp. 68–99; or David C. Hoy's discussion in "Philosophy as Rigorous Philology? Nietzsche and Post-structuralism," in *Fragments: Incompletion and Discontinuity (New York Literary Forum,* Vols. 8–9 [1981]), pp. 171–185; or George J. Stack's discussion in "Nietzsche and Perspectival Interpretation," in *Philosophy Today* (Fall 1981), pp. 221–241.

3. Bernd Magnus takes a similar approach in "Nietzsche Today: A View from America," *International Studies in Philosophy,* Vol. XV, No. 2 (1983), pp. 99–101. He argues that taking Nietzsche's perspectival remarks as a rhetorical device rather than a positive doctrine avoids the problem of self-reference, i.e., the problem of the truth value of the perspectivist claim itself when the doctrine of perspectivism appears to assert that there are no truths. If the perspectivist claim is not true, then we need not concern ourselves with it; and if it is true, then it refutes the basic thesis of perspectivism. See on this point the literature referred to in note 7 to Chapter Seven.

4. An appeal could be made to Nietzsche as a forerunner of the contemporary attack on the "Myth of the Given." Cornel West adopts this strategy in "Nietzsche's Prefiguration of Post-Modern American Philosophy," in the *boundary 2* symposium entitled "Why Nietzsche Now?" (*boundary 2, a journal of postmodern literature,* Vol. IX, No. 3 and Vol. X, No. 1 [Spring/Fall 1981], pp. 241–269). West examines three tendencies in the work of W. V. O. Quine, Nelson Goodman, Wilfred Sellars, Richard Rorty, and Thomas Kuhn: anti-realism or conventionalism in ontology; the demythologization of the Myth of the Given, or epistemological anti-foundationalism; and the "detranscendentalization of the subject." By interspersing citations from Nietzsche into the examination of these contemporary Anglo-American philosophers, West brings up some striking parallels. The following two citations typify the Nietzschean spirit that West locates in their work: "The movement is from unique truth and a world fixed and found to a diversity of right and even conflicting versions or worlds in the making" (Nelson Goodman, *Ways of Worldmaking* [Indianapolis: Hackett Press, 1978], p. x; quoted by West, p. 249). "The myth of physical objects is epistemologically superior to most in that it has proved more efficacious than other myths as a device for working a manageable structure into the flux of experience" (W. V. O. Quine, *From a Logical Point of View* [New York: Harper and Row, Publishers, Inc., 1963] p. 44; quoted by West, p. 251). Needless to say, Rorty's more recent work in *Consequences of Pragmatism* (Minneapolis: University of Minnesota Press, 1982) and *Contingency, Irony and Solidarity* (Cambridge: Cambridge University Press, 1989) makes his affinities toward Nietzsche even more explicit than his earlier works discussed by West.

5. Gilles Deleuze develops this call for nomadism in "Pensée Nomade," which appears in *Nietzsche aujourd'hui,* Vol. I, pp. 159–174; the bulk of this essay has been translated by David B. Allison as "Nomad Thought" in his anthology *The New Nietzsche,* pp. 142–149.

6. A notable exception is Karl Jaspers, who addresses this issue in his *Nietzsche: An Introduction to the Understanding of his Philosophical Activity;* see, in particular, the chapter entitled "World Exegesis."

7. Quoted in Jaspers, *Nietzsche,* p. 28.

8. In addition to his work on Greek and Roman rhetoric and grammar and on pre-Platonic philosophy, Nietzsche also lectured at Basel on many of the "classics" of Greek and Roman literature including, among others, the works of Aeschylus, Sophocles, Euripides, Homer, Hesiod, and Pindar. For a complete list of Nietzsche's academic work, see Curt Paul Janz, "Friedrich Nietzsches Akademische Lehrtätigkeit in Basel 1869 bis 1879," in *Nietzsche-Studien,* Band 3 (Berlin: Walter de Gruyter, 1974), pp. 192–203.

9. For example, in his methodological reflections on his reading of the Greeks, Nietzsche anticipates in an interesting way the Heideggerian formulation of the hermeneutic circle: "How much of this lies in the Greeks, and how much lies only in my ears, the ears of a very unskillful

man—that, even now, I cannot yet articulate with certainty" (*KGW*, IV, 3: 30[52]). Many of the points of contact between Nietzsche and hermeneutics are discussed by Davey in "Nietzsche's Aesthetics and the Question of Hermeneutic Interpretation," and Johann Figl in "Hermeneutische Voraussetzungen der philologische Kritik," *Nietzsche-Studien*, Band 13 (Berlin: Walter de Gruyter, 1984).

10. In his writings at Basel, Nietzsche frequently refers approvingly to Wolf's work in philology; see, for example, *We Philologists*, 53–62 (*KGW*, IV, 1: 3[passim]), and the concluding pages of "Homer and Classical Philology." For a discussion which attempts to integrate Nietzsche into nineteenth-century German philology, see James Whitman, "Nietzsche in the Magisterial Tradition of German Classical Philology," in *Journal of the History of Ideas*, Vol. XLVII, No. 3 (July–September 1986), pp. 453–468. At this point, a word regarding Nietzsche's relation to Schleiermacher is in order. In Nietzsche's discussions of philology, the only references to Schleiermacher come in the context of Schleiermacher's translations of the Platonic dialogues, and there are few comments concerning Schleiermacher's hermeneutic theory (see "Einleitung in das Studium der platonischen Dialoge," in *MA*, IV, pp. 365–443, esp. Section 1, pp. 367–377). There are also a few references to Schleiermacher in Nietzsche's published writings (see, e.g., *DS*, 6, 11; *HAH*, 132; *WS*, 216; *D*, 190; *EH*, CW3). Here Nietzsche views Schleiermacher in one of two contexts: either as a representative of the German idealist tradition of Hegel, Fichte, and Schelling, or as a representative of German Protestant theology. In each case, the view which Nietzsche adopts toward Schleiermacher is exceedingly hostile.

11. Cf. Nietzsche's discussion of the "Homeric question" and his view that "Homer" is an "aesthetic judgment" in *KGW*, II, 1: pp. 254–264.

12. Let me take this opportunity to explain in more detail the significance of my marking the link between Nietzschean *ephexis* and the phenomenological *epochē*. It strikes me that this is a crucial point for understanding where Nietzsche's transvalued philology and a hermeneutic based on Husserlian phenomenology differ. For Nietzsche, the philologist must *attempt* to bracket his or her interests and *strive* not to overdetermine the text's meaning, while recognizing that complete success in these ventures is never possible. For Husserl and some Husserlians, on the other hand, a *genuine* bracketing of one's interests seems not only desirable but quite possible. If one is to draw connections between Nietzsche and the phenomenological tradition on this point, the place to start would be with Maurice Merleau-Ponty who, we must recall, remarks in *Phenomenology of Perception* that "[t]he most important lesson which the reduction teaches us is the impossibility of a complete reduction" (Maurice Merleau-Ponty, *Phenomenology of Perception*, translated by Colin Smith [London: Routledge and Kegan Paul, 1962], p. xiv). On this point of the impossibility of a complete reduction, Merleau-Ponty like Nietzsche speaks of the inevitable perspectival limitations on knowledge and, although Merleau-Ponty is primarily concerned with those perspectives that accrue from our historical contextualization, the connections between Nietzsche and Merleau-Ponty on the question of the situatedness of knowledge are worth pursuing.

13. Jean Granier, *Le problème de la vérité dans la philosophie de Nietzsche*, p. 325.

14. Granier, p. 323.

15. Granier, p. 325.

16. Granier, pp. 501–502.

17. See Sarah Kofman, *Nietzsche et la métaphore*, p. 194.

18. Kofman, p. 196. Eric Blondel also emphasizes the genealogical dimension within philology; see *Nietzsche, le corps et la culture* (Paris: Presses Universitaires de France, 1986), esp. the chapters titled "Nietzsche et la philologie généalogique" (pp. 133–189) and "Critique du discours métaphysique: la généalogie philologique et la misologie" (pp. 191–274).

19. Kofman, p. 199.

20. See Kofman, p. 201. This point, which will be developed in the next chapter, is one of the central themes in Alexander Nehamas's *Nietzsche: Life as Literature*. See, for example, his discussion of Nietzsche's critique of the ascetic ideal on the grounds that it fails to present itself as a partial interpretation and does not invite its own questioning (pp. 128–129).

Chapter 7: Genealogy, Interpretation, Text

1. Jacques Derrida, *Writing and Difference*, p. 292.

2. Samuel Weber makes a similar point, noting that Derrida's discussion in "Structure, Sign, and Play" suggests a third style of reading which challenges the straightforward identification of Nietzsche with interpretation as innocent, affirmative play:

   > The allusion to Nietzsche suggests—but only implicitly, and hence only to a reader willing to interpret—that beyond the "irreducible difference" of nostalgic and affirmative interpretations, there is a third version, interpreting interpretation as a struggle to overwhelm and to dislodge an already existing, dominant interpretation and thus to establish its own authority. Could anything be less "innocent"? (*Institution and Interpretation* [Minneapolis: University of Minnesota Press, 1987], p. 5.)

   Although I agree, for the most part, with Weber's point, I will try to show that the goal of this third version, while dislodging the existing dominant interpretation, is not to "establish its own authority."

3. Michel Foucault develops this point in an essay entitled "Nietzsche, Genealogy, History," in *Language, Counter-Memory, Practice,* translated by Donald F. Bouchard and Sherry Simon (Ithaca: Cornell University Press, 1977), pp. 139–164. In this essay, which is in part directed toward disclosing a conception of *"wirkliche Historie* [Effective History]" in Nietzsche's genealogy, Foucault makes some important points regarding the different sorts of origins (e.g., *Ursprung* [origin], *Herkunft* [descent], *Entstehung* [emergence], *Geburt* [birth], *Anfang* [beginning], *Abkunft* [lineage]) which Nietzsche investigates, and the different genealogical practices which result from these different origins. What is perhaps most interesting in this essay are the parallels that emerge between his analysis of Nietzsche's genealogy and Foucault's own method of archaeology (*logos* of the *archē*). Foucault's archaeological method, like Nietzsche's genealogical method, engages in a critical re-reading of history, but from the perspective of the discursive rules and structures that were sanctioned at the origin, rather than the Nietzschean perspective of the life-affirming or life-negating instincts of those who did the original sanctioning. See, in this regard, Foucault's discussion of archaeology in *The Archaeology of Knowledge*, translated by A. M. Sheridan Smith (New York: Harper and Row, Publishers, Inc., 1972), especially pp. 131–148. For an interesting discussion of the use of both genealogy and archaeology in Foucault, see Hubert L. Dreyfus and Paul Rabinow, *Michel Foucault: Beyond Structuralism and Hermeneutics* (Chicago: University of Chicago Press, 1982), pp. 104–125.

4. The distinction I am making between the foundational search for origins and the psycho-genealogical inquiry that questions the forces operating in the construction of these origins should be compared to the distinction Foucault makes between the archaeological and genealogical dimensions of his analyses. The former makes it possible to examine forms while the latter makes possible an analysis of the processes of formation and modification of these forms. See Michel Foucault, *The Use of Pleasure*, translated by Robert Hurley (New York: Random House, Inc., 1985), pp. 11–12.

5. For a discussion of the function of hyperbole in Nietzsche, see Chapter One of Alexander Nehamas, *Nietzsche: Life as Literature*, pp. 22–32.

6. Alexander Nehamas also focuses on Nietzsche's style, but he does so to stress a different point. I agree with most of Nehamas's interpretation, and in particular, with his views that "Nietzsche's stylistic pluralism [. . .] is his solution to the problem involved in presenting positive views that do not, simply by virtue of being positive, fall back into dogmatism," and that "Nietzsche's interpretations announce themselves as such" (*Nietzsche: Life as Literature*, p. 40). Whereas Nehamas, in large part, directs Nietzsche's remarks on style to his (Nietzsche's) aestheticist project of creating an artwork out of himself, I am more interested in Nietzsche's stylistic multiplicity as a strategy for escaping the necessity of adopting an author(itarian) voice or dogmatic position along with his genealogical examination of others' styles. For an interesting interpretation of the aestheticist dimension of Nietzsche's work and his influence on modern and post-modern aesthetics, see Allan Megill's *Prophets of Extremity: Nietzsche, Heidegger, Foucault, Derrida*. Like Nehamas, Megill wants to broaden the term "aestheticism" in reference to Nietzsche. In an introductory comment, he writes: "I am using [aestheticism] not to refer to the condition of being enclosed within the limited territory of the aesthetic, but rather to an attempt to expand the aesthetic to embrace the whole of reality. To put it in another way, I am using it to refer to a tendency to see 'art' or 'language' or 'discourse' or 'text' as constituting the primary realm of human experience" (p. 2).

7. Arthur C. Danto raises this charge when he considers the "paradox" of perspectivism: "Does Perspectivism entail that Perspectivism itself is but a perspective, so that the truth of this doctrine entails that it is false?" See his *Nietzsche as Philosopher*, p. 80. Walter Kaufmann, in *Nietzsche: Philosopher, Psychologist, Antichrist*, also addresses this point of Nietzsche's possible self-refutation. For an alternative, though weaker solution to this charge than the one I provide, see Kaufmann, pp. 204–207. The question of self-reference has become one of the major issues being debated in the recent Nietzsche literature in English. See, for example, Alexander Nehamas's discussions in "Immanent and Transcendent Perspectivism in Nietzsche," *Nietzsche-Studien*, Band 12 (Berlin: Walter de Gruyter, 1983), pp. 473–490, and Chapter Two of his *Nietzsche: Life as Literature*, especially pp. 46–57 and 64–67. Nehamas offers a stronger solution than Kaufmann, arguing that Nietzsche falls victim to the problem of self-reference only if we accept the presupposition that "to consider a view an interpretation is to concede that it is false" (p. 66). In other words, Nietzsche's critics draw from his admission that perspectivism *might* be false the illegitimate inference that it *is* false. For other perspectives on this issue, see Bernd Magnus's discussion in "Nietzsche Today: A View from America," pp. 99–101, and Ruediger H. Grimm, "Circularity and Self-Reference in Nietzsche," *Metaphilosophy*, Vol. 10, Nos. 3–4 (July/October 1979), pp. 289–305. For a general review of this literature, see Willard Mittelman, "Perspectivism, Being, and Truth," *International Studies in Philosophy*, Vol. XVI, No. 2 (1984), pp. 3–22.

8. A comment should be made here regarding the relationship between this principle and the "principle of proliferation" espoused by Paul Feyerabend in *Against Method* (London: New Left Books, 1975). Feyerabend's pluralistic approach to philosophy of science clearly exhibits a Nietzschean flavor, as we see in the following remarks:

> Knowledge so conceived is not a series of self-consistent theories that converges towards an ideal view; it is not a gradual approach to the truth. It is rather an ever increasing *ocean of mutually incompatible (and perhaps even incommensurable) alternatives,* each single theory, each fairy tale, each myth that is part of the collection forcing the others into greater articulation and all of them contributing, via this process of competition, to the development of our consciousness. (p. 30)
>
> *Unanimity of opinion may be fitting for a church, for the frightened or greedy victims of some (ancient or modern) myth, or for the weak and willing followers of some*

tyrant. Variety of opinion is necessary for objective knowledge. And a method that encourages variety is also the only method that is compatible with a humanitarian outlook. (p. 46)

There may, however, be an important difference between Feyerabend's "theoretical anarchism" and Nietzsche's interpretive pluralism, and this concerns Feyerabend's affirmation of the principle "anything goes" (see especially pp. 28–33). If, by "anything goes," he means that we should not limit a priori the postulation of a theory on the grounds that it runs counter to what is currently accepted as "true," then he remains in basic agreement with the Nietzschean principle of proliferation. But if, by "anything goes," he means that all theories are equally acceptable, thereby determining the principle of proliferation to mean simply "the more theories the better," then he parts company with Nietzsche, whose call for a proliferation of interpretation refuses to sanction the principle that anything goes in interpretation.

9. There are obvious links between this way of characterizing a Nietzschean pluralist approach and Nelson Goodman's self-described relativism. To cite one example from Goodman which I find to be virtually identical to the position I am developing, consider the following:

> There are very many different equally true descriptions of the world, and their truth is the only standard of their faithfulness. And when we say of them that they all involve conventionalizations, we are saying that no one of these different descriptions is *exclusively* true, since the others are also true. None of them tells us *the* way the world is, but each of them tells *a* way the world is. If I were asked what is the food for men, I should have to answer "none". For there are many foods. And if I am asked what is the way the world is, I must likewise answer, "none". For the world is many ways. (Nelson Goodman, *Problems and Projects* [New York: Bobbs-Merrill, 1972], pp. 30–31.)

The way Goodman appeals to the relative merits of different kinds of foods anticipates the use I will make of Nietzsche's criterion of health to support an interpretive pluralism.

10. See in this regard Eric Blondel's discussion of the *Versuch* in *Nietzsche, le corps et la culture,* pp. 115–131. Deleuze has also focused on this theme, although his resistance to the hermeneutic tradition leads him to oppose experimentation to interpretation, as evidenced by the following remarks:

> The characters and the authors always have a little secret, on which the craze for interpretation feeds. Something must always remind us of something else, make us think of something else. [. . .] The great secret is when you no longer have anything to hide, and thus when no one can grasp you. A secret everywhere, no more to be said. Since the "signifier" has been invented, things have not fallen into place. Instead of language being interpreted by us, it has set about interpreting us, and interpreting itself. Significance and interpretosis are the two diseases of the earth, the pair of despot and priest. [. . .] On lines of flight, there can no longer be but one thing, experimentation-life. [. . .] Experiment, never interpret. Programme, never phantasize. (Deleuze and Parnet, *Dialogues,* pp. 46–48. Translation modified.)

11. For an interesting discussion of the "ethical" implications of Nietzsche's notion of justice, see Jean-Luc Nancy, *L'Impératif catégorique* (Paris: Aubier-Flammarion, 1983), Chapter Three: "Notre Probité," pp. 61–86.

12. Hélène Cixous discusses the problematics of possession in the language of appropriation in *The Newly Born Woman,* pp. 78–83. A similar point is made by Michèle Le Doeuff when she speaks of escaping from the prison of "commentary trapped between the alternatives of violation and fidelity" in "Women and Philosophy," translated by Debbie Pope, in *French Feminist Thought: A Reader,* edited by Toril Moi (Oxford: Basil Blackwell, 1987), p. 206. We might say, to bring Foucault's notion of the author-function into this context, that if the *modern* author-function is

determined in part as the possessor of his or her discourse (see "What is an Author?" in *Language, Counter-Memory, Practice*, pp. 124–125), a *post*-modern author-function may emerge out of the rejection of the language of appropriation. This is to say, the rejection of the notion of authors possessing texts underlies the post-modern author(ity) of writers like Cixous and Deleuze.

13.   On some of the distinctions between these two forms of the dilemma, see Richard J. Bernstein, *Beyond Objectivism and Relativism: Science, Hermeneutics and Praxis* (Philadelphia: University of Pennsylvania Press, 1983), pp. 8–16.

14.   Elsewhere, I have developed the links between this Nietzschean strategy and Derrida's deconstruction of binary oppositions. See Alan D. Schrift, "Genealogy and/as Deconstruction: Nietzsche, Derrida, and Foucault on Philosophy as Critique," in *Postmodernism and Continental Philosophy*, edited by Hugh Silverman and Donn Welton (Albany: State University of New York Press, 1988), pp. 193–213.

15.   Or, to put it another way, the pluralist will accept these labels only after having freed them from the context of what Bernstein has called the "Cartesian Anxiety" which led to their initial application. Bernstein draws this notion of the "Cartesian Anxiety" from his reading of Descartes's quest (one might say "obsession") for foundational certitude: "With a chilling clarity Descartes leads us with an apparent and ineluctable necessity to a grand and seductive Either/Or. *Either* there is some support for our being, a fixed foundation for our knowledge, *or* we cannot escape the forces of darkness that envelop us with madness, with intellectual and moral chaos" (*Beyond Objectivism and Relativism*, p. 18).

16.   Here I can only note the affinity between this approach and Cixous's description of *écriture féminine* as the "questioning/being questioned in the between of same and of other." See *The Newly Born Woman*, pp. 85ff.

17.   This strategy of recasting the choice between binary opposites as a continuum appears in the works of many contemporary French thinkers. As Jean-François Lyotard has put it, "oppositional thinking [. . .] is out of step with the most vital modes of postmodern knowledge" (Jean-François Lyotard, *The Postmodern Condition*, translated by Geoff Bennington and Brian Massumi [Minneapolis: University of Minnesota Press, 1983], p. 14). I would suggest that we situate Derrida's discussion of "writing" (set between the limits of speech and "writing in the narrow sense"), Deleuze's discussion of "desire" (between the limits of repression and production), Cixous's discussion of bisexuality (between the limits of the feminine and the masculine), Bourdieu's discussion of "doxa" (between the limits of orthodoxy and heterodoxy), and Foucault's discussion of "power" (between the limits of domination and subordination) among these "most vital modes of postmodern knowledge." Each of these thinkers recasts the forced choice or exclusive disjunction between binary opposites in terms of a pluralistic continuum: for Foucault, a continuum of power/knowledge; for Deleuze, of desiring production; for Cixous, of bisexuality as the non-exclusivity of sexual difference; for Bourdieu, of doxa and habitus; and for Derrida, of writing and difference. I think Nietzsche was attempting something similar with his introduction of the will to power, recasting all substantive differences in kind in terms of differences of degree of will to power. In his attempt to think difference differently, Nietzsche emerges as an initiator of post-modern thinking, and to trace this particular genealogy back a little further, we may recall Nietzsche's own discovery of a precursor in Spinoza (Letter to Overbeck, July 30, 1881) and his affinity for the thought of Heraclitus. For further discussion of this and other points of contact between Nietzsche and postmodern French philosophy, see my "The becoming-post-modern of philosophy," in *After the Future: Postmodern Times and Places*, edited by Gary Shapiro (Albany: State University of New York Press, 1990), pp. 99–113, and "Nietzsche's French Legacy," in *Cambridge Companions to Philosophy: Friedrich Nietzsche*, edited by Bernd Magnus (Cambridge: Cambridge University Press, forthcoming).

18. Philippe Lacoue-Labarthe, "La Dissimulation," in *Nietzsche aujourd'hui,* Vol. II, p. 12.

19. Richard Rorty has made a similar point in "explaining" Derrida's remark "*il n'y a pas des hors-texte*" as an attempt to "debunk Kantian philosophy generally" rather than as an ontological theory of textuality. See "Philosophy as a Kind of Writing: An Essay on Derrida," in *Consequences of Pragmatism,* p. 97.

Bibliography

Nietzsche

Collected Works in German

Nietzsches Werke, Grossoktavausgabe. Second Edition. Leipzig: Kröner, 1901–13.

Gesammelte Werke, Musarionausgabe. Munich: Musarion Verlag, 1920–29.

Werke in drei Bänden. Edited by Karl Schlechta. Munich: Carl Hanser, 1954–56.

Nietzsche Werke, Kritische Gesamtausgabe. Edited by Giorgio Colli and Mazzino Montinari. Berlin: Walter de Gruyter, 1967ff.

English Translations

"Lecture on Rhetoric." Translated by Carole Blair. In *Friedrich Nietzsche on Rhetoric and Language.* Edited by Sander L. Gilman, Carole Blair, and David J. Parent. Oxford: Oxford University Press, 1989.

The Birth of Tragedy. The Case of Wagner. Translated by Walter Kaufmann. New York: Random House, Inc., 1967.

The Future of Our Educational Institutions. Homer and Classical Philology. Translated by J. M. Kennedy. Volume III of *The Complete Works.* Edited by Dr. Oscar Levy. Edinburgh: T. N. Foulis, 1910.

"The Last Philosopher. The Philosopher. Reflections on the Struggle between Art and Knowledge." "On the Pathos of Truth." "The Philosopher as Cultural Physician." "On Truth and Lies in a Nonmoral Sense." "Thoughts on the Meditation: Philosophy in Hard Times." "The Struggle between Science and Wisdom." Translated and edited by Daniel Breazeale in *Philosophy and Truth: Selections from Nietzsche's Notebooks of the early 1870s.* Atlantic Highlands, N.J.: Humanities Press, 1979.

We Philologists. Translated by J. M. Kennedy. Volume VIII of *The Complete Works.* Edited by Dr. Oscar Levy. Edinburgh: T. N. Foulis, 1910.

Philosophy in the Tragic Age of the Greeks. Translated by Maximilian A. Mugge. Volume II of *The Complete Works.* Edited by Dr. Oscar Levy. Edinburgh: T. N. Foulis, 1910.

Untimely Meditations: David Strauss, the Confessor and the Writer; On the uses and disadvantages of history for life; Schopenhauer as Educator; Richard Wagner in Bayreuth. Translated by R. J. Hollingdale. Cambridge: Cambridge University Press, 1983.

Human, All-Too-Human. Volumes One and Two [*Assorted Opinions and Maxims. The Wanderer and His Shadow*]. Translated by R. J. Hollingdale. Cambridge: Cambridge University Press, 1986.

Daybreak. Translated by R. J. Hollingdale. Cambridge: Cambridge University Press, 1982.

The Gay Science. Translated by Walter Kaufmann. New York: Random House, Inc., 1974.

Thus Spoke Zarathustra. Twilight of the Idols. The Antichrist. Nietzsche Contra Wagner. In *The Viking Portable Nietzsche*. Translated and edited by Walter Kaufmann. New York: The Viking Press, 1967.

Beyond Good and Evil. Translated by Walter Kaufmann. New York: Random House, Inc., 1966.

On the Genealogy of Morals. Ecce Homo. Translated by Walter Kaufmann. New York: Random House, Inc., 1967.

Twilight of the Idols. The Antichrist. Translated by R. J. Hollingdale. Middlesex, England: Penguin Books, 1968.

The Will to Power. Translated by Walter Kaufmann and R. J. Hollingdale. New York: Random House, Inc., 1968.

Selected Letters. Edited and translated by Christopher Middleton. Chicago: University of Chicago Press, 1969.

Other Works Cited

Allison, David B., editor. *The New Nietzsche: Contemporary Styles of Interpretation*. New York: Dell Publishing Co., Inc., 1977.

Argyros, Alex. "The Warp of the World: Deconstruction and Hermeneutics." *Diacritics* (Fall 1986), pp. 47–55.

Bataille, Georges. *Sur Nietzsche*. Paris: Gallimard, 1945.

Berg, Elizabeth L. "The Third Woman." *Diacritics*, Vol. 12 (1982), pp. 11–20.

Bernstein, Richard J. *Beyond Objectivism and Relativism: Science, Hermeneutics, and Praxis*. Philadelphia: University of Pennsylvania Press, 1983.

Betti, Emilio. *Hermeneutics as the General Methodology of the Geisteswissenschaften*. Translated by Josef Bleicher. In Gayle L. Ormiston and Alan D. Schrift, editors, *The Hermeneutic Tradition: From Ast to Ricoeur*. Albany: State University of New York Press, 1990.

Blondel, Eric. *Nietzsche, le corps et la culture*. Paris: Presses Universitaires de France, 1986.

Breazeale, Daniel. "The Word, the World, and Nietzsche." *Philosophical Forum*, Vol. VI, Nos. 2–3 (Winter-Spring 1975), pp. 301–320.

Burke, Kenneth. *Permanence and Change*. New York: New Republic, Inc., 1935.

————. *A Grammar of Motives*. Cleveland: The World Publishing Co., 1962.

Cixous, Hélène, and Clément, Catherine. *The Newly Born Woman*. Translated by Betsy Wing. Minneapolis: University of Minnesota Press, 1986.

Danto, Arthur C. *Nietzsche as Philosopher*. New York: Columbia University Press, 1980.

Davey, Nicholas. "Nietzsche's Aesthetics and the Question of Hermeneutic Interpretation." *British Journal of Aesthetics*, Vol. 26, No. 4 (Autumn 1986), pp. 328–344.

————. "Nietzsche and Hume on Self and Identity." *Journal of the British Society for Phenomenology*, Vol. 18, No. 1 (January 1987), pp. 14–29.

————. "Nietzsche, the Self, and Hermeneutic Theory." *Journal of the British Society for Phenomenology*, Vol. 18, No. 3 (October 1987), pp. 272–284.

Deleuze, Gilles. *Nietzsche et la philosophie*. Paris: Presses Universitaires de France, 1962. [English translation: *Nietzsche and Philosophy* by Hugh Tomlinson. New York: Columbia University Press, 1983.]

————. *Foucault*. Translated by Seán Hand. Minneapolis: University of Minnesota Press, 1988.

Deleuze, Gilles, and Guattari, Félix. *Anti-Oedipus*. Translated by Robert Hurley, Mark Seem, and Helen R. Lane. Minneapolis: University of Minnesota Press, 1983.

————. *A Thousand Plateaus*. Translated by Brian Massumi. Minneapolis: University of Minnesota Press, 1987.

————. "Rhizome." Translated by Paul Patton. *I&C*, No. 8 (Spring 1981), pp. 52–62.

Deleuze, Gilles, and Parnet, Claire. *Dialogues*. Translated by Hugh Tomlinson and Barbara Habberjam. New York: Columbia University Press, 1987.

DeMan, Paul. *Allegories of Reading*. New Haven: Yale University Press, 1979.

Derrida, Jacques. *Of Grammatology*. Translated by Gayatri C. Spivak. Baltimore: Johns Hopkins University Press, 1974.

————. *Writing and Difference*. Translated by Alan Bass. Chicago: University of Chicago Press, 1978.

————. *Margins of Philosophy*. Translated by Alan Bass. Chicago: University of Chicago Press, 1982.

————. *Dissemination*. Translated by Barbara Johnson. Chicago: University of Chicago Press, 1981.

————. *Positions*. Translated by Alan Bass. Chicago: University of Chicago Press, 1981.

————. *Spurs: Nietzsche's Styles*. Translated by Barbara Harlow. Chicago: University of Chicago Press, 1979.

————. *Otobiographies: The Teaching of Nietzsche and the Politics of the Proper Name*. Translated by Avital Ronell. In *The Ear of the Other: Otobiography, Transference, Translation*. Edited by Christie V. McDonald. Translated by Peggy Kamuf. New York: Schocken Books, 1985.

————. *The Post Card: From Socrates to Freud and Beyond*. Translated by Alan Bass. Chicago: University of Chicago Press, 1987.

————. *Memoires for Paul de Man*. Translated by Cecile Lindsay, Jonathan Culler, and Eduardo Cadava. New York: Columbia University Press, 1986.

————. "Structure, Sign, and Play in the Discourse of the Human Sciences." Translated by Richard Macksey. In *The Structuralist Controversy: The Languages of Criticism and the Sciences of Man*. Edited by Richard Macksey and Eugenio Donato. Baltimore: Johns Hopkins University Press, 1970, pp. 247–272.

————. "The time of a thesis: punctuations." Translated by Kathleen McLaughlin. In *Philosophy in France Today*. Edited by Alan Montefiore. Cambridge: Cambridge University Press, 1983, pp. 34–50.

————. "TITLE (to be specified)." Translated by Tom Conley. *Sub-stance*, No. 31 (1981), pp. 5–22.

————. "Choreographies." Translated by Christie V. McDonald. *Diacritics*, Vol. 12: *Cherchez La Femme: Feminist Critique/Feminine Text* (Summer 1982), pp. 66–76.

Dilthey, Wilhelm. *Selected Writings*. Translated and edited by H. P. Rickman. Cambridge: Cambridge University Press, 1976.

Dreyfus, Hubert L., and Rabinow, Paul. *Michel Foucault: Beyond Structuralism and Hermeneutics*. Chicago: University of Chicago Press, 1982.

Feyerabend, Paul K. *Against Method*. London: New Left Books, 1975.

Figl, Johann. *Interpretation als philosophisches Prinzip: Friedrich Nietzsches universale Theorie der Auslegung im späten Nachlass*. Berlin: Walter de Gruyter, 1982.

————. "Nietzsche und die philosophische Hermeneutik des 20. Jahrhunderts." *Nietzsche-Studien*, Band 10–11. Berlin: Walter de Gruyter, 1981, pp. 408–430.

————. "Hermeneutische Voraussetzungen der philologische Kritik." *Nietzsche-Studien*, Band 13. Berlin: Walter de Gruyter, 1984.

Fink, Eugen. *Nietzsches Philosophie*. Stuttgart: W. Kohlhammer Verlag, 1960.

Forget, Philippe, editor. *Text und Interpretation*. Munich: Wilhelm Fink Verlag, 1984.

Foucault, Michel. *The Order of Things*. New York: Random House, Inc., 1973.

————. *The Archaeology of Knowledge*. Translated by A. M. Sheridan Smith. New York: Harper Colophon Books, 1972.

————. *Language, Counter-Memory, Practice*. Translated by D. F. Bouchard and S. Simon. Ithaca: Cornell University Press, 1977.

————. *The Use of Pleasure*. Translated by Robert Hurley. New York: Random House, Inc., 1985.

————. "Nietzsche, Freud, Marx." In *Nietzsche: Cahiers du Royaumont, Philosophie*, No. VI. Paris: Éditions de Minuit, 1967, pp. 183–200. [English translation by Alan D. Schrift. In *Transforming the Hermeneutic Context: From Nietzsche to Nancy*. Edited by Gayle L. Ormiston and Alan D. Schrift. Albany: State University of New York Press, 1990.]

Gadamer, Hans-Georg. *Truth and Method*. Second Edition. Translated and edited by Garrett Barden and John Cumming. London: Sheed and Ward, Ltd., 1975.

————. *Philosophical Hermeneutics*. Translated and edited by David E. Linge. Berkeley: University of California Press, 1976.

————. "Heidegger and the History of Philosophy." Translated by Karen Campbell. *The Monist*, Vol. 64, No. 4 (October 1981), pp. 435–444.

Gasché, Rodolphe. *The Tain of the Mirror: Derrida and the Philosophy of Reflection*. Cambridge: Harvard University Press, 1986.

Gearhart, Suzanne. "The Scene of Psychoanalysis: The Unanswered Questions of Dora." In *In Dora's Case: Freud—Hysteria—Feminism*. Edited by Charles Bernheimer and Claire Kahane. New York: Columbia University Press, 1985.

Goodman, Nelson, *Problems and Projects*. Indianapolis: Bobbs-Merrill Company, Inc., 1972.

————. *Ways of Worldmaking*. Indianapolis: Hackett Publishing Company, 1978.

Goth, Joachim. *Nietzsche und die Rhetorik*. Tübingen: Max Niemeyer Verlag, 1970.

Granier, Jean. *Le problème de la Vérité dans la philosophie de Nietzsche*. Paris: Éditions du Seuil, 1966.

Grimm, Ruediger H. "Circularity and Self-Reference in Nietzsche." *Metaphilosophy*, Vol. 10, Nos. 3–4 (July/October 1979), pp. 289–305.

Heidegger, Martin. *Being and Time*. Translated by John Macquarrie and Edward Robinson. London: SCM Press, Ltd., 1962.

————. *Kant and the Problem of Metaphysics*. Translated by James S. Churchill. Bloomington: Indiana University Press, 1962.

————. *Existence and Being*. Translated by Douglas Scott, R. F. C. Hull, and Alan Crick. Chicago: Henry Regnery Co., 1949.

————. *Platons Lehre von der Wahrheit*. Bern: Francke Verlag, 1947.

————. "Letter on Humanism." Translated by Frank A. Capuzzi. In *Basic Writings*. Edited by David F. Krell. New York: Harper and Row, Publishers, Inc., 1977, pp. 193–242.

————. *Holzwege*. Frankfurt am Main: Vittorio Klostermann, 1953.

————. *An Introduction to Metaphysics*. Translated by Ralph Manheim. Garden City, N.Y.: Doubleday and Company, Inc., 1961.

————. "The Anaximander Fragment." Translated by David F. Krell and Frank A. Capuzzi. In *Early Greek Thinking*. New York: Harper and Row, Publishers, Inc., 1975, pp. 13–58.

————. *What is Called Thinking?* Translated by J. Glenn Gray. New York: Harper and Row, Publishers, Inc., 1968.

————. *Vorträge und Aufsätze*. Pfullingen: Verlag Günther Neske, 1954.

————. *The Question of Being*. Bilingual edition of *Zur Seinsfrage*. Translated by W. Kluback and Jean T. Wilde. New York: Twayne Publishers, Inc., 1958.

————. *Identity and Difference*. Translated by Joan Stambaugh. New York: Harper and Row, Publishers, Inc., 1969.

————. *On the Way to Language*. Translated by Peter D. Hertz. San Francisco: Harper and Row, Publishers, Inc., 1971.

————. *Nietzsche*. Bands I and II. Pfullingen: Verlag Günther Neske, 1961.

————. *Nietzsche. Volume One: The Will to Power as Art*. Edited and translated by David F. Krell. San Francisco: Harper and Row, Publishers, Inc., 1979.

————. *Nietzsche. Volume Two: The Eternal Recurrence of the Same*. Edited and translated by David F. Krell. New York: Harper and Row, Publishers, Inc., 1984.

————. *Nietzsche. Volume Three: The Will to Power as Knowledge and Metaphysics*. Edited by David F. Krell. Translated by Joan Stambaugh, David F. Krell, and Frank A. Capuzzi. New York: Harper and Row, Publishers, Inc., 1987.

————. *Nietzsche. Volume Four: Nihilism*. Edited by David F. Krell. Translated by Frank A. Capuzzi. San Francisco: Harper and Row, Publishers, Inc., 1982.

————. *The End of Philosophy*. Translated by Joan Stambaugh. New York: Harper and Row, Publishers, Inc., 1973.

————. *The Question Concerning Technology and Other Essays*. Translated by William Lovitt. New York: Harper and Row, Publishers, Inc., 1977.

————. "The Way Back into the Ground of Metaphysics." Translated by Walter Kaufmann. In *Existentialism from Dostoevsky to Sartre*. New York: New American Library, 1975, pp. 265–279.

————. *On Time and Being*. Translated by Joan Stambaugh. New York: Harper and Row, Publishers, Inc., 1972.

Hinman, Lawrence M. "Nietzsche's Philosophy of Play." *Philosophy Today* (Summer 1974), pp. 106–124.

———. "Nietzsche, Metaphor, and Truth." *Philosophy and Phenomenological Research,* Vol. 43, No. 2 (December 1982), pp. 179–200.

Hirsch, E. D., Jr. *Validity in Interpretation.* New Haven: Yale University Press, 1967.

Hoy, David C. *The Critical Circle.* Berkeley: University of California Press, 1978.

———. "Forgetting the Text: Derrida's Critique of Heidegger." *boundary 2* (Fall 1979), pp. 223–235.

———. "Philosophy as Rigorous Philology? Nietzsche and Post-structuralism." *New York Literary Forum.* Vols. 8–9: *Fragments: Incompletion and Discontinuity* (1981), pp. 171–185.

———. "Nietzsche, Hume, and the Genealogical Method." In *Nietzsche as Affirmative Thinker.* Edited by Yirmiyahu Yovel. Dordrecht: Martinus Nijhoff, 1986, pp. 20–38.

IJsseling, Samuel. *Rhetoric and Philosophy in Conflict.* Translated by Paul Dunphy. The Hague: Martinus Nijhoff, 1976.

Janz, Curt Paul. "Friedrich Nietzsches Akademische Lehrtätigkeit in Basel 1869 bis 1879." *Nietzsche-Studien,* Band 3. Berlin: Walter de Gruyter, 1974, pp. 192–203.

Jaspers, Karl. *Nietzsche: An Introduction to the Understanding of his Philosophical Activity.* Translated by Charles F. Wallraff and Frederick J. Schmitz. Tucson: University of Arizona Press, 1965.

Kant, Immanuel. *Kant's Introduction to Logic.* Translated by T. K. Abbott. New York: Philosophical Library, 1963.

Kaufmann, Walter. *Nietzsche: Philosopher, Psychologist, Antichrist.* Princeton: Princeton University Press, 1974.

Klossowski, Pierre. *Nietzsche et le cercle vicieux.* Paris: Mercure de France, 1969.

Kofman, Sarah. *Nietzsche et la métaphore.* Paris: Payot, 1972.

———. "Nietzsche and the Obscurity of Heraclitus." Translated by Françoise Lionnet-McCumber. *Diacritics,* Vol. 17, No. 3 (Fall 1987), pp. 39–55.

Krell, David Farrell, and Wood, David, editors. *Exceedingly Nietzsche: Aspects of Contemporary Nietzsche Interpretation.* London: Routledge and Kegan Paul, Ltd., 1988.

Lacoue-Labarthe, Philippe. "Le détour (Nietzsche et la rhétorique)." *Poétique* 5 (1971), pp. 53–76.

———. *Le Sujet de la philosophie (Typographies I).* Paris: Aubier-Flammarion, 1979.

Lacoue-Labarthe, Philippe, and Nancy, Jean-Luc, "Rhétorique et langage." *Poétique* 5 (1971), pp. 99–142.

Le Doeuff, Michèle. "Women and Philosophy." Translated by Debbie Pope. In *French Feminist Thought: A Reader*. Edited by Toril Moi. Oxford: Basil Blackwell, 1987.

Lyotard, Jean-François. *The Postmodern Condition*. Translated by Geoff Bennington and Brian Massumi. Minneapolis: University of Minnesota Press, 1983.

Magnus, Bernd. *Heidegger's Metahistory of Philosophy: Amor Fati, Being and Truth*. The Hague: Martinus Nijhoff, 1970.

————. *Nietzsche's Existential Imperative*. Bloomington: Indiana University Press, 1978.

————. "Nietzsche Today: A View from America." *International Studies in Philosophy*, Vol. XV, No. 2 (1983), pp. 95–103.

————. "Nietzsche's Philosophy in 1888: *The Will to Power* and the *Übermensch*." *The Journal of the History of Philosophy*, Vol. 24, No. 1 (January 1986), pp. 79–98.

————. "Self-Consuming Concepts." *International Studies in Philosophy*, Vol. XXI, No. 2 (1989), pp. 63–71.

Megill, Allan. *Prophets of Extremity: Nietzsche, Heidegger, Foucault, Derrida*. Berkeley: University of California Press, 1985.

Meijers, Anthonie. "Gustav Gerber und Friedrich Nietzsche." *Nietzsche-Studien*, Band 17. Berlin: Walter de Gruyter, 1988, pp. 369–390.

Merleau-Ponty, Maurice. *Phenomenology of Perception*. Translated by Colin Smith. London: Routledge and Kegan Paul, 1962.

Michelfelder, Diane P., and Palmer, Richard E., editors. *Dialogue and Deconstruction: The Gadamer-Derrida Encounter*. Albany: State University of New York Press, 1989.

Mittelman, Willard. "Perspectivism, Being, and Truth." *International Studies in Philosophy*, Vol. XVI, No. 2 (1984), pp. 3–22.

Nancy, Jean-Luc. *L'Impératif catégorique*. Paris: Aubier-Flammarion, 1983.

Nehamas, Alexander. *Nietzsche: Life as Literature*. Cambridge: Harvard University Press, 1985.

————. "Immanent and Transcendent Perspectivism in Nietzsche." *Nietzsche-Studien*, Band 12. Berlin: Walter de Gruyter, 1983, pp. 473–490.

Nietzsche aujourd'hui. 2 Vols. Paris: Union Générale D'Éditions, 1973.

Norris, Christopher. "Deconstruction against Itself: Derrida and Nietzsche." *Diacritics*, Vol. 16, No. 4 (Winter 1986), pp. 61–69.

Ormiston, Gayle L., and Schrift, Alan D., editors. *The Hermeneutic Tradition: From Ast to Ricoeur*. Albany: State University of New York Press, 1990.

————. *Transforming the Hermeneutic Context: From Nietzsche to Nancy*. Albany: State University of New York Press, 1990.

Palmer, Richard E. *Hermeneutics.* Evanston: Northwestern University Press, 1969.

Pautrat, Bernard. *Versions du soleil. Figures et système de Nietzsche.* Paris: Éditions du Seuil, 1971.

Quine, Willard Van Orman. *From a Logical Point of View.* New York: Harper and Row, Publishers, Inc., 1963.

Rey, Jean-Michel. *L'enjeu des signes. Lecture de Nietzsche.* Paris: Éditions du Seuil, 1971.

Richardson, William J., S.J. *Heidegger: Through Phenomenology to Thought.* The Hague: Martinus Nijhoff, 1963.

Ricoeur, Paul. *Freud and Philosophy: An Essay on Interpretation.* Translated by Denis Savage. New Haven: Yale University Press, 1970.

————. *The Rule of Metaphor: Multi-disciplinary studies of the creation of meaning in language.* Translated by Robert Czerny, with Kathleen McLaughlin and John Costello, S.J. Toronto: University of Toronto Press, 1977.

————. *The Philosophy of Paul Ricoeur.* Edited by Charles E. Reagan and David Stewart. Boston: Beacon Press, 1978.

————. *Hermeneutics and the Human Sciences.* Translated and edited by John B. Thompson. Cambridge: Cambridge University Press, 1981.

Rickels, Laurence A. editor. *Looking After Nietzsche.* Albany: State University of New York Press, 1990.

Rorty, Richard M. *Philosophy and the Mirror of Nature.* Princeton: Princeton University Press, 1979.

————. *Consequences of Pragmatism.* Minneapolis: University of Minnesota Press, 1982.

Sartre, Jean-Paul. *Literature and Existentialism.* Translation of *Qu'est-ce que la littérature? [What is Literature?]* by Bernard Frechtman. Secaucus, N.J.: The Citadel Press, 1972.

Schacht, Richard. *Nietzsche.* London: Routledge and Kegan Paul, Ltd., 1983.

Schleiermacher, Friedrich D. E. *Hermeneutics: The Handwritten Manuscripts.* Edited by Heinz Kimmerle. Translated by James Duke and Jack Forstman. Missoula, Mont.: Scholars Press, 1977.

Schrift, Alan D. "Genealogy and/as Deconstruction: Nietzsche, Derrida, and Foucault on Philosophy as Critique." In *Postmodernism and Continental Philosophy.* Edited by Hugh Silverman and Donn Welton. Albany: State University of New York Press, 1988, pp. 193–213.

————. "The becoming-post-modern of philosophy." In *After the Future: Postmodern Times and Places.* Edited by Gary Shapiro. Albany: State University of New York Press, 1990, pp. 99–113.

————. "Nietzsche's French Legacy." In *Cambridge Companions to Philosophy: Friedrich Nietzsche*. Edited by Bernd Magnus. Cambridge: Cambridge University Press, forthcoming.

Scott, Charles E. *The Language of Difference*. Atlantic Highlands, N.J.: Humanities Press International, Inc., 1987.

Shapiro, Gary, and Sica, Alan, editors. *Hermeneutics: Questions and Prospects*. Amherst: University of Massachusetts Press, 1984.

Stack, George J. "Nietzsche and Perspectival Interpretation." *Philosophy Today* (Fall 1981), pp. 221–241.

Thomas, R. Hinton. *Nietzsche in German politics and society, 1890–1918*. Manchester: Manchester University Press, 1983.

Weber, Samuel. *Institution and Interpretation*. Minneapolis: University of Minnesota Press, 1987.

West, Cornel. "Nietzsche's Prefiguration of Post-Modern American Philosophy." *boundary 2*. Special issue: *Why Nietzsche Now?* Vol. IX, No. 3 and Vol. X, No. 1 (Spring/Fall 1981), pp. 241–269.

White, Hayden. *Metahistory: The Historical Imagination in Nineteenth-Century Europe*. Baltimore: Johns Hopkins University Press, 1973.

Whitman, James. "Nietzsche in the Magisterial Tradition of German Classical Philology." *Journal of the History of Ideas*, Vol. XLVII, No. 3 (July–September 1986), pp. 453–468.

Yovel, Yirmiyahu, editor. *Nietzsche as Affirmative Thinker*. Dordrecht: Martinus Nijhoff, 1986.

Index